Conference of the North American Chapter of the Association for Computational Linguistics: Human Language Technologies (NAACL HLT 2021)

Student Research Workshop

Online
6 – 11 June 2021

ISBN: 978-1-7138-3012-2

Printed from e-media with permission by:

Curran Associates, Inc.
57 Morehouse Lane
Red Hook, NY 12571

Some format issues inherent in the e-media version may also appear in this print version.

Printed with permission by Curran Associates, Inc. (2021)

For permission requests, please contact the Association for Computational Linguistics at the address below.

Association for Computational Linguistics
209 N. Eighth Street
Stroudsburg, Pennsylvania 18360

Phone: 1-570-476-8006
Fax: 1-570-476-0860

acl@aclweb.org

Additional copies of this publication are available from:

Curran Associates, Inc.
57 Morehouse Lane
Red Hook, NY 12571 USA
Phone: 845-758-0400
Fax: 845-758-2633
Email: curran@proceedings.com
Web: www.proceedings.com

NAACL-HLT 2021

The 2021 Conference of the North American Chapter of the Association for Computational Linguistics: Human Language Technologies

Proceedings of the Student Research Workshop

June 6 - 11, 2021

Introduction

Welcome to the NAACL 2021 Student Research Workshop!

The NAACL 2021 Student Research Workshop (SRW) is a forum for student researchers in computational linguistics and natural language processing. The workshop provides a unique opportunity for student participants to present their work and receive valuable feedback from the international research community as well as from faculty mentors.

Following the tradition of the previous student research workshops, we have two tracks: research papers and thesis proposals. The research paper track is a venue for Ph.D. students, Masters students, and advanced undergraduates to describe completed work or work-in-progress along with preliminary results. The thesis proposal track is offered for advanced Masters and Ph.D. students who have decided on a thesis topic and are interested in feedback on their proposal and ideas about future directions for their work.

This year, we received 50 submissions in total. We accepted 22 papers, with an acceptance rate of 44

Mentoring is at the heart of the SRW. In keeping with previous years, we had a pre-submission mentoring program before the submission deadline. A total of 12 papers participated in the pre-submission mentoring program. This program offered students the opportunity to receive comments from an experienced researcher to improve the writing style and presentation of their submissions.

We are deeply grateful to our sponsor, the National Science Foundation. We thank our program committee members for their careful reviews of each paper and all of our mentors for donating their time to provide feedback to our student authors. Thank you to our faculty advisors, Nanyun Peng and Yu Su, for their essential advice and guidance, and to the NAACL 2021 organizing committee for their support. Finally, thank you to our student participants!

Organizers

Esin Durmus - Cornell University
Vivek Gupta - University of Utah
Nelson Liu - Stanford University

Faculty Advisors

Nanyun Peng - University of California, Los Angeles
Yu Su - The Ohio State University

Pre-submission Mentors

Mohit Bansal - University of North Carolina, Chapel Hill
Valerio Basile - University of Turin
Eduardo Blanco - University of North Texas
Dallas Card - Stanford University
Kai-Wei Chang - University of California, Los Angeles
Eunsol Choi - University of Texas, Austin
Lucia Donatelli - Saarland University
Greg Durrett - University of Texas, Austin
Yansong Feng - Peking University
Matt Gardner - Allen Institute for Artificial Intelligence
Luke Holman - University of North Texas
Robin Jia - Facebook AI Research / University of Southern California
Debanjan Mahata - Bloomberg
Vincent Ng - University of Texas, Dallas
Barbara Plank - IT University of Copenhagen
Sai Krishna Rallabandi - Carnegie Mellon University
Melissa Roemmele - SDL
Masoud Rouhizadeh - Johns Hopkins University
Sebastian Ruder - DeepMind
Roy Schwartz - Hebrew University of Jerusalem
Vered Shwartz - Allen Institute for Artificial Intelligence
Maneesh Singh - Verisk Inc.
Amanda Stent - Bloomberg
Swabha Swayamdipta - Allen Institute for Artificial Intelligence
Jesse Thomason - Amazon / University of Southern California
Aline Villavicencio - Federal University of Rio Grande do Sul
Bonnie Webber - University of Edinburgh
Arkaitz Zubiaga - Queen Mary University of London

Program Committee

Piush Aggarwal
Afroz Ahamad
Chaitanya Ahuja
Abeer AL-Dayel
Sedeeq Al-khazraji

Miguel A. Alonso
Rami Aly
Bharat Ram Ambati
Calude Andreea
Maria Antoniak
Kristjan Arumae
Ehsaneddin Asgari
Vidhisha Balachandran
Loïc Barrault
Valerio Basile
Roberto Basili
Rachel Bawden
Eduardo Blanco
Rishi Bommasani
Marine Carpuat
Arlene Casey
Arun Chaganty
lisa andreevna chalaguine
Mingda Chen
Xinchi Chen
Jifan Chen
Leshem Choshen
Siddharth Dalmia
Samvit Dammalapati
Alok Debnath
Louise Deléger
Chris Develder
Flavio Di Palo
Anne Dirkson
Radina Dobreva
Zi-Yi Dou
Micha Elsner
Denis Emelin
Carlos Escolano
Tina Fang
Murhaf Fares
Amir Feder
Yansong Feng
Jared Fernandez
Dayne Freitag
Yoshinari Fujinuma
Saadia Gabriel
Diana Galvan-Sosa
Marcos Garcia
Matt Gardner
Dan Goldwasser
Sarah Gupta
Abhinav Gupta
Vivek Gupta
Hardy Hardy
Mareike Hartmann

Junxian He
Christopher Homan
saghar Hosseini
Mohammad Javad Hosseini
Nina Hosseini-Kivanani
Phu Mon Htut
Jeff Jacobs
Aaron Jaech
Glorianna Jagfeld
Labiba Jahan
Jyoti Jha
Zhengbao Jiang
Chen Junjie
Jad Kabbara
Tomoyuki Kajiwara
Ehsan Kamalloo
Zara Kancheva
Sudipta Kar
Alina Karakanta
Philipp Koehn
Taiwo Kolajo
Mamoru Komachi
Parisa Kordjamshidi
Mandy Korpusik
Kalpesh Krishna
Jonathan K. Kummerfeld
Kemal Kurniawan
Yash Kumar Lal
Alexandra Lavrentovich
Bowen Li
Yiyuan Li
Lei Li
Tao Li
Xiang Lorraine Li
Junwei Liang
Jasy Suet Yan Liew
Kevin Lin
Kevin Lin
Fangyu Liu
Debanjan Mahata
Valentin Malykh
Emma Manning
Pedro Henrique Martins
Bruno Martins
Puneet Mathur
Dheeraj Mekala
Omid Memarrast
Rui Meng
Antonio Valerio Miceli Barone
Sabrina J. Mielke
Zulfat Miftahutdinov

Tsvetomila Mihaylova
Farjana Sultana Mim
Sewon Min
Koji Mineshima
Swaroop Mishra
Rohan Mishra
Amita Misra
Jesse Mu
Nora Muheim
Masaaki Nagata
Nihal V. Nayak
Dat Quoc Nguyen
Vincent Nguyen
Shinji Nishimoto
Pegah Nokhiz
Yasumasa Onoe
Naoki Otani
Endang Wahyu Pamungkas
Isabel Papadimitriou
Thiago Pardo
Chan Young Park
Roma Patel
Archita Pathak
Siyao Peng
Hai Pham
Adithya Pratapa
Ivaylo Radev
Sree Harsha Ramesh
Surangika Ranathunga
Vikas Raunak
Paul Rayson
Kirk Roberts
Alexander Robertson
Guy Rotman
Maria Ryskina
sepideh sadeghi
Younes Samih
Jainisha Sankhavara
Ryohei Sasano
Carolina Scarton
Michael Sejr Schlichtkrull
Sebastian Schuster
Giovanni Semeraro
Olga Seminck
Indira Sen
Gautam Kishore Shahi
Sina Sheikholeslami
A.B. Siddique
Kushagra Singh
Pradyumna Sinha
Sunayana Sitaram

Katira Soleymanzadeh
Thamar Solorio
Richard Sproat
Tejas Srinivasan
Marija Stanojevic
Alane Suhr
Jeniya Tabassum
Shabnam Tafreshi
Nicholas Tomlin
Trang Tran
Sowmya Vajjala
Alakananda Vempala
Rob Voigt
Teodora Vukovic
Eric Wallace
Bonnie Webber
John Wieting
Steven Wilson
Patrick Xia
Yumo Xu
Rongtian Ye
Da Yin
Michael Yoder
Xiaodong Yu
Meishan Zhang
Tianyi Zhang
Yanpeng Zhao
Arkaitz Zubiaga
Talha Çolakoğlu

Table of Contents

Sampling and Filtering of Neural Machine Translation Distillation Data
Vilém Zouhar 1

IceSum: An Icelandic Text Summarization Corpus
Jón Daðason, Hrafn Loftsson, Salome Sigurðardóttir and Þorsteinn Björnsson 9

Negation typology and general representation models for cross-lingual zero-shot negation scope resolution in Russian, French, and Spanish.
Anastassia Shaitarova and Fabio Rinaldi 15

Representations of Meaning in Neural Networks for NLP: a Thesis Proposal
Tomáš Musil 24

Towards Layered Events and Schema Representations in Long Documents
Hans Ole Hatzel and Chris Biemann 32

Parallel Text Alignment and Monolingual Parallel Corpus Creation from Philosophical Texts for Text Simplification
Stefan Paun 40

Syntax-Based Attention Masking for Neural Machine Translation
Colin McDonald and David Chiang 47

Multi-Modal Image Captioning for the Visually Impaired
Hiba Ahsan, Daivat Bhatt, Kaivan Shah and Nikita Bhalla 53

Open-Domain Question Answering with Pre-Constructed Question Spaces
Jinfeng Xiao, Lidan Wang, Franck Dernoncourt, Trung Bui, Tong Sun and Jiawei Han 61

A Sliding-Window Approach to Automatic Creation of Meeting Minutes
Jia Jin Koay, Alexander Roustai, Xiaojin Dai and Fei Liu 68

Exploration and Discovery of the COVID-19 Literature through Semantic Visualization
Jingxuan Tu, Marc Verhagen, Brent Cochran and James Pustejovsky 76

Shuffled-token Detection for Refining Pre-trained RoBERTa
Subhadarshi Panda, Anjali Agrawal, Jeewon Ha and Benjamin Bloch 88

Morphology-Aware Meta-Embeddings for Tamil
Arjun Sai Krishnan and Seyoon Ragavan 94

Seed Word Selection for Weakly-Supervised Text Classification with Unsupervised Error Estimation
Yiping Jin, Akshay Bhatia and Dittaya Wanvarie 112

Multi-Task Learning of Generation and Classification for Emotion-Aware Dialogue Response Generation
Tatsuya Ide and Daisuke Kawahara 119

Comparison of Grammatical Error Correction Using Back-Translation Models
Aomi Koyama, Kengo Hotate, Masahiro Kaneko and Mamoru Komachi 126

Parallel sentences mining with transfer learning in an unsupervised setting
Yu Sun, Shaolin Zhu, Feng Yifan and Chenggang Mi 136

Sentence Concatenation Approach to Data Augmentation for Neural Machine Translation
Seiichiro Kondo, Kengo Hotate, Tosho Hirasawa, Masahiro Kaneko and Mamoru Komachi . . . 143

Emotion Classification in a Resource Constrained Language Using Transformer-based Approach
Avishek Das, Omar Sharif, Mohammed Moshiul Hoque and Iqbal H. Sarker 150

Hie-BART: Document Summarization with Hierarchical BART
Kazuki Akiyama, Akihiro Tamura and Takashi Ninomiya 159

Conference Program

Saturday, June 5, 2021 UTC+0

16:00–17:20 SRW Session 1

Sampling and Filtering of Neural Machine Translation Distillation Data
Vilém Zouhar

Towards Multi-Modal Text-Image Retrieval to improve Human Reading
Florian Schneider, Özge Alacam, Xintong Wang and Chris Biemann

IceSum: An Icelandic Text Summarization Corpus
Jón Daðason, Hrafn Loftsson, Salome Sigurðardóttir and Þorsteinn Björnsson

Negation typology and general representation models for cross-lingual zero-shot negation scope resolution in Russian, French, and Spanish.
Anastassia Shaitarova and Fabio Rinaldi

Representations of Meaning in Neural Networks for NLP: a Thesis Proposal
Tomáš Musil

Towards Layered Events and Schema Representations in Long Documents
Hans Ole Hatzel and Chris Biemann

Parallel Text Alignment and Monolingual Parallel Corpus Creation from Philosophical Texts for Text Simplification
Stefan Paun

Saturday, June 5, 2021 UTC+0 (continued)

18:40–20:00 SRW Session 2

Syntax-Based Attention Masking for Neural Machine Translation
Colin McDonald and David Chiang

Multi-Modal Image Captioning for the Visually Impaired
Hiba Ahsan, Daivat Bhatt, Kaivan Shah and Nikita Bhalla

Open-Domain Question Answering with Pre-Constructed Question Spaces
Jinfeng Xiao, Lidan Wang, Franck Dernoncourt, Trung Bui, Tong Sun and Jiawei Han

A Character-and-Event-Based Framework for Detecting Literary Allusion in Internet Humor
Emily Shen

A Sliding-Window Approach to Automatic Creation of Meeting Minutes
Jia Jin Koay, Alexander Roustai, Xiaojin Dai and Fei Liu

Exploration and Discovery of the COVID-19 Literature through Semantic Visualization
Jingxuan Tu, Marc Verhagen, Brent Cochran and James Pustejovsky

Shuffled-token Detection for Refining Pre-trained RoBERTa
Subhadarshi Panda, Anjali Agrawal, Jeewon Ha and Benjamin Bloch

Morphology-Aware Meta-Embeddings for Tamil
Arjun Sai Krishnan and Seyoon Ragavan

Sunday, June 6, 2021 UTC+0

1:20–2:40 SRW Session 3

Seed Word Selection for Weakly-Supervised Text Classification with Unsupervised Error Estimation
Yiping Jin, Akshay Bhatia and Dittaya Wanvarie

Multi-Task Learning of Generation and Classification for Emotion-Aware Dialogue Response Generation
Tatsuya Ide and Daisuke Kawahara

Comparison of Grammatical Error Correction Using Back-Translation Models
Aomi Koyama, Kengo Hotate, Masahiro Kaneko and Mamoru Komachi

Parallel sentences mining with transfer learning in an unsupervised setting
Yu Sun, Shaolin Zhu, Feng Yifan and Chenggang Mi

Sentence Concatenation Approach to Data Augmentation for Neural Machine Translation
Seiichiro Kondo, Kengo Hotate, Tosho Hirasawa, Masahiro Kaneko and Mamoru Komachi

Emotion Classification in a Resource Constrained Language Using Transformer-based Approach
Avishek Das, Omar Sharif, Mohammed Moshiul Hoque and Iqbal H. Sarker

Hie-BART: Document Summarization with Hierarchical BART
Kazuki Akiyama, Akihiro Tamura and Takashi Ninomiya

Sampling and Filtering of Neural Machine Translation Distillation Data

Vilém Zouhar
Institute of Formal and Applied Linguistics, Charles University
zouhar@ufal.mff.cuni.cz

Abstract

In most of neural machine translation distillation or stealing scenarios, the goal is to preserve the performance of the target model (teacher). The highest-scoring hypothesis of the teacher model is commonly used to train a new model (student). If reference translations are also available, then better hypotheses (with respect to the references) can be upsampled and poor hypotheses either removed or undersampled.

This paper explores the importance sampling method landscape (pruning, hypothesis upsampling and undersampling, deduplication and their combination) with English to Czech and English to German MT models using standard MT evaluation metrics. We show that careful upsampling and combination with the original data leads to better performance when compared to training only on the original or synthesized data or their direct combination.

1 Introduction

Model distillation is a process of transferring the knowledge of one or more, usually larger, model(s) into another, usually smaller, model (Buciluă et al., 2006). A variation of this is training a new model in a way that its performance is similar to that of the already trained one. This is achieved by making use of either teacher predictions (black-box) or other products of the workings of the teacher, such as attention-score or decoder score (grey/glass-box). Assuming we have access to a parallel corpus, we focus on sampling the translation hypotheses and making use not only of the teacher scores but also of their comparison to the reference.

There are various possible motivations for model distillation. The student model can be much smaller than the teacher model, which has the benefit of faster inference speed (Germann et al., 2020). It can also be used for model stealing, where an adversary tries to copy the teacher functionality. This is a practical concern for production-level MT systems (Wallace et al., 2020).

One of the approaches for knowledge distillation is to use the teacher model to generate a new dataset for the student model to train on. Having access to a trained teacher model, this approach does not require parallel data and can leverage large monolingual corpora. Reference translations, however, help with determining which of the teacher's translations are good and which are of low quality.

We focus on this approach and propose and compare several importance sampling approaches to prepare training data for student models that leverage access to reference translations. These include pruning, upsampling and undersampling, deduplication and their combination. We show that a combination of these methods improves the student performance over just using the reference or the best hypothesis (by the decoder score), which is a common distillation practice.

The experiment code is available open-source.[1]

1.1 Related work

The general methodology for knowledge distillation in the form of teacher-student has been proposed by Hinton et al. (2015). For the MT task specifically, Tan et al. (2019) focus on vastly reducing the number of parameters, while retaining the performance of a multi-lingual teacher. Wei et al. (2019) and Gordon and Duh use distillation during training to further improve the model performance.

The work of Kim and Rush (2016) shows that taking either the top sentence with respect to the teacher decoder score or BLEU (Papineni et al., 2002) improves the performance. Germann et al. (2020) presented student models that distil knowledge from a larger teacher model with a negligible loss in performance. They manipulate the queried data based on target sentence quality, such as by removing sentences that are not correctly recognized

[1] github.com/zouharvi/reference-mt-distill

Proceedings of NAACL-HLT 2021: Student Research Workshop, pages 1–8
June 6–11, 2021.

by a language identifier. For the parallel part of the data, they extract the best BLEU scoring sentence out of 8 hypotheses. Freitag et al. (2017) experiment with pruning sentences that are below some TER (Snover et al., 2006) threshold (lower is better). They further document the effect of using an ensemble of teachers and also reducing the student model size.

2 Methods

The evaluation of every sampling method follows the following three-step process. First, the specific parallel corpus (Section 2.1) is translated by the teacher model (Section 2.2) for the considered translation direction. New datasets based on metrics are then created. The reference is taken into consideration during the hypothesis selection. We train new models (students) on these datasets and measure their performance. There are 12 hypotheses (default in Marian NMT) provided by the teacher using beam search for every source sentence which we consider when composing a new dataset.

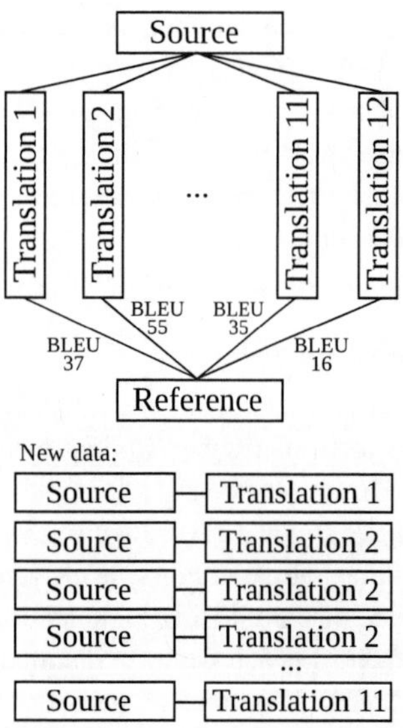

Figure 1: Scheme of an example of hypothesis sampling with BLEU metric.

Figure 1 shows an example of the sampling process with BLEU. Twelve translations are made of *Source* and each receives a score against the provided reference. The new data contain *Translation 2* three times, because of its high score. *Translation 12* is omitted because of its low score. This upsampling is explained in detail in Section 2.3.

2.1 Data

We make use of the Europarl v10 parallel corpus (Koehn, 2005) for English-Czech (0.6M sentences) and English-German (1.8M sentences). The sentences are longer (23 target words per sentence on average) than in the WMT News Task domain (Barrault et al., 2020). To modern standards, this dataset is relatively small and very domain restricted. This was chosen deliberately because of computational limitations.[2] Despite that it demonstrates the results of the different sampling methods with respect to each other. These results may not be transferable to large parallel corpora in which training data is abundant.

For every language pair, we randomly sample 15k sentences as development dataset (used only for determining the best epoch and early stopping) and 15k sentences for final test evaluation which is reported. The WMT News test dataset is not used for student evaluation, because the students are trained on a limited amount of data and on a different domain. Out of the WMT20 News tokens, 0.18% are not present in the Europarl training set. This would introduce a higher variance into the WMT News test evaluation, which would be largely dependent on the diversity of the teacher vocabulary.

2.2 Models

The teachers[3] in this experiment are transformer-based (Vaswani et al., 2017), speed optimized and were themselves created by knowledge distillation from state-of-the-art models (Popel et al., 2020; Junczys-Dowmunt, 2019), as proposed by Germann et al. (2020). The Czech↔English model is described by Germann et al. (2020) and the English→German model by Bogoychev et al. (2020). Our student models follow the teacher's architecture with half the size of the embedding vector (256 instead of 512) and half of the attention heads (4 instead of 8). Student models were trained with an early stopping of 20 evaluations on validation data with evaluation performed every 10k sentences. Vocabularies were not shared from the teacher because they did not affect the results, and not using them makes fewer assumptions regarding the level of access to the teacher model. Marian NMT (Junczys-Dowmunt et al., 2018) is used for teacher decoding and student training.

[2] ~4500 GPU hours in total for the whole experiment
[3] Version *student.base* at github.com/browsermt/students

Table 1 shows the teacher performance measured on WMT20 News and the test subset of Europarl. Czech models performed better on the Europarl than on the News task, while for the German model the trend was the opposite. This may be caused by the fact that the models were distilled from a system that had Europarl as part of the training data, CzEng 2.0 (Kocmi et al., 2020).

Dataset:	CS→EN	EN→CS	EN→DE
BLEU:			
WMT20 News	28.2	35.8	42.7
Europarl	46.1	38.2	32.1
ChrF:			
WMT20 News	0.57	0.55	0.66
Europarl	0.69	0.64	0.61
TER:			
WMT20 News	0.57	0.71	0.51
Europarl	0.41	0.50	0.61

Table 1: Teacher models BLEU, ChrF and TER scores on WMT20 News Task dataset and Europarl domain.

2.3 Sampling

Concerning the sampling metrics (always between the considered hypothesis and the reference), we make use of BLEU, ChrF (Popović, 2015), TER (negative), the difference (negative of absolute value) in subword unit counts by SentencePiece (Kudo and Richardson, 2018) (SP) and decoder probability divided by the number of output tokens (score). TER and SP are negative in Section 3 so that higher is always better. The motivation for SP is to capture the difference in length of the hypotheses with respect to the reference. This is a very naive metric, but we can use it to see the performance and the behaviour of all the other metrics. Although BLEU is a document-level metric, it can also be used to determine sentence similarity. Standard machine translation metrics[4] are computed using Sacrebleu (Post, 2018). Different sampling methods are used even though the goal is to maximize the BLEU scores of the student models. There is no reason to assume that sampling only based on BLEU will lead to the best results.

The number of training sentences differs for every method. We define the following notation.

- T - top; T^n_{metric} takes n top translation hypotheses according to *metric*; equal to $S^{1,1,\ldots 1(n)}_{\text{metric}}$. The student model may benefit from seeing e.g. the second best hypothesis, even though it's not the best available. This results in n times the number of original sentences which are all different.
- S - skewed; $S^{k_1,k_2,\ldots k_n}_{\text{metric}}$ takes $k_1\times$ the top translation hypotheses according to *metric*, $k_2\times$ the second top translation, etc. As opposed to T^n_{metric}, this method tries to preserve the information of the ordering by setting $k_1 \geq k_2 \geq \ldots k_n$. This results in $(\sum k_i)$ times the number of original sentences but only n times of which are different sentences.
- $Dedup[X]$ deduplicates sentence pairs of X. It is used after joining the results of other methods. This method is useful for emulating the *or* operation: $Dedup[A + B]$ then means "all sentences in either A or B." The output size is strictly dependent on their overlap.
- G - greater than; G^m_{metric} takes all sentence translations with *metric* at least m. This results in sentences that are close to the reference according to the metric. The number of output sentences highly dependent on the threshold and is discussed in the corresponding section.

Sampling methods can be combined: $T^2_{\text{bleu}} + G^{-10}_{\text{score}}$ joins the top 2 sentences measured by BLEU and adds them to the hypotheses with decoder score of at least -10. Duplicates are intentionally not removed; thus, hypotheses in both sampling methods are upsampled.

3 Results

Baseline. Table 2 shows results for baseline sampling methods. *Original* corresponds to training only to the provided parallel corpus (references). T^1_{score} takes only the highest-scoring hypothesis from the decoder, which is related to the scenario where the reference is not available, and the decoder score is the best measure for hypothesis quality.[5] The sampling method T^{12}_{-} takes all available hypotheses (metric does not matter).

Training on the original data leads to better results than training on the best scoring hypotheses.

[4]Sacrebleu metrics version strings:
BLEU+case.mixed+numrefs.1+smooth.exp+tok.13a+v1.4.14
ChrF2+numchars.6+space.false+v1.4.14
TER+tok.tercom-nonorm-punct-noasian-uncased+v1.4.14

[5]MT quality estimation tools could be used to approximate the sentence translation quality or language models to use sentence fluency in lieu of translation quality.

Dataset	CS→EN	EN→CS	EN→DE
Original	41.6	31.8	25.1
T^1_{score}	40.0	31.2	28.5
T^{12}_{-}	41.1	31.6	28.4

Table 2: BLEU scores for students trained on baseline datasets

Training on all hypotheses results in slightly lower BLEU performance. This may be caused by the small amount of training data available in which case taking all hypotheses just improves the vocabulary and language modelling capacity.

Best hypotheses. The results of datasets created by taking either the best one or the four best hypotheses for every source sentence is shown in Table 3. In the case of multiple hypotheses having the same score, the one with the highest decoder score is chosen. The top one and top four hypotheses were chosen to show that the optimum is neither the top one nor the top twelve (all) hypotheses.

On average, the hypothesis overlap[6] in sampling between metrics is 29% for T^1 and 51% for T^4. This is expected and shows that when more top hypotheses are taken into the new dataset, the individual metrics tend to matter less.

Dataset	CS→EN	EN→CS	EN→DE
T^1_{BLEU}	42.6	34.4	29.5
T^1_{ChrF}	43.8	33.9	30.5
T^1_{TER}	43.0	36.1	28.5
T^1_{SP}	39.9	29.5	28.2
T^4_{BLEU}	44.0	33.3	29.3
T^4_{ChrF}	44.3	34.9	29.6
T^4_{TER}	44.2	32.0	28.8
T^4_{SP}	41.8	32.3	27.9
T^4_{score}	44.2	32.0	28.8

Table 3: BLEU scores for students trained on best-one and best-four hypotheses datasets

Taking only the top-scoring hypothesis of reference-based metrics, T^1 showed better results than the baseline (training on the original data, taking the highest decoder scoring hypothesis or taking all hypotheses). In all cases the T^4 outperformed T^1. The main gains were on CS→EN and EN→CS. Although the results on EN→DE are only slightly better than the baseline, they are systematic across all metrics except for SP. The effect of choosing the metric for the top four hypotheses seems marginal, even compared to sampling based on the decoder score. The only exception is the SP difference, which leads to lower results.

[6]Overlap computed as average$_{m1\neq m2}|T^1_{m1} \cap T^1_{m2}|/n$ and average$_{m1\neq m2}|T^4_{m1} \cap T^4_{m2}|/(4n)$. Original data size is n.

Thresholding. Determining a single threshold for all datasets leads to a vastly different number of hypotheses being selected (the use of G^{65}_{BLEU} results in $1.3\times$ the original dataset for CS→EN, but 0.6 for EN→DE). Therefore, we establish different metric thresholds for every dataset so that the new datasets are $1\times$ to $1.5\times$ the original size for consistent results across language pairs.

Some of the source sentences were easier to translate, and more of their hypotheses were put into the new dataset. Others had no hypothesis above a given threshold and were not included in the new data at all. On average only 25% of original sentences were preserved for BLEU, ChrF, TER and SP. For the decoder score metric, it is 46%. The high loss of source sentences is expected since most of the hypotheses share large portions of the target sentence and only differ in a few words. All of them will then behave similarly with respect to the metric.

Dataset	CS→EN	EN→CS	EN→DE
G_{BLEU}	39.0_{65}	30.2_{60}	27.2_{55}
G_{ChrF}	$37.4_{0.82}$	$29.2_{0.81}$	$26.5_{0.80}$
G_{TER}	$37.8_{-0.2}$	$30.2_{-0.25}$	$25.2_{-0.24}$
G_{SP}	32.5_{-1}	19.6_{-2}	23.0_{-1}
G_{score}	$39.0_{-0.08}$	$32.0_{-0.09}$	$27.6_{-0.11}$

Table 4: BLEU scores for students trained on datasets made of hypotheses above threshold of different metrics. Metrics thresholds are in subscript.

The highest performance is achieved using G_{score} which can be explained by how much of the original sentences were preserved. G_{score} shows that it is possible to achieve a performance comparable to T^1_{score} with less than half of the source sentences by only taking all hypotheses with a decoder score above a threshold. G_{BLEU} gets worse results (on average -1.1 BLEU), but with only 27% source sentences preserved.

Better performance could be achieved by lowering the threshold to allow more source sentences and by intersecting the result with some of the other sampling methods, thus eliminating only the very low-quality sentence pairs. This is the approach (done with 5 hypotheses) done by Freitag et al. (2017): $T^1_{score} \cap G^{-0.8}_{TER}$.

Upsampling. In the first upsampling case, $S^{4,3,2,1}$, the best hypothesis is present four times, the second-best three times, the third-best two times and the fourth-best once. The reason for upsampling better hypotheses is that we want to force the optimizer to make bigger steps for sentence pairs that are of high quality, but at the same time, we want to present other hypotheses to enlarge the vocabulary and improve the student's language model. The most straightforward approach is to put multiple copies of the high-quality example into the dataset. We also experiment with $S^{2,2,1,1}$, because the upsampling intensity for every hypothesis rank is an independent variable as well. Both of these schemes are relatively conservative so that they can be compared to each other and to T^4. Results for upsampling within a single metric are shown in Table 5.

Dataset	CS→EN	EN→CS	EN→DE
$S^{4,3,2,1}_{\text{BLEU}}$	**45.2**	**37.1**	29.7
$S^{4,3,2,1}_{\text{ChrF}}$	42.9	36.6	**30.1**
$S^{4,3,2,1}_{\text{TER}}$	44.4	36.9	29.8
$S^{4,3,2,1}_{\text{SP}}$	41.8	30.7	28.5
$S^{4,3,2,1}_{\text{score}}$	41.4	33.7	27.9
$S^{2,2,1,1}_{\text{BLEU}}$	44.3	36.5	29.6
$S^{2,2,1,1}_{\text{ChrF}}$	45.2	36.1	29.8
$S^{2,2,1,1}_{\text{TER}}$	43.5	33.4	29.6
$S^{2,2,1,1}_{\text{SP}}$	41.8	33.3	28.9
$S^{2,2,1,1}_{\text{score}}$	43.5	33.4	29.6

Table 5: BLEU scores for students trained on datasets made by upsampling top hypotheses within a single metric using $S^{4,3,2,1}$ and $S^{2,2,1,1}$

Both versions of upsampling ($S^{4,3,2,1}$ and $S^{2,2,1,1}$) outperformed all of the previous results. There seems to be no systematic difference between $S^{4,3,2,1}$ and $S^{2,2,1,1}$. With the exception of SP and decoder score, the metrics are comparable. A direct comparison can be made to $T^4 = S^{1,1,1,1}$ because both T^4 and the upsampling methods contain all source sentences and even the same hypotheses. The only difference is that in the upsampling case, the better hypothesis is upsampled. In this case $S^{2,2,1,1}$ had higher results over T^4 with $p < 0.005$ by Student's t-test.[7]

Combination. For the combination scenarios, the newly sampled datasets are joined together. This is shown in Table 6. In the first four cases, the sampling methods were joined with the original data. A baseline to this is T^1_{score} + Original, which is commonly used for distillation.

Deduplicating the top four hypotheses according to BLEU or decoder score and adding them to the original data did not improve over the baseline. Combining the upsampling according to the decoder score with the original data also did not help. Replacing the decoder score with BLEU resulted in a significant improvement. The original data is upsampled so that the ratio of synthetic to original data is 4:1 in the first case and 2:1 in the second one.

For the rest of the cases, the methods are combined without the original data. Baselines are shown in Table 2. The combination of the top four hypotheses (T^4_{BLEU} or T^4_{score}) with all of the hypotheses, T^{12}_{-}, improved over the baseline, including T^{12}_{-}, but performed poorly with respect to the other methods. Taking hypotheses that are in the top four according to either BLEU or decoder score leads to the best results in this section. The top one hypothesis, according to BLEU, is upsampled at least two and at most four times. This seems to work best for EN→DE where the training data were three times larger.

Bigger student model. To demonstrate the data sampling method behaviour on slightly larger models, the common distillation baseline (T^1_{score} + Original) and the best performing proposed sampling method ($S^{4,3,2,1}_{\text{BLEU}} + 4 \times$ Original) were used to train a student of the same size as the used teacher (embedding vector dimension 512 and 8 attention heads). The results are shown in Table 7. They are systematically higher than for the smaller models, and the difference between the baseline and the best sampling is preserved.

[7] Average was subtracted from the three directions so that T^4 and $S^{2,2,1,1}$ could be treated as only two distributions.

Dataset	CS→EN	EN→CS	EN→DE
T^1_{score} + Original	44.4	36.4	28.3
$Dedup[T^4_{\text{BLEU}} + T^4_{\text{score}}]$ + Original	43.7	35.3	29.1
$S^{4,3,2,1}_{\text{score}}$ + 2 × Original	43.9	36.1	28.3
$S^{4,3,2,1}_{\text{BLEU}}$ + 2 × Original	**45.5**	**37.3**	28.8
$S^{4,3,2,1}_{\text{BLEU}}$ + 4 × Original	**45.5** ⋆	**37.4** ⋆	28.9
$T^4_{\text{score}} + T^{12}_{-}$	41.6	33.2	28.3
$T^4_{\text{BLEU}} + T^{12}_{-}$	42.6	33.9	28.7
$T^4_{\text{BLEU}} + T^4_{\text{score}}$	43.3	33.2	28.9
$Dedup[\sum T^2_{\text{metric}}]$	43.6	34.7	29.1
$Dedup[\sum T^2_{\text{metrics}}] + T^{12}_{-}$	40.8	32.0	27.2
$Dedup[T^4_{\text{BLEU}} + T^4_{\text{score}}] + T^1_{\text{BLEU}} + T^1_{\text{score}}$	43.5	34.7	29.2
$Dedup[T^4_{\text{BLEU}} + T^4_{\text{score}}] + Dedup[T^1_{\text{BLEU}} + T^1_{\text{score}}]$	42.6	34.9	**29.6** ⋆
$Dedup[T^4_{\text{BLEU}} + T^4_{\text{score}}]$	43.5	35.0	**29.3**

Table 6: BLEU scores for students trained on datasets made of combination of sampling methods. $\sum_{\text{metric}}$ sums over all used metrics (BLEU, ChrF, TER, SP, score).

Dataset	CS→EN	EN→CS	EN→DE
T^1_{score} + Original	44.7	36.2	28.3
$Dedup[T^4_{\text{BLEU}} + T^4_{\text{score}}]$+ Original	44.3	36.2	28.5
$S^{4,3,2,1}_{\text{BLEU}}$ + 2 × Original	**46.9**	**38.5**	**28.8**
$S^{4,3,2,1}_{\text{BLEU}}$ + 4 × Original	**47.4** ⋆	**38.9** ⋆	**28.9**

Table 7: BLEU scores for students trained on datasets made of combination of top hypothesis and original data. Trained with parameters equal to the teacher's: embedding vector dimension 512 and 8 attention heads.

4 Summary

Although widely used, taking only the highest-scoring sentence (with respect to the decoder score or any reference-based metrics, such as BLEU) does not lead to the best results. In the context of the proposed experiments, these are achieved by a combination of top hypotheses and the original data, such as $S^{4,3,2,1}_{\text{BLEU}}$ +4× Original (upsampling according to BLEU and joining with the original data duplicated four times). Here, an improvement of an average +2 BLEU points against T^1_{score} + Original was achieved.

The choice of the sampling metric does not significantly influence the results, especially in cases where more than the top one hypothesis is sampled. Because of this, in most scenarios the decoder score can be used instead, reducing the need for translation references.

Future work. We worked with only two upsampling schemes: $S^{4,3,2,1}$ and $S^{2,2,1,1}$. However, the two vectors are arbitrary and more of the vast vector space should be explored, especially with more than the top four hypotheses considered or more skewed towards the best hypothesis. More sophisticated methods based on the value of the metric instead of just the ordering could also be tried out.

The effects of large models (both teacher and student) and data access should be explored to verify the transferability of the results of the current setup. Specifically, the teacher model should not be a distilled model itself. The robustness of the training should also be established.

Even though this paper focused solely on MT, the importance sampling methods could also be applied and verified on other NLP tasks, possibly even on more general machine learning problems.

Acknowledgements

Sincere thanks to Philipp Zimmermann, Martin Popel and both PBML reviewers for their helpful suggestions and comments.

This study was supported by the Czech Science Foundation (grant n. 19-26934X, NEUREM3).

The work described also used services provided by the LINDAT/CLARIAH-CZ Research Infrastructure (lindat.cz), supported by the Ministry of Education, Youth and Sports of the Czech Republic (Project No. LM2018101).

References

Loïc Barrault, Magdalena Biesialska, Ondřej Bojar, Marta R Costa-jussà, Christian Federmann, Yvette Graham, Roman Grundkiewicz, Barry Haddow, Matthias Huck, Eric Joanis, et al. 2020. Findings of the 2020 conference on machine translation (wmt20). In *Proceedings of the Fifth Conference on Machine Translation*, pages 1–55.

Nikolay Bogoychev, Roman Grundkiewicz, Alham Fikri Aji, Maximiliana Behnke, Kenneth Heafield, Sidharth Kashyap, Emmanouil-Ioannis Farsarakis, and Mateusz Chudyk. 2020. Edinburgh's submissions to the 2020 machine translation efficiency task. In *Proceedings of the Fourth Workshop on Neural Generation and Translation*, pages 218–224, Online. Association for Computational Linguistics.

Cristian Buciluă, Rich Caruana, and Alexandru Niculescu-Mizil. 2006. Model compression. In *Proceedings of the 12th ACM SIGKDD international conference on Knowledge discovery and data mining*, pages 535–541.

Markus Freitag, Yaser Al-Onaizan, and Baskaran Sankaran. 2017. Ensemble distillation for neural machine translation. *arXiv preprint arXiv:1702.01802*.

Ulrich Germann, Roman Grundkiewicz, Martin Popel, Radina Dobreva, Nikolay Bogoychev, and Kenneth Heafield. 2020. Speed-optimized, compact student models that distill knowledge from a larger teacher model: the uedin-cuni submission to the wmt 2020 news translation task. pages 190–195, Online. Association for Computational Linguistics.

Mitchell A Gordon and Kevin Duh. Distill, adapt, distill: Training small, in-domain models for neural machine translation. *ACL 2020*, page 110.

Geoffrey Hinton, Oriol Vinyals, and Jeff Dean. 2015. Distilling the knowledge in a neural network. *arXiv preprint arXiv:1503.02531*.

Marcin Junczys-Dowmunt. 2019. Microsoft translator at wmt 2019: Towards large-scale document-level neural machine translation. In *Proceedings of the Fourth Conference on Machine Translation (Volume 2: Shared Task Papers, Day 1)*, pages 225–233.

Marcin Junczys-Dowmunt, Roman Grundkiewicz, Tomasz Dwojak, Hieu Hoang, Kenneth Heafield, Tom Neckermann, Frank Seide, Ulrich Germann, Alham Fikri Aji, Nikolay Bogoychev, André F. T. Martins, and Alexandra Birch. 2018. Marian: Fast neural machine translation in C++. In *Proceedings of ACL 2018, System Demonstrations*, pages 116–121, Melbourne, Australia. Association for Computational Linguistics.

Yoon Kim and Alexander M Rush. 2016. Sequence-level knowledge distillation. In *Proceedings of the 2016 Conference on Empirical Methods in Natural Language Processing*, pages 1317–1327.

Tom Kocmi, Martin Popel, and Ondrej Bojar. 2020. Announcing czeng 2.0 parallel corpus with over 2 gigawords. *arXiv preprint arXiv:2007.03006*.

Philipp Koehn. 2005. Europarl: A parallel corpus for statistical machine translation. In *MT summit*, volume 5, pages 79–86. Citeseer.

Taku Kudo and John Richardson. 2018. Sentencepiece: A simple and language independent subword tokenizer and detokenizer for neural text processing. In *Proceedings of the 2018 Conference on Empirical Methods in Natural Language Processing: System Demonstrations*, pages 66–71.

Kishore Papineni, Salim Roukos, Todd Ward, and Wei-Jing Zhu. 2002. Bleu: a method for automatic evaluation of machine translation. In *Proceedings of the 40th annual meeting of the Association for Computational Linguistics*, pages 311–318.

Martin Popel, Marketa Tomkova, Jakub Tomek, Łukasz Kaiser, Jakob Uszkoreit, Ondřej Bojar, and Zdeněk Žabokrtský. 2020. Transforming machine translation: a deep learning system reaches news translation quality comparable to human professionals. *Nature communications*, 11(1):1–15.

Maja Popović. 2015. chrf: character n-gram f-score for automatic mt evaluation. In *Proceedings of the Tenth Workshop on Statistical Machine Translation*, pages 392–395.

Matt Post. 2018. A call for clarity in reporting bleu scores. In *Proceedings of the Third Conference on Machine Translation: Research Papers*, pages 186–191.

Matthew Snover, Bonnie Dorr, Richard Schwartz, Linnea Micciulla, and John Makhoul. 2006. A study of translation edit rate with targeted human annotation. In *Proceedings of association for machine translation in the Americas*, volume 200. Cambridge, MA.

Xu Tan, Yi Ren, Di He, Tao Qin, Zhou Zhao, and Tie-Yan Liu. 2019. Multilingual neural machine translation with knowledge distillation. *arXiv preprint arXiv:1902.10461*.

Ashish Vaswani, Noam Shazeer, Niki Parmar, Jakob Uszkoreit, Llion Jones, Aidan N. Gomez, Lukasz Kaiser, and Illia Polosukhin. 2017. Attention is all you need.

Eric Wallace, Mitchell Stern, and Dawn Song. 2020. Imitation attacks and defenses for black-box machine translation systems. In *Proceedings of the 2020 Conference on Empirical Methods in Natural Language Processing (EMNLP)*, pages 5531–5546.

Hao-Ran Wei, Shujian Huang, Ran Wang, Xinyu Dai, and Jiajun Chen. 2019. Online distilling from checkpoints for neural machine translation. In *Proceedings of the 2019 Conference of the North American Chapter of the Association for Computational Linguistics: Human Language Technologies, Volume 1 (Long and Short Papers)*, pages 1932–1941.

IceSum: An Icelandic Text Summarization Corpus

Jón Friðrik Daðason
Hrafn Loftsson
Department of Computer Science

Reykjavik University
Iceland
{jond19, hrafn}@ru.is

Salome Lilja Sigurðardóttir
Þorsteinn Björnsson
Department of Icelandic and
Comparative Cultural Studies
University of Iceland
Iceland
{sls32, thb123}@hi.is

Abstract

Automatic Text Summarization (ATS) is the task of generating concise and fluent summaries from one or more documents. In this paper, we present IceSum, the first Icelandic corpus annotated with human-generated summaries. IceSum consists of 1,000 online news articles and their extractive summaries. We train and evaluate several neural network-based models on this dataset, comparing them against a selection of baseline methods. The best model obtains a ROUGE-2 recall score of 71.06, outperforming all baseline methods. Furthermore, we evaluate how the amount of training data affects the quality of the generated summaries. Our results show that while the corpus is sufficiently large to train a well-performing model, there could still be significant gains from increasing the size of the training set. We release the corpus and the models with an open license.

1 Introduction

Due to the increasing number of articles being published online every day, there is a growing need for robust Automatic Text Summarization (ATS) systems, which provide readers with a concise and fluent summary of their contents.

ATS systems are often divided into two main types (Gambhir and Gupta, 2017). First, based on the number of source documents used to generate a given summary, i.e. either *single-document* or *multi-document* summarization. In single document summarization, a single document is used for generating the summary, whereas in multi-document summarization many documents are used as the source for the generated summary.

The second type is based on the method used to generate the individual sentences in the summary, i.e. either *extractive* or *abstractive* summarization. Extractive summaries typically consist of sentence-level excerpts from the source document(s), and therefore tend to be grammatically correct and fluent. In contrast, abstractive summaries may contain words, phrases and sentences that do not occur in the original text. These summaries may also introduce grammatical errors and contain statements that are inconsistent with the source text.

Research on ATS for Icelandic has been limited to the evaluation of simple statistical methods (Christiansen, 2014) (described in Section 2). Furthermore, to our best knowledge, no ATS system is currently in use in companies or institutions in Iceland.

In this paper, we present *IceSum*, a corpus of 1,000 Icelandic news articles that can be used to train and evaluate Icelandic ATS systems. We continue previous work on summarizing Icelandic text by evaluating more recently proposed methods for extractive summarization, using neural network-based encoder-decoder models and pre-trained language models. We benchmark several single-document ATS models on this dataset and compare them against previously published methods. The best performing model obtains a ROUGE-2[1] (Lin, 2004) recall score of 71.06. This is the first ATS model for Icelandic which obtains a better result than the Lead baseline method (described in Section 4), which obtains a score of 69.14.

Lemmatization is often employed as a preprocessing step for NLP tasks in Icelandic, as it dramatically reduces the size of the vocabulary. Although it has been shown to be beneficial for tasks such as named entity recognition (Ingólfsdóttir et al., 2020), information extraction (Steingrímsson et al., 2020) and machine translation (Barkarson and Steingrímsson, 2019), previous experiments with non-neural network-based models failed to show any improvement for extractive text summarization. We find that the same holds true for neural network-based models. Finally, we examine

[1]ROUGE-n refers to the overlap of n-grams between the system and the gold summaries.

Proceedings of NAACL-HLT 2021: Student Research Workshop, pages 9–14
June 6–11, 2021. ©2021 Association for Computational Linguistics

the relationship between the size of the training set and the quality of the generated summaries and find that increasing the size of the corpus would likely lead to significantly better results. We release the corpus[2] and the models[3] with an open license.

The rest of this paper is structured as follows. We discuss related work in Section 2 and present the summarization corpus in Section 3. The methods are presented in Section 4 and the experimental setup in Section 5. We present and discuss the evaluation results in Section 6, and, finally, we conclude in Section 7.

2 Related Work

A standard approach to extractive summarization involves allocating a score to each sentence, taking into account certain features, and selecting the most important sentences according to this score. Many different approaches have been proposed for this task, including statistical-based methods such as *TF-IDF* (Salton and McGill, 1986) and graph-based methods such as *TextRank* (Mihalcea and Tarau, 2004). Other methods include supervised machine learning approaches like Support Vector Machines (Hirao et al., 2002; Begum et al., 2009), Hidden Markov Models (Conroy and O'Leary, 2001), Conditional Random Fields (Shen et al., 2007), and genetic algorithms (Mendoza et al., 2014). These approaches obtain better results than purely statistical or graph-based methods (Gambhir and Gupta, 2017), but often require some feature engineering or rely on additional language resources, such as WordNet-like databases (Hirao et al., 2002), which may not be available for many low or medium-resource languages.

The use of neural network-based methods has become commonplace in ATS in recent years. One of the advantages of these methods is that the features are normally inferred automatically as opposed to being learnt with the help of hand-crafted feature templates as in feature-engineered systems. Cheng and Lapata (2016) proposed a neural network-based encoder-decoder model for extractive summarization. In their model, a Convolutional Neural Network (CNN) encoder is used to generate sentence representations which are fed to a Recurrent Neural Network (RNN) encoder that chooses which sentences to extract for the summary. This approach has been improved upon by Nallapati et al. (2017), who instead use a two-layer, bidirectional RNN, and later by Kedzie et al. (2018) who use a sequence-to-sequence model with attention. Encoder-decoder models have been shown to perform well, even with small training sets (Kedzie et al., 2018). More recently, Liu and Lapata (2019) use a pre-trained language model to generate sentence representations, and a two-layer transformer-based sequence classifier to determine which sentences should appear in the summary.

To date, there has been very limited research on text summarization for Icelandic. Christiansen (2014) evaluated the TF-IDF and TextRank (Mihalcea and Tarau, 2004) algorithms on a collection of 20 Icelandic news articles. Despite attempts at improving their performance through pre-processing (e.g., lemmatization and part-of-speech filtering), both algorithms were outperformed by a baseline summarizer which always selects the first few sentences of a document.

As presented in (Dernoncourt et al., 2018), the vast majority of existing text summarization corpora are in English. Of the 21 data sets listed in that paper, only two contain summaries in other languages than English, i.e. Arabic and Chinese. Our work, of compiling an Icelandic text summarization corpus, thus increases the pool of languages available to researchers and developers of ATS systems.

3 The Corpus

Our summarization corpus, IceSum, consists of 1,000 news articles from `mbl.is`, an Icelandic news site. This corpus is similar in size to manually annotated datasets for other languages, such as the DUC-2001 and DUC-2002 single document summarization datasets which contain 607 and 657 news texts, respectively (Kedzie et al., 2018). The goal was originally to assemble around 600 news articles, using the DUC-2001 dataset as a model. The summaries were generated by two annotators who are native speakers with a background in general linguistics and Icelandic literature. Ultimately, the total number of summarized news articles was 1,000, as mentioned above. The articles were split evenly among the two annotators, with each generating a single summary for 500 articles.

The articles in IceSum span a period of 22 years, published between 1998 and 2019, and the dataset was weighted towards more recent articles. It consists of four news categories: local (50%), world

[2]`http://hdl.handle.net/20.500.12537/96`
[3]`https://github.com/cadia-lvl/icesum`

(26%), business (14%) and sports news (10%). The summaries, generated by the two annotators, are extractive, consisting of full sentences or independent clauses from the source text. The majority of the summaries consist of full sentences, i.e. unaltered strings, ending in a full stop.

The sentences were carefully selected based on their informative value. The sentences extracted from the text more often than not contained nouns, especially proper nouns, that were of high importance for the context of the summary. If the agent of a sentence was a pronoun, the referent had to be included in earlier sentences in the summary. In this manner, the summaries always needed to be considered as a whole, rather than a series of sentences, functioning as independent entities. In the case of exceptionally long sentences, independent clauses were extracted from the sentence. In these cases, clauses were cut off right before or after a conjunction, so that the extracted clause would make an independent grammatical sentence in a summary.

The original goal was to compose summaries of 3–6 sentences for each article. Moreover, each summary was meant to contain no more than 50% of the original word count of the article itself. In the case of exceptionally long articles, the total number exceeded the original limit of 6 sentences, resulting in the upper limit of 8 sentences. This resulted in an average of 102 words per summary where the average length of the full articles was 302 words, or roughly three times longer.

4 Methods

We evaluated two types of models. First, three non-machine learning based models, which we refer to as the baseline models. Second, several neural network-based encoder-decoder models.

4.1 Baseline methods

Lead is a simple baseline method that creates a summary consisting of the first several sentences of a document. Despite its simplicity, it has historically proven to be extremely challenging for ATS models to outperform when summarizing news articles (Nenkova, 2005).

We also compared the neural network-based models against the two methods evaluated by Christiansen (2014) on Icelandic news articles, i.e. TextRank and TF-IDF. The graph-based TextRank algorithm is language-independent and requires no training. It uses co-occurrences in the text to identify similarities between sentences and uses the PageRank (Page et al., 1998) algorithm to rank each sentence. The TF-IDF algorithm assigns weights to words based on their frequency, typically obtained from a large text corpus. Sentence weights can be calculated as the average weight of the words they contain.

4.2 Encoder-decoder models

We evaluated an encoder-decoder model using four different extractors implemented in the *nnsum*[4] library:

- **Cheng & Lapata**: a unidirectional sequence-to-sequence based model where the inputs are weighed by the previous extraction probabilities (Cheng and Lapata, 2016).
- **SummaRuNNer**: a bidirectional, two-layer RNN-based sequence classifier that calculates the extraction probability based on several different sources, such as salience and position (Nallapati et al., 2017).
- **RNN**: a bidirectional, RNN-based tagging model (Kedzie et al., 2018).
- **Seq2Seq**: a bidirectional, sequence-to-sequence model with attention (Kedzie et al., 2018).

We additionally evaluate an encoder-decoder model trained using the TransformerSum[5] library, which is heavily based on the BertSum extractive text summarization model (Liu and Lapata, 2019). Sentence vectors are generated using a pre-trained language model, which is then fine-tuned with an additional classification layer.

5 Experimental Setup

We used 70% of the corpus for training, 15% for validation and 15% for testing. Each set consists of articles from the same time range and contains approximately the same proportion of news categories.

For models trained using the nnsum library, we use an averaging encoder, which obtains sentence representations by averaging out word embeddings. We used pre-trained GloVe embeddings (Pennington et al., 2014) with 300 dimensions, trained on

[4]https://github.com/kedz/nnsum

[5]https://github.com/HHousen/TransformerSum

the Icelandic Gigaword Corpus (IGC) (Steingrímsson et al., 2018), which contains approximately 1.5 billion tokens. All models are trained for 50 epochs, and we report results obtained on the test set for the model that achieved the highest ROUGE-2 recall score on the validation set.

The Transformer model was trained using IceBERT (Símonarson et al., 2021), which is fine-tuned using the TransformerSum library. We use a linear classifier and train for 5 epochs. Default settings were used for all experiments, unless otherwise noted. Like Kedzie et al. (2018), we continue adding sentences to our summary until it contains at least 100 words, and truncate summaries to 100 words when computing ROUGE scores.

We also investigated whether lemmatizing the text improves the quality of the summaries. For lemmatization, we first used ABLTagger (Steingrímsson et al., 2019) to assign part-of-speech tags to each token and then Nefnir (Ingólfsdóttir et al., 2019) to lemmatize the text. The Tokenizer[6] library was used to tokenize the source text. For models trained using nnsum, we use GloVe embeddings trained on a lemmatized version of the IGC.

The summarization methods we evaluated extract full sentences from a single document. During training, input sentences are labelled as 1 if they should be extracted and 0 otherwise. As the sentences in the gold summary contain both independent clauses and full sentences, we generated a sentence-level oracle summary for each document, using the same algorithm as Kedzie et al. (2018). For a given document, we greedily select the sentences which result in the highest possible ROUGE-2 score against the gold summary, which are then used to label the training data. We report ROUGE recall scores, calculated without stemming.

6 Results

The results of the evaluation are summarized in Table 1. The encoder-decoder model with the sequence-to-sequence extractor achieves the best performance, obtaining a ROUGE-2 score of 71.06, outperforming the Lead baseline as well as other previously evaluated methods.

For the first time, we have demonstrated an ATS system for Icelandic that outperforms baseline methods. Although Transformer-based models have obtained state-of-the-art performance for extractive summarization (Liu and Lapata, 2019; Zhong et al., 2020), the TransformerSum model does not outperform the Seq2Seq or SummaRuNNeR models in our experiments. This may be due to lack of hyperparameter tuning or the small size of the training set.

Model	R-1	R-2	R-L
Oracle	92.04	89.31	91.92
Lead	76.19	69.14	75.67
TextRank	60.43	47.09	59.07
TF-IDF	63.46	51.77	62.30
Cheng & Lapata	76.60	69.34	76.10
SummaRuNNer	**76.98**	**69.80**	**76.43**
RNN	76.84	69.79	76.26
Seq2Seq	**77.98**	**71.06**	**77.48**
TransformerSum	**76.80**	**69.59**	**76.23**

Table 1: ROUGE scores for all evaluated models. Scores in bold are statistically indistinguishable from the best model (paired t-test; $p < 0.05$).

As shown in Table 2, we find that lemmatizing the input text results in lower ROUGE scores. Our results are consistent with those of Christiansen (2014), who also finds that lemmatization has a negative impact on the quality of generated summaries.

Model	R-1	R-2	R-L
Oracle	92.04	89.31	91.92
Lead	**76.19**	**69.14**	**75.67**
TextRank	60.40	47.02	59.00
TF-IDF	62.25	50.21	61.24
Cheng & Lapata	**75.98**	**68.67**	**75.43**
SummaRuNNer	**75.82**	**68.17**	**75.20**
RNN	**76.17**	**69.07**	**75.64**
Seq2Seq	**76.33**	**69.19**	**75.80**

Table 2: ROUGE scores for all evaluated models when the text has been lemmatized. The TransformerSum model is omitted as it was pre-trained on unlemmatized text. Scores in bold are statistically indistinguishable from the best model (paired t-test; $p < 0.05$).

To estimate how the ROUGE score is affected by the size of the training set, we split it into 7 equally sized portions, each containing the same proportion of news categories. Figure 1 shows the ROUGE-2 recall score for the Seq2Seq model on the test set for a varying number of articles in the training set.

Notably, the Seq2Seq model almost matches the ROUGE-2 recall score of the Lead baseline method

[6] `https://github.com/mideind/Tokenizer`

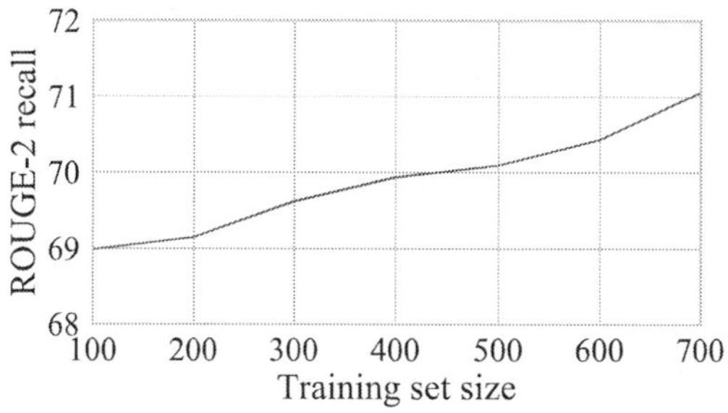

Figure 1: ROUGE-2 recall scores of the Seq2Seq model with varying amounts of training data.

with a training set of only 100 news articles. Furthermore, the ROUGE-2 score is still rising at a steady pace with a training set of 700 articles, suggesting that there may be significant benefits to enlarging the size of the corpus.

7 Conclusion

We presented the first Icelandic corpus annotated with human-generated summaries and showed that it can be used to to create an ATS system that outperforms baseline methods. We also showed that lemmatizing the source text does not result in improved performance. Finally, we evaluated how the size of the training corpus affects the quality of the generated summaries. The corpus and models have been released with an open license.

For future work, we intend to experiment further with Transformer-based models, performing hyperparameter tuning for a selection of Transformer models, such as RoBERTa-Base and ELECTRA-Base. We also plan to experiment with abstractive summarization using a much larger, unannotated corpus of Icelandic news articles. We also hope to add more summaries to the IceSum corpus in the future, and to examine inter-annotator agreement.

Acknowledgements

This work was funded by the Icelandic Strategic Research and Development Programme for Language Technology 2019, grant no. 180037-5301.

References

Starkaður Barkarson and Steinþór Steingrímsson. 2019. Compiling and Filtering ParIce: An English-Icelandic Parallel Corpus. In *Proceedings of the 22nd Nordic Conference on Computational Linguistics*, pages 140–145, Turku, Finland. Linköping University Electronic Press.

Nadira Begum, Mohamed A. Fattah, and Fuji Ren. 2009. Automatic Text Summarization Using Support Vector Machine. *International Journal of Innovative Computing, Information and Control*, 5(7):1987–1996.

Jianpeng Cheng and Mirella Lapata. 2016. Neural Summarization by Extracting Sentences and Words. In *Proceedings of the 54th Annual Meeting of the Association for Computational Linguistics (Volume 1: Long Papers)*, pages 484–494, Berlin, Germany. Association for Computational Linguistics.

Karin Christiansen. 2014. Summarization of Icelandic Texts. Master's thesis, Reykjavik University, Reykjavik, Iceland.

John M. Conroy and Dianne P. O'Leary. 2001. Text Summarization via Hidden Markov Models. In *Proceedings of the 24th Annual International ACM SIGIR Conference on Research and Development in Information Retrieval*, SIGIR '01, page 406–407, New Orleans, Louisiana, USA. Association for Computing Machinery.

Franck Dernoncourt, Mohammad Ghassemi, and Walter Chang. 2018. A Repository of Corpora for Summarization. In *Proceedings of the Eleventh International Conference on Language Resources and Evaluation*, LREC 2018, Miyazaki, Japan. European Language Resources Association (ELRA).

Mahak Gambhir and Vishal Gupta. 2017. Recent Automatic Text Summarization Techniques: A Survey. *Artificial Intelligence Review*, 47(1):1–66.

Tsutomu Hirao, Hideki Isozaki, Eisaku Maeda, and Yuji Matsumoto. 2002. Extracting Important Sentences with Support Vector Machines. In *Proceedings of the 19th International Conference on Computational Linguistics - Volume 1*, COLING '02, page 1–7, Taipei, Taiwan. Association for Computational Linguistics.

Svanhvít L. Ingólfsdóttir, Ásmundur A. Guðjónsson, and Hrafn Loftsson. 2020. Named Entity Recognition for Icelandic: Annotated Corpus and Models. In *Statistical Language and Speech Processing*, pages 46–57, Cham. Springer International Publishing.

Svanhvít Lilja Ingólfsdóttir, Hrafn Loftsson, Jón Friðrik Daðason, and Kristín Bjarnadóttir. 2019. Nefnir: A high accuracy lemmatizer for Icelandic. In *Proceedings of the 22nd Nordic Conference on Computational Linguistics*, pages 310–315, Turku, Finland. Linköping University Electronic Press.

Chris Kedzie, Kathleen McKeown, and Hal Daumé III. 2018. Content Selection in Deep Learning Models of Summarization. In *Proceedings of the 2018 Conference on Empirical Methods in Natural Language Processing*, pages 1818–1828, Brussels, Belgium. Association for Computational Linguistics.

Chin-Yew Lin. 2004. ROUGE: A Package for Automatic Evaluation of Summaries. In *Text Summarization Branches Out*, pages 74–81, Barcelona, Spain. Association for Computational Linguistics.

Yang Liu and Mirella Lapata. 2019. Text Summarization with Pretrained Encoders. In *Proceedings of the 2019 Conference on Empirical Methods in Natural Language Processing and the 9th International Joint Conference on Natural Language Processing (EMNLP-IJCNLP)*, pages 3730–3740, Hong Kong, China. Association for Computational Linguistics.

Martha Mendoza, Susana Bonilla, Clara Noguera, Carlos Cobos, and Elizabeth León. 2014. Extractive Single-Document Summarization Based on Genetic Operators and Guided Local Search. *Expert Systems with Applications*, 41(9):4158–4169.

Rada Mihalcea and Paul Tarau. 2004. TextRank: Bringing Order into Text. In *Proceedings of the 2004 Conference on Empirical Methods in Natural Language Processing*, pages 404–411, Barcelona, Spain. Association for Computational Linguistics.

Ramesh Nallapati, Feifei Zhai, and Bowen Zhou. 2017. SummaRuNNer: A Recurrent Neural Network Based Sequence Model for Extractive Summarization of Documents. In *Proceedings of the Thirty-First AAAI Conference on Artificial Intelligence*, AAAI'17, page 3075–3081, San Francisco, California, USA. AAAI Press.

Ani Nenkova. 2005. Automatic Text Summarization of Newswire: Lessons Learned from the Document Understanding Conference. In *Proceedings of the 20th National Conference on Artificial Intelligence - Volume 3*, AAAI'05, page 1436–1441, Pittsburgh, Pennsylvania. AAAI Press.

Larry Page, Sergey Brin, Rajeev Motwani, and Terry Winograd. 1998. The PageRank citation ranking: Bringing order to the Web. In *Proceedings of the 7th International World Wide Web Conference*, pages 161–172, Brisbane, Australia.

Jeffrey Pennington, Richard Socher, and Christopher Manning. 2014. Glove: Global Vectors for Word Representation. In *Proceedings of the Conference on Empirical Methods in Natural Language Processing*, EMNLP 2014, Doha, Qatar.

Gerard Salton and Michael J. McGill. 1986. *Introduction to Modern Information Retrieval*. McGraw-Hill, Inc., USA.

Dou Shen, Jian-Tao Sun, Hua Li, Qiang Yang, and Zheng Chen. 2007. Document Summarization Using Conditional Random Fields. In *Proceedings of the 20th International Joint Conference on Artifical Intelligence*, IJCAI'07, page 2862–2867, Hyderabad, India. Morgan Kaufmann Publishers Inc.

Steinþór Steingrímsson, Örvar Kárason, and Hrafn Loftsson. 2019. Augmenting a BiLSTM Tagger with a Morphological Lexicon and a Lexical Category Identification Step. In *Proceedings of the International Conference on Recent Advances in Natural Language Processing*, RANLP 2019, pages 1161–1168, Varna, Bulgaria. INCOMA Ltd.

Steinþór Steingrímsson, Sigrún Helgadóttir, Eiríkur Rögnvaldsson, Starkaður Barkarson, and Jón Guðnason. 2018. Risamálheild: A Very Large Icelandic Text Corpus. In *Proceedings of the Eleventh International Conference on Language Resources and Evaluation*, LREC 2018, Miyazaki, Japan.

Steinþór Steingrímsson, Ágústa Þorbergsdóttir, Hjalti Daníelsson, and Gunnar Thor Örnólfsson. 2020. TermPortal: A Workbench for Automatic Term Extraction from Icelandic Texts. In *Proceedings of the 6th International Workshop on Computational Terminology*, pages 8–16, Marseille, France. European Language Resources Association.

Haukur B. Símonarson, Vésteinn Snæbjarnarson, Pétur O. Ragnarsson, and Hafsteinn Einarsson. 2021. ByteBERT: Masked language modeling for morphologically rich languages (IceBERT). Unpublished manuscript.

Ming Zhong, Pengfei Liu, Yiran Chen, Danqing Wang, Xipeng Qiu, and Xuanjing Huang. 2020. Extractive summarization as text matching. In *Proceedings of the 58th Annual Meeting of the Association for Computational Linguistics*, pages 6197–6208, Online. Association for Computational Linguistics.

Negation typology and general representation models for cross-lingual zero-shot negation scope resolution in Russian, French, and Spanish

Anastassia Shaitarova
Department of Computational Linguistics
University of Zurich, Switzerland
anastassia.shaitarova@uzh.ch

Fabio Rinaldi
Dalle Molle Institute for Artificial
Intelligence Research, Switzerland
fabio.rinaldi@idsia.ch

Abstract

Negation is a linguistic universal that poses difficulties for cognitive and computational processing. Despite many advances in text analytics, negation resolution remains an acute and continuously researched question in Natural Language Processing. Reliable negation parsing affects results in biomedical text mining, sentiment analysis, machine translation, and many other fields. The availability of multilingual pre-trained general representation models makes it possible to experiment with negation detection in languages that lack annotated data. In this work we test the performance of two state-of-the-art contextual representation models, Multilingual BERT and XLM-RoBERTa. We resolve negation scope by conducting zero-shot transfer between English, Spanish, French, and Russian. Our best result amounts to a token-level F1-score of 86.86% from Spanish to Russian. We correlate these results with a linguistic negation typology and lexical capacity of the models.

1 Introduction

Negation continues to occupy the minds of many researchers. It is a fascinating and complicated linguistic phenomenon that is still not entirely understood or conceptualized. Moreover negation is an important thought process. The ability to negate is a deeply human trait that is also universal, therefore any given language is bound to have negation (Horn, 2001).

Negation has the power to change the truth value of a proposition. Thus its identification in text is of utmost importance for the reliability of results since negated information should either be discarded or presented separately from the facts. This is particularly relevant for biomedical text mining and sentiment analysis but is also important for most Natural Language Processing (NLP) tasks. The identification of negated textual spans, however, is far from trivial. Negation exhibits great diversity in its syntactic and morphological representation.

Like many other NLP tasks, most work on negation detection has been done on the English language, though there is a growing amount of research on negation detection in Spanish, Chinese and some other languages. Despite the need for quality text analytics around the world, annotated data is still sparse in many languages. This motivates the further exploration of approaches like transfer learning where models are trained on available resources and subsequently tested on a different target language.

In this paper we use a cross-lingual transfer-learning approach for negation scope detection using two state-of-the-art general purpose representation models: mBERT (Multilingual BERT, Devlin, 2018) and XLM-R (XLM-RoBERTa, Conneau et al., 2020). We fine-tune the models on freely accessible annotated corpora in English, Spanish, and French and test them cross-lingually. Additionally we test the models on a small dataset in Russian which was specially annotated for the experiment. Our research is guided by three objectives:

- We compare the performance of two state-of-the-art models on the task of cross-lingual zero-shot negation scope resolution in Spanish, French, and Russian;
- We experiment with Russian which is an under-sourced and under-researched language regarding the task of negation detection;
- We study the four involved languages typologically and correlate our findings with the experiment results.

In Section 2 we perform a brief typological analysis of the languages in relation to negation. Additionally, we overview previous work on cross-

Proceedings of NAACL-HLT 2021: Student Research Workshop, pages 15–23
June 6–11, 2021.

lingual negation scope resolution. Section 3 discusses the datasets and highlights their annotation differences. We describe the experiments and present the results in Section 4, and in Sections 5 and 6 we discuss the results and draw conclusions.

2 Negation and its processing

Linguistics and typology. A number of psycholinguistic studies show that humans require extra time in order to process negation during language comprehension (Gulgowski and Błaszczak, 2020). This is attributed to the fact that humans first construct a positive counterpart of the argument and only then embed its negative aspect as an extra step (Tian and Breheny, 2016). Indeed, negative sentences exhibit a more complicated, marked-up structure on a lexico-syntactic level which is a universal feature (Barigou et al., 2018). The main building blocks of this markup are negative words and expressions, also known as negative markers, cues, or triggers.

When a sentence contains more than one negation trigger, Negative Concord (NC) languages treat them as one, letting relevant negative markers intensify one another. The majority of languages including French, Spanish, and Russian belong to the NC group. Standard English, on the other hand, is a Double Negation (DN) language where each negative marker is interpreted separately.

Hossain et al. (2020) compared English to a number of languages in regards to negation features drawn from the World Atlas of Language Structures (WALS)[1]. They showed that the number of negation-related errors in machine translation corresponds to how close the languages are in a typology based on negation.

Inspired by their discoveries we construct a negation-based typology for our languages and merge it with the classification from Dahl (1979). Even though English, French, Spanish, and Russian are in the same linguistic family and feature the same subject-verb-object pattern, the typology based on negation assigns them to different categories (Table 1).

We expect a negation-based linguistic typology to help us predict and interpret our results. According to our classification, Russian is most similar to Spanish and least similar to English. Thus we hypothesise that zero-shot transfer from Spanish into Russian will be most successful.

[1]https://wals.info/

Lang	predNeg	symm	NC/DN	Dahl et al.
RU	yes	symm	NC	S11 12
ES	mixed	symm	NC	S11 12
FR	no	symm	NC	$S11^2$ 12/22
EN	no	both	DN	S11/S3 22

Table 1: Negation-based typology of languages. **PredNeg** indicates whether negative indefinite pronouns require an additional negative particle. Symmetricity of negation (**symm**) shows whether the presence of a negation marker causes grammatical changes in the sentence. **NC/DN** means Negative Concord vs. Double Negation. In **Dahl**'s typology S11 represents a class of languages where an uninflected particle must be added while the finite verb does not change. $S11^2$ signals the use of double particles. Number 12 categorizes languages where a negative marker immediately precedes a finite element (verb) whereas 22 indicates that the marker immediately follows it. S3 shows the use of noninflected markers together with dummy auxiliaries.

Automated negation detection consists of two tasks: identification of negation cues, and detection of sentence parts that are affected by these cues. The latter is called *negation scope resolution*, the task that interests us most.

Negation detection began in the medical domain with the goal of improving information retrieval from Electronic Health Records (EHRs). Rule-based algorithms such as NegExpander (Aronow et al., 1999), NegFinder (Mutalik et al., 2001), NegEx (Chapman et al., 2001), and their adaptations were used in order to find medical concepts and then determine whether they are negated. The scope of negation was often understood as a distance between a negation cue and a medical term that it affects.

These algorithms were successful and some are still in wide use due to their explainability, customizability, and independence from annotated data. NegEx is incorporated into various modern computational libraries[2] and is successfully used for biomedical texts (Cotik et al., 2016; Elazhary, 2017). Despite the aforementioned qualities, rule-based algorithms suffer from an inherent inability to generalize (Wu et al., 2014; Sergeeva et al., 2019; Sykes et al., 2020).

The release of the BioScope corpus (Szarvas

[2]cTAKES:https://pypi.org/project/ctakes-parser/, pyConTextNLP:https://github.com/chapmanbe/pyConTextNLP, negspaCy: https://spacy.io/universe/project/negspacy, etc.

et al., 2008; Vincze et al., 2008) became a pivotal moment for negation detection by providing data for machine learning. Negation scope resolution was formalized by Morante et al. (2008); Morante and Daelemans (2009), who established it as a problem of sequence classification. Using gold-standard cues and an ensemble of three different classifiers, they achieved the best F1-score of 84.71% on the Full Papers subcorpus of BioScope and 90.67% on the Abstracts subcorpus. The latter result was later surpassed by Fancellu et al. (2017) who employed neural networks and reached a score of 92.11%.

The Shared Task on Resolving the Scope and Focus of Negation (Morante and Blanco, 2012) addressed the issue of negation scope resolution directly and released another annotated corpus (ConanDoyle-neg, Morante and Daelemans, 2012). The best system (Packard et al., 2014) used an enhanced hybrid model by Read et al. (2012) and a semantic parser. They reached an F1-score of 88.2% using gold-standard cues. These results were surpassed by Li and Lu (2018) who used the Conditional Random Fields classifier and reached an F1-score of 89.4%.

Additionally, Fancellu et al. (2016) secured an F1-score of 89.93% on the SFU Review-NEG corpus (Konstantinova et al., 2012), another publicly available corpus annotated for negation scope. The results on these three corpora remained the benchmark for negation scope resolution until the Bidirectional Encoder Representation from Transformers (BERT, Devlin et al., 2019) became the new state of the art. Moreover, BERT became widely used for transfer learning due to its enhanced ability to generalize using attention and general purpose language representations. NegBERT (Khandelwal and Sawant, 2020) set new records for negation scope resolution on all three publicly available corpora.

Cross-lingual negation scope work. Many languages remain under-researched regarding negation detection and particularly scope resolution. One of the main problems is the lack of annotated data. There currently exist a handful of corpora in English, two in Spanish, and one corpus each in Swedish, German, Dutch, Chinese, Italian, and Portuguese which are not all publicly available (Jiménez-Zafra et al., 2020).

Negation work on Spanish has been growing in recent years but it has mostly concerned sentiment analysis (Brooke et al., 2009; Vilares et al., 2013; Jimenez Zafra et al., 2019). Rivera Zavala and Martinez (2020) are the first ones to work with sense embeddings to detect negation cues and scopes in the Spanish biomedical and general domain texts. They also worked with mBERT but in a monolingual setting. The research on negation in French is particularly limited. Aside from a few papers describing rule-based approaches (Deléger and Grouin, 2012; Abdaoui et al., 2017) and the implementation of BiLSTMs by Dalloux et al. (2019, 2020), there is barely any other research available on the topic.

Cross-lingual work on negation detection is even more limited. Fancellu et al. (2018) developed a truly cross-lingual system that uses no language specific features. They worked with English and Chinese and used universal dependencies to abstract away from the word order. Their Bidirectional Dependency LSTM model reached an F1-score of 72.46%.

Finally, Shaitarova et al. (2020) employed Multilingual BERT to perform zero-shot transfer for negation scope resolution and showed good preliminary results. We build on this work and compare mBERT with a new multilingual general purpose representation model, XLM-R. Unlike mBERT, XLM-R was pre-trained on more than two terabytes of filtered data collected by CommonCrawl. Instead of WordPiece units it uses SentencePiece (Kudo and Richardson, 2018) units and features a bigger size of shared vocabulary (250K).

3 Data

In our experiments we work with a corpus of clinical texts in French (Dalloux et al., 2020), and SFU ReviewSP-NEG, a Spanish corpus of online reviews (Jiménez-Zafra et al., 2018). The English data includes the biological paper abstracts and full scientific articles in the domain of bioinformatics from BioScope (Vincze et al., 2008), all available subcorpora of the ConanDoyle-neg corpus (Morante and Daelemans, 2012) as well as SFU (SFU Review-NEG, Konstantinova et al., 2012), a large multi-domain corpus of product reviews.

We use the English corpora separately and also combine them into one training dataset. The three corpora belong to different domains and feature certain variations in scope annotation guidelines. Despite these significant problems we combine the datasets based on the successful cross-corpora knowledge transfer described by Khandelwal and Sawant (2020).

The BioScope annotators set the precedent by ultimately basing scope annotation on syntax. They employed a maximal scope size strategy and extended annotation to the biggest syntactic unit possible. The normal direction of scope was assumed to be to the right of the cue. The subject is not included in the scope, unless the sentence has a passive voice.

Morante et al. (2011) argued that semantically the subject should be always annotated within the scope. Thus, unlike the BioScope corpus, ConanDoyle-neg includes the subject yet excludes the cue. Additionally, it features morphological negations. The SFU corpus mostly adheres to the BioScope's annotation guidelines but does not include cues into the scope of negation.

The French data is described in Dalloux et al. (2020) and is publicly available on request[3]. It combines two subcorpora of clinical narratives. Its format and annotations are loosely modeled on the ConanDoyle-neg corpus. The data in the Spanish SFU ReviewSP-NEG corpus can be requested from Simon Fraser University. Its annotations reflect the guidelines of the English corpora but are also based on Spanish grammar.

In our experiments we only use sentences that contain at least one negation. We duplicate sentences with multiple negations into several copies containing a single negation. Table 2 shows the statistics for all the corpora. For the sake of consistency we excluded cues from scope annotation across all corpora.

	ConDo	BioScope	SFU	SP	FR
uniq	1215	1935	3112	3258	1682
negs+	1421	2095	3528	4327	1870

Table 2: Corpora statistics. `uniq` indicates the original number of unique sentences with negations. `neg+` shows the number of negation sentences after the duplication of sentences with multiple negations.

3.1 The Russian test set

To the best of our knowledge, there are no publicly available negation corpora in Russian or any other Slavic language. Thus, there is almost no available research on negation detection in Russian on either the English or Russian speaking Internet, with Funkner et al. (2020) being the only relevant publication.

In order to work with Russian in our experiments, we created a small dataset annotated with negation cues and negation scopes[4]. It is a Russian counterpart to one of the ConanDoyle-neg's test sets, The Adventure of the Cardboard Box. The number of sentences containing negation amounts to 120.

The annotation was performed by one native Russian speaker using Prodigy[5], an annotation tool created by explosion.ai. Since there are no known publications about negation detection for Russian, the annotation was based on linguistic intuition, Russian grammar, and a generalization of annotation schema from the other corpora.

In accordance with the guidelines, the scope in the Russian test set corresponds to a syntactic component. A maximal scope rule was implemented as in BioScope. The subject is included in the scope when the negation cue directly affects the main verb. Cues are not included in the scope. Since morphological cues appear only in ConanDoyle-neg, they were not considered during annotation.

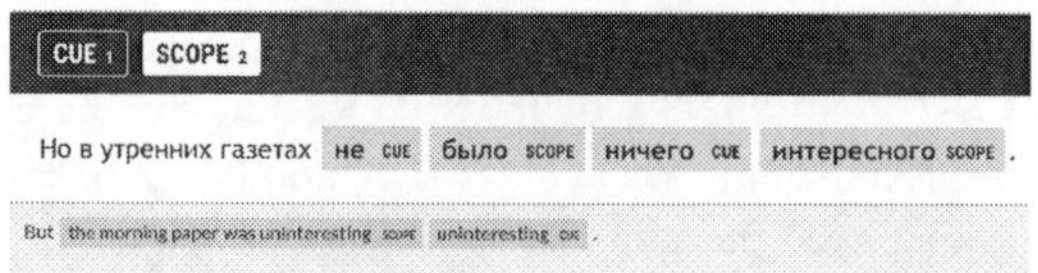

Figure 1: Annotation of negation cues and scopes in a Russian sentence with the use of the Prodigy annotation tool.

4 Experiments and results

We used NegBERT (Khandelwal and Sawant, 2020) as the main architecture and employed `bert-base-multilingual-cased` and `xlm-roberta-base-model` models. We fine-tuned the two models on the three datasets: English (**en**), Spanish (**es**), and French (**fr**). All the models were trained with the same set of hyperparameters. Early stopping method with patience set to 9 was used to prevent overfitting. The maximum input length was adjusted to 250 to prevent truncated sentences.

The word-level token class is determined by using the argmax function on the averaged softmax

[3] `http://people.irisa.fr/Clement.Dalloux/`

[4] `https://doi.org/10.5281/zenodo.4537833`

[5] (Montani and Honnibal, 2018)

probabilities of all subword units. We use gold-standard negation cues and report token-level F1-scores for negation scope resolution (Table 3).

Despite the fact that the English corpora are of different domains, models fine-tuned on the combined English data brought better cross-lingual results than models that were fine-tuned on each corpus individually. Even the model fine-tuned on the ConanDoyle-neg corpus did not perform better on the Russian version of the text. Thus, we only discuss the results of the model trained on the entirety of the English data.

Since the datasets differ in size, we ran additional experiments where we equalized the number of training examples to the smallest corpus (French). We drew a random sample of 1870 sentences from the English and the Spanish data and retrained the models. Row ru2 in Table 3 shows these evaluation results.

	EN		**FR**		**ES**	
fr	82.61	83.22	–	–	79.33	79.79
es	78.62	78.83	76.81	78.17	–	–
ru	83.47	86.49	76.50	80.07	81.40	86.73
ru2	80.07	85.35	76.50	80.07	81.24	86.86

Table 3: Evaluation results for mBERT (grey columns) and XLM_RoBERTa (white columns). The models were fine-tuned on English (**EN**), French (**FR**), and Spanish (**ES**) and tested on French (**fr**), Spanish (**sp**), and Russian (**ru**). Row **ru2** shows evaluations of models that were fine-tuned on equal size data.

5 Discussion and error analysis

There have been many debates on whether BERT-like models truly "understand" negation. Zhao and Bethard (2020) showed evidence for shallow encoding of this phenomenon in both BERT and RoBERTa. Meanwhile Staliūnaitė and Iacobacci (2020) demonstrated that these models lack linguistic abstraction abilities and fail when confronted with compositional semantic aspects of language.

In our experiments, the XLM-R model performed significantly better than mBERT for all language pairs. As an additional metric, we measured how well both models identified scopes with 100% precision. Averaged across all languages, both models performed equally well, with mBERT solving 46.23% of exact scopes, and XLM-R - 46.66%. The best result for Russian was produced by the XLM-R model fine-tuned on Spanish (53% of exact scopes).

In fact, Russian benefited most from a transfer from Spanish and least from French, irrespective of training data size or model type. We can assume that the success of the Spanish-Russian transfer is partially due to the commonalities described in Table 1. Nevertheless, the negation typology does not explain the poor results of the French-Russian pair.

We investigated several factors that might have negatively affected the French-Russian knowledge transfer. For example, we examined the vocabularies of the models and calculated lexical overlap between the datasets based on a model-specific tokenization. The comparison in Table 4 shows a lower percentage of lexical overlap between the Russian and the French datasets than between Russian and other languages. According to this observation, however, English-Russian transfer should have been the most successful one.

	vocab size		shared vocab					
	SubW	SentP	**en**		**fr**		**es**	
en	10550	10592	–	–	23	21	28	26
es	8453	8934	35	31	22	17	–	–
fr	5101	5032	47	44	–	–	36	31
ru	1280	1329	35	31	23	21	28	26

Table 4: Vocabulary distribution across the data. Numbers in grey are calculated on the basis of mBERT's SubWord units. White columns show XLM-R's SentencePiece units. Numbers in the shared vocab section indicate percentages. For example, the French data shares 47% of its WordPieces and 44% of its SentencePieces with the English dataset, while only 23% of the English SubWords and 21% of its SentencePieces appear in the French dataset.

Next, we took a closer look at our negation typology. We investigated a prominent phenomenon that emerges in several categories, namely negative indefinite pronouns (words like *nothing, nowhere, nobody*). The way a languages handles these pronouns is reflected in both the **predNeg** and the **NC/DN** columns in Table 1. This phenomenon classifies Russian and English as polar opposites.

We found 19 sentences in the Russian dataset that contain negation structures with negative indefinite pronouns. Despite the fact that these pronouns are always marked as cues, the English XLM-R model included them into the scope 9 times. The English mBERT model made that same mistake 3 times. On the other hand, neither Spanish, nor French models had this problem. We can hypothesise that a model fine-tuned on English could not coordinate a negative particle with an indefinite negative pronoun in the same sentence since this does not occur in English.

During the examination of these 19 sentences we stated that the models fine-tuned on the French data persistently omit the subject of a sentence in the annotation of scope. The English models also suffered from this problem but to a lesser extent. This can be traced to the difference in annotation. The subject is not annotated in the French corpus while only part of the English data features that annotation. Figure 2 illustrates the issue of negative indefinite pronouns as well the annotation of a sentence's subject.

ES: Нет, [я] **ничего** [такого] **не** [видел].
EN: Нет, я [**ничего** такого] **не** [видел].
FR: Нет, я **ничего** [такого] **не** [видел].
No, I nothing such not saw.

No, [I saw] **nothing**.

Figure 2: A Russian sentence with a negative indefinite pronoun featuring annotations by three XLM-R models fine-tuned on Spanish (ES), English (EN), and French(FR). The fourth line contains a literal translation. The bottom line is the original sentence and annotation from the ConanDoyle-neg corpus.

Additionally we investigated scope annotations which were precisely identified by one type of model but not the other. We chose to look at the highest scoring language pair Spanish-Russian where the models were trained on 1870 sentences. There are 15 sentences where the XLM-R model found scope with a perfect precision while mBERT did not. In most cases mBERT made a mistake in the leftward direction from a negation cue.

We found only four cases where mBERT scored perfectly while XLM-R made a mistake. The mistakes are rather random and do not seem to belong to a particular pattern. Overall, we detected several situations where mistakes made by the models could be scrutinized due to questionable annotation. We acknowledge that the lack of additional annotators and an inter-annotator agreement is a weakness that should be addressed in further work.

6 Conclusion

The short excursion into negation scope resolution in Russian using zero-shot model transfer has shown good preliminary results. Despite controversial previous findings, multilingual general purpose representation models perform rather well on negation scope resolution. XLM-RoBERTa scored consistently better than mBERT in all language pairs.

We constructed a typology that classifies English, Spanish, French, and Russian according to their negation-based features. Since indefinite negative pronouns play a role in several typological categories, we investigated their effect on zero-shot transfer. We found that fine-tuning models on English compromises their performance with this phenomenon when transferring to Russian, which correlates with the negation typology.

Transferring syntactic negation knowledge from Spanish brought the most benefit for Russian. This result is fully in line with the negation typology of the four languages. Despite the clear correlation between the negation typology and the results of the Spanish-Russian transfer, not all outcomes are easily explainable. The relatively poor performance of the French-Russian transfer might be related to the domain mismatch and the difference in annotation schemes. A lower lexical overlap between the vocabularies could have had an effect as well.

Future work involves growing the Russian corpus of negations, ideally benefiting from multiple annotators. It may prove beneficial to perform a systematic examination of all the categories constituting the negation typology and to expose their effects on knowledge transfer across languages.

References

Amine Abdaoui, Andon Tchechmedjiev, William Digan, Sandra Bringay, and Clement Jonquet. 2017. French ConText: Détecter la négation, la temporalité et le sujet dans les textes cliniques Français.

David B. Aronow, Feng Fangfang, and W. Bruce Croft. 1999. Ad Hoc Classification of Radiology Reports. *Journal of the American Medical Informatics Association : JAMIA*, 6(5):393–411.

Baya Naouel Barigou, Fatiha Barigou, and Baghdad Atmani. 2018. Handling Negation to Improve Information Retrieval from French Clinical Reports. *Journal of e-Learning and Knowledge Society*, 14(1). Number: 1.

Julian Brooke, Milan Tofiloski, and Maite Taboada. 2009. Cross-Linguistic Sentiment Analysis: From English to Spanish. In *Proceedings of the International Conference RANLP-2009*, pages 50–54, Borovets, Bulgaria. Association for Computational Linguistics.

Wendy W. Chapman, Will Bridewell, Paul Hanbury, Gregory F. Cooper, and Bruce G. Buchanan. 2001. A Simple Algorithm for Identifying Negated Findings and Diseases in Discharge Summaries. *Journal of Biomedical Informatics*, 34(5):301–310.

Alexis Conneau, Kartikay Khandelwal, Naman Goyal, Vishrav Chaudhary, Guillaume Wenzek, Francisco Guzmán, Edouard Grave, Myle Ott, Luke Zettlemoyer, and Veselin Stoyanov. 2020. Unsupervised Cross-lingual Representation Learning at Scale. *arXiv:1911.02116 [cs]*. ArXiv: 1911.02116.

Viviana Cotik, Roland Roller, Feiyu Xu, Hans Uszkoreit, Klemens Budde, and Danilo Schmidt. 2016. Negation Detection in Clinical Reports Written in German. In *Proceedings of the Fifth Workshop on Building and Evaluating Resources for Biomedical Text Mining (BioTxtM2016)*, pages 115–124, Osaka, Japan. The COLING 2016 Organizing Committee.

Östen Dahl. 1979. Typology of sentence negation. *Linguistics*, 17(1-2):79–106. Publisher: De Gruyter Mouton Section: Linguistics.

Clément Dalloux, Vincent Claveau, and Natalia Grabar. 2019. Speculation and Negation detection in French biomedical corpora. In *Proceedings of the International Conference on Recent Advances in Natural Language Processing (RANLP 2019)*, pages 223–232, Varna, Bulgaria. INCOMA Ltd.

Clément Dalloux, Vincent Claveau, Natalia Grabar, Lucas Emanuel Silva Oliveira, Claudia Maria Cabral Moro, Yohan Bonescki Gumiel, and Deborah Ribeiro Carvalho. 2020. Supervised learning for the detection of negation and of its scope in French and Brazilian Portuguese biomedical corpora. *Natural Language Engineering*, pages 1–21. Publisher: Cambridge University Press.

Louise Deléger and Cyril Grouin. 2012. Detecting Negation of Medical Problems in French Clinical Notes. In *Proc of Int Health Inform*, Miami Beach, FL.

Jacob Devlin. 2018. Multilingual BERT Readme document. Library Catalog: github.com.

Jacob Devlin, Ming-Wei Chang, Kenton Lee, and Kristina Toutanova. 2019. BERT: Pre-training of Deep Bidirectional Transformers for Language Understanding. *arXiv:1810.04805 [cs]*. ArXiv: 1810.04805.

Hanan Elazhary. 2017. NegMiner: An Automated Tool for Mining Negations from Electronic Narrative Medical Documents.

Federico Fancellu, Adam Lopez, and Bonnie Webber. 2016. Neural Networks For Negation Scope Detection. In *Proceedings of the 54th Annual Meeting of the Association for Computational Linguistics (Volume 1: Long Papers)*, pages 495–504, Berlin, Germany. Association for Computational Linguistics.

Federico Fancellu, Adam Lopez, Bonnie Webber, and Hangfeng He. 2017. Detecting negation scope is easy, except when it isn't. In *Proceedings of the 15th Conference of the European Chapter of the Association for Computational Linguistics: Volume 2, Short Papers*, pages 58–63, Valencia, Spain. Association for Computational Linguistics.

Federico Fancellu, Adam Lopez, and Bonnie L. Webber. 2018. Neural Networks for Cross-lingual Negation Scope Detection. *ArXiv*, abs/1810.02156.

Anastasia Funkner, Ksenia Balabaeva, and Sergey Kovalchuk. 2020. Negation Detection for Clinical Text Mining in Russian. *arXiv:2004.04980 [cs]*. ArXiv: 2004.04980 version: 1.

Piotr Gulgowski and Joanna Błaszczak. 2020. Psycholinguistic Investigation of the Immediate Interpretation of Plural Nouns in the Scope of Sentential Negation in Polish. *Journal of Psycholinguistic Research*, 49(5):741–760.

Laurence R. Horn. 2001. *A natural history of negation*. The David Hume series. CSLI, Stanford, Calif.

Md Mosharaf Hossain, Antonios Anastasopoulos, Eduardo Blanco, and Alexis Palmer. 2020. It's not a Non-Issue: Negation as a Source of Error in Machine Translation. *arXiv:2010.05432 [cs]*. ArXiv: 2010.05432.

Salud Maria Jimenez Zafra, M. Teresa Martin Valdivia, Eugenio Martinez Camara, and L Alfonso Urena Lopez. 2019. Studying the Scope of Negation for Spanish Sentiment Analysis on Twitter. *IEEE Transactions on Affective Computing*, 10(1):129–141.

Salud María Jiménez-Zafra, M. Teresa Martín-Valdivia, M. Dolores Molina-González, and L. Alfonso Ureña-López. 2018. Relevance of the SFU ReviewSP-NEG corpus annotated with the scope of negation for supervised polarity classification in Spanish. *Information Processing & Management*, 54(2):240–251.

Salud María Jiménez-Zafra, Roser Morante, María Teresa Martín-Valdivia, and L. Alfonso Ureña-López. 2020. Corpora Annotated with Negation: An Overview. In *Computational Linguistics*, volume 0, pages 1–87.

Aditya Khandelwal and Suraj Sawant. 2020. NegBERT: A Transfer Learning Approach for Negation Detection and Scope Resolution. In *LREC*.

Natalia Konstantinova, Sheila C.M. de Sousa, Noa P. Cruz, Manuel J. Maña, Maite Taboada, and Ruslan Mitkov. 2012. A review corpus annotated for negation, speculation and their scope. In *Proceedings of the Eighth International Conference on Language Resources and Evaluation (LREC'12)*, pages 3190–3195, Istanbul, Turkey. European Language Resources Association (ELRA).

Taku Kudo and John Richardson. 2018. SentencePiece: A simple and language independent subword tokenizer and detokenizer for Neural Text Processing. In *Proceedings of the 2018 Conference on Empirical Methods in Natural Language Processing: System Demonstrations*, pages 66–71, Brussels, Belgium. Association for Computational Linguistics.

Hao Li and Wei Lu. 2018. Learning with Structured Representations for Negation Scope Extraction. In *Proceedings of the 56th Annual Meeting of the Association for Computational Linguistics (Volume 2: Short Papers)*, pages 533–539, Melbourne, Australia. Association for Computational Linguistics.

I Montani and M Honnibal. 2018. Prodigy: A new annotation tool for radically efficient machine teaching. *Artificial Intelligence*.

Roser Morante and Eduardo Blanco. 2012. *SEM 2012 Shared Task: Resolving the Scope and Focus of Negation. In **SEM 2012: The First Joint Conference on Lexical and Computational Semantics – Volume 1: Proceedings of the main conference and the shared task, and Volume 2: Proceedings of the Sixth International Workshop on Semantic Evaluation (SemEval 2012)*, pages 265–274, Montréal, Canada. Association for Computational Linguistics.

Roser Morante and Walter Daelemans. 2009. Learning the Scope of Hedge Cues in Biomedical Texts. In *Proceedings of the BioNLP 2009 Workshop*, pages 28–36, Boulder, Colorado. Association for Computational Linguistics.

Roser Morante and Walter Daelemans. 2012. ConanDoyle-neg: Annotation of negation in Conan Doyle stories. page 6.

Roser Morante, Anthony Liekens, and Walter Daelemans. 2008. Learning the Scope of Negation in Biomedical Texts. In *Proceedings of the 2008 Conference on Empirical Methods in Natural Language Processing*, pages 715–724, Honolulu, Hawaii. Association for Computational Linguistics.

Roser Morante, Sarah Schrauwen, and Walter Daelemans. 2011. Corpus-based approaches to processing the scope of negation cues: an evaluation of the state of the art. In *Proceedings of the Ninth International Conference on Computational Semantics (IWCS 2011)*.

Pradeep Mutalik, Aniruddha M. Deshpande, and Prakash M. Nadkarni. 2001. Research Paper: Use of General-purpose Negation Detection to Augment Concept Indexing of Medical Documents: A Quantitative Study Using the UMLS. *JAMIA*.

Woodley Packard, Emily M. Bender, Jonathon Read, Stephan Oepen, and Rebecca Dridan. 2014. Simple Negation Scope Resolution through Deep Parsing: A Semantic Solution to a Semantic Problem. In *Proceedings of the 52nd Annual Meeting of the Association for Computational Linguistics (Volume 1: Long Papers)*, pages 69–78, Baltimore, Maryland. Association for Computational Linguistics.

Jonathon Read, Erik Velldal, Lilja Øvrelid, and Stephan Oepen. 2012. UiO1: Constituent-Based Discriminative Ranking for Negation Resolution. In **SEM 2012: The First Joint Conference on Lexical and Computational Semantics – Volume 1: Proceedings of the main conference and the shared task, and Volume 2: Proceedings of the Sixth International Workshop on Semantic Evaluation (SemEval 2012)*, pages 310–318, Montréal, Canada. Association for Computational Linguistics.

Renzo Rivera Zavala and Paloma Martinez. 2020. The Impact of Pretrained Language Models on Negation and Speculation Detection in Cross-Lingual Medical Text: Comparative Study. *JMIR Medical Informatics*, 8(12):e18953.

Elena Sergeeva, Henghui Zhu, Peter Prinsen, and Amir Tahmasebi. 2019. Negation Scope Detection in Clinical Notes and Scientific Abstracts: A Feature-enriched LSTM-based Approach. *AMIA Summits on Translational Science Proceedings*, 2019:212–221.

Anastassia Shaitarova, Lenz Furrer, and Fabio Rinaldi. 2020. Cross-lingual transfer-learning approach to negation scope resolution. In *CEUR Workshop Proceedings*, Zurich. CEUR-WS. ISSN: 1613-0073.

Ieva Staliūnaitė and Ignacio Iacobacci. 2020. Compositional and Lexical Semantics in RoBERTa, BERT and DistilBERT: A Case Study on CoQA. In *Proceedings of the 2020 Conference on Empirical Methods in Natural Language Processing (EMNLP)*, pages 7046–7056, Online. Association for Computational Linguistics.

D. Sykes, A. Grivas, C. Grover, R. Tobin, C. Sudlow, W. Whiteley, A. Mcintosh, H. Whalley, and B. Alex. 2020. Comparison of rule-based and neural network models for negation detection in radiology reports. *Natural Language Engineering*, pages 1–22.

György Szarvas, Veronika Vincze, Richárd Farkas, and János Csirik. 2008. The BioScope corpus: annotation for negation, uncertainty and their scope in biomedical texts. In *Proceedings of the Workshop on Current Trends in Biomedical Natural Language Processing*, pages 38–45, Columbus, Ohio. Association for Computational Linguistics.

Ye Tian and Richard Breheny. 2016. Dynamic Pragmatic View of Negation Processing. In Pierre Larrivée and Chungmin Lee, editors, *Negation and Polarity: Experimental Perspectives*, Language, Cognition, and Mind, pages 21–43. Springer International Publishing, Cham.

David Vilares, Miguel Ángel Alonso, and Carlos Gómez-Rodríguez. 2013. Supervised polarity classification of Spanish tweets based on linguistic knowledge. In *Proceedings of the 2013 ACM symposium on Document engineering*, DocEng '13, pages 169–172, Florence, Italy. Association for Computing Machinery.

Veronika Vincze, György Szarvas, Richárd Farkas, György Móra, and János Csirik. 2008. The BioScope corpus: biomedical texts annotated for uncertainty, negation and their scopes. *BMC Bioinformatics*, 9(S11):S9.

Stephen Wu, Timothy Miller, James Masanz, Matt Coarr, Scott Halgrim, David Carrell, and Cheryl Clark. 2014. Negation's Not Solved: Generalizability Versus Optimizability in Clinical Natural Language Processing. *PLOS ONE*, 9(11):1–11.

Yiyun Zhao and Steven Bethard. 2020. How does BERT's attention change when you fine-tune? an analysis methodology and a case study in negation scope. In *Proceedings of the 58th Annual Meeting of the Association for Computational Linguistics*, pages 4729–4747, Online. Association for Computational Linguistics.

Representations of Meaning in Neural Networks for NLP: a Thesis Proposal

Tomáš Musil
Charles University, Faculty of Mathematics and Physics
Institute of Formal and Applied Linguistics
Prague, Czech Republic
musil@ufal.mff.cuni.cz

Abstract

Neural networks are the state-of-the-art method of machine learning for many problems in natural language processing (NLP). Their success in machine translation and other NLP tasks is phenomenal, but their interpretability is challenging. We want to find out how neural networks represent meaning. We will focus on lexical semantics in the embedding layer of the network. We propose to examine the distribution of meaning in the vector space representation of words in neural networks trained for NLP tasks. Furthermore, we propose to consider various theories of meaning in the philosophy of language and to find a methodology that would enable us to connect these areas.

1 NLP, Language, and Meaning

Language has been one of the central topics of artificial intelligence (AI) research ever since Turing (1950) considered the question "Can machines think?" and proposed to replace it with the "imitation game", based purely on textual communication.

Even though language is still one of the hardest problems in AI, there has been a tremendous development in recent years in NLP. Machine translation systems achieve super-human performance (at least in a competition setting) (Barrault et al., 2019; Popel et al., 2020). Voice assistants are getting better and better. Some text generation models are so powerful that their authors consider them to pose a danger to society (Radford et al., 2019a).

Artificial neural networks are behind a lot of these achievements. The models that are used in NLP can have billions of parameters. The same architecture is often used for various tasks. Consequently, neural networks are often regarded as black boxes, and interpretation of the trained models presents a major scientific challenge (Belinkov et al., 2019).

Certain specific questions, such as whether a layer of a particular model contains information about part of speech (POS) can be answered with various methods. Other, more general questions, are proving more difficult. How do neural machine translation (NMT) systems achieve the level of translation quality comparable to humans? Are there any fundamental limitations in language understanding for artificial neural networks? Do neural networks represent meaning and if they do, then how?

It is the last question we are interested in. The nature of meaning is itself a subject of debate in the philosophy of language. This presents a challenging methodological problem: on the one hand, we need a definition of meaning for the question to make sense; on the other hand, we do not want to restrict our research to a predefined concept of meaning, because then we are in danger of assuming the conclusion and presenting a circular argument. The solution would be to refine the sought-after concept of meaning gradually, based on careful justification supported by empirical observations.

The focus of this work is on lexical semantics in the embedding layer the neural network. We believe that this is a good place to start, as it is the interface between the input text and the network. Furthermore, there are interesting models for obtaining words embeddings without any hidden layers.

1.1 Thesis Proposal

The thesis will consist of two parts. In the first part, described in Section 2, we will consider various theories and properties of meaning from the point of view of philosophy of language. We will find which aspects of these theories are useful to describe the process of representing meaning in neural networks in NLP.

In the second part, described in Section 3, we will examine the distribution of word representations in the embedding spaces with respect to meaning. We propose to use mostly unsupervised meth-

Proceedings of NAACL-HLT 2021: Student Research Workshop, pages 24–31
June 6–11, 2021.

ods, such as clustering, principal component analysis (PCA), independent component analysis (ICA) and unsupervised mapping of embedding spaces.

The goal of the thesis is to show which theories of meaning offer a conceptual framework that would be useful for understanding the empirical results of the analysis of the embeddings.

2 NLP and Philosophy of Language

There is no agreed-upon general definition of 'meaning' (or 'sense', 'semantics', ...; see e.g. Stokhof (2013), Bender and Koller (2020)).

To be able to talk about representations of meaning, we will have to review different conceptualizations of meaning and find one that is useful for describing the phenomena we encounter when we examine how neural networks work in NLP. We will contrast meaning representations in neural language models with representations in other applications, with emphasis on NMT.

There is very little related work that connects NLP with the philosophy of language. Honkela (2007) links neural language models, self-organizing maps and Quine's semantic holism. The works of Melby (1994, 1995) are discussed in Section 2.5.

2.1 The Distributional Hypothesis

Many NLP applications only use raw text for training data (language models, models for embedding pretraining, arguably even NMT models, although the alignment in parallel corpora may be considered an additional source of information). If they represent meaning, the information must be derived from the training corpus, usually presented to the model through a sliding window of tokens. This may be the reason behind the popularity of the distributional hypothesis in neural language model (LM) literature. The famous saying by Firth (1957), "You shall know a word by the company it keeps!", is quoted in most papers concerned with vector space models of language.

The general distributional hypothesis states that the meaning of a word is given by the contexts in which it occurs. It is, however, worth noticing that in Firth's theory, collocation is just one among multiple levels of meaning, and his text does not support the idea of meaning being based on the context alone.

The distributional hypothesis would explain why word embeddings capture meaning. However, by itself it tells us nothing about what meaning is and how it relates to the world or people who are using the language.

2.2 The *Use Theory* of Meaning

The *use theory* of meaning can be summed up as "the meaning of a word is its use in the language" (Wittgenstein, 1953, § 43). It is associated with late Wittgenstein's concept of language game. Meaning determines which combinations of words are "in circulation", excluding the senseless combinations and therefore "bounding of the domain of language" (Wittgenstein, 1953, § 499), which is precisely what a LM does; therefore, the use theory may be one way to connect language modelling and semantics.

That "knowledge of language emerges from language use" is also one of the main hypotheses of cognitive linguistics (Croft and Cruse, 2004).

This approach tells us a bit more about how meaning relates to entities outside language: people are *using* language to accomplish something in the world.

2.3 Structuralism

In structuralism, the meaning of a word is given by its relation to the other words of the language (de Saussure, 1916). The nature of the sign is arbitrary. This holds for word representations in artificial neural networks as well. Due to the random initialization, the vectors are different every time the model is trained. The individual dimensions of an embedding vector do not have any preconceived interpretation and their values are arbitrary. The embedding vectors do not have any meaning other than their position among the rest of the vectors, and a single vector does not have any significance outside the model.

2.4 Semantic Holism and Atomism

Semantic holism (or *meaning holism*) is "the thesis that what a linguistic expression means depends on its relations to many or all other expressions within the same totality. [...] The totality in question may be the language to which the expressions belong or a theory formulation in that language" (Fodor and Lepore, 1992). The opposing view is called *semantic atomism*, and it claims that there are expressions (typically words), whose meaning does not depend on the meaning of other expressions. The meaning of these expressions is given by something outside language (e.g. their relation to physical or mental objects).

2.5 Objectivism and Experientialism

Study of metaphor and its connection to experience led Lakoff and Johnson (1980) to criticize what they call the *objectivist* approach to language. Melby (1994) applies this critique to machine translation (MT) and says that "most work in machine translation is explicitly or implicitly based on [the objectivist framework]." He lists the following beliefs as characteristic for objectivism:

1. Words and expressions are mapped to senses.
2. Each sense exists independently and has the properties of mathematical sets.
3. The meaning of a sentence can be obtained by combining the word senses from the bottom up.

Melby (1995) claimed that then-current techniques of machine translation will never be extended to handle general language texts and that entirely new techniques that avoid the assumptions of objectivism will be needed; the systems need to understand dynamic metaphor and exhibit flexibility in handling new situations. If Lakoff and Johnson's theory of metaphor holds, this is a trivial consequence: since understanding metaphor is based on experience and contemporary translation systems do not experience anything, they cannot understand and translate metaphors. The *experientialist* view of language places emphasis on the shared experience of the world, which is structured by metaphors.

More than 25 years later, NMT is based on principles that can hardly be construed as an extension of the old techniques. They are more flexible and produce significantly better translations. Do neural networks somehow evade the pitfalls of objectivism? Maybe going repeatedly through the enormous quantity of textual data constitutes a kind of experience; perhaps it is possible to extract the experience of others from the data? May that be one of the reasons for their sudden success in MT and other NLP applications?

2.6 Meaning and Understanding

Can a LM really understand natural language? Bender and Koller (2020) argue that methods based only on text cannot learn meaning. They define *meaning* as mapping from words to *communicative intent*. Because text itself does not contain communicative intent, it is impossible to learn to understand it from a textual corpora alone.

Our approach works in the opposite direction: instead of picking a theory of meaning and projecting restrictions on technical possibilities, we want to start with what is already achieved in NLP. We will analyse the models and find out which aspects of language use are they able to understand. We will then find a theory of meaning that explains the results of the analysis well.

The way a computer solves the NLP tasks does not necessarily correspond to what a person does when solving the same. Therefore our results may not be usable for explaining how we experience language. However, the results would still be useful for understanding the linguistic behavior of black-box neural models. Comparing our results with neurological findings about biological representations of meaning would be interesting, however it is outside the scope of the proposed thesis.

2.7 Conclusion: Properties of Meaning

Based on the properties of word embeddings mentioned in the preceding sections, we want the concept of meaning that we are looking to be compatible with the distributional hypothesis, structuralism, and semantic holism. Based on the arguments given by Lakoff and Johnson (1980); Melby (1995) and others, we believe that the correct account of meaning should not be objectivist.

We propose to investigate a possibility of a concept of meaning of an expression as a combination of various components. These components would emerge from the use of the expression in context (*semantic holism, distributional hypothesis*). Each of them would represent a specific relation to other expressions (*structuralism*). The components would be continuous and will not form a simple tree hierarchy, therefore avoiding the most problematic aspects of *objectivism*. Instead of definition or enumeration, the components would be described by prototypes (*experientialism, cognitive linguistics*). ICA of word embeddings is a plausible candidate for such conceptualization.

3 Properties of Word Embeddings

In this section, we present methods for analysis of words embeddings and provide examples of results obtained with these methods.

We will concentrate on embeddings from unsupervised learning algorithms, language models and NMT. Unsupervised learning algorithms for obtaining word representations, such as Word2vec (Mikolov et al., 2013a), GloVe (Pennington et al., 2014) or FastText (Bojanowski et al., 2017), have the advantage of being simple, both conceptually and regarding computational costs. Language modelling is the most general language task. Pretrained models, such as masked LMs from the BERT family (Devlin et al., 2018), can be finetuned for many NLP tasks. Large generative LMs can even be used for various tasks with little or no fine-tuning (Radford et al., 2019b; Brown et al., 2020). NMT is a mature NLP application and the task itself is closely connected to the concept of meaning. By comparing embeddings from different models, we hope to distinguish between properties of the specific model and general properties of continuous word representations.

We will also investigate contextual representations in current Transformer models (e.g. Radford et al., 2019a). It is possible to reduce contextual embedding to static embeddings (Bommasani et al., 2020) and apply the methods for analyzing static embeddings.

In this section we present methods for analyzing word embeddings and their results. Related work on examining vector representations in NLP was surveyed by Bakarov (2018). Further information can also be found in the overview of methods for analyzing deep learning models for NLP by Belinkov and Glass (2019). For more on interpretation in general and unsupervised methods in examining word embeddings, see Mareček et al. (2020, Chapters 3 and 4).

Probing is the most common approach for examining linguistic properties in neural network components (Belinkov and Glass, 2019). It is the method of using a supervised classifier to predict these properties from activations of the neural network. The methodology may present problems with train/test overlap (Rosa et al., 2020).

Probing is most useful when there are high quality annotated data for the property that is being probed. Even though we plan to occasionally use probing in such cases, we will generally emphasize unsupervised methods of interpretation, because we do not want to bias the results by restricting the possible outcome by probing for specific features.

Component Analysis is an unsupervised method for factoring the vector space of embeddings into meaningful components.

PCA is a generally well known example. It is often used for dimensionality reduction. The resulting components are ordered by their importance and they maximize variance of the data given all the previous components.

ICA (Jutten and Herault, 1991; Comon, 1994; Hyvärinen and Oja, 2000) is an algorithm originally developed for finding separate sources in a mixed signal, such as a recording of multiple people in the same room speaking at the same time. It was used, for example, to extract features from distribution representations of the words (Honkela et al., 2010). The ICA algorithm consists of: optional dimension reduction, usually with PCA; centering the data and *whitening* them (setting variance of each component to 1); iteratively finding directions in the data that are the most non-Gaussian. The last step is based on the assumption of the central limit theorem: the mixed signal is a sum of independent variables, therefore it should be closer to the normal distribution, than the variables themselves.

Clustering is another unsupervised method for examining embeddings. The t-SNE clustering algorithm is often used for visualizing embeddings (e.g. Maaten and Hinton, 2008). Word embeddings are clustered according to meaning in t-SNE (Liu et al., 2018).

We show elsewhere (Musil et al., 2019) that clusters of embeddings of derivational relations mostly match manually annotated semantic categories of these relations (e.g. the relation 'bake–baker' belongs to the category 'actor', and a correct clustering puts it into the same cluster as 'govern–governor').

Unsupervised Mapping There are unsupervised methods for finding a mapping between two embedding spaces that can be used for simple word-for-word translation, as a starting point for creating an unsupervised NMT system (Lample et al., 2017).

Mapping of embedding spaces from different corpora of the same language can lead to interesting insights, as demonstrated by KhudaBukhsh et al. (2020), who show polarization in US political comments by highlighting different use of specific words or phrases by supporters of different political parties.

We have found that a neural translation model divides words into POS classes (Musil, 2019). It also distinguishes between proper names and general nouns. The structure of representation varies between the encoder and the decoder of the NMT system.

The structure of the representation of the same data in the word2vec model is different, for example, in that it distinguishes infinitive forms of verbs or modal verbs. A completely different structure is found in the space of representations of words in the neural model for sentiment analysis. All of these facts can be shown without annotated data and thus without deciding beforehand what we will look for in the space of representations. For this reason, we find these results more convincing than if they had been obtained through probing.

3.1 Semantic properties

Hollis and Westbury (2016) have found that principal components of word2vec embedding space are correlated with various psycholinguistic and semantic properties of words.

One example of a semantic property we have found is that the shape of the space of word embeddings in a convolutional neural network (CNN) model trained for sentiment analysis is triangular Musil (2019).

With the help of PCA, we show that the first principal component represents the polarity of the words (good/bad); the second component represents intensity (strong/neutral). The triangular shape may be explained by the fact that words that are far from the center on the polarity axis are always of high intensity. This is an example of component analysis showing more than a probing classifier about the structure of the representation.

This may in fact be all the information that the CNN uses to classify the sentiment. We propose to test this empirically by projecting the embeddings on the first two principal components, retraining the rest of the network and measuring the impact of this on its performance.

3.2 Word2vec and Semantic Holism

Word representations obtained from the word2vec model (Mikolov et al., 2013a) exhibit interesting semantic properties. They obey the vector arithmetic of meanings illustrated by the following equation:

$$v_{king} - v_{man} + v_{woman} \approx v_{queen},$$

meaning that if we start with the word "king", by subtracting the vector for the word "man" and adding the vector for the word "woman" we arrive at a vector that is nearest in the vector space to the one that corresponds to the word "queen". This means that *queen* is to *woman* as *king* is to *man*.

This is usually explained by referring to the general distributional hypothesis. We propose a more specific approach based on Frege's holistic and functional approach to meaning.

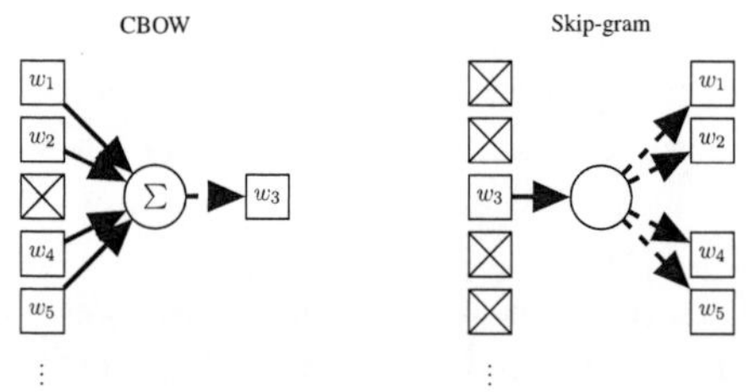

Figure 1: CBOW and Skip-gram language models according to (Mikolov et al., 2013a).

There are two variants of the word2vec model (Mikolov et al., 2013a). The CBOW variant predicts a missing word based on the context; the Skip-gram variant predicts context words based on a single word (see Figure 1). The Skip-gram variant performs better in analogy tasks (Mikolov et al., 2013b). We show that the training process the Skip-gram variant of word2vec is analogous to a holistic definition of meaning.

Taking Tugendhat's formal reinterpretation of Frege's holistic approach to meaning (Tugendhat, 1970) as a starting point, we demonstrate that it is analogical to the process of training the Skip-gram model and it offers a possible explanation of its semantic properties. Tugendhat's definition of meaning as truth-value potential is:

> [T]wo expressions φ and ψ have the same truth-value potential if and only if, whenever each is completed by the same expression to form a sentence, the two sentences have the same truth-value.

This definition has one crucial aspect in common with the Skip-gram version of the word2vec model: while we examine the meaning of an expression, the expression is fixed, and the context is changing for comparison. Therefore, it presupposes the context as the source of meaning, in the same way, that Skip-gram learns the representation of a word from the representation of the context. The fact that the holistic Skip-gram version of word2vec works better in analogy tasks than the complementary atomistic CBOW version supports the holistic approach to meaning.

3.3 Independent Component Analysis

Our preliminary experiments with ICA indicate, that the independent components represent both morpho-syntactic and semantic features. For our data, we are able to explain roughly 10% of the dimensions by morphological/syntactic features (by using correlations with annotated data). The other 90% seem to be semantic, although the distinction between syntactic and semantic properties is blurry in this context.

ICA of word embeddings seems to be a good candidate for a non-hierarchical system for describing relations between words, as expressed in Section 2.7.

4 Conclusion and Future Work

Interpretability is an important challenge for neural networks in NLP. There is a limited amount of findings about linguistic phenomena that we are able to predict from embeddings. Much less is known about the semantic properties of the embedding space. The proposed approach to finding a description of the process of representing meaning in neural networks for NLP both from the technological and philosophical perspective would contribute to our understanding of the technology and of the concept of meaning.

Future work could also address the relation between neural networks for natural language inference and the philosophy of *inferentialism* (Brandom, 1994).

This proposal leaves out important methodological questions: we are using machine learning methods to run experiments on the results of other machine learning methods. It may be a challenging task to interpret experiments correctly and attribute the discovered properties to the original model or to the model we are using to examine it. The question of how to incorporate results of machine learning into the scientific workflow is starting to come up in other sciences as well, e.g. biology (Currie, 2019).

This question is perhaps too broad and general to be solved as a part of this thesis. However, we hope to at least formulate in detail the challenges that we are facing when performing this kind of research, as we encounter them while completing the work proposed in the previous sections.

5 Acknowledgements

This research was partially supported by SVV project number 260 575 and Grant Agency of Charles University in Prague project GAUK 370721 "Analýza nezávislých komponent vektorových reprezentací slov".

I would like to thank Sebastian Ruder for valuable feedback on the manuscript.

References

Amir Bakarov. 2018. A Survey of Word Embeddings Evaluation Methods. *arXiv:1801.09536 [cs]*. ArXiv: 1801.09536.

Loïc Barrault, Ondřej Bojar, Marta R. Costa-jussà, Christian Federmann, Mark Fishel, Yvette Graham, Barry Haddow, Matthias Huck, Philipp Koehn, Shervin Malmasi, Christof Monz, Mathias Müller, Santanu Pal, Matt Post, and Marcos Zampieri. 2019. Findings of the 2019 Conference on Machine Translation (WMT19). In *Proceedings of the Fourth Conference on Machine Translation (Volume 2: Shared Task Papers, Day 1)*, pages 1–61, Florence, Italy. Association for Computational Linguistics.

Yonatan Belinkov, Nadir Durrani, Fahim Dalvi, Hassan Sajjad, and James Glass. 2019. On the Linguistic Representational Power of Neural Machine Translation Models. *arXiv:1911.00317 [cs]*. ArXiv: 1911.00317.

Yonatan Belinkov and James Glass. 2019. Analysis Methods in Neural Language Processing: A Survey. *Transactions of the Association for Computational Linguistics*, 7:49–72.

Emily M. Bender and Alexander Koller. 2020. Climbing towards NLU: On meaning, form, and understanding in the age of data. In *Proceedings of the 58th Annual Meeting of the Association for Computational Linguistics*, pages 5185–5198, Online. Association for Computational Linguistics.

Piotr Bojanowski, Edouard Grave, Armand Joulin, and Tomas Mikolov. 2017. Enriching Word Vectors with Subword Information. *Transactions of the Association for Computational Linguistics*, 5:135–146. ArXiv: 1607.04606.

Rishi Bommasani, Kelly Davis, and Claire Cardie. 2020. Interpreting Pretrained Contextualized Representations via Reductions to Static Embeddings. In *Proceedings of the 58th Annual Meeting of the Association for Computational Linguistics*, pages 4758–4781, Online. Association for Computational Linguistics.

Robert Brandom. 1994. *Making it explicit: Reasoning, representing, and discursive commitment*. Harvard university press.

Tom B Brown, Benjamin Mann, Nick Ryder, Melanie Subbiah, Jared Kaplan, Prafulla Dhariwal, Arvind Neelakantan, Pranav Shyam, Girish Sastry, Amanda Askell, et al. 2020. Language models are few-shot learners. *arXiv preprint arXiv:2005.14165*.

Pierre Comon. 1994. Independent component analysis, a new concept? *Signal processing*, 36(3):287–314.

William Croft and D. Alan Cruse. 2004. *Cognitive Linguistics*, 1 edition. Cambridge University Press.

David J. Currie. 2019. Where Newton might have taken ecology. *Global Ecology and Biogeography*, 28(1):18–27.

Ferdinand de Saussure. 1916. *Course in General Linguistics*. Duckworth, London.

Jacob Devlin, Ming-Wei Chang, Kenton Lee, and Kristina Toutanova. 2018. Bert: Pre-training of deep bidirectional transformers for language understanding. *arXiv preprint arXiv:1810.04805*.

John R Firth. 1957. A synopsis of linguistic theory, 1930-1955. *Studies in linguistic analysis*.

Jerry A Fodor and Ernest Lepore. 1992. *Holism: A shopper's guide*. Blackwell.

Geoff Hollis and Chris Westbury. 2016. The principals of meaning: Extracting semantic dimensions from co-occurrence models of semantics. *Psychonomic bulletin & review*, 23(6):1744–1756.

Timo Honkela. 2007. Philosophical aspects of neural, probabilistic and fuzzy modeling of language use and translation. In *Neural Networks, 2007. IJCNN 2007. International Joint Conference on*, pages \mbox2881–2886. IEEE.

Timo Honkela, Aapo Hyvärinen, and Jaakko J. Väyrynen. 2010. WordICA—emergence of linguistic representations for words by independent component analysis. *Natural Language Engineering*, 16(3):277–308.

A. Hyvärinen and E. Oja. 2000. Independent component analysis: algorithms and applications. *Neural Networks*, 13(4-5):411–430.

Christian Jutten and Jeanny Herault. 1991. Blind separation of sources, part I: An adaptive algorithm based on neuromimetic architecture. *Signal processing*, 24(1):1–10.

Ashiqur R KhudaBukhsh, Rupak Sarkar, Mark S Kamlet, and Tom M Mitchell. 2020. We don't speak the same language: Interpreting polarization through machine translation. *arXiv preprint arXiv:2010.02339*.

George Lakoff and Mark Johnson. 1980. *Metaphors we live by*. University of Chicago press.

Guillaume Lample, Alexis Conneau, Ludovic Denoyer, and Marc'Aurelio Ranzato. 2017. Unsupervised machine translation using monolingual corpora only. *arXiv preprint arXiv:1711.00043*.

Shusen Liu, Peer-Timo Bremer, Jayaraman J. Thiagarajan, Vivek Srikumar, Bei Wang, Yarden Livnat, and Valerio Pascucci. 2018. Visual Exploration of Semantic Relationships in Neural Word Embeddings. *IEEE Transactions on Visualization and Computer Graphics*, 24(1):553–562.

Laurens van der Maaten and Geoffrey Hinton. 2008. Visualizing data using t-SNE. *Journal of machine learning research*, 9(Nov):2579–2605.

David Mareček, Jindřich Libovický, Tomáš Musil, Rudolf Rosa, and Tomasz Limisiewicz. 2020. *Hidden in the Layers: Interpretation of Neural Networks for Natural Language Processing*, volume 20 of *Studies in Computational and Theoretical Linguistics*. Institute of Formal and Applied Linguistics, Prague, Czechia. Backup Publisher: Institute of Formal and Applied Linguistics.

Alan Melby. 1994. Machine Translation and Philosophy of Language. In *Machine Translation — Ten Years On*, Cranfield, Bedford. Cranfield University Press.

Alan K. Melby. 1995. *The Possibility of Language : a Discussion of the Nature of Language, with Implications for Human and Machine Translation*. John Benjamins Publishing Company.

Tomas Mikolov, Kai Chen, Gregory S. Corrado, and Jeffrey Dean. 2013a. Efficient Estimation of Word Representations in Vector Space. *CoRR*, abs/1301.3781.

Tomas Mikolov, Wen-tau Yih, and Geoffrey Zweig. 2013b. Linguistic Regularities in Continuous Space Word Representations. In *Proceedings of the 2013 Conference of the North American Chapter of the Association for Computational Linguistics: Human Language Technologies*, pages 746–751, Atlanta, Georgia. Association for Computational Linguistics.

Tomáš Musil. 2019. Examining Structure of Word Embeddings with PCA. In *Text, Speech, and Dialogue*, pages 211–223, Cham. Springer International Publishing.

Tomáš Musil, Jonáš Vidra, and David Mareček. 2019. Derivational Morphological Relations in Word Embeddings. In *Proceedings of the 2019 ACL Workshop BlackboxNLP: Analyzing and Interpreting Neural Networks for NLP*, pages 173–180, Florence, Italy. Association for Computational Linguistics.

Jeffrey Pennington, Richard Socher, and Christopher Manning. 2014. Glove: Global Vectors for Word Representation. In *Proceedings of the 2014 Conference on Empirical Methods in Natural Language Processing (EMNLP)*, pages 1532–1543, Doha, Qatar. Association for Computational Linguistics.

Martin Popel, Marketa Tomkova, Jakub Tomek, Łukasz Kaiser, Jakob Uszkoreit, Ondřej Bojar, and Zdeněk Žabokrtský. 2020. Transforming machine translation: a deep learning system reaches news translation quality comparable to human professionals. *Nature Communications*, 11(1):4381.

Alec Radford, Jeffrey Wu, Dario Amodei, Jack Clark, Amanda Askell, Miles Brundage, and Ilya Sutskever. 2019a. Better Language Models and Their Implications.

Alec Radford, Jeffrey Wu, Rewon Child, David Luan, Dario Amodei, and Ilya Sutskever. 2019b. Language models are unsupervised multitask learners. *OpenAI blog*, 1(8):9.

Rudolf Rosa, Tomáš Musil, and David Mareček. 2020. Measuring memorization effect in word-level neural networks probing. In *Text, Speech, and Dialogue*, pages 180–188, Cham. Springer International Publishing.

Martin Stokhof. 2013. Formal semantics and Wittgenstein: An alternative? *The Monist*, 96(2):205–231.

Ernst Tugendhat. 1970. The meaning of 'Bedeutung' in Frege. *Analysis*, 30(6):177–189.

Alan M. Turing. 1950. Computing Machinery and Intelligence. *Mind*, LIX(236):433–460.

Ludwig Wittgenstein. 1953. *Philosophical Investigations*. Wiley-Blackwell.

Towards Layered Events and Schema Representations in Long Documents

Hans Ole Hatzel
Language Technology Group
Universität Hamburg, Germany
hatzel@informatik.uni-hamburg.de

Chris Biemann
Language Technology Group
Universität Hamburg, Germany
biemann@informatik.uni-hamburg.de

Abstract

In this thesis proposal, we explore event extraction and event representation on literary texts. Due to its variety of genres and varying document length, literature is a challenging domain, yet the representation of literary content has received relatively little attention. As most individual events contribute little to the overall semantics of literary documents, we model events at different granularities. On the conceptual level, we adapt the previous definition of schemas as sequences of events, all describing a single process connected through shared participants, and extend the notion to allow modeling a document's content using sequences of schemas. Technically, the segmentation of event sequences into schemas is approached by modeling such sequences, making use of the narrative cloze task, which is the prediction of masked events in event sequence contexts. We propose building on sequences of event embeddings to form schema representations, thereby summarizing sections of documents using a fixed-size representation. This approach will give rise to comparisons of sections such as chapters up to the comparison of entire literary works on the level of their schema structure, paving the way to a computational approach to quantitative literary research.

1 Introduction

Events generally describe any change of state (Hogenboom et al., 2016) and are often used in information extraction scenarios (Gaizauskas and Wilks, 1998; Niklaus et al., 2018). The modeling of sequences of events has the potential of aiding literary scientists in understanding narrative patterns and devices. Determining which events in a narrative are crucial is challenging and relates to a variety of related tasks, such as summarization, comparison, or even story generation. Understanding the contexts of an event requires modeling its arguments and semantics. A simple representation can be the subject and object relating to a given verb, in conjunction with the verb's lemma (Chambers and Jurafsky, 2008).

If one only wants to include events involving a single character in a story, it is necessary to consider only those predicates with arguments coreferring to the character. The narrative coherence assumption says that "verbs sharing coreferring arguments are semantically connected by virtue of narrative discourse structure" (Chambers and Jurafsky, 2008). Verbs connected in this way are, under the assumption, considered to be part of the same so-called narrative chain (Chambers and Jurafsky, 2008). Previous work has focused on finding chains as representations of narratives in short documents, combining individual narrative chains, each focused on one character, into a schema involving multiple chains and thereby multiple characters (Chambers and Jurafsky, 2009). While the overall narrative in a long document could be regarded as a large schema, a variety of sub-schemas exists describing each scene using individual events. As a result, a typical document in our domain contains multiple schemas.

Figure 1 illustrates a potential separation of an event sequence into schemas. For each event E_n^C in any given text we know, based on coreference resolution, which entities C are involved with it (i.e.: occur as its arguments). Intuitively a separation boundary is preferably found between non-connected events. The verbs *"leaving"* and *"arriving"*, for example, are strongly connected events; we expect them to often appear in sequence. After modeling the likelihood of different events occurring in sequence, we can calculate the model's perplexity with regard to a specific event and use this information for the separation of chains. Even in our simple example (Fig. 1) it is not clear where exactly to place separations, E_7 could, for example, form a *social gathering* schema with E_5 and E_6 instead of a separate *transportation* schema.

Proceedings of NAACL-HLT 2021: Student Research Workshop, pages 32–39
June 6–11, 2021. ©2021 Association for Computational Linguistics

$E_0^{\{B\}}$	Bob **enters** the store.
$E_1^{\{B\}}$	He **picks up** some milk.
$E_2^{\{B\}}$	After he **pays** for it he
$E_3^{\{B\}}$	**leaves** in his car.
$E_4^{\{B\}}$	Bob **arrives** home.
$E_5^{\{A,B\}}$	Alice **visits** him.
$E_6^{\{A,B\}}$	They **watch** a movie.
$E_7^{\{A\}}$	Alice **drives** home.

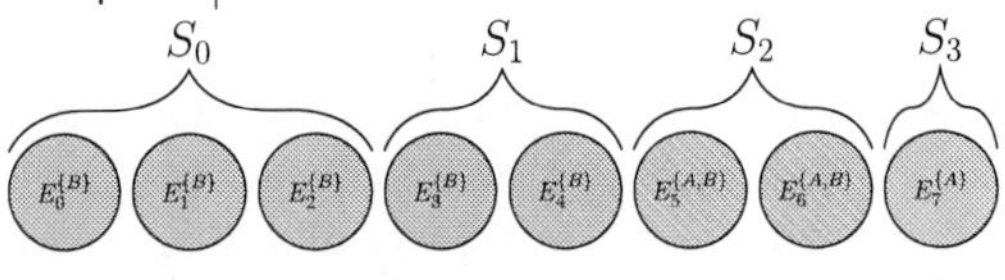

Figure 1: One possible separation of the events into four schemas splits the event up into a *shopping*, a *transportation*, a *social gathering*, and another *transportation* schema.

2 Related Work

2.1 Event Processing

The detection of events has mostly focused on domains outside of literature, such as news (Doddington et al., 2004; Chambers and Jurafsky, 2008). More recently, Sims et al. (2019) created a new dataset of annotated literary texts.

2.2 Semantic Frame Induction

Semantic frames, in the context of FrameNet (Baker et al., 1998), are definitions of word senses where each sense can be evoked by multiple different words. The "Commerce_buy" frame, for example, can be evoked by the verbs "buy", "aquire" and "purchase", among others. FrameNet is an annotated dataset, marking for each predicate the frame that it evokes. A German frame resource called SALSA (Burchardt et al., 2006) builds on the frame lexicon provided by FrameNet.

The induction of specific frames has received much attention (Gildea and Jurafsky, 2000; Das et al., 2014). Generally, frame-semantic parsing is split into two sub-tasks of relevance to us: **(i)** target detection, the discovery of predicates evoking frames, and **(ii)** frame induction, the classification tasks of deciding which frame a predicate evokes (Das et al., 2014, p. 19). For the SemEval-2007 shared task (Pradhan et al., 2007), the work by Johansson and Nugues (2007) relies on the FrameNet lexicon specifying all possible frames for a predicate, with their model only deciding between the defined options. To handle predicates not covered by FrameNet but occurring in the evaluation data they map uncovered verbs to existing ones using WordNet (Fellbaum, 1998).

Our proposal is closely related to QasemiZadeh et al. (2019), who introduce a shared task for unsupervised frame induction. Unlike the FrameNet dataset, they only provide frame annotations for verbs.

2.3 Event Sequences

Chambers and Jurafsky (2008) worked on learning narrative chains, sequences of events sharing a common protagonist. They operate on news data, introducing the narrative cloze task (the task of, given its surrounding events, predicting an event in a narrative chain). Chambers and Jurafsky (2009) extend the concept of narrative chains to narrative schemas, which involve more than one character and capture the interactions of different chains. Our approach is an extension of this work in that we aim to extract multiple schemas from a single long document. We assume that a document contains the descriptions of multiple processes or scenarios where each forms a schema.

Distinguishing real from generated event chains has been used in discriminative setups for story generation. Goldfarb-Tarrant et al. (2020) use event sequences as a building block to allow language models to generate globally consistent stories based on short prompts. Their model is trained to discern shuffled event sequences (using different shuffling strategies) from real ones. Guan et al. (2020) generate common-sense stories based on external knowledge bases. To our knowledge, no existing event modeling literature operates on longer chains of events as found in the domain of long-form literature.

Our approach is closely related to the one by Chambers and Jurafsky (2008) and Chambers and Jurafsky (2009), extending their approach to use vector representations over verb forms and to the operation on longer texts with multiple schemas.

2.4 Coreference Resolution

Coreference resolution is the task of identifying spans of text referring to the same entity within a document. Spans of text that refer to an entity are called mentions, in the sentence "[Alice] got up to greet [her] friend.", for example, both "Alice" and "her" refer to the same entity. The output of a coreference system is a set of mentions for each entity in the text. With the recent success of contextual embedding based coreference resolution approaches (Xu and Choi, 2020; Joshi et al., 2019, 2020) and its adaptation to longer documents on English data (Xia et al., 2020; Toshniwal et al., 2020), it seems possible that learning-based approaches could outperform rule-based ones, even on documents the length of entire novels. For English, the CoNLL-2012 shared task, based on the OntoNotes 5.0 dataset, is universally used for evaluation (Pradhan et al., 2012). The improvement in performance on this task in the recent past has largely been attributed to the improvements in underlying embeddings (Xu and Choi, 2020). Existing approaches on German news-domain data (Roesiger and Kuhn, 2016) are based on rule-based systems.

LitBank (Bamman et al., 2020) is a dataset of English novels with coreference annotations. Recent approaches by Xia et al. (2020) and Toshniwal et al. (2020) have evaluated their approach on this dataset. Krug et al. (2015) have approached the domain of German literature using rule-based coreference resolution. They point out issues with machine learning approaches, namely the fact that literary text is very different from the news data usually used for training, and provide a corpus for evaluation (Krug et al., 2018). The availability and quality of pre-trained embeddings as well as the absence of very large annotated German literary datasets are hindrances to applying state-of-the-art English approaches. Recently neural networks, however, have been found to perform similarly to rule-based approaches in our domain, with weaknesses in global consistency (Krug, 2020, chap. 8).

3 Research Questions

Generally, the proposed thesis seeks to model broader narratives by building up from single events. We aim to build two-layered models, building from events to schemas by segmenting chains of events into semantically related sub-chains. Those sub-chains sharing coreferring arguments form what we call a schema. Over a simple sequence model of events, this has the potential benefits of allowing for human analysis and simplifying comparisons between multiple texts.

RQ 1: How can events be represented? We approach the detection of events by processing verb occurrences. We aim to make use of dense vector representations of frames instead of using discrete frames. This is motivated by coverage concerns as well as the intuitive insight that frames have varying semantic distances between each other, which we hope can be represented by vector space distances. The approach will be evaluated on existing semantic frame resources as well as regarding their contribution towards schemas.

RQ 2: How can schemas be represented? Through the use of sequence models, we will attempt to find semantically related sequences of events. This may mean finding common-sense event sequences. For example *"take cart"* – *"take fruit"* – *"queue up"* – *"pay"* clearly is a sequence of events typical for grocery shopping, even though no individual event is uniquely indicative of grocery shopping. In this way, we may find semantic structures in texts that only emerge from the combination of several events.

We will experiment with different approaches to transforming sequences of events into schema representations. A simple approach may be averaging of event representations; more advanced approaches involving neural sequence models are also to be explored.

RQ 3: Which role does coreference play in schema representations? Coreference allows us to resolve the arguments of frames to their entities. Predicates that share corefering arguments may, depending on the segmentation, be part of the same schema. Entities will be chosen based on their prevalence, only entities with multiple occurrences are of interest. As a result, all predicates not involved with entities of interest are discarded immediately; this is an implied filtering step removing many predicates that do not constitute events. Descriptions of scenery for example would usually be discarded in such a scenario. The evaluation of coreference resolution can be performed on existing datasets. Literary datasets generally only annotate characters, rather than all entities.

It is conceivable that representation learning on events in text order may, in our case, be an appropriate replacement for coreference resolution. In this case, the presence of multiple events in proximity would be modeled rather than an explicit interaction. Initial filtering of non-event predicates is, in this case, required to not include predicates irrelevant to the story at large.

RQ 4: How can event and schema representations be adapted to literary works. We hypothesize to encounter the following challenges in our approach to literary works: document length, vocabulary mismatch with pre-trained models, and a diversity of domains (i.e.: different literary genres). To address these, we will explore the role of segmentation for processing documents in sections, the viability of incremental processing, and the role of pre-training and unsupervised fine-tuning. Aside from intrinsic evaluations of schemas based on their similarity and predicates based on them constituting events, we plan to derive summaries from the schema structure and compare them to human-generated summaries in literary lexicons (e.g. Arnold, 2009).

4 Methodology

From the research questions, two immediate directions emerge: event extraction, including coreference, and event representations. Later in the research process, we plan to build two-layer models transforming sequences of events into schemas.

4.1 Datasets

We operate on historical German literature in the form of the d-Prose dataset (Gius et al., 2020). Event annotations will, in cooperation with literary scientists, be created on a small subset of this data. In this subset, all verbs will be annotated, indicated whether or not they represent an event. For any verb that does represent an event, a set of binary features will be recorded, indicating several binary features based on concepts from narratology (Schmid, 2014). These features capture such criteria as reversibility, unexpectedness, and relevance of events.

4.2 Frame Identification for Event Representation

Initially, we assume each verb to evoke a frame and to represent an event, thereby addressing target detection using a parser-based heuristic. One notable exception, to the assumption of all verbs evoking frames, is stative verbs, *"Water is cold"* does not describe an event. Other cases such as inductive generalizations like *"Metal expands in the heat"* are more difficult to handle and may require machine learning approaches. Our initial approaches will only rely on the text order of events; we choose not to apply temporal ordering approaches (Mirroshandel et al., 2009; Mostafazadeh et al., 2016).

Concerns over insufficient coverage in the frame annotation data are motivated by an assumed diverse vocabulary in the domain of German literature. We separate coverage issues with frame resources into two categories, expecting both to occur with our data: **(i)** missing frames where, as pointed out by Yong and Torrent (2020), some semantics may not be covered, and **(ii)** missing lexical units where not-before-seen verbs evoke known frames.

While previous work by Yong and Torrent (2020) addressed missing frame coverage concerns by generating new frames, our approach does not necessitate discrete frame representations, rather we see multiple potential benefits to using continuous representations instead. Vector representations for different frames may model their semantic distances, different frames of communication such as *"Statement"* and *"Reporting"*, for example, are relatively closely related. Further, continuous representations may cover gradual distinctions between frames. The lexical unit *"say"* will typically evoke the *"Statement"* frame, while the verb *"scream"* will evoke the *"Communication_noise"* frame; gradual decisions could be made as to which frame the example *"she spoke loudly"* should evoke. Lastly, continuous representations are a good fit for processing neural models, no additional embedding layer is needed.

Our initial approach mirrors the one described as "Bottom-up Prototype" by Sikos and Padó (2019). In this approach, for each frame, the average vector representation of all training examples is computed, with the resulting centroid representing the entire frame. With this approach, using BERT-based embeddings, assigning frames based on the closest centroid embedding, (Devlin et al., 2019) we only barely reached double-digit results (in terms of frame classification F1-score) without lexical unit filtering while predicting German SALSA frames. These current results are not comparable with existing ones that we are aware of but we will make sure to apply our approach to existing datasets (e.g. Pradhan et al., 2007) in the future to facilitate comparisons. To retain the wider applicability of our embeddings, while improving results, we decided to use an approach similar to the "Bottom-up plus Top-down Prototype" one taken by QasemiZadeh et al. (2019). We train a BERT network to decide if a pair of lexical units in their contexts evoke the same frame. Unlike QasemiZadeh et al. (2019), we rely on embedding similarity to frame centroids at evaluation time.

Model Name	Max F1-Score
bert-german	71.73
bert-dbmdz	72.71
multilingual-bert	73.36
bert-electra	**75.86**
IMS HotCoref DE[1]	48.54

Table 1: Preliminary F1 scores for German coreference resolution on the TüBa-D/Z 10 validation set for different underlying embeddings using early stopping, with previous results listed for comparison.

4.3 Coreference Resolution

Coreference resolution is required to extract chains of events sharing a specific entity. Our initial results are promising, showing that current neural approaches using modern embeddings perform very well on German data.

In the experiments we present in this proposal, we train and evaluate German coreference models on the TüBa-D/Z dataset (Telljohann et al., 2004), adapting English approaches that are trained on OntoNotes (Pradhan and Ramshaw, 2017). We intend to train and evaluate further on the DROC (Krug et al., 2018) and DraCor (Pagel and Reiter, 2020) datasets adapting our models to perform character based coreference resolution. In the context of event extraction, the focus on characters could benefit us by irrelevant events being discarded, on the other hand, the removal of non-character related events relevant to the plot (e.g.: an earthquake) could be detrimental.

Table 1 shows our best results for each model on the validation set (with which early stopping is performed). All models were tested in their base variant. We use the training, validation, and test splits suggested by Roesiger and Kuhn (2016). Multilingual BERT (Devlin et al., 2019) performs about on par with the two older German models but is outperformed by the more recently released Electra model[2].

On the test set, our approach also performs well, reaching an F1 score of 75.44 using the evaluation script by Pradhan et al. (2014). Existing German results on the same data, using the same prediction setup (i.e. without using gold mentions), reach a maximum F1 score of 48.54 (Roesiger and Kuhn, 2016). Our preliminary results show that the existing approach by Xu and Choi (2020) adapts well to German data, out-performing previous rule-based systems. We attribute this clear improvement over the current state of the art mostly to the improvements in word embeddings; previous approaches on German data have not made use of transformer-based models. Comparisons with English provide limited insight due to the difference in datasets.

In our context tuning coreference systems for precision could be an option, but it remains to be seen how this would affect overall performance.

4.4 Narrative Schemas

As mentioned in Section 1, as a first step a schema segmentation needs to be performed. From surface-level features (like paragraphs) to content-based ones (like perplexity of event sequence models), we will openly explore different approaches. The evaluation of segmentations will pose a challenge, due to the lack of evaluation data; we will start with manual evaluation, potentially extending it to metric-based evaluation later on. There is also the issue of unclear definitions of schema boundaries, it is not clear, for example, if a *social gathering* schema should contain events for transportation to said social gathering (recall the example in Figure 1).

When considering the document from the perspective of an entity e, we get a sequence of events $E_0^{\{e,...\}}$ through $E_n^{\{e,...\}}$ where each ellipsis in the superscript may represent any number of additional entities involved with the event. Splitting event chains from each entities' perspective (based on, for example, a sequence model's perplexity) could be a suitable first step in creating schemas, resulting in a set of event chains for each entity. The second step would then unify all event chains sharing common events into schemas. Taking a more global approach involving all events in sequence, in conjunction with the entities related to them will also be considered.

After segmentation, each individual chain will be processed into a single fixed-size vector representation. We intend to evaluate the naïve approach of averaging event representations. Sequence models, such as LSTMs (Hochreiter and Schmidhuber, 1997), will also be evaluated, training them on the narrative cloze task we hope to use their state vectors as representations for schemas. Such schema vectors would, ideally, be close, in vector space,

[1]Result from Roesiger and Kuhn (2016)

[2]`https://huggingface.co/german-nlp-group/electra-base-german-uncased`

to semantically similar schemas. Due to the presumed length of event sequences, we will focus on recurrent models that allow for arbitrary input sizes.

5 Conclusion

We proposed segmenting chains of events to form multiple schemas in long documents, mentioning different approaches to the representation of events and to their segmentation. Further, we discussed the options for representing schemas to allow for their analysis and thereby the comparison of different documents. An open question for us is if the two-layer approach to schemas and events is sufficient, if needed a hierarchical approach involving levels of schemas will be considered.

As part of the event extraction process in this thesis, work on both semantic frame induction and coreference resolution for German language content will be advanced. The representation of events using continuous frame embeddings is a new approach in the domain of information extraction.

Specifics of sequence modeling and feature learning on events are vague, iterations on the proposed concepts are planned. The open question of how exactly schemas boundaries are to be defined still needs to be explored.

We intend to help enable the computational analysis of literary texts. Schema representations may be used for finding previously hard to find similarities in different documents, whereas event features can be used to identify events that are important to the narrative. Statistical and machine-learning-based approaches to event modeling will advance the understanding of events in a domain that yet received relatively little attention.

Acknowledgements

This work was supported by the DFG through the project "Evaluating Events in Narrative Theory (EvENT)" (grants BI 1544/11-1 and GI 1105/3-1) as part of the priority program "Computational Literary Studies (CLS)" (SPP 2207).

References

Heinz Ludwig Arnold. 2009. *Kindlers Literatur-Lexikon (KLL)*. J.B. Metzler, Stuttgart/Weimar.

Collin F. Baker, Charles J. Fillmore, and John B. Lowe. 1998. The Berkeley FrameNet Project. In *36th Annual Meeting of the Association for Computational Linguistics and 17th International Conference on Computational Linguistics, Volume 1*, pages 86–90, Montreal, Quebec, Canada. Association for Computational Linguistics.

David Bamman, Olivia Lewke, and Anya Mansoor. 2020. An annotated dataset of coreference in English literature. In *Proceedings of the 12th Language Resources and Evaluation Conference*, pages 44–54, Marseille, France. European Language Resources Association.

Aljoscha Burchardt, Katrin Erk, Anette Frank, Andrea Kowalski, Sebastian Padó, and Manfred Pinkal. 2006. The SALSA corpus: a German corpus resource for lexical semantics. In *Proceedings of the Fifth International Conference on Language Resources and Evaluation (LREC'06)*, pages 969–974, Genoa, Italy. European Language Resources Association (ELRA).

Nathanael Chambers and Dan Jurafsky. 2008. Unsupervised Learning of Narrative Event Chains. In *Proceedings of ACL-08: HLT*, pages 789–797, Columbus, Ohio, USA. Association for Computational Linguistics.

Nathanael Chambers and Dan Jurafsky. 2009. Unsupervised learning of narrative schemas and their participants. In *Proceedings of the Joint Conference of the 47th Annual Meeting of the ACL and the 4th International Joint Conference on Natural Language Processing of the AFNLP: Volume 2 - ACL-IJCNLP '09*, volume 2, pages 602–610, Suntec, Singapore. Association for Computational Linguistics.

Dipanjan Das, Desai Chen, André FT Martins, Nathan Schneider, and Noah A. Smith. 2014. Frame-semantic parsing. *Computational linguistics*, 40(1):9–56.

Jacob Devlin, Ming-Wei Chang, Kenton Lee, and Kristina Toutanova. 2019. BERT: Pre-training of deep bidirectional transformers for language understanding. In *Proceedings of the 2019 Conference of the North American Chapter of the Association for Computational Linguistics: Human Language Technologies, Volume 1 (Long and Short Papers)*, pages 4171–4186, Minneapolis, Minnesota, USA. Association for Computational Linguistics.

George Doddington, Alexis Mitchell, Mark Przybocki, Lance Ramshaw, Stephanie Strassel, and Ralph Weischedel. 2004. The automatic content extraction (ACE) program – tasks, data, and evaluation. In *Proceedings of the Fourth International Conference on Language Resources and Evaluation (LREC'04)*, pages 837–840, Lisbon, Portugal. European Language Resources Association (ELRA).

Christiane Fellbaum, editor. 1998. *WordNet: An electronic lexical database*. Language, speech, and communication. MIT Press, Cambridge, MA.

Robert Gaizauskas and Yorick Wilks. 1998. Information extraction: beyond document retrieval. *Journal of Documentation*, 54(1):70–105.

Daniel Gildea and Daniel Jurafsky. 2000. Automatic labeling of semantic roles. In *Proceedings of the 38th Annual Meeting of the Association for Computational Linguistics*, pages 512–520, Hong Kong. Association for Computational Linguistics.

Evelyn Gius, Svenja Guhr, and Benedikt Adelmann. 2020. d-Prose 1870-1920. Type: dataset.

Seraphina Goldfarb-Tarrant, Tuhin Chakrabarty, Ralph Weischedel, and Nanyun Peng. 2020. Content planning for neural story generation with Aristotelian rescoring. In *Proceedings of the 2020 Conference on Empirical Methods in Natural Language Processing (EMNLP)*, pages 4319–4338, Online. Association for Computational Linguistics.

Jian Guan, Fei Huang, Zhihao Zhao, Xiaoyan Zhu, and Minlie Huang. 2020. A Knowledge-Enhanced Pretraining Model for Commonsense Story Generation. *Transactions of the Association for Computational Linguistics*, 8:93–108.

Sepp Hochreiter and Jürgen Schmidhuber. 1997. Long short-term memory. *Neural computation*, 9(8):1735–1780.

Frederik Hogenboom, Flavius Frasincar, Uzay Kaymak, Franciska de Jong, and Emiel Caron. 2016. A survey of event extraction methods from text for decision support systems. *Decision Support Systems*, 85(C):12–22.

Richard Johansson and Pierre Nugues. 2007. Using WordNet to extend FrameNet coverage. In *Proceedings of the workshop on building frame-semantic resources for scandinavian and baltic languages, at NODALIDA*, pages 27–30, Tartu, Estonia.

Mandar Joshi, Danqi Chen, Yinhan Liu, Daniel S. Weld, Luke Zettlemoyer, and Omer Levy. 2020. SpanBERT: Improving Pre-training by Representing and Predicting Spans. *Transactions of the Association for Computational Linguistics*, 8:64–77. Publisher: MIT Press.

Mandar Joshi, Omer Levy, Luke Zettlemoyer, and Daniel Weld. 2019. BERT for Coreference Resolution: Baselines and Analysis. In *Proceedings of the 2019 Conference on Empirical Methods in Natural Language Processing and the 9th International Joint Conference on Natural Language Processing (EMNLP-IJCNLP)*, pages 5803–5808, Hong Kong. Association for Computational Linguistics.

Markus Krug. 2020. *Techniques for the Automatic Extraction of Character Networks in German Historic Novels*. Ph.D. thesis, Universität Würzburg.

Markus Krug, Frank Puppe, Fotis Jannidis, Luisa Macharowsky, Isabella Reger, and Lukas Weimar. 2015. Rule-based coreference resolution in German historic novels. In *Proceedings of the Fourth Workshop on Computational Linguistics for Literature*, pages 98–104, Denver, Colorado, USA. Association for Computational Linguistics.

Markus Krug, Lukas Weimer, Isabella Reger, Luisa Macharowsky, Stephan Feldhaus, Frank Puppe, and Fotis Jannidis. 2018. Description of a corpus of character references in German novels-DROC [Deutsches ROman Corpus]. *DARIAH-DE Working Papers*, 27.

Seyed Abolghasem Mirroshandel, Gholamreza Ghassem-Sani, and Mahdy Khayyamian. 2009. Using tree kernels for classifying temporal relations between events. In *Proceedings of the 23rd Pacific Asia Conference on Language, Information and Computation, Volume 1*, pages 355–364, Hong Kong. City University of Hong Kong.

Nasrin Mostafazadeh, Alyson Grealish, Nathanael Chambers, James Allen, and Lucy Vanderwende. 2016. CaTeRS: Causal and temporal relation scheme for semantic annotation of event structures. In *Proceedings of the Fourth Workshop on Events*, pages 51–61, San Diego, California, USA. Association for Computational Linguistics.

Christina Niklaus, Matthias Cetto, André Freitas, and Siegfried Handschuh. 2018. A Survey on Open Information Extraction. In *Proceedings of the 27th International Conference on Computational Linguistics*, pages 3866–3878, Santa Fe, New Mexico, USA. Association for Computational Linguistics.

Janis Pagel and Nils Reiter. 2020. GerDraCor-Coref: A Coreference Corpus for Dramatic Texts in German. In *Proceedings of the 12th Language Resources and Evaluation Conference*, pages 55–64, Marseille, France. European Language Resources Association.

Sameer Pradhan, Edward Loper, Dmitriy Dligach, and Martha Palmer. 2007. SemEval-2007 Task-17: English Lexical Sample, SRL and All Words. In *Proceedings of the Fourth International Workshop on Semantic Evaluations (SemEval-2007)*, pages 87–92, Prague, Czech Republic. Association for Computational Linguistics.

Sameer Pradhan, Xiaoqiang Luo, Marta Recasens, Eduard Hovy, Vincent Ng, and Michael Strube. 2014. Scoring coreference partitions of predicted mentions: A reference implementation. In *Proceedings of the 52nd Annual Meeting of the Association for Computational Linguistics (Volume 2: Short Papers)*, pages 30–35, Baltimore, Maryland, USA. Association for Computational Linguistics.

Sameer Pradhan, Alessandro Moschitti, Nianwen Xue, Olga Uryupina, and Yuchen Zhang. 2012. CoNLL-2012 Shared Task: Modeling Multilingual Unrestricted Coreference in OntoNotes. In *Joint Conference on EMNLP and CoNLL - Shared Task*, pages 1–40, Jeju Island, Korea. Association for Computational Linguistics.

Sameer Pradhan and Lance Ramshaw. 2017. OntoNotes: Large Scale Multi-Layer, Multi-Lingual, Distributed Annotation. In Nancy Ide and James Pustejovsky, editors, *Handbook of Linguistic Annotation*, pages 521–554. Springer Netherlands, Dordrecht.

Behrang QasemiZadeh, Miriam R. L. Petruck, Regina Stodden, Laura Kallmeyer, and Marie Candito. 2019. SemEval-2019 task 2: Unsupervised lexical frame induction. In *Proceedings of the 13th International Workshop on Semantic Evaluation*, pages 16–30, Minneapolis, Minnesota, USA. Association for Computational Linguistics.

Ina Roesiger and Jonas Kuhn. 2016. IMS HotCoref DE: A Data-driven Co-reference Resolver for German. In *Proceedings of the Tenth International Conference on Language Resources and Evaluation (LREC'16)*, pages 155–160, Portorož, Slovenia. European Language Resources Association (ELRA).

Wolf Schmid. 2014. *Elemente der Narratologie*, 3., erweiterte und überarbeitete auflage edition. De-Gruyter-Studium. de Gruyter, Berlin/Boston.

Jennifer Sikos and Sebastian Padó. 2019. Frame identification as categorization: Exemplars vs prototypes in embeddingland. In *Proceedings of the 13th International Conference on Computational Semantics - Long Papers*, pages 295–306, Gothenburg, Sweden. Association for Computational Linguistics.

Matthew Sims, Jong Ho Park, and David Bamman. 2019. Literary event detection. In *Proceedings of the 57th Annual Meeting of the Association for Computational Linguistics*, pages 3623–3634, Florence, Italy. Association for Computational Linguistics.

Heike Telljohann, Erhard Hinrichs, and Sandra Kübler. 2004. The Tüba-D/Z Treebank: Annotating German with a Context-Free Backbone. In *Proceedings of the Fourth International Conference on Language Resources and Evaluation (LREC'04)*, pages 2229–2232, Lisbon, Portugal. European Language Resources Association (ELRA).

Shubham Toshniwal, Sam Wiseman, Allyson Ettinger, Karen Livescu, and Kevin Gimpel. 2020. Learning to Ignore: Long Document Coreference with Bounded Memory Neural Networks. In *Proceedings of the 2020 Conference on Empirical Methods in Natural Language Processing (EMNLP)*, pages 8519–8526, Online. Association for Computational Linguistics.

Patrick Xia, João Sedoc, and Benjamin Van Durme. 2020. Incremental neural coreference resolution in constant memory. In *Proceedings of the 2020 Conference on Empirical Methods in Natural Language Processing (EMNLP)*, pages 8617–8624, Online. Association for Computational Linguistics.

Liyan Xu and Jinho D. Choi. 2020. Revealing the myth of higher-order inference in coreference resolution. In *Proceedings of the 2020 Conference on Empirical Methods in Natural Language Processing (EMNLP)*, pages 8527–8533, Online. Association for Computational Linguistics.

Zheng Xin Yong and Tiago Timponi Torrent. 2020. Semi-supervised deep embedded clustering with anomaly detection for semantic frame induction. In *Proceedings of the 12th Language Resources and Evaluation Conference*, pages 3509–3519, Marseille, France. European Language Resources Association.

Parallel Text Alignment and Monolingual Parallel Corpus Creation from Philosophical Texts for Text Simplification

Stefan Paun
University of Twente / Enschede, Netherlands
s.paun@student.utwente.nl

Abstract

Text simplification is a growing field with many potential useful applications. Training text simplification algorithms generally requires a lot of annotated data, however there are not many corpora suitable for this task. We propose a new unsupervised method for aligning text based on Doc2Vec embeddings and a new alignment algorithm, capable of aligning texts at different levels. Initial evaluation shows promising results for the new approach. We used the newly developed approach to create a new monolingual parallel corpus composed of the works of English early modern philosophers and their corresponding simplified versions.

1 Introduction

There has been a clear growth in research in the field of text simplification in recent years (Shardlow, 2014). Text simplification has many potential advantages, such as helping people who suffer from impairments like dyslexia (Alva-Manchego et al., 2020). Most recent approaches are data-driven and require learning text simplification transformations such as sentence splitting or word substitution from a parallel corpus.

Such a parallel corpus consists of a source document and a target document, which is the simplified version of it. The most widespread parallel corpora for text simplification are the parallel English Simple Wikipedia corpus (Zhu et al., 2010) and the more recent Newsela corpus (Xu et al., 2015).

A parallel corpus is obtained by aligning the units of text between the original-simplified pairs. The alignment can be done at different levels, however most research in the field is focused on sentence simplification (Alva-Manchego et al., 2020), thus sentence level alignments is the gold standard. Automated methods which can asses text similarity are highly desirable in order to produce such parallel corpora.

There are few tools that can easily align text in an unsupervised way. MASSAlign[1] by Paetzold et al. (2017) is a Python library which can produce alignments at both paragraph and sentence level in an unsupervised manner using a TF-IDF model. However, according to Campr and Ježek (2015), a Doc2Vec model would yield results which would imitate human estimates closer than a TF-IDF model when computing text similarity.

The current work has a twofold contribution. Firstly, we extend the existing MASSAlign tool with a Doc2Vec language model to better capture text similarity and a new alignment algorithm to complement the language model. We manually label two pairs of original-simpliefied documents and use these pairs to evaluate the performance of the Doc2Vec-based method. We find some promising results, however more evaluation is needed in order to draw a strong conclusion.

Secondly, we create a novel monolingual parallel corpus from philosophical texts. The novelty lies in the type of texts that constitute the corpus, specifically original philosophical works written by early modern English philosophers and their simplified variants re-written by a group of editors, with the scope to make the texts more accessible while preserving the meaning. The newly developed parallel corpus is created using the improved text alignment tool and is intended to be used as training data for existing text simplification systems. We sample alignments at random to get an idea of the quality of the corpus. Our initial findings show that the generated corpus seems to be of high quality.

2 Related Work

Paetzold et al. (2017) have proposed and developed an easy-to-use text alignment tool in the form of a Python library. Their approach relies on a simple TF-IDF model coupled with a Vicinity-Driven

[1]Github.com/ghpaetzold/massalign

Proceedings of NAACL-HLT 2021: Student Research Workshop, pages 40–46
June 6–11, 2021. ©2021 Association for Computational Linguistics

alignment method described in Paetzold and Specia (2016). Their alignment relies on the assumption that the order in which the information appears is consistent in both text pairs. Their system can identify one-to-many, many-to-one and many-to-many alignments, as opposed to the method proposed by Xu et al. (2015). This allows for capturing of text simplification operations such as splitting and compressing. Additionally, they employ a two stage approach, in which they first align paragraphs and then align sentences in the already aligned paragraphs. Our research expands and builds upon the work of Paetzold and Specia (2016).

Štajner et al. (2018) have presented CATS[2], a tool for the alignment of text simplification corpora. They employ two alignment methods, one which works under the same assumption as Paetzold et al. (2017), namely that the order of information is consistent in both pairs of text, and one which relaxes that assumption. Both approaches use the same strategy of aligning each sentence from the simplified-version of the document with the most similar sentence from original document, on the basis of textual similarity metrics. Similarly, their tool also allows for one-to-many and many-to-one alignments, and offers the option for a two staged alignment approach. One of their findings is that employing the assumption of consistent information ordering leads to an increase in the number of partial matches, at the cost of the number of full matches. However, this allows for the better capturing of the deletion operation specific to text simplification.

Xu et al. (2015) argue that the Simple Wikipedia corpus is a bottle neck for the text simplification field because the corpus is prone to automatic alignment errors, has inadequate simplifications and does not transfer well to other styles of texts. They present a new parallel corpus, Newsela, as an alternative to the Simple Wikipedia dataset. This new corpus improves on the shortcomings of the Wikipedia corpus since it consists of news articles professionally rewritten by editors. Our work provides an additional, novel corpus in order to advance the field of text simplification.

3 Dataset

The parallel dataset created is built from the works of four early modern philosophers, whose works were originally written in English: George Berkeley, David Hume, John Locke and John Stuart Mill. We obtained the original documents, which were in the public domain, from Project Gutenberg[3]. We obtained their simplified counter-parts of from Early Modern Texts[4]. The simplified version of texts were re-written by a team of editors, with the specific goal of making the original document more accessible while keeping the original ideas intact.

In order to be able to generate the parallel corpus, we cleaned-up and pre-processed the gathered data such that each document consists of a sentence per line, while empty lines represent the paragraph boundaries.

The pre-processing pipeline consists of multiple steps. First, using regular expressions we remove unwanted characters from the texts such as hashtags or underscores, or in the case of the simplified versions, characters that mark omissions or that are used for formatting purposes, which were added by the editors. The next step was to remove the newline characters found in the middle of sentences. This was also done by means of regular expressions. At the end of this step, the documents were formatted such that each line of the document represents a paragraph. Once this was achieved, a paragraph was split into sentences by using the Punkt Tokenizer provided in the NLTK[5] Python library. A list of common encountered abbreviations was supplied to the tokenizer such that sentences are not split midway.

4 Method

We use the open-source Python library, MASSAlign, developed by Paetzold et al. (2017) as the base for our new alignment algorithm. We expand the tool with a Doc2Vec language model and a new alignment algorithm which can take advantage of the new language model. Subsection 4.1 describes the language model, while Subsection 4.2 describes the alignment algorithm.

4.1 Language Model

Campr and Ježek (2015) evaluated a number of language models for the task of computing document similarity and found that TF-IDF embeddings are outperformed by Doc2Vec embeddings. This is in line with the intuition that a paragraph vector would capture meaning better than a simple bag of words

[2]Github.com/neosyon/SimpTextAlign

[3]Gutenberg.org

[4]EarlyModernTexts.com

[5]NLTK.org

approach since it makes better use of the context around words. Therefore, we decided to extend the MASSAlign tool with a Doc2Vec model.

The Doc2Vec model is used to create a vector embedding for the text unit to be aligned. In order to measure how similar two text units are, we use the cosine distance metric of the two vectors. We train a new Doc2Vec model each time an original-simplified pair of documents is to be aligned. The intuition behind is that this approach will better capture the specific style of the document.

We chose the parameters of the Doc2Vec model based on the insights from Lau and Baldwin (2016). Their empirical evaluation has shown that from the two methods employed by Doc2Vec, *dmpv* and *dbow*, the latter one yields better results, despite being less complex. They also find that instead of initializing word embeddings with random vectors, as it is typical with Doc2Vec, a step of *skip-gram* being performed before *dbow* leads to improvement in performance.

Therefore, the model is initialized with a vector size of 300, a window size of 15 and a negative sample of 5. The two parameters that are different from the findings of Lau and Baldwin (2016) are the number of training epochs and the minimum word count. Since some of the texts to be aligned are relatively short, a larger number of epochs and a smaller minimum word count is used in order to achieve more consistent results.

4.2 Alignment Algorithm

We developed an alignment algorithm to complement the Doc2Vec language model. The alignment algorithm is heavily inspired by the already existing Vicinity-Driven algorithm of (Paetzold and Specia, 2016). The need for another alignment algorithm was motivated by way the TF-IDF language model was used to determine whether two paragraphs are aligned. In the initial Vicinity-Driven method the similarity score of two paragraphs is given by the pair of sentences within the paragraph that have the highest similarity score. With the Doc2Vec model, a similarity score can be computed directly for the entire paragraph.

The new alignment algorithm starts from the beginning of the documents and looks for the first (original, simplified) pair of text units that are similar enough to consider. Once this candidate alignment pair is found, the next step is to try to improve alignment score, by expanding the initial alignment and looking for potential one-to-many and many-to-one alignments. Expanding the initial alignment is done by concatenating the current text units being considered with the next text unit from the original document, and, respectively, from the simplified document and computing new similarity scores. This expansion process continues until the newly computed similarity score stops improving. At this point the expansion process is stopped and the similarity score of this expanded candidate alignment pair is evaluated against a threshold. If the score is above the threshold, the candidate pair is considered aligned, otherwise, the algorithm looks for the next pair of text units which could be considered similar enough to try to align. The process continues until the end of both documents is reached. The algorithm allows for skipping of text units, to allow for the situation in which a particular text unit is not aligned to any text unit in the other document of the pair.

Similar to the original Vicinity-Driven method, the developed algorithm is capable of identifying one-to-one, many-to-one, one-to-many and many-to-many alignments. While it relies on the same assumptions as the original alignment algorithm, the approach described in this paper is able to relax one assumption, namely that the first paragraphs of the pair of documents are definitely aligned. Moreover, while the Vicinity-Driven approach employs two slightly different methods for aligning paragraphs and aligning sentences, the new method uses the same logic for both paragraph and sentence levels. This, coupled with the Doc2Vec model, makes the aligner capable of aligning text at different levels.

Unlike the already existing method, the new algorithm makes use of three different threshold levels. This is done for a number of reasons. First of all, a *certain threshold* is used to identify one-to-one alignments with a very high degree of similarity. A second, *hard threshold* is used to determine whether an alignment is good enough. A third threshold, *soft threshold* is employed in order to identify potential one-to-many, many-to-one or many-to-many alignments.

The thresholds are determined automatically by considering the distribution of the best similarity scores for each of the paragraphs or sentences of the simplified document from the initial similarity matrix. The *soft threshold* is determined by the lowest value of the similarity score distribution. Next, the 95% confidence interval where the median value of the similarity score falls is determined. The *hard threshold* is determined by taking the lower boundary of the confidence interval and subtracting the standard deviation of the distribution, while the *certain threshold* is determined by considering the upper boundary of the confidence interval and adding the standard deviation of the distribution.

5 Results

5.1 Doc2Vec algorithm

In order to evaluate the performance of the proposed alignment algorithm, we have manually aligned two pairs of documents and created a ground-truth document for each pair of texts. The document which were used for evaluation are George Berkeley's "Essay Towards a New Theory of Vision" (Berkeley1709) and John Locke's "A Letter Concerning Toleration" (Locke1689b). We compared the performance of the original TF-IDF based Vicinity-Driven algorithm against the Doc2Vec based proposed algorithm.

Due to the statistical nature of Doc2Vec, running the alignment algorithm multiple times with the same parameters leads to small jitters in the results. The variation from run to run is determined by the quality of the Doc2Vec model, in particular for the number of epochs the model is trained. If the model is under-trained, there will be large variations in results between runs, thus it is important to have a model adjusted to the particularities of the text.

In order to evaluate the two methods, we consider the task of aligning sentences as a binary classification task, where each pair of sentences or paragraphs considered are either classified as correctly aligned or incorrectly aligned. We report the performance in terms of precision, recall and F1 measure. For sentences we consider two cases, one where the alignment is fully correct and one where the alignment is partial. In addition, we provide descriptive statistics about the one-to-one (1-to-1), many-to-one (n-to-1) and one-to-many (1-to-n) alignments. A one-to-many alignment implies that one unit of text from the original document maps to more than one unit of text from the simplified document, hence the original unit of text was split into multiple units in the simplified version.

The results are shown in Table 1. As it can be observed, for the Berkeley pair of documents, the Doc2Vec-based method seems to be slightly superior to TF-IDF, however the Doc2Vec-based approach performs worse in the case of the Locke pair of documents. Since the evaluation was performed on a limited sample of documents, there is not enough data to be able to infer anything categorically about the Doc2Vec-based approach.

	Berkeley		**Locke**	
	TF-IDF	Doc2Vec	TF-IDF	Doc2Vec
	Paragraph			
Detected	155	153	75	71
Correct	147	146	70	59
1-to-1	122	121	52	49
n-to-1	1	0	5	1
1-to-n	24	25	13	9
Precision	0.948	0.954	0.933	0.830
Recall	0.936	0.929	0.945	0.797
F1	0.942	0.941	0.939	0.813
	Sentences			
Detected	540	557	414	350
Correct	459	482	307	227
1-to-1	384	397	279	203
n-to-1	21	22	15	15
1-to-n	54	63	13	9
Precision	0.850	0.865	0.741	0.648
Recall	0.796	0.836	0.685	0.506
F1	0.822	0.850	0.712	0.568
	Partial Sentences			
Precision	0.948	0.935	0.908	0.797
Recall	0.888	0.904	0.839	0.622
F1	0.917	0.919	0.872	0.699

Table 1: Evaluation of TF-IDF model and original alignment algorithm against Doc2Vec model and our alignment algorithm for two pairs of documents

Table 2 contains examples which illustrate both successful and unsuccessful sentence alignments. Examples 1, 3.1 and 3.2 are from Berkeley's work (Berkeley1709), while examples 2 and 4 are from Locke's work (Locke1689b). Example 1 showcases a one-to-many type of alignment, in which the original sentence corresponds to two sentences from the simplified version. Example 2 showcases a many-to-one type of alignment, where two sentences of the original version correspond to a single sentence from the simplified document. Unsuccessful alignments can be classified as either partial or erroneous. With partial alignments there is some overlap between the original and simplified sentences, however the alignment fails to capture the full semantic similarity. A partial alignment can introduce offset in the alignment process and can

Ex.	Original Document	Simplified Document
	Successful alignments	
1	*to which i answer, it is not faintness anyhow applied that suggests greater magnitude, there being no necessary but only an experimental connexion between those two things.*	*i answer that what suggests larger size is not faintness as such but faintness of a kind and in circumstances that have been observed to accompany the vision of large sizes. we're not dealing with a necessary connection here, but only an experimental connection between those two things.*
2	*nay, we must not content ourselves with the narrow measures of bare justice; charity, bounty, and liberality must be added to it. this the gospel enjoins, this reason directs, and this that natural fellowship we are born into requires of us.*	*indeed, we should go beyond mere justice, adding benevolence and charity; the gospel commands this, reason urges it, and it is favoured by the natural fellowship we are born into.*
	Unsuccessful alignments	
3.1	*but, say you, the picture of the man is inverted, and yet the appearance is erect: i ask, what mean you by the picture of the man, or, which is the same thing, the visible man's being inverted?*	*you object: the picture of the man is inverted, yet the appearance is erect.*
3.2	*you tell me it is inverted, because the heels are uppermost and the head undermost?*	*what do you mean by the picture of the man? or, the same question, what do you mean by the visible man's being inverted? you tell me that it's inverted because the heels are uppermost and the head undermost?*
4	*another more secret evil, but more dangerous to the commonwealth, is when men arrogate to themselves, and to those of their own sect, some peculiar prerogative covered over with a specious show of deceitful words, but in effect opposite to the civil right of the community.*	*for if these were proposed thus nakedly and plainly, they would soon attract the attention of the magistrate and arouse the commonwealth to be on its guard against the spreading of such a dangerous evil.*

Table 2: Examples of successful and unsuccessful alignments.

cause the following sentence pair to also be only partially aligned, as illustrated by examples 3.1 and 3.2, which are consecutive pieces of text in the documents. With erroneous alignments, illustrated by example 4, the sentences convey different messages.

5.2 Parallel Corpus

The gathered documents have been aligned using the Doc2Vec aligner method. In Table 3 it is shown what percentage of the paragraph and sentence of the simplified documents have been aligned. This value gives an indication of how much of the document could be aligned, however it does not reflect the recall performance of the aligner since the total number of alignments will always be less or equal to the number of initial paragraphs or sentences, due to many to one alignments.

It can be observed that the coverage percentage is very low for larger documents. The cause of this is two-fold. Firstly, the Doc2Vec model is most likely under-powered since the hyperparameter values have been tuned on the *Berkeley1709* pair which is shorter than for instance *Berkeley1732*. Secondly,

	Paragraphs			Sentences		
Doc ID	Total	Det.	Cov.	Total	Det.	Cov.
Berkeley1709	157	154	0.98	576	547	0.94
Berkeley1710	185	173	0.93	1046	800	0.76
Berkeley1713	223	211	0.94	331	290	0.87
Berkeley1732	291	42	0.14	4228	865	0.12
Hume1739	1378	248	0.17	6687	865	0.12
Hume1748	277	114	0.41	1158	488	0.42
Hume1751	364	129	0.35	1348	422	0.31
Hume1779	264	254	0.96	1237	1140	0.91
Locke1689a	309	119	0.38	948	325	0.34
Locke1689b	88	71	0.80	616	350	0.56
Mill1843	1556	168	0.10	68686	426	0.06
Mill1859	140	124	0.88	1263	1109	0.87
Mill1863	111	91	0.81	696	602	0.86
Mill1869	96	85	0.88	1186	755	0.63
Mill1873	208	181	0.87	1879	1625	0.86

Table 3: Total and detected (Det.) paragraph (P) and sentence (S) alignments using Doc2Vec alignment method. Coverage (Cov.) shows the percentage of the total number of paragraphs and sentences that have been aligned.

by inspecting the documents with a low coverage, it was observed that there were a large number of short paragraphs and short sentences, of few words. These short paragraphs or sentences affect the performance of the Doc2Vec model since there is a lot less context when compared to longer paragraphs.

The alignments have been manually inspected by randomly sampling alignments from the different documents. While the sampling and inspection have not been performed in a structured manner, this was sufficient to determine that the text pairs which achieved a low coverage score were not optimally aligned. Therefore it would be detrimental to include these document pairs in the final corpus. Conversely, the text pairs which achieved a high coverage score appeared to be well aligned.

Therefore, we concatenated together the document pairs with a coverage value of above 0.3 to form a new corpus. Two files are created, for aligned paragraphs and for aligned sentences. The sentence alignment file consists of 8453 aligned sentences comprised of 636652 words in total. Another random sampling inspection is performed on the resulting corpus made of aligned sentences. Out of 100 sentence alignments extracted, 98 alignments can be classified as good, while 2 alignments can be classified as partial. A partial alignment means that there is an overlap between the aligned sentences, however, one of the sentence contains additional information which is not present in the other sentence.

6 Discussion

The current work has a number of limitations. One of the biggest limitations is that the evaluation of the performance of the Doc2Vec model is done with limited data points. While, it shows some promising results, the limited evaluation is not enough to allow for a strong conclusion to be drawn. To overcome this, a more extensive intrinsic and extrinsic evaluation should be performed by testing with parallel corpora that have already been aligned, such as the Simple Wikipedia corpus or the Newsela corpus and compare the number and quality of alignments obtained against already established methods.

In addition to a better evaluation of the model, a method for determining the hyperparameters of the Doc2Vec model based on the characteristics of the texts to be aligned, such as number of sentences or number of words, would be highly beneficial and would improve the alignment process in terms of both quality and time investment. Moreover, more recent, neural-network based language models, such as Sentence-BERT or Universal Sentence Encoder, could be considered as an alternative to Doc2Vec.

Another limitation of the current work is the lack of evaluation of the produced parallel corpus. While the limited random sampling shows very promising results, this is not enough in order to draw a conclusion regarding the quality of the resulted dataset. A more structured approach to the random sampling method could give better insight into the quality of the dataset.

Another point of improvement is the preprocessing stage. Ensuring that all text formatting elements, such as chapter numbers or titles are removed, would result in a more robust Doc2Vec model being trained on those documents. Moreover, very short paragraphs or sentences are detrimental to the quality of the Doc2Vec embeddings and do not add a lot of value for the text simplification process, thus they should be filtered out.

7 Conclusion

An approach to unsupervised text alignment was presented in this paper which makes use of Doc2Vec text embeddings in order to asses similarity between two pieces of texts. Additionally, an alignment method derived from the Vicinity-Driven approach of Paetzold and Specia (2016) has been presented. Initial results have shown the current work has slightly better performance compared to the original approach when evaluated on a specific pair of texts, but it has worse results on a different pair of texts. However, due to the limited evaluation, the outcome cannot be readily generalized and more testing is required in order to draw a definitive conclusion. The MASSAlign Python library has been extended to include this new Doc2Vec model.

A new monolingual parallel corpus has been created from documents consisting of works of English early modern philosophers and their simplified, corresponding, versions, which were redacted by a group of editors with the goal of making the original documents easier to follow and understand, while preserving meaning.

The newly created parallel corpus, together with the extended version of MASSAlign are available at: github.com/stefanpaun/massalign.

References

Fernando Alva-Manchego, Carolina Scarton, and Lucia Specia. 2020. Data-driven sentence simplification: Survey and benchmark. *Computational Linguistics*, 46(1):135–187.

Michal Campr and Karel Ježek. 2015. Comparing semantic models for evaluating automatic document summarization. In *Text, Speech, and Dialogue*, pages 252–260, Cham. Springer International Publishing.

Jey Han Lau and Timothy Baldwin. 2016. An empirical evaluation of doc2vec with practical insights into document embedding generation. In *Proceedings of the 1st Workshop on Representation Learning for NLP*, pages 78–86, Berlin, Germany. Association for Computational Linguistics.

Gustavo Paetzold, Fernando Alva-Manchego, and Lucia Specia. 2017. MASSAlign: Alignment and annotation of comparable documents. In *Proceedings of the IJCNLP 2017, System Demonstrations*, pages 1–4, Tapei, Taiwan. Association for Computational Linguistics.

Gustavo Henrique Paetzold and Lucia Specia. 2016. Vicinity-driven paragraph and sentence alignment for comparable corpora. *ArXiv*, abs/1612.04113.

Matthew Shardlow. 2014. A survey of automated text simplification. *International Journal of Advanced Computer Science and Applications*, 4.

Sanja Štajner, Marc Franco-Salvador, Paolo Rosso, and Simone Paolo Ponzetto. 2018. CATS: A tool for customized alignment of text simplification corpora. In *Proceedings of the Eleventh International Conference on Language Resources and Evaluation (LREC 2018)*, Miyazaki, Japan. European Language Resources Association (ELRA).

Wei Xu, Chris Callison-Burch, and Courtney Napoles. 2015. Problems in current text simplification research: New data can help. *Transactions of the Association for Computational Linguistics*, 3:283–297.

Zhemin Zhu, Delphine Bernhard, and Iryna Gurevych. 2010. A monolingual tree-based translation model for sentence simplification. In *Proceedings of the 23rd International Conference on Computational Linguistics (Coling 2010)*, pages 1353–1361, Beijing, China. Coling 2010 Organizing Committee.

Syntax-Based Attention Masking for Neural Machine Translation

Colin McDonald and David Chiang
University of Notre Dame
Dept. of Computer Science and Engineering
{cmcdona8,dchiang}@nd.edu

Abstract

We present a simple method for extending transformers to source-side trees. We define a number of masks that limit self-attention based on relationships among tree nodes, and we allow each attention head to learn which mask or masks to use. On translation from English to various low-resource languages, and translation in both directions between English and German, our method always improves over simple linearization of the source-side parse tree and almost always improves over a sequence-to-sequence baseline, by up to +2.1% BLEU.

1 Introduction

The transformer model for machine translation (Vaswani et al., 2017) was originally defined as a mapping from sequences to sequences. More recent work has explored extensions of transformers to other structures: a tree transformer would be able to make use of syntactic information, and a graph transformer would be able to make use of semantic graphs or knowledge graphs.

There have been a number of proposals for transformers on trees, including phrase-structure trees and dependency trees for natural languages, and abstract syntax trees for programming languages. One common strategy is to *linearize* a tree into a sequence (Ahmad et al., 2020; Currey and Heafield, 2019). Another strategy is to recognize that transformers are fundamentally defined not on sequences but on bags; all information about sequential order is contained in the positional encodings, so all that is needed to construct a tree transformer is to define new positional encodings on trees (Shiv and Quirk, 2019; Omote et al., 2019).

In this paper, we present a third approach, which is to enhance the encoder's self-attention mechanism with *attention masks* (Shen et al., 2018), which restrict the possible positions an attention head can attend to. We extend this idea in two new ways. First, our attention masks are based on relationships among tree positions (for example, "is an ancestor of" or "is a descendant of") rather than sequence positions ("is left of" or "is right of"). Second, instead of pre-assigning different masks to each attention head, we allow each attention head to learn separately which mask or masks to use.

We experiment on machine translation of several low-resource language pairs (Section 3). Compared to linearization without masks, our method always improves accuracy, by up to +1.7 BLEU (all BLEU reported as percen t). Compared with a sequence-to-sequence baseline, our method improves accuracy by up to +2.1 BLEU. On tasks where linearization hurts, our method is usually, but not always, able to turn the loss into a gain.

2 Methods

Like several previous approaches, we use linearized syntax trees. But whereas the usual linearization traverses a node both before and after its descendants, we use a preorder traversal of the tree. In other words, our linearization does not have closing brackets. Our linearization does not have enough information to reconstruct the original tree; this information is contained in the attention masks, which we describe next.

Shen et al. (2018) introduce the idea of using *masks* in a string transformer to allow attention heads to attend only to the left or only to the right. We apply this idea to tree transformers, with two modifications. First, instead of masking out the left or right context, we use masks based on the structure of the tree. Second, instead of allocating a fixed number of heads to each mask, we let the model learn which mask(s) to use for each attention head.

Given a query $Q \in \mathbb{R}^{n \times d_k}$, key $K \in \mathbb{R}^{n \times d_k}$, and value $V \in \mathbb{R}^{n \times d_v}$ (where n is the number of input tokens and $d_k = d_v$ is d_{model} divided by the number of attention heads), scaled dot-product attention is

Proceedings of NAACL-HLT 2021: Student Research Workshop, pages 47–52
June 6–11, 2021.

normally computed as

$$\alpha = \text{softmax}\frac{QK^T}{\sqrt{d_k}}$$
$$\text{Att}(Q, K, V) = \alpha V$$

where $\alpha \in \mathbb{R}^{n \times n}$ is the matrix of attention weights, and the softmax is performed per row. We modify the definition of α to

$$\alpha = \text{softmax}\left(\frac{QK^T}{\sqrt{d_k}} - \exp\sum_m s^m M^m\right)$$

where, for each m, the matrix $M^m \in \{0, 1\}^{n \times n}$ is a fixed mask and s^m is its corresponding strength, which is learnable. If $[M^m]_{ij} = 1$ and s^m is large, then the attention at position i is prevented from attending to position j. If $[M^m]_{ij} = 0$ or s^m is very negative, then position i is free to attend to position j. With multiple attention heads, each head has its own strength parameters.

The strength parameters are initialized to zero and learned by backpropagation with the rest of the model. In this way, each attention head can learn separately which mask or masks to use.

It remains to define the masks M^m. A mask can be defined for any imaginable string or tree relationship. Because the model can always choose not to use a mask, we can add as many masks as we want. We use the following set:

self position i is equal to position j

parent position i is the parent of position j

child position i is a child of position j

left-sib position i is a left sibling of position j

right-sib position i is a right sibling of position j

anc position i is an ancestor (but not a parent) of position j

desc position i is a descendent (but not a child) of position j

left-other position i has none of the above relationships with position j, but is left of position j

right-other position i has none of the above relationships with position j, but is right of position j

Task	Lines			Avg. source	
	train	dev	test	words	nodes
En-Vi	131k	1,553	1,268	22.9	36.4
En-De	100k*	3,000	3,003	28.5	45.5
De-En	100k*	3,000	3,003	29.6	34.6
En-Tu	59k	1,114	544	28.7	39.1
En-Ha	45k	914	497	26.5	39.3
En-Ur	11k	1,271	652	22.5	30.7

Table 1: Dataset statistics. Nodes: average number of *interior* nodes. *The original German–English dataset had 4.5M lines, but we only trained on subsets of up to 100k lines.

Although none of the above masks overlap, there would be no problem with defining masks that do.

Please see Figure 1 for an example. In (a) is an English tree; (b) shows the same tree after applying byte pair encoding (BPE) subword segmentation (see Section 3 below); and (c) shows the relationships of all the nodes with the second NP (the one dominating *my father*).

3 Experiments

3.1 Data

We tested on the following datasets:

en-vi English to Vietnamese, from the IWSLT 2015 shared task.[1] To test for dependence of our method on training data size, we also used random subsets of 20k and 50k.

de-en, en-de German↔English, from the WMT 2016 news translation task.[2] For training, we used random subsets of 20k, 50k, and 100k. We used news-test2013 for validation and news-test2014 for testing.

en-tu, en-ha, en-ur English to Turkish, Hausa, and Urdu, from the DARPA LORELEI program.

Some statistics of the datasets are shown in Table 1. This table lists the average number of source words and source *interior* nodes, from which the average number of tokens in the **linearized** and **mask** systems can be derived.

We tokenized using the Moses tokenizer, then divided words into subwords using BPE (Sennrich

[1] `https://nlp.stanford.edu/projects/nmt/`

[2] `https://www.statmt.org/wmt16/translation-task.html`

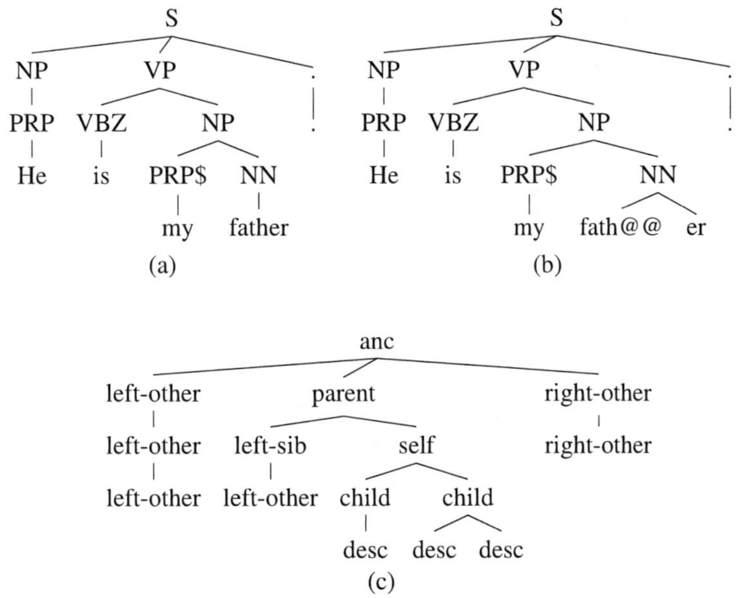

Figure 1: (a) Example tree. (b) With BPE. (c) Relationships of all nodes to the second NP (dominating *my father*).

et al., 2016). For en-vi, en-tu, en-ha, and en-ur, we used 8k joint BPE operations, and for en-de and de-en, we used 32k operations.

To parse English or German sentences, we used the Berkeley Neural Parser (Kitaev and Klein, 2018; Kitaev et al., 2019) with the included `benepar_en2` model for English and `benepar_de` for German. The parser reads in untokenized strings and writes out tokenized trees; we used the parser's tokenization, but applied BPE to the leaves, as shown in Figure 1b.

3.2 Evaluation

We compare against two baselines: **Sequence** is a standard sequence-to-sequence model, run on words only. **Linearized** is a standard sequence-to-sequence model, run on linearized trees. A leaf node w is linearized as w. An interior node X is linearized as $\boxed{(X}$ followed by the linearization of its children followed by $\boxed{)}$. Against these baselines, we compare our model, **Mask**, which uses a pre-order traversal of the tree together with the masks described above in Section 2.

All systems are implemented on top of Witwicky,[3] an open-source implementation of the transformer. We use all default settings; in particular, layer normalization is performed after residual connections (Nguyen and Salazar, 2019).

[3]`https://github.com/tnq177/witwicky`

We score detokenized system outputs using case-sensitive BLEU against raw references (except on en-vi, where we use tokenized outputs and references), using bootstrap resampling (Koehn, 2004; Zhang et al., 2004) for significance testing.

3.3 Results

The results are shown in Table 2. Relative to the **linearized** baseline, our method (**mask**) always improves, by up to +1.7 BLEU for English–Turkish. The difference is statistically significant ($p < 0.05$) except for English–Urdu.

Relative to the **sequence** baseline, the story is more complex. Whenever **linearized** helps over **sequence**, our method helps more, up to a total of +2.1 BLEU for German↔English (50k). But when **linearized** hurts, our method sometimes helps overall (all tasks with 20k lines of training) and sometimes doesn't (e.g., English–Urdu, with only 11k lines of training). A simple possible explanation is that additional tokens make training more difficult on the very smallest datasets, and the effect is stronger for **linearized**, which has twice as many extra tokens.

4 Analysis

4.1 Which masks get used

Figure 3 shows a heatmap of mask strengths for the English–German task (100k lines), and Figure 2

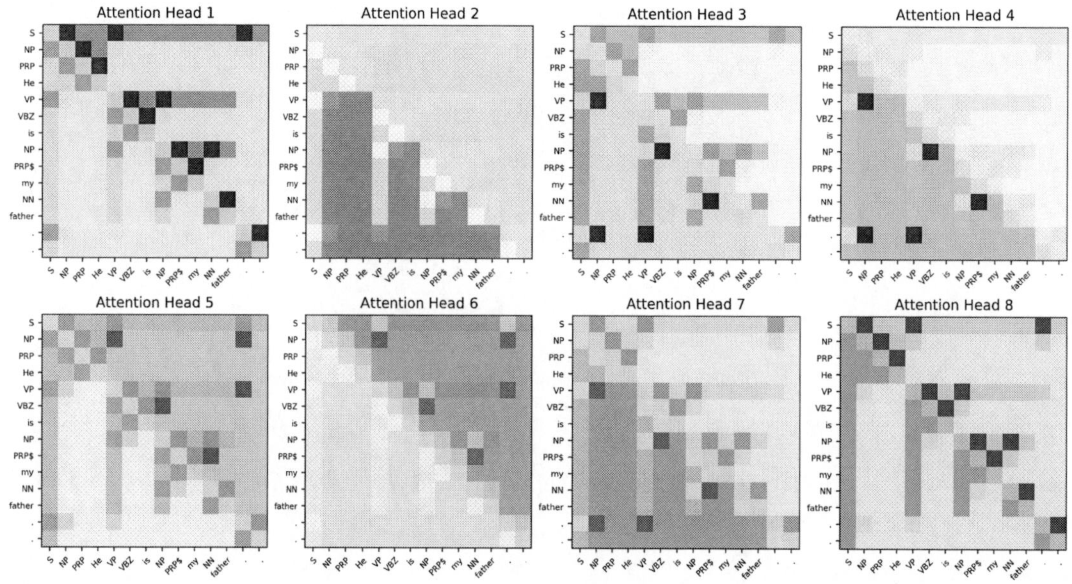

Figure 2: English–German attention masks. The cell in row i, column j shows the strength of the attention mask for node i attending to node j. Light is the strongest (least attention) and dark is the weakest (most attention); see Figure 3 for scale.

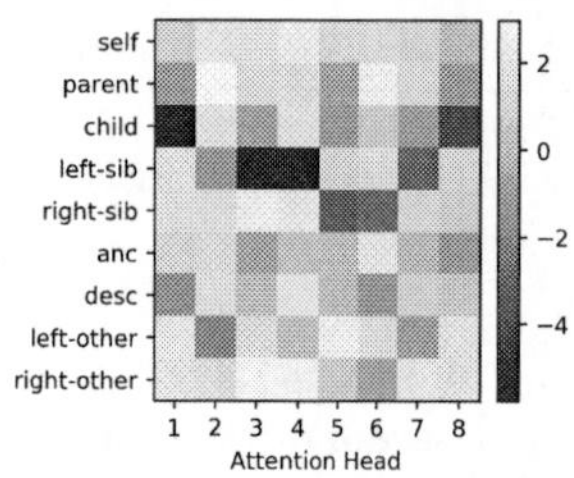

Figure 3: English–German mask strengths. Light is the strongest (least attention) and dark is the weakest (most attention).

Dataset	Min	Max	Range	ΔBLEU
en-vi (full)	−7.52	3.32	10.84	−0.24
en-de (100k)	−5.77	2.96	8.73	1.49
de-en (100k)	−6.29	2.59	8.88	1.41
en-tu	−6.88	3.03	9.91	1.89
en-ha	−4.49	2.41	6.90	1.16
en-ur	−0.32	0.23	0.55	−1.32

Figure 4: Minimum, maximum, and range of mask strengths. ΔBLEU = Change in test BLEU relative to Sequence baseline.

displays the resulting sum of the masks for each attention head for the parse tree of the sentence, "He is my father." There's a strong left-right asymmetry, with heads 2–4 and 7 attending to the left and heads 1 and 5–6 attending to the right. There's also a strong preference to attend to nodes that are nearby in the tree, with strongest weights on the child, left-sib, and right-sib relations.

4.2 Usefulness of masks

Figure 4 shows the minimum, maximum, and range of the mask strengths learned for various tasks. Generally, a mask's range correlates with its usefulness to the model. In particular, on Urdu–English, where we saw the syntax-based models perform the worst, we also see the masks being used the least and distinguished the least. English-Vietnamese is clearly an exception to this, however, with the highest maximum and widest range, but a small (insignificant) loss in BLEU.

5 Conclusion

In this paper, we've shown that syntax can be both helpful and easy to incorporate into low-resource neural machine translation. We introduced learnable attention masks for the transformer that allow each attention head to focus more narrowly on certain node relationships in the syntax tree, improving translation across a variety of low-resource datasets by up to +2.1 BLEU.

English–Vietnamese (en-vi)			
	lines		
	20k	50k	131k
Sequence	19.44	**27.23**	**31.99**
Linearized	19.20	25.92	31.06
Mask	**21.41**	26.34	**31.75**

English–German (en-de)			
	lines		
	20k	50k	100k
Sequence	**2.77**	10.83	15.45
Linearized	2.18	11.78	16.42
Mask	**2.88**	**12.95**	**16.94**

German–English (de-en)			
	lines		
	20k	50k	100k
Sequence	4.19	13.37	18.64
Linearized	3.57	13.81	19.54
Mask	**4.73**	**15.45**	**20.05**

English to Other Languages			
	target language / lines		
	tu	ha	ur
	59k	45k	11k
Sequence	22.30	23.46	**12.98**
Linearized	22.47	23.16	11.52
Mask	**24.19**	**24.62**	11.66

Table 2: Experiment results. In each column, the best score and any scores not significantly different from the best ($p \geq 0.05$) are printed in boldface.

6 Acknowledgements

We would like to thank Toan Nguyen for providing a base implementation of the transformer and answering questions about it, and the anonymous reviewers for their helpful comments.

References

Wasi Ahmad, Saikat Chakraborty, Baishakhi Ray, and Kai-Wei Chang. 2020. A transformer-based approach for source code summarization. In *Proc. ACL*, pages 4998–5007.

Anna Currey and Kenneth Heafield. 2019. Incorporating source syntax into transformer-based neural machine translation. In *Proc. Conference on Machine Translation*, pages 24–33.

Nikita Kitaev, Steven Cao, and Dan Klein. 2019. Multilingual constituency parsing with self-attention and pre-training. In *Proceedings of the 57th Annual Meeting of the Association for Computational Linguistics*, pages 3499–3505, Florence, Italy. Association for Computational Linguistics.

Nikita Kitaev and Dan Klein. 2018. Constituency parsing with a self-attentive encoder. In *Proceedings of the 56th Annual Meeting of the Association for Computational Linguistics (Volume 1: Long Papers)*, pages 2676–2686, Melbourne, Australia. Association for Computational Linguistics.

Philipp Koehn. 2004. Statistical significance tests for machine translation evaluation. In *Proceedings of the 2004 Conference on Empirical Methods in Natural Language Processing*, pages 388–395, Barcelona, Spain. Association for Computational Linguistics.

Toan Q. Nguyen and Julian Salazar. 2019. Transformers without tears: Improving the normalization of self-attention. In *Proc. Workshop on Spoken Language Translation*.

Yutaro Omote, Akihiro Tamura, and Takashi Ninomiya. 2019. Dependency-based relative positional encoding for transformer NMT. In *Proc. RANLP*, pages 854–861.

Rico Sennrich, Barry Haddow, and Alexandra Birch. 2016. Neural machine translation of rare words with subword units. In *Proceedings of the 54th Annual Meeting of the Association for Computational Linguistics (Volume 1: Long Papers)*, pages 1715–1725, Berlin, Germany. Association for Computational Linguistics.

Tao Shen, Tianyi Zhou, Guodong Long, Jing Jiang, Shirui Pan, and Chengqi Zhang. 2018. DiSAN: Directional self-attention network for RNN/CNN-free language understanding. In *Proc. AAAI*.

Vighnesh Shiv and Chris Quirk. 2019. Novel positional encodings to enable tree-based transformers. In *Advances in Neural Information Processing Systems*, volume 32, pages 12081–12091. Curran Associates, Inc.

Ashish Vaswani, Noam Shazeer, Niki Parmar, Jakob Uszkoreit, Llion Jones, Aidan N. Gomez, Łukasz Kaiser, and Illia Polosukhin. 2017. Attention is all you need. In *Advances in Neural Information Processing Systems 30*, pages 5998–6008.

Ying Zhang, Stephan Vogel, and Alex Waibel. 2004. Interpreting BLEU/NIST scores: How much improvement do we need to have a better system? In *Proceedings of the Fourth International Conference on Language Resources and Evaluation (LREC'04)*, Lisbon, Portugal. European Language Resources Association (ELRA).

Multi-Modal Image Captioning for the Visually Impaired

Hiba Ahsan* **Nikita Bhalla*** **Daivat Bhatt*** **Kaivankumar Shah***
{hahsan,nbhalla,dbhatt,kaivankumars}@umass.edu
University of Massachusetts Amherst

Abstract

One of the ways blind people understand their surroundings is by clicking images and relying on descriptions generated by image captioning systems. Current work on captioning images for the visually impaired do not use the textual data present in the image when generating captions. This problem is critical as many visual scenes contain text. Moreover, up to 21% of the questions asked by blind people about the images they click pertain to the text present in them (Bigham et al., 2010). In this work, we propose altering AoANet, a state-of-the-art image captioning model, to leverage the text detected in the image as an input feature. In addition, we use a pointer-generator mechanism to copy the detected text to the caption when tokens need to be reproduced accurately. Our model outperforms AoANet on the benchmark dataset VizWiz, giving a 35% and 16.2% performance improvement on CIDEr and SPICE scores, respectively.

1 Introduction

Image Captioning as a service has helped people with visual impairments to learn about images they take and to make sense of images they encounter in digital environments. Applications such as (TapTapSee, 2012) allow the visually impaired to take photos of their surroundings and upload them to get descriptions of the photos. Such applications leverage a human-in-the-loop approach to generate descriptions. In order to bypass the dependency on a human, there is a need to automate the image captioning process. Unfortunately, the current state-of-the-art (SOTA) image captioning models are built using large, publicly available, crowd-sourced datasets which have been collected and created in a contrived setting. Thus, these models perform poorly on images clicked by blind people largely because the images clicked by blind people differ dramatically from the images present in the datasets. To encourage solving this problem, Gurari et al. (2020) released the VizWiz dataset, a dataset comprising of images taken by the blind. Current work on captioning images for the blind do not use the text detected in the image when generating captions (Figures 1a and 1b show two images from the VizWiz dataset that contain text). The problem is critical as many visual scenes contain text and up to 21% of the questions asked by blind people about the images clicked by them pertain to the text present in them. This makes it more important to improvise the models to focus on objects as well as the text in the images.

With the availability of large labelled corpora, image captioning and reading scene text (OCR) have seen a steady increase in performance. However, traditional image captioning models focus only on the visual objects when generating captions and fail to recognize and reason about the text in the scene. This calls for incorporating OCR tokens into the caption generation process. The task is challenging since unlike conventional vocabulary tokens which depend on the text before them and therefore can be inferred, OCR tokens often cannot be predicted from the context and therefore represent independent entities. Predicting a token from vocabulary and selecting an OCR token from the scene are two rather different tasks which have to be seamlessly combined to tackle this task.

In this work, we build a model to caption images for the blind by leveraging the text detected in the images in addition to visual features. We alter AoANet, a SOTA image captioning model to consume embeddings of tokens detected in the image using Optical Character Recognition (OCR). In many cases, OCR tokens such as entity names or dates need to be reproduced exactly as they are in the caption. To aid this copying process, we employ a pointer-generator mechanism. Our contributions

* Equal contribution

Proceedings of NAACL-HLT 2021: Student Research Workshop, pages 53–60
June 6–11, 2021. ©2021 Association for Computational Linguistics

are 1) We build an image captioning model for the blind that specifically leverages text detected in the image. 2) We use a pointer-generator mechanism when generating captions to copy the detected text when needed.

(a) **Model**: a bottle of water is on top of a table
Ground Truth: a clear plastic bottle of Springbourne brand spring water

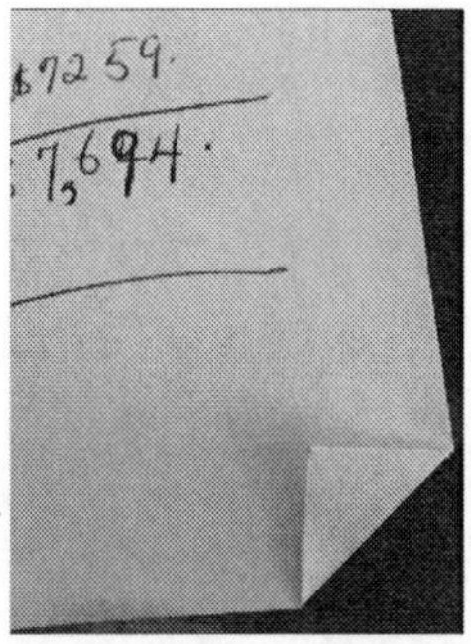

(b) **Model**: A piece of paper with text on it
Ground Truth: In a yellow paper written as 7259 and totally as 7694

2 Related Work

Automated image captioning has seen a significant amount of recent work. The task is typically handled using an encoder-decoder framework; image-related features are fed to the encoder and the decoder generates the caption (Aneja et al., 2018; Yao et al., 2018; Cornia et al., 2018). Language modeling based approaches have also been explored for image captioning (Kiros et al., 2014; Devlin et al., 2015). Apart from the architecture, image captioning approaches are also diverse in terms of the features used. Visual-based image captioning models exploit features generated from images. Multi-modal image captioning approaches exploit other modes of features in addition to image-based features such as candidate captions and text detected in images (Wang et al., 2020; Hu et al., 2020).

The task we address deals with captioning images specifically for the blind. This is different from traditional image captioning due to the authenticity of the dataset compared to popular, synthetic ones such as MS-COCO (Chen et al., 2015) and Flickr30k (Plummer et al., 2015) . The task is relatively less explored. Previous works have solved the problem using human-in-the-loop approaches (Aira, 2017; BeSpecular, 2016; TapTapSee, 2012) as well as automated ones (Microsoft; Facebook). A particular challenge in this area has been the lack of an authentic dataset of photos taken by the blind. To address the issue, Gurari et al. (2020) created VizWiz-Captions, a dataset that consists of descriptions of images taken by people who are blind. In addition, they analyzed how the SOTA image captioning algorithms performed on this dataset. Concurrent to our work, Dognin et al. (2020) created a multi-modal transformer that consumes ResNext based visual features, object detection-based textual features and OCR-based textual features. Our work differs from this approach in the following ways: we use AoANet as our captioning model and do not account for rotation invariance during OCR detection. We use BERT to generate embeddings of the OCR tokens instead of fastText. Since we use bottom-up image feature vectors extracted using a pre-trained Faster-RCNN, we do not use object detection-based textual features. Similarly, since the Faster-RCNN is initialized with ResNet-101 pre-trained for classification, we do not explicitly use classification-based features such as those generated by ResNext.

We explored copy mechanism in our work to aid copying over OCR tokens from the image to the caption. Copy mechanism has been typically employed in textual sequence-to-sequence learning for tasks such as summarization (See et al., 2017; Gu et al., 2016). It has also been used in image captioning to aid learning novel objects (Yao et al., 2017; Li et al., 2019). Also, Sidorov et al. (2020) introduced an M4C model that recognizes text, relates it to its visual context, and decides what part of the text to copy or paraphrase, requiring spatial, semantic, and visual reasoning between multiple text tokens and visual entities such as objects.

3 Dataset

The Vizwiz Captions dataset (Gurari et al., 2020) consists of over $39,000$ images originating from people who are blind that are each paired with five captions. The dataset consists of $23,431$ training images, $7,750$ validation images and $8,000$ test images. The average length of a caption in the train set and the validation set was 11. We refer readers to the VizWiz Dataset Browser (Bhattacharya and Gurari, 2019) as well as the original paper by Gurari et al. (2020) for more details about the dataset.

4 Approach

We employ AoANet as our baseline model. AoANet extends the conventional attention mechanism to account for the relevance of the attention results with respect to the query. An attention module $f_{att}(Q, K, V)$ operates on queries Q, keys K and values V. It measures the similarities between Q and K and using the similarity scores to compute a weighted average over V.

$$a_{i,j} = f_{sim}(q_i, k_j), \alpha = \frac{e^{a_{i,j}}}{\sum_j e^{a_{i,j}}} \quad (1)$$

$$\hat{v}_i = \sum_j \alpha_{i,j} v_{i,j} \quad (2)$$

$$f_{sim}(q_i, k_j) = \text{softmax}(\frac{q_i k_j^T}{\sqrt{D}}) v_i \quad (3)$$

where $q_i \in Q$ is the ith query, $k_j \in K$ and $v_j \in V$ are the jth key/value pair, f_{sim} is the similarity function, D is the dimension of q_i and $\hat{v}_i$ is the attended vector for query q_i.

The AoANet model introduces a module AoA which measures the relevance between the attention result and the query. The AoA module generates an "information vector", i, and an "attention gate", g, both of which are obtained via separate linear transformations, conditioned on the attention result and the query:

$$i = W_q^i q + W_v^i \hat{v} + b^i \quad (4)$$

$$g = \sigma(W_q^g q + W_v^g \hat{v} + b^g) \quad (5)$$

where $W_q^i, W_v^i, b^i, W_q^g, W_v^g, b^g$ are parameters. AoA module then adds another attention by applying the attention gate to the information vector to obtain the attended information $\hat{i}$.

$$\hat{i} = g \odot i \quad (6)$$

The AoA module can thus be formulated as:

$$AoA(f_{att}, Q, K, V) = \sigma(W_q^g Q + W_v^g f_{att}(Q, K, V) + b^g) \odot (W_q^i Q + W_v^i f_{att}(Q, K, V) + b^i) \quad (7)$$

The AoA module is applied to both the encoder and decoder. The model is trained by minimizing the cross-entropy loss:

$$L(\theta) = -\sum_{t=1}^{T} \log(p_\theta(y_t^* | y_{1:t-1}^*)) \quad (8)$$

where $y_{1:T}^*$ is the ground truth sequence. We refer readers to the original work (Huang et al., 2019) for more details. We altered AoANet using two approaches described next.

4.1 Extending Feature Set with OCR Token Embeddings

Our first extension to the model was to increase the vocabulary by incorporating OCR tokens. We use an off-the-shelf text detector available - Google Cloud Platform's vision API (Google). After extracting OCR tokens for each image using the API, we use a standard stopwords list[1] as part of necessary pre-processing. We use this API to detect text in an image and then generate an embedding for each OCR token that we detect using a pre-trained base, uncased BERT (Devlin et al., 2019) model. The image and text features are fed together into the AoANet model. We expect the BERT embeddings to help the model direct its attention towards the textual component of the image. Although we also experiment with a pointer-generator mechanism explained in Section 4.2, we wanted to leverage the model's inbuilt attention mechanism that currently performs as a state of the art model and guide it towards using these OCR tokens.

Once the OCR tokens were detected, we conducted two different experiments with varying sizes of thresholds. We first put a count threshold of 5 i.e. we only add words to the vocabulary which occur 5 or more times. With this threshold, the total words added were $4,555$. We then put a count threshold of 2. With such a low threshold, we expect a lot of noise to be present in the OCR tokens vocabulary - half-detected text, words in a different language, or words that do not make sense. With this threshold, the total words added were $19,781$. A quantitative analysis of the OCR tokens detected and their frequency is shown in Figure 2.

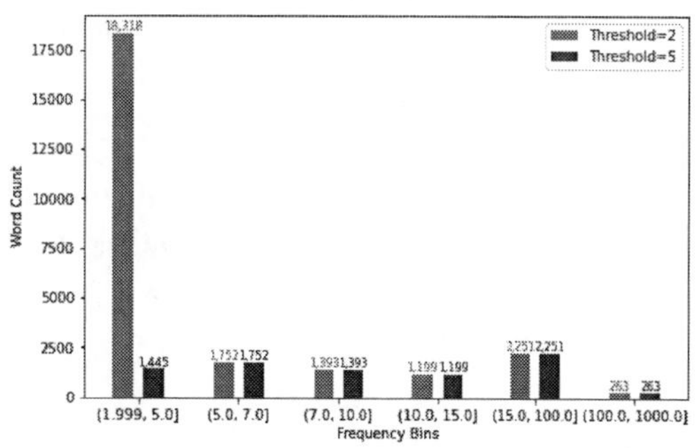

Figure 2: Word counts and frequency bins for threshold = 2 and threshold = 5

[1]https://gist.github.com/sebleier/554280

4.2 Copying OCR Tokens via Pointing

In sequence-to-sequence learning, there is often a need to copy certain segments from the input sequence to the output sequence as they are. This can be useful when sub-sequences such as entity names or dates are involved. Instead of heavily relying on meaning, creating an explicit channel to aid copying of such sub-sequences has been shown to be effective (Gu et al., 2016).

In this approach, in addition to augmenting the input feature set with OCR token embeddings, we employ the pointer-generator mechanism (See et al., 2017) to copy OCR tokens to the caption when needed. The decoder then becomes a hybrid that is able to copy OCR tokens via pointing as well as generate words from the fixed vocabulary. A soft-switch is used to choose between the two modes. The switching is dictated by *generation probability*, p_{gen}, calculated at each time-step, t, as follows:

$$p_{gen} = \sigma(w_h^T c_t + w_s^T h_t + w_x^T x_t + b_{ptr}) \quad (9)$$

where σ is the sigmoid function and w_h, w_s, w_x and b_{ptr} are learnable parameters. c_t is the context vector, h_t is the decoder hidden state and x_t is the input embedding at time t in the decoder. At each step, p_{gen} determines whether a word has to be generated using the fixed vocabulary or to copy an OCR token using the attention distribution at time t. Let *extended vocabulary* denote a union of the fixed vocabulary and the OCR words. The probability distribution over the *extended vocabulary* is given as:

$$P(w) = p_{gen} P_{vocab}(w) + (1 - p_{gen}) \sum_{i:w_i=w} a_i^t \quad (10)$$

P_{vocab} is the probability of w using the fixed vocabulary and a is the attention distribution. If w does not appear in the fixed vocabulary, then P_{vocab} is zero. If w is not an OCR word, then $\sum_{i:w_i=w} a_i^t$ is zero.

5 Experiments

In our experiments, we alter AoANet as per the approaches described in Section 4 and compare these with the baseline model. AoANet-E refers to AoANet altered as per the approach described in Section 4.1. To observe the impact of the number of OCR words added to the extended vocabulary, we train two Extended variants: (1) E5: Only OCR words with frequency greater than or equal to 5. (2) E2: Only OCR words that occur with frequency greater than or equal to 2. AoANet-P refers to AoANet altered as per the approach described in Section 4.2. The extended vocabulary consists of OCR words that occur with frequency greater than or equal to 2.

We use the code[2] released by the authors of AoANet to train the model. We cloned the repository and made changes to extend the feature set and the vocabulary using OCR tokens as well as to incorporate the copy mechanism during decoding [3]. We train our models on a Google Cloud VM instance with 1 Tesla K80 GPU. Like the original work, we use a Faster-RCNN (Ren et al., 2015) model pre-trained on ImageNet (Deng et al., 2009) and Visual Genome (Krishna et al., 2017) to extract bottom-up feature vectors of images. The OCR token embeddings are extracted using a pre-trained base, uncased BERT model. The AoANet models are trained using the Adam optimizer and a learning rate of $2e-5$ annealed by 0.8 every 3 epochs as recommended in Huang et al. (2019). The baseline AoANet is trained for 10 epochs while AoANet-E and AoANet-P are trained for 15 epochs.

6 Results

We show quantitative metrics for each of the models that we experimented with in Table 1. We show qualitative results where we compare captions generated by different models in Table 2. Note that none of the models were pre-trained on the MS-COCO dataset as Gurari et al. (2020) have done as part of their experimenting process.

We compare different models and find that merely extending the vocabulary helps to improve model performance on the dataset. We see that the AoAnet-E5 matches the validation scores for AoANet but we see an improvement in the CIDEr score. Moreover, we see a massive improvement in validation and test CIDEr scores for AoANet-E2. Similarly, we see a gain in the other metrics too. This goes to show that the BERT embeddings generated for each OCR token for the images do provide an important context to the task of generating captions. Moreover, we see the AoANet-P scores, where we use pointer-generator to copy

[2]https://github.com/husthuaan/AoANet

[3]https://github.com/hiba008/AlteredAoA

Model	Validation Scores				Test Scores			
	BLEU-4	ROUGE_L	SPICE	CIDEr	BLEU-4	ROUGE_L	SPICE	CIDEr
AoANet	21.4	43.8	11.1	40.0	19.5	43.1	12.2	40.8
AoANet-E5	21.4	43.6	10.8	41.4	19.8	42.9	11.9	40.2
AoANet-E2	**24.3**	**46.1**	**12.9**	**54.1**	**22.3**	**45.0**	**14.1**	**53.8**
AoANet-P	21.6	43.6	11.5	46.1	19.9	42.7	12.8	45.4

Table 1: Validation and Test scores for AoANet, AoANet-E5 (extended vocabulary variant with OCR frequency threshold as 5), AoANet-E2 (extended vocabulary variant with OCR frequency threshold as 2) and AoANet-P (pointer-generator variant).

OCR tokens after extending the vocabulary also perform better than our baseline AoANet model. This goes to show that an OCR copy mechanism is an essential task in generating image captions. Intuitively, it makes sense because we would expect to humans to use these words while generating lengthy captions ourselves.

We feel that *top-k* sampling is a worthwhile direction of thought especially when we would like some variety in the captions. Beam-search is prone to preferring shorter captions, as the probability values for longer captions accumulates smaller values as discussed by Holtzman et al. (2019).

7 Error Analysis

Although there have been concerns about the robustness of the GCP API towards noise (Hosseini et al., 2017), we focused our attention on the model's captioning performance and on the pointer-generator mechanism. We agree that the API's performance might hinder the quality of the captions generated but we expected it to not have a large enough impact.

We first look at how the Extended variants compare with the baseline. We observe that adding text-based features to the feature set imparts useful information to the model. In 2a, AoANet perceives the card as a box of food. Addition of text features enables AoANet-E5 to perceive it as a box with black text. While not entirely correct, it is an improvement over the baseline. The alteration also encourages it to be more specific. When the model is unable to find the token that entails specificity, it resorts to producing UNK. Extending the vocabulary to accommodate more OCR words helps address this problem. In image 2b, baseline AoANet is unable to recognize that the bottle is a supplements bottle. AoANet-E5 attempts to be specific but since 'dietary' and 'supplement' are not present in the extended vocabulary, it outputs UNK. AoANet-E2 outputs a much better caption. We see a similar pattern in 2c.

We now look at how the Pointer variant performs compared to the baseline and the Extended variant. Incorporating copy mechanism helps the Pointer variant in copying over OCR tokens to the caption. AoANet-P is able to copy over 'oats' and 'almonds' in 2d and the token 'rewards' in 2e. But the model is prone to copying tokens multiple times as seen in images 2b and 2f. This is referred to as repetition which is a common problem in sequence-to-sequence models (Tu et al., 2016) as well as in pointer generator networks. Coverage mechanism (Tu et al., 2016; See et al., 2017) is used to handle this and we wish to explore this in the future.

8 Conclusion

In this work, we propose a pointer-generator based image captioning model that deals specifically with images taken by people with visual disabilities. Our alteration of AoANet shows significant improvement on the VizWiz dataset compared to the baseline. As stated in Section 7, we would like to explore coverage mechanism in the future. Dognin et al. (2020) recently discussed their winning entry to the VizWiz Grand Challenge. In addition, Sidorov et al. (2020) introduced a model that has shown to gain significant performance improvement by using OCR tokens. We intend to compare our model with these and improve our work based on the observations made.

9 Acknowledgements

The authors would like to thank Mohit Iyyer and Kalpesh Krishna at the University of Massachusetts, Amherst for their invaluable guidance and suggestions. The authors would also like to thank the University of Massachusetts, Amherst for providing the necessary resources throughout the course of this project.

Image	Captions
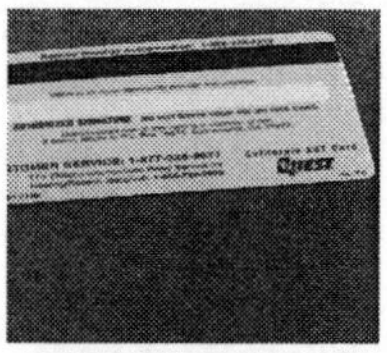 (a)	**AoANet**: the back of a box of food that is yellow **AoANet-E5**: the back of a yellow box with black text **AoANet-E2**: the back of a card with a barcode on it **AoANet-P**: the back of a UNK UNK card **GT1**: The back of an EBT card that is placed on a black surface. **GT2**: The back of a California EBT debit card. **GT3**: A yellow EBT card on a dark fabric surface. **GT4**: The backside of a beige EBT card with a magnetic strip. **GT5**: back of yellow Quest card with black text on it and a white empty signature box
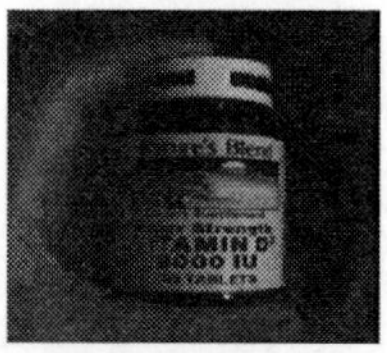 (b)	**AoANet**:a person is holding a bottle of seasoning **AoANet-E5**: a person is holding a bottle of UNK **AoANet-E2**: a person is holding a bottle of dietary supplement **AoANet-P**: a person is holding a bottle of super tablets tablets tablets tablets tablets tablets **GT1**: A bottle of Nature's Blend Vitamin D3 2000 IU with 100 tablets. **GT2**: bottle of Nature's Blend brand vitamin D3 tablets, 100 count, 2000 IU per tab **GT3**: A hand is holding a container of vitamin D. **GT4**: Someone is holding a black bottle with a yellow lid. **GT5**: A person's hand holds a bottle of Vitamin D3 tablets.
 (c)	**AoANet**: a a green bottle with a green and white label **AoANet-E5**: a green bottle of UNK UNK UNK UNK **AoANet-E2**: a bottle of body lotion is on a table **AoANet-P**: a bottle of vanilla lotion is sitting on a table **GT1**: A container of vanilla bean body lotion is on a white table. **GT2**: A bottle of body lotion sits on top of a white table **GT3**: a plastic bottle of vanilla bean body lotion from bath and body works **GT4**: A bottle of body lotion that says Noel on it sitting on a table with a phone behind it and other items around it. **GT5**: A body lotion bottle is on top of table with several papers behind it and a set of keys in the background.
 (d)	**AoANet**: a box of frozen dinner is on top of a table **AoANet-E5**: a box of UNK 's UNK brand UNK UNK **AoANet-E2**: a box of granola granola granola granola bars **AoANet-P**: a box of oats 's almond almond bars **GT1**: A box of nature valley roasted almond crunchy bars is on a table. **GT2**: A box of granola bars sitting on a floral cloth near a wooden object. **GT3**: A granola bar box sits on a table cloth with other items. **GT4**: Green box with roasted almond granola bar place tablecloth with flower prints. **GT5**: A package of granola bars is lying on top of a table.
 (e)	**AoANet**: a hand holding a box of chocolate 's brand **AoANet-E5**: a person is holding a package of food **AoANet-E2**: a hand holding a card with a number on it **AoANet-P**: a person is holding a box of rewards card **GT1**: Appears to be a picture of a reward card **GT2**: A plastic card that says speedy rewards membership card. **GT3**: A Speedy Rewards membership card with a large gold star displayed on it. **GT4**: a human hold some cards like credit cards and reward cards **GT5**: Rewards membership card from the Speedway chain of stores.
 (f)	**AoANet**: a bottle of water is on top of a table **AoANet-E5**: a bottle of water is on top of a table **AoANet-E2**: a bottle of vanilla vanilla coffee mate creamer **AoANet-P**: a bottle of vanilla vanilla vanilla vanilla vanilla **GT1**: A bottle of coffee creamer has a plastic flip top cap that can also be twisted off. **GT2**: A blue bottle of coffee creamer is sitting on a counter top next to a black cup. **GT3**: A container of Coffee Mate French Vanilla showing part of the front and part of the back. **GT4**: A bottle of French vanilla coffee creamer sits in front of a mug on the table. **GT5**: A bottle of creamer is on top of a table.

Table 2: Examples of captions generated by AoANet, AoANet-E5 (extended vocabulary variant with OCR frequency threshold as 5), AoANet-E2 (extended vocabulary variant with OCR frequency threshold as 2) and AoANet-P (pointer-generator variant) for validation set images along with their respective ground truth captions.

References

Aira. 2017. Aira: Connecting you to real people instantly to simplify daily life.

Jyoti Aneja, Aditya Deshpande, and Alexander G Schwing. 2018. Convolutional image captioning. In *Proceedings of the IEEE conference on computer vision and pattern recognition*, pages 5561–5570.

BeSpecular. 2016. Bespecular: Let blind people see through your eyes.

Nilavra Bhattacharya and Danna Gurari. 2019. Vizwiz dataset browser: A tool for visualizing machine learning datasets. *arXiv preprint arXiv:1912.09336*.

Jeffrey P. Bigham, Chandrika Jayant, Hanjie Ji, Greg Little, Andrew Miller, Robert C. Miller, Robin Miller, Aubrey Tatarowicz, Brandyn White, Samual White, and Tom Yeh. 2010. Vizwiz: Nearly real-time answers to visual questions. In *Proceedings of the 23nd Annual ACM Symposium on User Interface Software and Technology*, UIST '10, page 333–342, New York, NY, USA. Association for Computing Machinery.

Xinlei Chen, Hao Fang, Tsung-Yi Lin, Ramakrishna Vedantam, Saurabh Gupta, Piotr Dollár, and C. Lawrence Zitnick. 2015. Microsoft COCO captions: Data collection and evaluation server. *CoRR*, abs/1504.00325.

Marcella Cornia, Lorenzo Baraldi, Giuseppe Serra, and Rita Cucchiara. 2018. Paying more attention to saliency: Image captioning with saliency and context attention. *ACM Transactions on Multimedia Computing, Communications, and Applications (TOMM)*, 14(2):1–21.

Jia Deng, Wei Dong, Richard Socher, Li-Jia Li, Kai Li, and Li Fei-Fei. 2009. Imagenet: A large-scale hierarchical image database. In *2009 IEEE conference on computer vision and pattern recognition*, pages 248–255. Ieee.

Jacob Devlin, Ming-Wei Chang, Kenton Lee, and Kristina Toutanova. 2019. BERT: Pre-training of deep bidirectional transformers for language understanding. In *Proceedings of the 2019 Conference of the North American Chapter of the Association for Computational Linguistics: Human Language Technologies, Volume 1 (Long and Short Papers)*, pages 4171–4186, Minneapolis, Minnesota. Association for Computational Linguistics.

Jacob Devlin, Hao Cheng, Hao Fang, Saurabh Gupta, Li Deng, Xiaodong He, Geoffrey Zweig, and Margaret Mitchell. 2015. Language models for image captioning: The quirks and what works. *arXiv preprint arXiv:1505.01809*.

Pierre Dognin, Igor Melnyk, Youssef Mroueh, Inkit Padhi, Mattia Rigotti, Jarret Ross, Yair Schiff, Richard A Young, and Brian Belgodere. 2020. Image captioning as an assistive technology: Lessons learned from vizwiz 2020 challenge. *arXiv preprint arXiv:2012.11696*.

Facebook. How does automatic alt text work on Facebook? — Facebook Help Center.

Google. Google cloud vision. (Accessed on 11/30/2020).

Jiatao Gu, Zhengdong Lu, Hang Li, and Victor OK Li. 2016. Incorporating copying mechanism in sequence-to-sequence learning. *arXiv preprint arXiv:1603.06393*.

Danna Gurari, Yinan Zhao, Meng Zhang, and Nilavra Bhattacharya. 2020. Captioning images taken by people who are blind.

Ari Holtzman, Jan Buys, Maxwell Forbes, and Yejin Choi. 2019. The curious case of neural text degeneration. *CoRR*, abs/1904.09751.

H. Hosseini, B. Xiao, and R. Poovendran. 2017. Google's cloud vision api is not robust to noise. In *2017 16th IEEE International Conference on Machine Learning and Applications (ICMLA)*, pages 101–105.

Ronghang Hu, Amanpreet Singh, Trevor Darrell, and Marcus Rohrbach. 2020. Iterative answer prediction with pointer-augmented multimodal transformers for textvqa. In *Proceedings of the IEEE/CVF Conference on Computer Vision and Pattern Recognition*, pages 9992–10002.

Lun Huang, Wenmin Wang, Jie Chen, and Xiao-Yong Wei. 2019. Attention on attention for image captioning. In *Proceedings of the IEEE International Conference on Computer Vision*, pages 4634–4643.

Ryan Kiros, Ruslan Salakhutdinov, and Richard S Zemel. 2014. Unifying visual-semantic embeddings with multimodal neural language models. *arXiv preprint arXiv:1411.2539*.

Ranjay Krishna, Yuke Zhu, Oliver Groth, Justin Johnson, Kenji Hata, Joshua Kravitz, Stephanie Chen, Yannis Kalantidis, Li-Jia Li, David A Shamma, et al. 2017. Visual genome: Connecting language and vision using crowdsourced dense image annotations. *International journal of computer vision*, 123(1):32–73.

Yehao Li, Ting Yao, Yingwei Pan, Hongyang Chao, and Tao Mei. 2019. Pointing novel objects in image captioning. In *Proceedings of the IEEE Conference on Computer Vision and Pattern Recognition*, pages 12497–12506.

Microsoft. Add alternative text to a shape, picture, chart, smartart graphic, or other object. (Accessed on 11/30/2020).

Bryan A Plummer, Liwei Wang, Chris M Cervantes, Juan C Caicedo, Julia Hockenmaier, and Svetlana Lazebnik. 2015. Flickr30k entities: Collecting region-to-phrase correspondences for richer image-to-sentence models. In *Proceedings of the IEEE international conference on computer vision*, pages 2641–2649.

Shaoqing Ren, Kaiming He, Ross Girshick, and Jian Sun. 2015. Faster r-cnn: Towards real-time object detection with region proposal networks. In *Advances in neural information processing systems*, pages 91–99.

Abigail See, Peter J Liu, and Christopher D Manning. 2017. Get to the point: Summarization with pointer-generator networks. *arXiv preprint arXiv:1704.04368*.

O. Sidorov, Ronghang Hu, Marcus Rohrbach, and Amanpreet Singh. 2020. Textcaps: a dataset for image captioning with reading comprehension. *ArXiv*, abs/2003.12462.

TapTapSee. 2012. Taptapsee - blind and visually impaired assistive technology - powered by the cloudsight.ai image recognition api.

Zhaopeng Tu, Zhengdong Lu, Yang Liu, Xiaohua Liu, and Hang Li. 2016. Modeling coverage for neural machine translation. *arXiv preprint arXiv:1601.04811*.

Jing Wang, Jinhui Tang, and Jiebo Luo. 2020. Multimodal attention with image text spatial relationship for ocr-based image captioning. In *Proceedings of the 28th ACM International Conference on Multimedia*, pages 4337–4345.

Ting Yao, Yingwei Pan, Yehao Li, and Tao Mei. 2017. Incorporating copying mechanism in image captioning for learning novel objects. In *Proceedings of the IEEE conference on computer vision and pattern recognition*, pages 6580–6588.

Ting Yao, Yingwei Pan, Yehao Li, and Tao Mei. 2018. Exploring visual relationship for image captioning. In *Proceedings of the European conference on computer vision (ECCV)*, pages 684–699.

Open-Domain Question Answering with Pre-Constructed Question Spaces

Jinfeng Xiao[†], **Lidan Wang**[*], **Franck Dernoncourt**[*], **Trung Bui**[*], **Tong Sun**[*], **Jiawei Han**[†]
[†]University of Illinois at Urbana-Champaign
{jxiao13,hanj}@illinois.edu
[*]Adobe Research
{lidwang,franck.dernoncourt,bui,tsun}@adobe.com

Abstract

Open-domain question answering aims at locating the answers to user-generated questions in massive collections of documents. Retriever-readers and knowledge graph approaches are two big families of solutions to this task. A retriever-reader first applies information retrieval techniques to locate a few passages that are likely to be relevant, and then feeds the retrieved text to a neural network reader to extract the answer. Alternatively, knowledge graphs can be constructed and queried to answer users' questions. We propose an algorithm with a novel reader-retriever design that differs from both families. Our reader-retriever first uses an offline reader to read the corpus and generate collections of all answerable questions associated with their answers, and then uses an online retriever to respond to user queries by searching the pre-constructed question spaces for answers that are most likely to be asked in the given way. We further combine one retriever-reader and two reader-retrievers into a hybrid model called R^6 for the best performance. Experiments with large-scale public datasets show that R^6 achieves state-of-the-art accuracy.

1 Introduction

Open-domain question answering, abbreviated as *OpenQA* in this paper, aims at enabling computers to answer user-submitted natural language questions based on a large collection of documents (a.k.a. a corpus). There are two big families of state-of-the-art OpenQA algorithms. One family, namely retriever-readers (Fig. 1, left branch), first retrieves from the corpus some documents or paragraphs that are likely to be relevant to the question, and then uses neural networks to read the retrieved passages and locate the answer. Another line of work, namely question answering using knowledge bases (abbreviated as *QA using KB* in this paper; Fig. 1, middle branch), first constructs a knowledge base (KB) from the corpus, then queries the KB with the given question. Either family of algorithms has some pros and cons: all retriever-readers face a trade-off between efficiency and accuracy; QA using KB methods are good at answering simple factoid questions within the KB schema but weak at complex or out-of-schema questions.

We propose a novel reader-retriever design for OpenQA (Fig. 1, right branch). First, we use deep neural networks to read the corpus offline, detect named entities, generate questions, and aggregate the results into two collections of questions that are answerable with the corpus. We use *question spaces* to term the two collections. When users submit queries online, a retriever compares user queries with the pre-constructed question spaces to retrieve the answers that are most likely to be asked in the given way. We combine two reader-retrievers (one for each question space) and one retriever-reader into a hybrid model called R^6 to predict the most likely answer based on the consistency among the three sub-models. Experiments with large-scale public datasets show that the pre-constructed question spaces boost the performance for OpenQA, and R^6 performs better than state-of-the-art methods by a large margin. The source code of R^6 is publicly available at `https://github.com/JinfengXiao/R6`.

2 Related Work

2.1 Retriever-Readers

Retriever-readers solve OpenQA by converting it to easier single-passage QA tasks. Examples of popular algorithms in this family include DrQA (Chen et al., 2017), which has a TF-IDF retriever followed by a recurrent neural network reader, and BERTserini (Yang et al., 2019), which consists of a BM25 retriever and a BERT reader.

All retriever-readers face a trade-off between efficiency and accuracy. When the retriever module is

Proceedings of NAACL-HLT 2021: Student Research Workshop, pages 61–67
June 6–11, 2021.

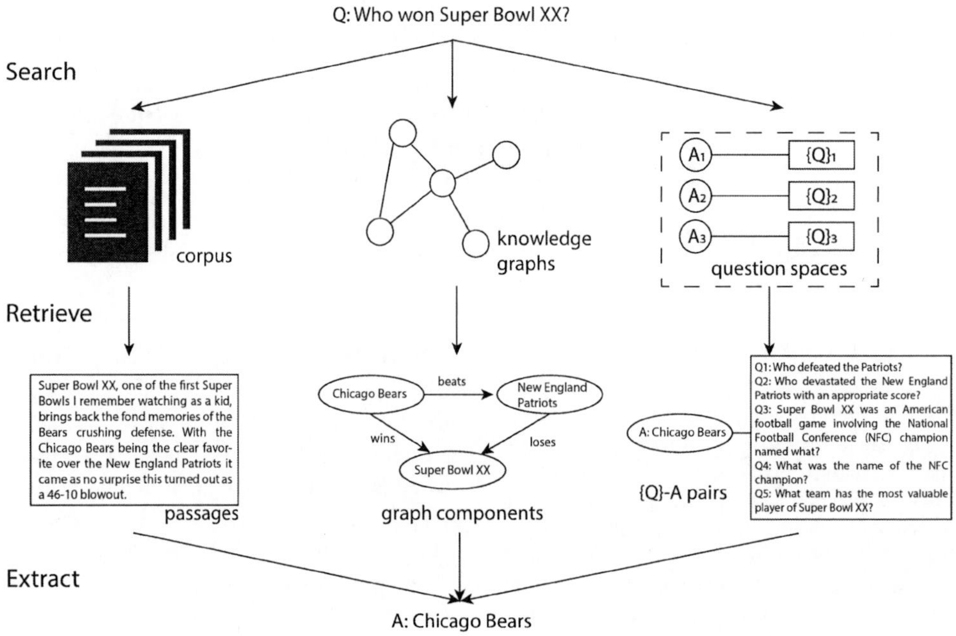

Figure 1: Retriever-readers (left), QA using KB (middle), and reader-retrievers (right).

computationally efficient, the retrieved results are not very reliable, and the performance of the subsequent reader is also constrained (Htut et al., 2018). On the other hand, there exist systems such as R^3 (Wang et al., 2018) and DS-QA (Lin et al., 2018) that have sophisticated retrievers jointly trained with the readers, but they are computationally expensive and thus not scalable to large corpora (Das et al., 2019).

2.2 QA Using KB

There are solutions that solve OpenQA with knowledge bases (KB). QA using KB applications include Google Knowledge Graph and Bing Satori (Uyar and Aliyu, 2015). Such approaches involve an offline knowledge graph construction module and an online graph query module. The graph construction module scans the corpus to build a knowledge base that contains one or more knowledge graphs. Each graph usually involves some types of entities, attributes and relations. Once a knowledge base is constructed, OpenQA tasks can then be converted to graph search tasks, which can be done in various ways including template decomposition (Zheng et al., 2018) or graph embedding (Huang et al., 2019).

There are a lot of challenges remaining for QA using KB. Examples include how to convert complex natural language questions into structured KB queries, how to alleviate error propagation from the KB construction step to the graph query step, and how to handle questions whose answers do not fall within the KB schema. Due to those complexities, the community is observing a recent trend that retriever-readers are dominating the leaderboards of public QA datasets but KB-based methods are not. Therefore, we choose to focus on the comparison with retriever-readers when experimentally evaluating our proposed algorithm.

3 Approach

3.1 Question Spaces

Definition 1. A *question space* is a bipartite graph with two disjoint and independent node sets A and Q representing the answers and associated questions. We herein define two types of question spaces: QA Spaces and {Q}A (read as Q-set-A) Spaces. In a *QA Space*, each element $a_{i,j}$ of A represents the jth mention in the corpus of the ith distinct named entity, and each element $q_{i,j}$ of Q is a question generated from the context of $a_{i,j}$ with a_i as its answer. For every i and j, $a_{i,j}$ and $q_{i,j}$ form a *QA pair* and are connected in the graph. In a *{Q}A Space*, each element a_i of A represents the ith distinct named entity, and each element q_i of Q is a collection of the $q_{i,j}$'s for all j in the QA Space. For every i, a_i and q_i form a *{Q}A pair* and are connected in the graph. In short, a QA space contains pairs of answer mentions and generated questions, while a {Q}A space contains pairs of distinct answer entities and collections of all generated questions with that answer.

For example, given the five questions in the right branch of Fig. 1 whose answer is "Chicago Bears", the QA Space will have five QA pairs: {$a_{1,1}$ = "Chicago Bears", $q_{1,1}$ = "Who defeated the Patriots?"}, ..., {$a_{1,5}$ = "Chicago Bears", $q_{1,5}$ = "What team has the most valuable player of Super Bowl XX?"}, and the {Q}A space will have one {Q}A pair: {a_1 = "Chicago Bears", q_1 = {"Who defeated the Patriots?", ..., "What team has the most valuable player of Super Bowl XX?"}}.

3.2 Algorithm

A detailed illustration of our algorithm is given in Figure 2. The components above the grey dashed line are offline. They construct the QA Space and the{Q}A Space as defined in Definition 1. The modules below the grey dashed line are all executed online.

3.2.1 NER, Question-Generating Reader and Question Aggregator

Given a corpus, a named entity recognition (NER) tool called TAGME (Ferragina and Scaiella, 2010, 2012) is applied to detect named entities from the corpus and link the entities to Wikipedia titles. Those entities form the set of candidate answers A in Definition 1. Then a question-generating (QG) reader is applied to the set of candidate answers to generate a question for each answer based on the local context. This reader features an encoder-decoder model structure with a question-answering reward and a question fluency reward tuned with policy gradient optimization (Yuan et al., 2017; Hosking and Riedel, 2019). Then we use a question aggregator to build the {Q}A Space by putting together all the questions with the same answer entity.

3.2.2 Passage Retriever and QA Reader

Given a query, the passage retriever uses the dot product of the query embedding and passage embedding vectors generated by Google Universal Sentence Encoder (Google USE) (Cer et al., 2018) to retrieve from the corpus a passage that is semantically most similar to the query. We then use BERT (Devlin et al., 2019), fine-tuned on SQuAD, to read the retrieved passage, predict the answer, and record the predicted answer as *Answer 1*. The pipeline in Figure 2 that goes from Input Corpus to Passage and then Answer 1 is a valid retriever-reader workflow, and we denote this workflow as **Retriever-Reader-BERT-Large** or **Retriever-Reader-BERT-Base**, depending on which BERT model is used.

3.2.3 Individual Question Retriever

Given a query, the individual question retriever uses Google USE to retrieve from the QA space k questions that are semantically most similar to the query. We record the ordered list of answers associated with the top k retrieved questions as *{Answer 2}*. A majority vote (where ties are resolved by average orders) over {Answer 2} can produce a single answer denoted as *Voted Answer 2*. Then the pipeline in Figure 2 that goes from Input Corpus to Candidate Answers, QA Space, {Answer 2}, and finally Voted Answer 2 (not shown in the figure) is a valid reader-retriever workflow. We denote this workflow as **Reader-Retriever-QA-Space**.

3.2.4 Aggregated Question Retriever

Given a query, the aggregated question retriever uses the BM25 score (Robertson and Zaragoza, 2009) to retrieve from the {Q}A space the answer whose associated set of questions is most similar to the given query. We query the {Q}A Space by treating each q_i as a single document which contains $q_{i,j}$ for all j as sentences. In practice, we observe that BM25 works better for long documents and Google USE works better for short passages. That is why we use BM25 as the aggregated question retriever but use Google USE for the passage retriever and the individual question retriever. We record the answer a_i associated to the top-ranked question set q_i as *Answer 3*. The pipeline in Figure 2 that goes from Input Corpus to Candidate Answers, QA Space, {Q}A Space and finally Answer 3 is a valid reader-retriever workflow. We denote this workflow as **Reader-Retriever-{Q}A-Space**.

3.2.5 Answer Aggregator

Now that we have Answer 1, {Answer 2}, and Answer 3, the last step is to aggregate them into one single answer to return to the user. Our answer aggregation works as follows: if Answer 1 appears in the set {Answer 2}, then accept Answer 1 and return it; otherwise reject Answer 1 and return Answer 3. In other words, the answer aggregator checks the consistency between the retriever-reader results and the reader-retriever ones, trust the retriever-reader more if they agree to some extent,

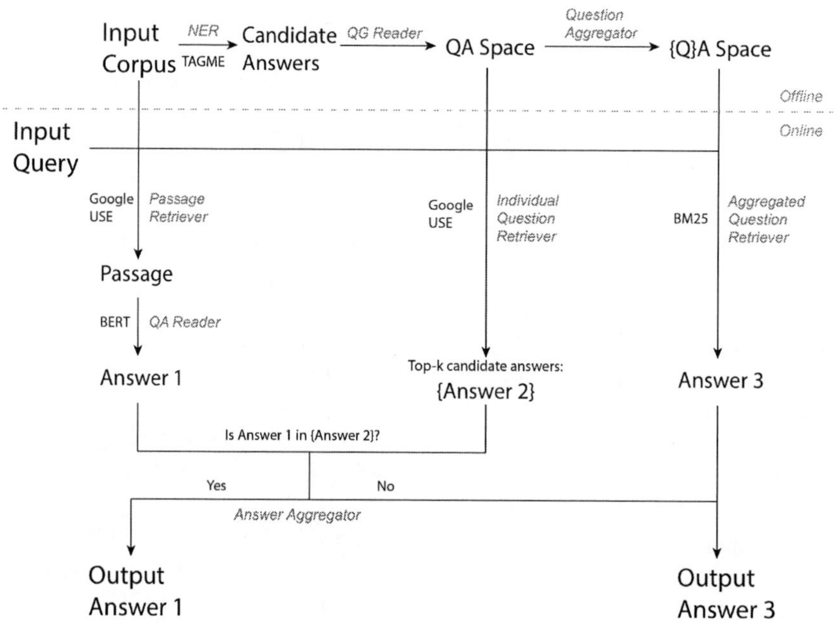

Figure 2: Detailed structure of the proposed method.

and trust the reader-retriever more if the results do not agree at all. We denote the complete workflow depicted in Figure 2 as $\mathbf{R^6}$.

4 Experiments

We evaluate the OpenQA performance of our proposed method R^6 and baseline methods using two public QA datasets, SQuAD (Rajpurkar et al., 2016) and TriviaQA (Joshi et al., 2017). We adopt a rather challenging setting that all trainable components of the models are trained on SQuAD, while the final models are tested on TriviaQA. Furthermore, we use TriviaQA in an open-domain setting by removing all annotated associations between questions and documents and enforcing the systems to answer every question with the entire corpus. We write **TriviaQA-Open** to distinguish such an open-domain setting from those officially adopted by TriviaQA.

One may wonder why we choose to use different datasets for training and testing. Because our goal of the experiments is to compare the effectiveness of our proposed methods to others, as long as all the methods are evaluated fairly under the same setting, we can achieve the goal. Such experimental settings are also used by the authors of DrQA (Chen et al., 2017). In addition, using SQuAD for training enables us to utilize pre-trained models and author-suggested hyper-parameters to the greatest extent, so that we can make sure we correctly reproduce others' work and do not put their models into disadvantages when comparing them with ours. More experimental details are available in Section 4.2. Although not critical to this study, using different datasets for training and testing has one additional benefit that it shows the ability of the systems to adapt to new corpora.

4.1 Models

We evaluate six different OpenQA methods with the exact match accuracy in the predicted answers on TriviaQA-Open. Five of them are introduced in Section 3, and the other is DrQA as introduced in Section 2. Here we summarize the basic structure of all six methods in Table 1.

4.2 Reproducibility Notes

This section aims at providing as many details as possible that are needed to reproduce our results. All experiments are run on an Ubuntu 16.04 machine with eight GeForce GTX 1080 GPUs (CUDA version 10.1) and 24 CPUs. The entity score threshold for TAGME is set at 0.2 by tuning that value and manually inspecting the NER quality for 20 documents sampled from TriviaQA. The k value for the individual question retriever that generates {Answer 2} is set to 10. For TriviaQA, we treat each paragraph with at least 50 characters as a passage,

Table 1: Model structures. Arrows show orders of modules.

Model	Description
R^6	Two reader-retrievers + Retriever-Reader-BERT-Base
DrQA	TF-IDF retriever → RNN reader
Retriever-Reader-BERT-Large	Google USE retriever → BERT-large reader
Retriever-Reader-BERT-Base	Google USE retriever → BERT-base reader
Reader-Retriever-QA-Space	QG reader → Google USE retriever
Reader-Retriever-{Q}A-Space	QG reader → Question aggregator → BM25 retriever

Table 2: Test accuracy on TriviaQA-Open. Columns are explained in Section 4.3.

Method	Accuracy	Proposed vs SOTA	Complete vs Components
R^6	**0.30**	•	•
DrQA	0.18	•	
Retriever-Reader-BERT-Large	0.16	•	•
Retriever-Reader-BERT-Base	0.15	•	•
Reader-Retriever-QA-Space	0.07		•
Reader-Retriever-{Q}A-Space	0.21		•

and drop paragraphs shorter than that. BERT is downloaded from the pytorch-transformers GitHub repository[1] and fine-tuned on SQuAD following the documentation. The question-generating reader is obtained from the question-generation GitHub repository[2] and trained on SQuAD with default settings. DrQA codes are downloaded from its GitHub repository[3], the model trained by the authors on SQuAD is obtained as instructed, and the hyperparameter n-docs is set to 1 at prediction time for fair comparisons with R^6. The Google USE retrievers are implemented by re-ranking the top one thousand BM25-retrieved passages with dot products between Google USE embedding vectors obtained with TensorFlow[4].

4.3 Overall Test Accuracy

Table 2 reports the overall test accuracy on TriviaQA-Open of our proposed method R^6, three state-of-the-art methods (DrQA, Retriever-Reader-BERT-Large, and Retriever-Reader-BERT-Base), and the two novel workflows we introduce (Reader-Retriever-QA-Space and Reader-Retriever-{Q}A-Space). The column "Proposed vs SOTA" indicates which rows to look at for comparing our method with state-of-the-art OpenQA methods, while the column "Complete vs Components" indicates which rows to look at for analyzing the contribution of each individual component to the complete model R^6.

Our proposed method R^6 outperforms both DrQA and BERT by a margin six times larger than that between DrQA and BERT. If the 2% difference between DrQA and BERT represents the consequence of differences in the detailed design of the retriever and reader modules in a retriever-reader model (e.g. TF-IDF vs semantic embedding, RNN vs BERT), then the 12% margin between R^6 and DrQA should be largely credited to the essential differences in the overall model structures.

When individual components of R^6 are inspected, our novel reader-retriever component on the {Q}A Space also outperforms DrQA and BERT, with a smaller margin though. Our reader-retriever component on the QA Space is not working well by itself, but as an integral part of the answer aggregation mechanism, it helps push up the performance of our complete model R^6.

4.4 Test Accuracy for Various Answer Types

We further examine how the discussed algorithms work for different answer types. Following the same practice as in the TriviaQA paper (Joshi et al., 2017), we sample 200 question-answer pairs from TriviaQA-Open and manually analyze their properties. We find that about 36% of those questions

[1]https://github.com/huggingface/transformers
[2]https://github.com/bloomsburyai/question-generation
[3]https://github.com/facebookresearch/DrQA
[4]https://tfhub.dev/google/universal-sentence-encoder/2

Table 3: Test accuracy on TriviaQA-Open-200 for various answer types.

Method	Overall	Person/Org (36%)	Location (26%)	Others (38%)
R^6	**0.34**	**0.56**	**0.46**	0.05
DrQA	0.22	0.33	0.23	**0.11**
Retriever-Reader-BERT-Base	0.20	0.39	0.23	0
Reader-Retriever-QA-Space	0.10	0.22	0.08	0
Reader-Retriever-{Q}A-Space	0.22	0.28	0.38	0.05

have person names or organization names as answers, 26% ask for locations, and 38% are expecting other types of answers including entities with other types, numbers, and other free texts. This sample distribution is roughly consistent with what TriviaQA authors have reported (32%, 23%, and 45% respectively) with their random sample. We then use this sampled dataset **TriviaQA-Open-200** to evaluate the test accuracy of the methods for different answer types. We drop Retriever-Reader-BERT-Large for this analysis because its overall accuracy is very close to Retriever-Reader-BERT-Base (Table 2) but it consumes much more computational resources.

The results of this experiment are shown in Table 3. Among the three types, questions that ask for Person/Organization names or locations look significantly easier to answer for all algorithms than those asking for other miscellaneous things, and our proposed method R^6 takes the lead. Among the other models, it looks like BERT is good at questions about Person/Organization names and our newly proposed reader-retriever algorithm on the {Q}A Space is good at answering questions for locations. On the other hand, when the expected answer is neither a person/organization nor a location, DrQA still has some chance of getting the right answer, while all other methods including ours almost always fail. This is probably due to the fact that our methods rely on NER (Figure 2) but DrQA does not. It is possible that better NER methods that are good at handling miscellaneous entity types and numbers could further boost the performance of R^6, and how to better answer those miscellaneous questions is left for future work.

4.5 Notes on Question Space Quality

A manual inspection into the constructed question spaces revealed three aspects worth discussion. 1) Many questions look reasonable, and those generated questions shown in Figure 1 are actually real examples taken from our {Q}A Space that are associated with the answer "Chicago Bears". 2) There are also many questions that to some extent deviate from being a "correct" question to ask for a given answer. One frequently observed mistake is the use of a wrong question word. 3) Some highly context-dependent questions like "who did Bob talk to" are generated. Although they are reasonable and answerable given the context, they do not really make sense when being asked in an open-domain setting. Since R^6 relies on the generated questions, its performance is hopeful to get further enhanced if the quality of the question spaces can be improved. How to generate better question spaces for OpenQA remains an interesting future direction.

5 Conclusion

We propose R^6, a novel algorithm that constructs question spaces from corpora and uses them to improve OpenQA. R^6 consists of two novel reader-retriever modules and one classic retriever-reader. Experiments on public datasets show that R^6 outperforms state-of-the-art retriever-readers by a large margin. Our method has the potential to get further improved if solutions can be proposed in future work to better handle questions about less typical answer types or generate questions with higher quality.

References

Daniel Cer, Yinfei Yang, Sheng-yi Kong, Nan Hua, Nicole Limtiaco, Rhomni St John, Noah Constant, Mario Guajardo-Cespedes, Steve Yuan, Chris Tar, et al. 2018. Universal sentence encoder. *arXiv preprint arXiv:1803.11175*.

Danqi Chen, Adam Fisch, Jason Weston, and Antoine Bordes. 2017. Reading Wikipedia to answer open-domain questions. In *Proceedings of the 55th Annual Meeting of the Association for Computational Linguistics (Volume 1: Long Papers)*, pages 1870–

1879, Vancouver, Canada. Association for Computational Linguistics.

Rajarshi Das, Shehzaad Dhuliawala, Manzil Zaheer, and Andrew McCallum. 2019. Multi-step retriever-reader interaction for scalable open-domain question answering. In *7th International Conference on Learning Representations, ICLR 2019, New Orleans, LA, USA, May 6-9, 2019*. OpenReview.net.

Jacob Devlin, Ming-Wei Chang, Kenton Lee, and Kristina Toutanova. 2019. BERT: Pre-training of deep bidirectional transformers for language understanding. In *Proceedings of the 2019 Conference of the North American Chapter of the Association for Computational Linguistics: Human Language Technologies, Volume 1 (Long and Short Papers)*, pages 4171–4186, Minneapolis, Minnesota. Association for Computational Linguistics.

Paolo Ferragina and Ugo Scaiella. 2010. TAGME: on-the-fly annotation of short text fragments (by wikipedia entities). In *Proceedings of the 19th ACM Conference on Information and Knowledge Management, CIKM 2010, Toronto, Ontario, Canada, October 26-30, 2010*, pages 1625–1628. ACM.

Paolo Ferragina and Ugo Scaiella. 2012. Fast and accurate annotation of short texts with wikipedia pages. *IEEE Softw.*, 29(1):70–75.

Tom Hosking and Sebastian Riedel. 2019. Evaluating rewards for question generation models. In *Proceedings of the 2019 Conference of the North American Chapter of the Association for Computational Linguistics: Human Language Technologies, Volume 1 (Long and Short Papers)*, pages 2278–2283, Minneapolis, Minnesota. Association for Computational Linguistics.

Phu Mon Htut, Samuel Bowman, and Kyunghyun Cho. 2018. Training a ranking function for open-domain question answering. In *Proceedings of the 2018 Conference of the North American Chapter of the Association for Computational Linguistics: Student Research Workshop*, pages 120–127, New Orleans, Louisiana, USA. Association for Computational Linguistics.

Xiao Huang, Jingyuan Zhang, Dingcheng Li, and Ping Li. 2019. Knowledge graph embedding based question answering. In *Proceedings of the Twelfth ACM International Conference on Web Search and Data Mining, WSDM 2019, Melbourne, VIC, Australia, February 11-15, 2019*, pages 105–113. ACM.

Mandar Joshi, Eunsol Choi, Daniel Weld, and Luke Zettlemoyer. 2017. TriviaQA: A large scale distantly supervised challenge dataset for reading comprehension. In *Proceedings of the 55th Annual Meeting of the Association for Computational Linguistics (Volume 1: Long Papers)*, pages 1601–1611, Vancouver, Canada. Association for Computational Linguistics.

Yankai Lin, Haozhe Ji, Zhiyuan Liu, and Maosong Sun. 2018. Denoising distantly supervised open-domain question answering. In *Proceedings of the 56th Annual Meeting of the Association for Computational Linguistics, ACL 2018, Melbourne, Australia, July 15-20, 2018, Volume 1: Long Papers*, pages 1736–1745. Association for Computational Linguistics.

Pranav Rajpurkar, Jian Zhang, Konstantin Lopyrev, and Percy Liang. 2016. SQuAD: 100,000+ questions for machine comprehension of text. In *Proceedings of the 2016 Conference on Empirical Methods in Natural Language Processing*, pages 2383–2392, Austin, Texas. Association for Computational Linguistics.

Stephen E. Robertson and Hugo Zaragoza. 2009. The probabilistic relevance framework: BM25 and beyond. *Found. Trends Inf. Retr.*, 3(4):333–389.

Ahmet Uyar and Farouk Musa Aliyu. 2015. Evaluating search features of google knowledge graph and bing satori: Entity types, list searches and query interfaces. *Online Inf. Rev.*, 39(2):197–213.

Shuohang Wang, Mo Yu, Xiaoxiao Guo, Zhiguo Wang, Tim Klinger, Wei Zhang, Shiyu Chang, Gerry Tesauro, Bowen Zhou, and Jing Jiang. 2018. R^3: Reinforced ranker-reader for open-domain question answering. In *Proceedings of the Thirty-Second AAAI Conference on Artificial Intelligence, (AAAI-18), the 30th innovative Applications of Artificial Intelligence (IAAI-18), and the 8th AAAI Symposium on Educational Advances in Artificial Intelligence (EAAI-18), New Orleans, Louisiana, USA, February 2-7, 2018*, pages 5981–5988. AAAI Press.

Wei Yang, Yuqing Xie, Aileen Lin, Xingyu Li, Luchen Tan, Kun Xiong, Ming Li, and Jimmy Lin. 2019. End-to-end open-domain question answering with BERTserini. In *Proceedings of the 2019 Conference of the North American Chapter of the Association for Computational Linguistics (Demonstrations)*, pages 72–77, Minneapolis, Minnesota. Association for Computational Linguistics.

Xingdi Yuan, Tong Wang, Caglar Gulcehre, Alessandro Sordoni, Philip Bachman, Saizheng Zhang, Sandeep Subramanian, and Adam Trischler. 2017. Machine comprehension by text-to-text neural question generation. In *Proceedings of the 2nd Workshop on Representation Learning for NLP*, pages 15–25, Vancouver, Canada. Association for Computational Linguistics.

Weiguo Zheng, Jeffrey Xu Yu, Lei Zou, and Hong Cheng. 2018. Question answering over knowledge graphs: Question understanding via template decomposition. *Proc. VLDB Endow.*, 11(11):1373–1386.

A Sliding-Window Approach to Automatic Creation of Meeting Minutes

Jia Jin Koay, Alexander Roustai, Xiaojin Dai, Fei Liu

Computer Science Department
University of Central Florida, Orlando, FL 32816

{jjkoay,alexroustai,xd.zangyiwu}@knights.ucf.edu
feiliu@cs.ucf.edu

Abstract

Meeting minutes record any subject matters discussed, decisions reached and actions taken at meetings. The importance of minuting cannot be overemphasized in a time when a significant number of meetings take place in the virtual space. In this paper, we present a sliding window approach to automatic generation of meeting minutes. It aims to tackle issues associated with the nature of spoken text, including lengthy transcripts and lack of document structure, which make it difficult to identify salient content to be included in the meeting minutes. Our approach combines a sliding window and a neural abstractive summarizer to navigate through the transcripts to find salient content. The approach is evaluated on transcripts of natural meeting conversations, where we compare results obtained for human transcripts and two versions of automatic transcripts and discuss how and to what extent the summarizer succeeds at capturing salient content.

1 Introduction

Meetings are ubiquitous across organizations of all shapes and sizes, and it takes a tremendous effort to record any subject matters discussed, final decisions reached and actions taken at meetings. With the rise of remote workforce, virtual meetings are more important than ever. An increasing number of video conferencing providers including Zoom, Microsoft Team, Amazon Chime and Google Meet allow meetings to be transcribed (Martindale, 2021). However, without automatic minuting, consolidating notes and creating meeting minutes is still regarded as a tedious and time-consuming task for meeting participants. There is thus an urgent need to develop advanced techniques to better summarize and organize meeting content.

Meeting summarization has been attempted on a small scale before the era of deep learning. Previous work includes efforts to extract utterances and keyphrases from meeting transcripts (Galley, 2006; Murray and Carenini, 2008; Gillick et al., 2009; Liu et al., 2009), detect meeting decisions (Hsueh and Moore, 2008), compress or merge utterances to generate abstracts (Liu and Liu, 2009; Wang and Cardie, 2013; Mehdad et al., 2013) and make use of acoustic-prosodic and speaker features (Maskey and Hirschberg, 2005; Zhu et al., 2009; Chen and Metze, 2012) for utterance extraction. The continued development of automatic transcription and its easy accessibility have sparked a renewed interest in meeting summarization (Shang et al., 2018; Li et al., 2019; Koay et al., 2020; Song et al., 2020; Zhu et al., 2020; Zhong et al., 2021), where neural representations are explored for this task. We believe the time is therefore ripe for a reconsideration of the approach to automatic minuting.

It may be tempting to apply neural abstractive summarization to meetings given its remarkable recent success on summarization benchmarks, e.g., CNN/DM (See et al., 2017; Chen and Bansal, 2018; Gehrmann et al., 2018; Laban et al., 2020). However, the challenge lies not only in handling hallucinations that are seen in abstractive models (Kryscinski et al., 2019; Lebanoff et al., 2019; Maynez et al., 2020) but also the models' strong positional bias that occurs as a consequence of fine-tuning on news articles (Kedzie et al., 2018; Grenander et al., 2019). Neural summarizers also assume a maximum sequence length, e.g., Perez-Beltrachini et al. (2019) use the first 800 tokens of the document as input. With an estimated speaking rate of 122 words per minute (Polifroni et al., 1991), it indicates that the summarizer may only process a relatively short transcript – about 5 minutes in duration.

In this paper, we instead study an extractive meeting summarizer to identify salient utterances from the transcripts. It leverages a sliding window to navigate through a transcript of any length and a neural abstractive summarizer to find salient local content. In particular, we aim to address three key questions: (1) what are suitable window and stride sizes? (2)

Proceedings of NAACL-HLT 2021: Student Research Workshop, pages 68–75
June 6–11, 2021. ©2021 Association for Computational Linguistics

can the abstractive summarizer effectively identify salient local content? (3) how should we consolidate local abstracts into meeting-level summaries? Our approach is intuitive and appealing, as humans make a sequence of local decisions when navigating through very long recordings. It is evaluated on transcripts of natural meeting conversations (Janin et al., 2003), where we obtained human transcripts and two versions of automatic transcripts produced by the AMI speech recognizer (Hain et al., 2006) and Google Cloud's Speech-to-Text API.[1] Our contributions in this paper are as follows.

- We study the feasibility of a sliding-window approach to automatic generation of meeting minutes that draws on a pretrained neural abstractive summarizer to make local decisions on utterance saliency. It does not require any annotated data and can be extended to meetings of various types and domains.
- We examine results obtained from human transcripts and two versions of automatic transcripts, and show that our summarizer either outperforms or performs comparably to competitive baselines given both automatic and human evaluations. We discuss how and to what extent the summarizer succeeds at capturing salient content.[2]

2 Background: The BART Summarizer

BART (Lewis et al., 2020) has demonstrated strong performance on neural abstractive summarization. It consists of a bidirectional encoder and a left-to-right autoregressive decoder, each contains multiple layers of Transformers (Vaswani et al., 2017). The model is pretrained using a denoising objective that, given a corrupted input text, the encoder strives to learn meaningful representations and the decoder reconstructs the original text using the representations. In this study, we use `BART-large-cnn` as a base summarizer. It contains 12 layers in each of the encoder and decoder and uses a hidden size of 1024. The model is then fine-tuned on the CNN dataset for abstractive summarization.

There are two obstacles that should be overcome in order for BART to generate meeting summaries from transcripts. Firstly, BART is trained on written text, rather than spoken text. The pretraining data contain 160G of news, books, stories, and web text. It remains unclear if the model can effectively identify salient content on spoken text and, how it is to reduce lead bias that is not as frequent in spoken text as in news writing (Grenander et al., 2019). Secondly, a transcript can far exceed the maximum input length of the model, which is restricted by the GPU memory size. This is the case even for recent variants such as Reformer (Kitaev et al., 2020) and Longformer (Beltagy et al., 2020).

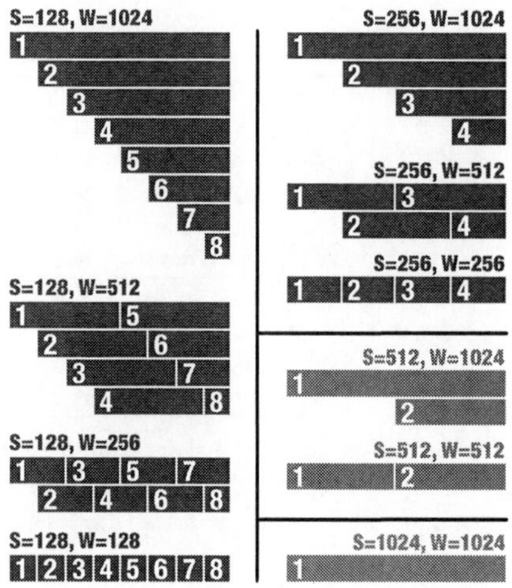

Figure 1: A total of 10 combinations of window (`W`) and stride (`S`) sizes examined in this study. A small stride allows a text region to be repeatedly visited by the summarizer. The numbers (`1-8`) indicate local windows.

3 Our Approach

A sliding-window approach to generating meeting minutes is appealing because it breaks lengthy transcripts into small and manageable local windows, allowing a set of "mini-summaries" to be produced from such windows which are then assembled into meeting-level summaries. There are two essential decisions to be made when using a sliding window. Firstly, one must decide on the size of the local window. Our window size is bounded by the maximum sequence length of BART as the utterances in a window are concatenated into a flat sequence that serves as input to it. We consider a number of window sizes with `W`={128, 256, 512, 1024} tokens. Secondly, a transcript may be partitioned into non-overlapping or partially overlapping windows. We set the stride size to be `S`={128, 256, 512, 1024} tokens to support both ($W \geq S$). When they are of equal size, a transcript is divided into a sequence of non-overlapping windows.

In Figure 1, we enumerate all 10 combinations of window and stride sizes. For example, we ex-

[1] `https://cloud.google.com/speech-to-text`

[2] Our transcripts and system outputs are released publicly at `https://github.com/ucfnlp/meeting-sliding-window`

Input	System	ROUGE-1 P(%)	ROUGE-1 R(%)	ROUGE-1 F(%)	ROUGE-2 P(%)	ROUGE-2 R(%)	ROUGE-2 F(%)	Summary Len %Uttrs	Summary Len #Wrds
Human	KL-Sum	57.2	31.9	40.8	19.0	10.6	13.6	19.6	754
	SumBasic	61.6	67.1	62.4	24.8	28.1	25.6	19.6	1,730
	LexRank	36.8	84.3	50.9	21.2	49.2	29.4	19.6	3,528
	TextRank	28.2	91.6	42.9	19.4	63.5	29.5	19.6	4,954
	(Koay et al., 2020)	52.6	81.0	62.5	29.4	46.1	35.2	21.7	2,321
	SW (HumanTrans)	**36.5**	**90.9**	**51.9**	**23.2**	**58.4**	**33.1**	19.6	3,741
ASR	(Shang et al., 2018)	27.6	36.3	31.0	4.4	5.6	4.8	n/a	n/a
	(Koay et al., 2020)	51.3	78.6	61.3	25.7	39.9	30.9	16.7	2,224
	SW (AMI ASR)	**36.1**	**88.3**	**51.2**	**19.4**	**47.8**	**27.6**	18.2	3,514
	SW (Google ASR)	**61.9**	**65.7**	**62.9**	**26.5**	**28.1**	**26.9**	23.2	1,460

Table 1: Results on the ICSI test set using human transcripts and two versions of automatic transcripts (AMI vs. Google) as input. The length is defined as percentage of selected utterances over all utterances of the meetings and average number of words in the summaries. The sliding-window (SW) summarizer uses (`S`=128, `W`=1024).

periment with four window sizes of 128, 256, 512 and 1,024 tokens using the same stride size of 128 tokens, shown in dark blue (left). A larger window gives additional context to BART for recognizing salient content. Using a window of 1,024 and stride of 128 tokens allow each utterance of the transcript to be visited 8 times, whereas using a window of 512 tokens reduces that to 4 times.

Consolidation. BART abstracts generated from local windows cannot be simply concatenated to form meeting-level summaries as they contain redundancy. When local windows are partially overlapping, they can cause the same content to be included in different abstracts. Instead, we identify *supporting utterances* of each abstract from the transcript. Particularly, we compute the ROUGE-L scores between each utterance in the window and the abstract. If the utterance is longer than 5 tokens, achieves a recall score $r > 0.5$ and precision score $p > 0.1$, we call it a supporting utterance.[3] The same utterance can support multiple abstracts. We include an utterance into the meeting summary if it is designated as the supporting utterance for at lease one local abstract. It lends flexibility and improves ease of consolidation of local abstractive summaries produced by BART.

4 Results

Dataset. Our experiments are performed on the ICSI meeting corpus (Janin et al., 2003), which is a challenging benchmark for meeting summarization. The corpus contains 75 meeting recordings, each is about an hour long. We use 54 meetings for training and report results on the standard test set containing 6 meetings. Each training meeting has been annotated with an extractive summary. Each test meeting has three human-annotated extractive summaries, which we use as gold-standard summaries. The original corpus include human transcripts and automatic speech recognition (ASR) output generated by the AMI ASR team (Hain et al., 2006). We are able to generate a new version of automatic transcripts by using Google's Speech-to-Text API as an off-the-shelf system.[4] Comparing results on different versions of transcripts allows us to better assess the generality of our findings.

Our baselines include both general-purpose extractive summarizers and meeting-specific summarizers. LexRank (Erkan and Radev, 2004) and TextRank (Mihalcea and Tarau, 2004) are graph-based extractive methods. SumBasic (Vanderwende et al., 2007) selects sentences if they contain frequently occurring content words. KL-Sum (Haghighi and Vanderwende, 2009) adds sentences to the summary to minimize KL divergence. We additionally experiment with two meeting summarizers. Shang et al. (2018) group utterances into clusters, generate an abstractive sentence from each cluster using sentence compression, then select best elements from these sentences under a budget constraint. Koay et al. (2020) develop a supervised BERT summarizer to identify summary utterances.

We report test set results in Table 1, where system summaries are compared with gold-standard extractive summaries using ROUGE metrics (Lin, 2004). The summary length is computed as the percentage of selected utterances over all utterances of the meetings and average number of words per test summary. This information is reported wherever

[3]The thresholds were determined heuristically on the training set by observing the resulting alignment.

[4]Due to lack of documentation, we are unable to report the word error rates of Google and AMI speech recognizers.

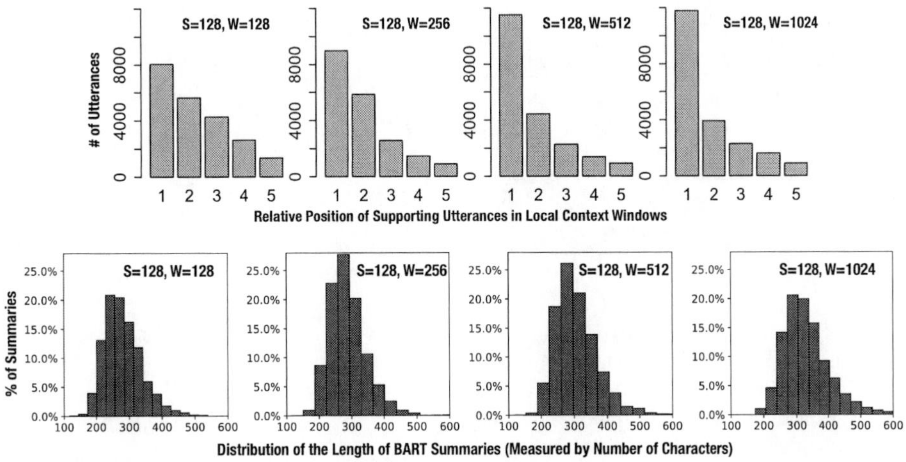

Figure 2: (TOP) Relative position of supporting utterances in their local windows. We find that BART tends to take summary content from the first 150-200 tokens of the input sequence. With a large window (W=1024), summary content is likely taken from the first 20% of input. (BOTTOM) Length distribution of BART abstracts, measured by number of characters. Using windows ranging from 128 to 1024 tokens, the average abstract length increases from 281 to 332 characters, i.e., 56 to 66 words assuming 5 characters per word for English texts (Shannon, 1951). Results are obtained on the ICSI training set using human transcripts.

available, and baseline summarizers are set to output the same number of summary utterances as the sliding-window (SW) approach. Our SW approach can outperform or perform comparably to competitive baselines when evaluated on human and ASR transcripts. We note that Koay et al. (2020) utilize a supervised BERT summarizer, whereas our SW approach is unsupervised.[5] It does not require annotated summaries and only uses the training set to determine window and stride sizes (S=128, W=1024, details later).

A closer examination reveals that Google transcripts contain substantially less filled pauses (*um, uh, mm-hmm*), disfluencies (*go-go-go away*), repetitions and verbal interruptions. The Google service also tends to produce lengthier utterances. Table 2 provides an example comparing human, AMI and Google transcripts. The summaries produced with Google transcripts contain fewer utterances and less number of words per summary. They achieve a higher precision and lower recall when compared to those of AMI and human transcripts.

We are curious to know where supporting utterances appear in the local windows. In Figure 2, we discretize the position information into 5 bins and plot the distributions for four settings that use different window sizes (W={128,256,512,1024}) but the same stride size (S=128). We observe that BART

Transcription	Human	AMI	Google
# of utter. per meeting	1330	1410	188
# of words per utterance	7.7	7.0	33.0
(Human) and um There one of our diligent workers has to sort of volunteer to look over Tilman's shoulder while he is changing the grammars to English			
(AMI) And um And they're one of our a The legend to work paris has to sort of volunteer to Look over time and shorter what he is changing that gram was to english			
(Google) and they are one of our diligent workers has to sit or volunteer to look over two months shoulder while he is changing the Grandma's to English			

Table 2: Compared to human and AMI transcripts, utterances produced by Google's transcription service are lengthier and there are fewer utterances per meeting.

tends to select content from the first 150 to 200 tokens of the input and add them to the abstract. It indicates that the model exhibits strong lead bias even for spoken text, which differs from news writing (Grenander et al., 2019). Additionally, we examine the length of BART abstracts, measured by the number of characters in an abstract. Using windows from 128 to 1024 tokens, we find that the avg. abstract length increases from 281 to 332 characters, ≈56 to 66 words assuming 5 characters per word on average for English texts (Shannon, 1951). While a larger window can lead to a longer abstract, the abstract size is disproportionate to the window

[5]We use pyrouge with default options to evaluate all summaries. The scores are different from that of Koay et al. (2020) which removed stopwords during evaluation by using '-s'.

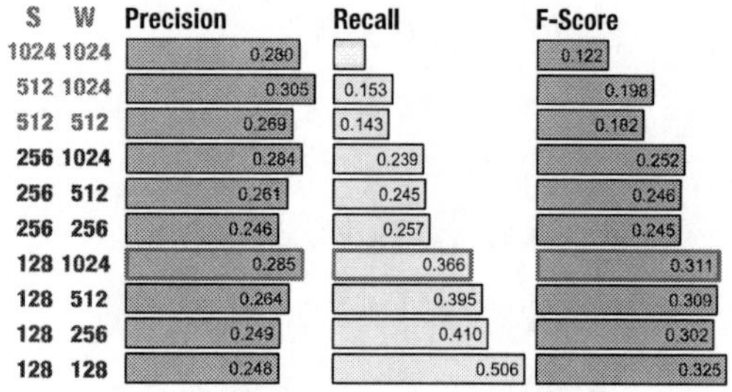

Figure 3: Precision, recall and F-scores of summary utterance selection using different combinations of stride (`S`) and window (`W`) sizes. Results are obtained on the ICSI training set using human transcripts. We find that (`S`=128, `W`=1024) attains a good balance between precision and recall, whereas using small, non-overlapping windows (`S`=128, `W`=128) yields high recall due to more utterances are included in the summary.

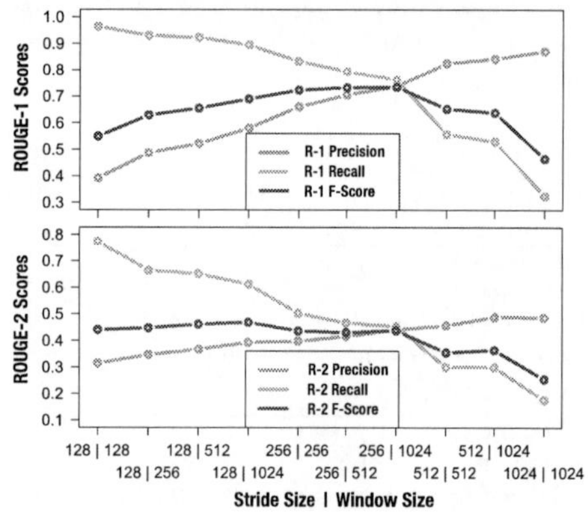

Figure 4: R-1 and R-2 scores when different combinations of stride (`S`) and window (`W`) sizes are used. Results are obtained on the ICSI training set for human transcripts. With (`S`=256, `W`=1024), we obtain balanced precision and recall scores. The best R-2 F-score is achieved with (`S`=128, `W`=1024).

size. These results are obtained on the training set using human transcripts as input.

In Figure 3, we investigate various combinations of stride (`S`) and window sizes (`W`) and report their precision, recall and F-scores on summary utterance selection. Similarly, the results are obtained on the training set using human transcripts as input. We highlight some interesting findings. We observe that a large context window (`W`=1024) tends to give high precision. A small window combined with small stride yields high recall due to more utterances are selected for the summary. For example, both settings (`W`=512, `S`=128) and (`W`=1024, `S`=256) allow an utterance to be visited 4 times. The former achieves a higher recall (0.395 vs. 0.239) due to

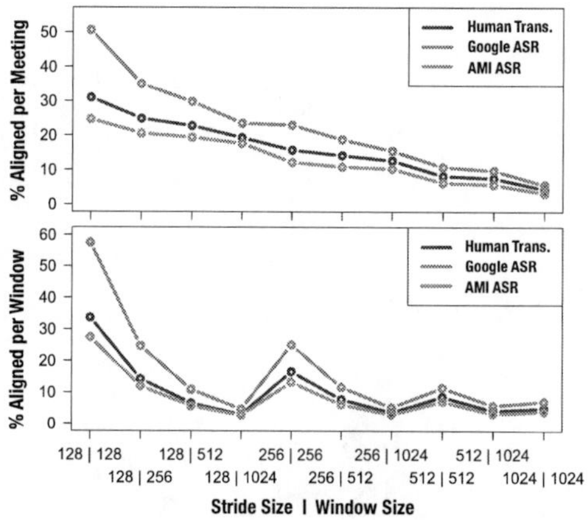

Figure 5: Percentage of supporting utterances per meeting (TOP) and per local window (BOTTOM). Results are obtained on the ICSI training set with different combinations of stride (`S`) and window (`W`) sizes, for human transcripts and two versions of automatic transcripts (Google vs. AMI).

System	Utterance Rating		
	Score-2	Score-1	Score-0
TextRank	8.58%	25.66%	65.77%
Supervised-BERT	11.35%	28.96%	59.69%
Sliding Window	**11.46%**	**26.11%**	**62.43%**

Table 3: Percentage of summary utterances rated as highly relevant (2), relevant (1) and irrelevant (0) by human evaluators. The systems for comparison are TextRank, a supervised BERT summarizer (Koay et al., 2020) and Sliding Window.

its smaller window and stride sizes. In Figure 4, we show R-1 and R-2 scores obtained on the training set for all combinations of stride and window sizes. We find that recall scores decrease substantially using large stride sizes (>=512 tokens). With (`S`=256, `W`=1024), we obtain balanced precision and recall scores. The best R-2 F-score is achieved with (`S`=128, `W`=1024) which is used at test time.

In Figure 5, we present the percentage of supporting (summary) utterances per meeting and per window, for various combinations of window and stride sizes. On human transcripts, we observe that combining small stride and window sizes (`S`=128, `W`=128) has led to ~30% utterances to be selected per meeting. In contrast, (`S`=128, `W`=1024) selects 19% of the utterances. Human transcripts and automatic transcripts generated by AMI ASR appear to show similar behavior, but the Google transcriber breaks up utterances differently.

We further conduct a human evaluation on the six test meetings. Three human evaluators (two native speakers and a non-native speaker) are employed

Speaker	Utterance	BERT	SW	Gold
fn002	I - Hynek last week say that if I have time I can to begin to - to study	1	1	1
fn002	well seriously the France Telecom proposal to look at the code and something like that	1	1	1
me013	Mm-hmm.	0	0	0
fn002	to know exactly what they are doing because maybe that we can have some ideas	1	0	0
me013	Mm-hmm.	0	0	0
fn002	but not only to read the proposal. Look look	0	0	0
fn002	carefully what they are doing with the program and I begin to - to work also in that.	1	0	1
fn002	But the first thing that I don't understand is that they	0	1	1
fn002	are using	0	0	1
fn002	the uh log energy that this quite - I don't know why they have some	0	1	1
fn002	constant in the expression of the lower energy. I don't know what that means.	0	1	1
me018	They have a constant in there, you said?	0	1	0

Table 4: Extractive summaries produced by the sliding-window approach (SW) appear to read more coherently than those of the supervised BERT summarizer. Consecutive sentences in SW summaries are more likely to be associated with the same idea/speaker compared to supervised-BERT. "Gold" are ground-truth summary utterances.

for this task. They rate each summary utterance as highly relevant (2), relevant (1) or irrelevant (0) by matching the utterance with the meeting abstract provided by the ICSI corpus. The systems for comparison are SW, TextRank and the fully supervised BERT summarizer (Koay et al., 2020). In Table 3, we report the percentage of summary utterances assigned to each category (Fleiss' Kappa=0.29). Our summarizer obtains promising results. It outperforms TextRank and performs comparably to supervised-BERT. We find that the SW summarizer navigates through the transcript in an *equally detailed* manner. It leads to coherent and sometimes verbose summaries, compared to other extractive summaries. A snippet of the transcript and its accompanying summaries are shown in Table 4.

5 Conclusion

We investigate the feasibility of a sliding-window approach to generating meeting minutes and obtain promising results on both human and automatic transcripts. The approach does not require annotated data and it has a great potential to be extended to meetings of various domains. Our future work includes, in the near horizon, experimenting with a look-ahead mechanism to enable the summarizer to skip over insignificant transcript segments.

Acknowledgements

We thank the anonymous reviewers for their helpful feedback. We would also like to thank Kaiqiang Song for helping transcribe the meetings using Google's Speech-to-Text API. Xiaojin Dai was supported by NSF DUE-1643835. We thank Amazon for partially sponsoring the research and computation in this study through the Amazon AWS Machine Learning Research Award.

References

Iz Beltagy, Matthew E. Peters, and Arman Cohan. 2020. Longformer: The long-document transformer.

Yen-Chun Chen and Mohit Bansal. 2018. Fast abstractive summarization with reinforce-selected sentence rewriting. In *Proceedings of the 56th Annual Meeting of the Association for Computational Linguistics (Volume 1: Long Papers)*, pages 675–686, Melbourne, Australia. Association for Computational Linguistics.

Yun-Nung Chen and Florian Metze. 2012. Two-layer mutually reinforced random walk for improved multi-party meeting summarization. In *2012 IEEE Spoken Language Technology Workshop (SLT), Miami, FL, USA, December 2-5, 2012*, pages 461–466. IEEE.

Günes Erkan and Dragomir R. Radev. 2004. LexRank: Graph-based lexical centrality as salience in text summarization. *Journal of Artificial Intelligence Research.*

Michel Galley. 2006. A skip-chain conditional random field for ranking meeting utterances by importance. In *Proceedings of the 2006 Conference on Empirical Methods in Natural Language Processing*, pages 364–372, Sydney, Australia. Association for Computational Linguistics.

Sebastian Gehrmann, Yuntian Deng, and Alexander Rush. 2018. Bottom-up abstractive summarization. In *Proceedings of the 2018 Conference on Empirical Methods in Natural Language Processing*, pages 4098–4109, Brussels, Belgium. Association for Computational Linguistics.

Daniel Gillick, Korbinian Riedhammer, Benoît Favre, and Dilek Hakkani-Tur. 2009. A global optimization framework for meeting summarization. In *2009 IEEE International Conference on Acoustics, Speech and Signal Processing*, pages 4769–4772.

Matt Grenander, Yue Dong, Jackie Chi Kit Cheung, and Annie Louis. 2019. Countering the effects of lead bias in news summarization via multi-stage training and auxiliary losses. In *Proceedings of the 2019 Conference on Empirical Methods in Natural Language Processing and the 9th International Joint Conference on Natural Language Processing (EMNLP-IJCNLP)*, pages 6019–6024, Hong Kong, China. Association for Computational Linguistics.

Aria Haghighi and Lucy Vanderwende. 2009. Exploring content models for multi-document summarization. In *Proceedings of the North American Chapter of the Association for Computational Linguistics (NAACL)*.

Thomas Hain, Lukas Burget, John Dines, Giulia Garau, Martin Karafiat, Mike Lincoln, Iain McCowan, Darren Moore, Vincent Wan, Roeland Ordelman, and Steve Renals. 2006. The 2005 ami system for the transcription of speech in meetings. In *Machine Learning for Multimodal Interaction*, pages 450–462, Berlin, Heidelberg. Springer Berlin Heidelberg.

Pei-Yun Hsueh and Johanna D. Moore. 2008. Automatic decision detection in meeting speech. In *Machine Learning for Multimodal Interaction*, pages 168–179, Berlin, Heidelberg. Springer Berlin Heidelberg.

A. Janin, D. Baron, J. Edwards, D. Ellis, D. Gelbart, N. Morgan, B. Peskin, T. Pfau, E. Shriberg, A. Stolcke, and C. Wooters. 2003. The icsi meeting corpus. In *2003 IEEE International Conference on Acoustics, Speech, and Signal Processing, 2003. Proceedings. (ICASSP '03).*, volume 1, pages I–I.

Chris Kedzie, Kathleen McKeown, and Hal Daumé III. 2018. Content selection in deep learning models of summarization. In *Proceedings of the 2018 Conference on Empirical Methods in Natural Language Processing*, pages 1818–1828, Brussels, Belgium. Association for Computational Linguistics.

Nikita Kitaev, Lukasz Kaiser, and Anselm Levskaya. 2020. Reformer: The efficient transformer. In *International Conference on Learning Representations*.

Jia Jin Koay, Alexander Roustai, Xiaojin Dai, Dillon Burns, Alec Kerrigan, and Fei Liu. 2020. How domain terminology affects meeting summarization performance. In *Proceedings of the 28th International Conference on Computational Linguistics*, pages 5689–5695, Barcelona, Spain (Online). International Committee on Computational Linguistics.

Wojciech Kryscinski, Nitish Shirish Keskar, Bryan McCann, Caiming Xiong, and Richard Socher. 2019. Neural text summarization: A critical evaluation. In *Proceedings of the 2019 Conference on Empirical Methods in Natural Language Processing and the 9th International Joint Conference on Natural Language Processing (EMNLP-IJCNLP)*, pages 540–551, Hong Kong, China. Association for Computational Linguistics.

Philippe Laban, Andrew Hsi, John Canny, and Marti A. Hearst. 2020. The summary loop: Learning to write abstractive summaries without examples. In *Proceedings of the 58th Annual Meeting of the Association for Computational Linguistics*, pages 5135–5150, Online. Association for Computational Linguistics.

Logan Lebanoff, John Muchovej, Franck Dernoncourt, Doo Soon Kim, Seokhwan Kim, Walter Chang, and Fei Liu. 2019. Analyzing sentence fusion in abstractive summarization. In *Proceedings of the 2nd Workshop on New Frontiers in Summarization*, pages 104–110, Hong Kong, China. Association for Computational Linguistics.

Mike Lewis, Yinhan Liu, Naman Goyal, Marjan Ghazvininejad, Abdelrahman Mohamed, Omer Levy, Veselin Stoyanov, and Luke Zettlemoyer. 2020. BART: Denoising sequence-to-sequence pretraining for natural language generation, translation, and comprehension. In *Proceedings of the 58th Annual Meeting of the Association for Computational Linguistics*, pages 7871–7880, Online. Association for Computational Linguistics.

Manling Li, Lingyu Zhang, Heng Ji, and Richard J. Radke. 2019. Keep meeting summaries on topic: Abstractive multi-modal meeting summarization. In *Proceedings of the 57th Annual Meeting of the Association for Computational Linguistics*, pages 2190–2196, Florence, Italy. Association for Computational Linguistics.

Chin-Yew Lin. 2004. ROUGE: A package for automatic evaluation of summaries. In *Text Summarization Branches Out*, pages 74–81, Barcelona, Spain. Association for Computational Linguistics.

Fei Liu and Yang Liu. 2009. From extractive to abstractive meeting summaries: Can it be done by sentence compression? In *Proceedings of the ACL-IJCNLP 2009 Conference Short Papers*, pages 261–264, Suntec, Singapore. Association for Computational Linguistics.

Feifan Liu, Deana Pennell, Fei Liu, and Yang Liu. 2009. Unsupervised approaches for automatic keyword extraction using meeting transcripts. In *Proceedings of Human Language Technologies: The 2009 Annual Conference of the North American Chapter of the Association for Computational Linguistics*, pages 620–628, Boulder, Colorado. Association for Computational Linguistics.

Jon Martindale. 2021. Google meet tips and tricks. *https://www.digitaltrends.com/computing/google-meet-tips-tricks/*.

Sameer Maskey and Julia Hirschberg. 2005. Comparing lexical, acoustic/prosodic, structural and discourse features for speech summarization. In *INTERSPEECH*, pages 621–624. ISCA.

Joshua Maynez, Shashi Narayan, Bernd Bohnet, and Ryan McDonald. 2020. On faithfulness and factuality in abstractive summarization. In *Proceedings of the 58th Annual Meeting of the Association for Computational Linguistics*, pages 1906–1919, Online. Association for Computational Linguistics.

Yashar Mehdad, Giuseppe Carenini, Frank Tompa, and Raymond T. Ng. 2013. Abstractive meeting summarization with entailment and fusion. In *Proceedings of the 14th European Workshop on Natural Language Generation*, pages 136–146, Sofia, Bulgaria. Association for Computational Linguistics.

Rada Mihalcea and Paul Tarau. 2004. TextRank: Bringing order into text. In *Proceedings of the 2004 Conference on Empirical Methods in Natural Language Processing*, pages 404–411, Barcelona, Spain. Association for Computational Linguistics.

Gabriel Murray and Giuseppe Carenini. 2008. Summarizing spoken and written conversations. In *Proceedings of the 2008 Conference on Empirical Methods in Natural Language Processing*, pages 773–782, Honolulu, Hawaii. Association for Computational Linguistics.

Laura Perez-Beltrachini, Yang Liu, and Mirella Lapata. 2019. Generating summaries with topic templates and structured convolutional decoders. In *Proceedings of the 57th Annual Meeting of the Association for Computational Linguistics*, pages 5107–5116, Florence, Italy. Association for Computational Linguistics.

Joseph Polifroni, Stephanie Seneff, and Victor W. Zue. 1991. Collection of spontaneous speech for the ATIS domain and comparative analyses of data collected at MIT and TI. In *Speech and Natural Language: Proceedings of a Workshop Held at Pacific Grove, California, February 19-22, 1991.*

Abigail See, Peter J. Liu, and Christopher D. Manning. 2017. Get to the point: Summarization with pointer-generator networks. In *Proceedings of the 55th Annual Meeting of the Association for Computational Linguistics (Volume 1: Long Papers)*, pages 1073–1083, Vancouver, Canada. Association for Computational Linguistics.

Guokan Shang, Wensi Ding, Zekun Zhang, Antoine Tixier, Polykarpos Meladianos, Michalis Vazirgiannis, and Jean-Pierre Lorré. 2018. Unsupervised abstractive meeting summarization with multi-sentence compression and budgeted submodular maximization. In *Proceedings of the 56th Annual Meeting of the Association for Computational Linguistics (Volume 1: Long Papers)*, pages 664–674, Melbourne, Australia. Association for Computational Linguistics.

C. E. Shannon. 1951. Prediction and entropy of printed english. *Bell System Technical Journal.*

Yan Song, Yuanhe Tian, Nan Wang, and Fei Xia. 2020. Summarizing medical conversations via identifying important utterances. In *Proceedings of the 28th International Conference on Computational Linguistics*, pages 717–729, Barcelona, Spain (Online). International Committee on Computational Linguistics.

Lucy Vanderwende, Hisami Suzuki, Chris Brockett, and Ani Nenkova. 2007. Beyond SumBasic: Task-focused summarization with sentence simplification and lexical expansion. *Information Processing and Management*, 43(6):1606–1618.

Ashish Vaswani, Noam Shazeer, Niki Parmar, Jakob Uszkoreit, Llion Jones, Aidan N Gomez, Ł ukasz Kaiser, and Illia Polosukhin. 2017. Attention is all you need. In *Advances in Neural Information Processing Systems*, volume 30, pages 5998–6008. Curran Associates, Inc.

Lu Wang and Claire Cardie. 2013. Domain-independent abstract generation for focused meeting summarization. In *Proceedings of the 51st Annual Meeting of the Association for Computational Linguistics (Volume 1: Long Papers)*, pages 1395–1405, Sofia, Bulgaria. Association for Computational Linguistics.

Ming Zhong, Da Yin, Tao Yu, Ahmad Zaidi, Mutethia Mutuma, Rahul Jha, Ahmed H. Awadallah, Asli Celikyilmaz, Yang Liu, Xipeng Qiu, and Dragomir Radev. 2021. QMSum: A new benchmark for query-based multi-domain meeting summarization. In *Proceedings of the 2021 Conference of the North American Chapter of the Association for Computational Linguistics.*

Chenguang Zhu, Ruochen Xu, Michael Zeng, and Xuedong Huang. 2020. A hierarchical network for abstractive meeting summarization with cross-domain pretraining. In *Findings of the Association for Computational Linguistics: EMNLP 2020*, pages 194–203, Online. Association for Computational Linguistics.

Xiaodan Zhu, Gerald Penn, and Frank Rudzicz. 2009. Summarizing multiple spoken documents: finding evidence from untranscribed audio. In *Proceedings of the Joint Conference of the 47th Annual Meeting of the ACL and the 4th International Joint Conference on Natural Language Processing of the AFNLP*, pages 549–557, Suntec, Singapore. Association for Computational Linguistics.

Exploration and Discovery of the COVID-19 Literature through Semantic Visualization

Jingxuan Tu[1], **Marc Verhagen**[1], **Brent Cochran**[2], **James Pustejovsky**[1]
[1]Brandeis University [2]Tufts University School of Medicine
{jxtu,verhagen,jamesp}@brandeis.edu
brent.cochran@tufts.edu

Abstract

We propose *semantic visualization* as a linguistic visual analytic method. It can enable exploration and discovery over large datasets of complex networks by exploiting the semantics of the relations in them. This involves extracting information, applying parameter reduction operations, building hierarchical data representation and designing visualization. We also present the accompanying COVID-SEMVIZ, a searchable and interactive visualization system for knowledge exploration of COVID-19 data to demonstrate the application of our proposed method.[1] In the user studies, users found that *semantic visualization*-powered COVID-SEMVIZ is helpful in terms of finding relevant information and discovering unknown associations.

1 Introduction

COVID-19 is the first global pandemic within a century. To facilitate the scientific and medical effort to stop this pandemic, most publishers are making full text of COVID-19 related manuscripts freely available.[2] However, every year, the number of published papers is growing at a rate that makes full use of these resources a daunting task (Johnson et al., 2018), and it is getting severer especially during the COVID-19 pandemic when new information is rapidly emerging.

To facilitate the research over these articles, many researchers also publish corpora of preprocessed and curated COVID-19 articles such as LidCovid (Chen et al., 2020) and CORD-19 (Wang et al., 2020). However, for most users and researchers, it is still challenging to fully explore such a corpus due to the complexity of scientific content it contains (for example, complicated pathways in biomedical field (Mercatelli et al., 2020)).

Finding connections among multiple corpora is another challenge. Even for corpora that are targeting a specific topic like *COVID-19*, they may contain information at different scale for different purposes. For example, one dataset provides parsed text and meta information of articles (Wang et al., 2020), and another provides detailed protein-protein interactions extracted from sentences (Gyori et al., 2017). It is difficult to gain full insight by looking either one of those individually. Although search engine is supported for some corpora and portals, this query-based and targeted search is limited in finding connections and patterns that are not obvious from individual articles or sentences (White and Roth, 2009).

To enhance the scientific discovery over complex corpora, we propose *semantic visualization*, a set of text processing and visualization techniques and accompanying tool COVID-SEMVIZ for enhanced knowledge exploration of COVID-19 data (Figure 1). *Semantic visualization* transforms large datasets of complex networks into rich semantic-aware text data; processes text data in a hierarchical manner; and provides visualizations for the indexed data.

The tool COVID-SEMVIZ allows for searchable and interactive visualization of data through word clouds, heat maps, graphs, etc. Unlike other work (See Section 4), we focus on constructing and navigating information from biomedical datasets in a unified hierarchical structure. For example, the activation relations between proteins and COVID-19 can be constructed as the functional type "COVID-19 activators". By reducing relations to a single functional type, it enables the visualization of higher order relations (*e.g.* relations between COVID-19 activators and other protein inhibitors) through a simple 2-dimensional heat map. Other types of visualizations will also appear on the side such as a word cloud of proteins that activate COVID-19, and a tabular form of evidencing sentences. All these visualizations compose a *habitat*

[1]https://www.semviz.org/

[2]https://www.who.int/emergencies/diseases/novel-coronavirus-2019/global-research-on-novel-coronavirus-2019-ncov

Proceedings of NAACL-HLT 2021: Student Research Workshop, pages 76–87
June 6–11, 2021.

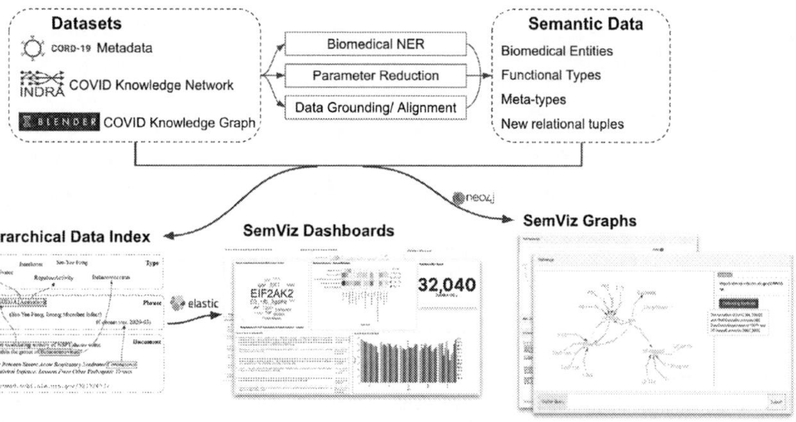

Figure 1: A system overview of COVID-SEMVIZ. The top shows the processing of raw corpora into semantic-aware data. At the bottom it shows the semantic data along with the original corpora are processed in the hierarchical manner and fitted in to the data index or transformed into graph data. Finally data is explored via dashboards and graphs.

of information about COVID-19. Through this, we aim to provide researchers with a global view of selected relationship subtypes drawn from hundreds or thousands of papers at a single glance. This enables the ready identification of novel relationships that would typically be missed by directed keyword searches.

We summarize our main contributions as the follows: (1) Proposed *semantic visualization*, a linguistic visual analytic method that enhances the exploration and visualization of scientific text datasets; (2) Implemented COVID-SEMVIZ, a working prototype for enhanced knowledge exploration of COVID-19 datasets; (3) User studies that evaluate the effectiveness of our system to the biomedical research community as well as future improvements.

2 Semantic Visualization

We propose *Semantic visualization* as a general linguistic visual analytic method for enabling exploration and discovery over large text datasets by exploiting the semantics of the relations in them. This involves (i) collecting data and applying NLP to extract named entities, relations and knowledge graphs from the original text; (ii) indexing the output and creating hierarchical representations for all relevant entities, relations and text that can be visualized in many different ways such as tag clouds, heat maps, graphs, etc.; (iii) applying parameter reduction operations to the extracted relations, creating *functional types* that can also be visualized using the same methods, allowing the visualization of multiple relations, partial graphs, and exploration across multiple dimensions.

2.1 Data collection and Extraction

The first step of semantic visualization involves collecting multiple text datasets of same domain and applying NLP techniques for information extraction to complement original data.

Recently, there is some important work that focuses on publishing new corpora and mining useful text from literature related to COVID-19. In our implementation, we choose to use the following three datasets of COVID-19 literature:

COVID-19 Open Research Dataset (CORD-19) is one of the most comprehensive resource of articles on COVID-19 (Wang et al., 2020). It contains metadata and parsed full text of each article collected from various sources.

Harvard INDRA CORD-19 causal assertions dataset (CKN) [3] contains over 320,000 causal assertions (CAs) extracted from the full text of CORD-19 articles by multiple machine reading systems including REACH (Valenzuela-Escárcega et al., 2018) and Sparser (Mcdonald, 1992). Extracted events were assembled by INDRA[4] and 24 relation types were defined (Gyori et al., 2017).

Blender lab Covid Knowledge Graphs (Blender KG) [5] contains knowledge including entities, re-

[3] https://emmaa.indra.bio

[4] https://github.com/sorgerlab/indra

[5] http://blender.cs.illinois.edu/covid19/

CKN DATASET	
Evidence:	**Ocrelizumab**$_{\texttt{[Protein]}}$ and Cladribine may **increase the risk of acquiring**$_{\texttt{[Relation]}}$ **COVID-19**$_{\texttt{[Protein]}}$.
Relation:	*(ocrelizumab, COVID-19, Activation)*
BLENDER KG	
Evidence:	**10074-G5**$_{\texttt{[Chemical]}}$ results in **decreased expression**$_{\texttt{[Relation]}}$ of **MYC**$_{\texttt{[Gene]}}$ protein.
Relation:	*(10074-G5, MYC, Decrease Expression)*

Table 1: Example data from CKN and Blender KG.

lations, and events that are extracted from the CORD-19 dataset through deep learning methods (Lin et al., 2020).

Table 1 shows data samples from both the INDRA CKN and Blender KG. Each sample contains a biomedical relation and a corresponding evidencing sentence of that relation. For CORD-19, we extracted and normalized `PMID`, `Title`, `Abstract`, `Authors`, `Publish time` and `Journal` as the metadata for each article.[6] For the CKN dataset, we applied the ScispaCy NER model (Neumann et al., 2019) trained on the BIONLP13CG corpus (Pyysalo et al., 2013) on the original evidencing sentences to extract biomedical named entities, and constructed knowledge graph over encoded relations. For the Blender KG, we use the chemical-gene, chemical-disease, gene-disease relation extraction results. It has over 1,640,000 relations with evidencing sentences from biomedical articles.

In general, semantic visualization suggests information extraction of different granularity. General practice includes named entity recognition, relation extraction, document summarization and graph completion.

2.2 Parameter Reduction

Relational information usually is denoted as *(entity1, entity2, relation-type)* tuples. While individual relations can be visualized through 2-dimensional display techniques like heat maps, demonstrating how multiple relations relate to each other when chained together can be tricky to visualize, requiring cumbersome network visualization techniques (Mercatelli et al., 2020; Nelson et al., 2019). In the biomedical data we are processing, the large number of nodes and connections along with the heterogeneity of both node types (proteins, chemicals, diseases) and edges (structural, functional, and causal interactions) complicates the visualization (Agapito et al., 2013; Salazar et al., 2014; Baryshnikova, 2016).

Particularly for relational information from the data, we propose semantic parameter reduction, a method that reduces relations to *functional types*, allowing them to be treated as individuals. *Functional types* can show more capability and flexibility in terms of encoding information and visualization. The term "parameter reduction" has been used in computer science to refer to reducing model parameters (Kim et al., 2017; Glaws et al., 2020), and our proposed method has the same spirit that aims to reduce the complexity of multiple relations.

Formally, in our current model M, for any given relation tuple $(x,\ y,\ rel)$, we define the function of relation type rel as:

$$[\![rel]\!]^M = [\lambda y \in D_e.[\lambda x \in D_e.\ 1\ \textit{iff}\ (x,\ y,\ rel) \in M]] \quad (1)$$

where x and y denote the entities appear in this relation tuple; D_e denotes the set of all entities. Take the tuple *(ocrelizumab, COVID-19, Activation)* as an example, if we pass in *COVID-19* as the first argument to the relation function of *activation*, we will be able to get:

$$[\![\textit{activation}]\!]^M = [\lambda x \in D_e.\ 1\ \textit{iff}\ (x,\ \textit{COVID-19},\ \textit{activation}) \in M] \quad (2)$$

Through the parameter reduction, we can get the functional type of Equation (2) such that:

$$[\![\textit{ocrelizumab}]\!]^M \in \textit{COVID-19 activator} \quad (3)$$

where the functional type *COVID-19 activator* can be treated as an individual entity instead of a relation. *ocrelizumab* is a member of the functional type in this example. We make the names of functional types both semantically and biologically meaningful based on the relation types, *e.g. activation→activator, phosphorylation→kinase*, etc.

Instead of visualizing relations in a heat map, the generated functional types can be visualized using single dimensional display techniques such as tag clouds as shown in Figure 2.

Functional types can also be arguments that will be passed into the relation function, enabling a chain of relations to be expressed in a conventional heat map visualization. For example, Equation (4) is the function of relations between an entity and the functional type *TNF regulator*:

$$[\![rel]\!]^M = [\lambda x \in D_e.\ 1\ \textit{iff}\ (x,\ \textit{TNF regulator},\ rel) \in M]] \quad (4)$$

[6]The release date of the dateset we use is 2020-7-5 to match the latest version of Blender KG. It contains over 180,000 scientific papers on COVID-19 and related historical coronavirus research. Download from www.semanticscholar.org/cord19/download.

Figure 2: Functional Types as Regulators Tag Cloud from COVID-SEMVIZ.

Figure 3 illustrates such a dense heat map in the Blender KG dataset, where a functionally typed protein is implicated in a disease relation (e.g., "those proteins that are down regulators of TNF which are implicated in obesity")[7].

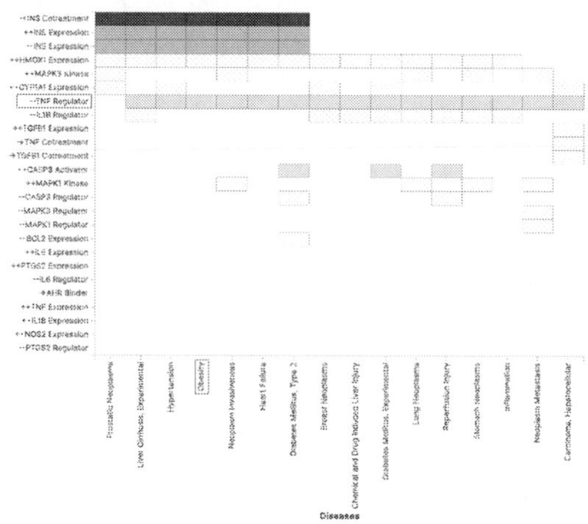

Figure 3: Regulatory Processes-Disease Interactions Heat Map from COVID-SEMVIZ.

2.3 Hierarchical Data Structure

Conceptually, semantic visualization suggests processing and representing data in a hierarchical manner. The resulting data structure composes of three different generic layers that enables better utility of information of various granularity and a global view of data. Although previous work has explored different text structure in data mining (Section 4), they didn't make a clear mapping from information in different layers to various visualization techniques. With the semantic parameter reduction, data can be also be passed and decomposed between different layers from the hierarchical structure.

Type-level layer Represents data that are entities or can be "parameter reduced" as functional types. In our data, individual arguments such as `COVID-19` and `MYC` that are involved in the relation (Table 1), can be seen as entities. In addition, the argument and predicate of a relation can be reduced as a functional type. The causal assertion *(ocrelizumab, COVID-19, Activation)* (Table 1) can be reduced to the entity `COVID-19 Activator`. Subsequently, it is implied that *ocrelizumab* is also included in the `COVID-19 Activators` set.

Phrase-level layer Represents data that can be transformed into "term tuples". A term tuple can be a natural relation that is identified in the datasets, e.g. the relation *(10074-G5, MYC, Decrease Expression)* in Table 1. It can also be built from entities and functional types. Term tuple *(COVID-19, Viruses)* contains the entity `COVID-19` that appears in the abstract of an article, and entity `Viruses` is the journal name where this article is from.

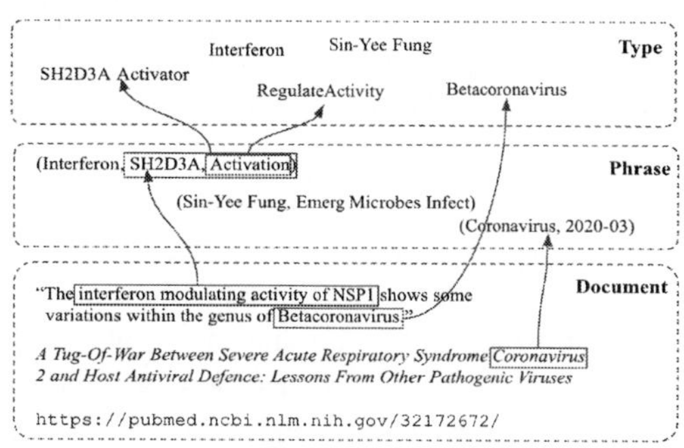

Figure 4: Hierarchical data representation for the datasets. Boxes from bottom to top show how data is represented in different layers. Arrows show how data is passed and decomposed between layers.

Document-level layer Represents data as documents that provide context information to the functional entities and term tuples. The document text is of variable length and it can be a phrase, sentence, or a whole paragraph. In our implementation, we index evidencing sentences, article titles and abstracts as documents. A clickable PubMed URL is also indexed to show the provenance of each

[7]We use the following symbols to indicate the "action" in each relation: "++" = increase, "−−" = decrease, "→" = affect.

evidencing sentence and article title.

Figure 4 shows how the data is processed into the hierarchical data representation. Arrows indicate some extracted relations and entities can be fitted into the other layers. For example, `Coronavirus` from document layer can be used to form a new term tuple with `2020-03` of type *(keyword in abstract, Publish time)*. In the phrase layer, the author name `Sin-Yee Fung` and journal name `Emerg Microbes Infect` that from the CORD-19 dataset can be processed into a new relational tuple. In the type layer, the generated entity `RegulateActivity` and the functional type `SH2D3A Activator` are all associated with a tuple in the phrase level.[8]

2.4 Visualization Techniques

We choose and apply multiple visualization techniques and combinations that are compatible with the hierarchical data representation and allows users to design and build semantically meaningful interactive visualization strategies. In practice, the following general visualization techniques are suggested to be considered: *Word Cloud* (a group of words), *Heat Map* (2D grid matrices for relational data), *Bar Chart* (for categorical data), *Line Chart* (for series of data), *Network* (graphs for complex pathways, KGs, etc), *Tabular Form* (tables for unstructured text) and *Indicator* (displays of the meta information of datasets).

2.5 COVID-SEMVIZ Overview

We release processed data and an implementation of COVID-SEMVIZ visualization system that has been applied with semantic visualization techniques. It contains three dashboards that use different subsets of the data. The Covid CA dashboard holds various visualizations designed principally for CKN dataset and CORD-19, and the Covid KGs dashboard contains visualizations designed for Blender KG and CORD-19. Covid Graph dashboard contains graph-based visualizations to show the all-connected knowledge graph and protein pathways. Due to the space limit, we will provide a detailed overview and technical aspects of the system in the extra page upon accepted.

[8]`RegulateActivity` is the parent relation of `Activation`.

3 User Studies and Evaluation

We present user studies from five researchers (**T1**-**T5**) by letting them interacting with COVID-SEMVIZ in their own research on coronaviruses.[9]

Finding supporting evidence and articles. Based on the search of anti-SARS CoV-2 antibodies, **T1** found most of the relevant literature and "allowed me to quickly zero in on the papers and evidencing sentences I would highlight." **T2** is interested in HEs activities in SARS CoV-2 and found "Many of the common and well known players were revealed in the word cloud".

Discovering unknown interactions. From the protein functional type word cloud, **T2** also found "`TTN Complex` that we had not previously considered." **T3** searched for AT2R and IL-6 inhibition and found the "linkage between those terms and respiratory distress", but the strategy in the linked literature "is not a viable therapeutic strategy in patients of certain conditions". **T4** also found "new links to follow up on, like glycosylation of the coronavirus M protein".

Raising new questions. Based on the search result for AT1R, **T3** found "AT2R activation may have a similar effect on IL-6 levels without impacting blood pressure", and "this is one that I can explore in my research". **T5** searched for TMPRSS2, and found TMPRSS4 appears in the same regulator word cloud. through the checking of linked evidence, **T5** found "Both TMPRSS2 and 4 can cleave the viral fusion protein. This raises the question whether the same is true for COVID-19".

Table 2 shows a summary of what levels of information from the hierarchical data structure that users have mentioned in their comments. We notice that all users find functional types are useful, suggesting the richness of information contained in the functional types from parameter reduction. Interestingly, only two users interacted with phrase-level information. This is probably due to the partial overlapping between phrases and functional types.

We also identify the limitations of our proposed system. One comes from the frequency-based method for displaying data, which means terms or relations that have larger counts are more "salient" in the visualizations (e.g. larger font in the word cloud or darker grids in the heat map). This might

[9]**T1** and **T5** study tumor virus and cancer cells; **T2**'s research focuses on the interface of chemistry, medicine and biology; **T3** studies medicine and nutrition and **T4** studies viral proteins.

User	Term	Functional Type	Phrase	Document
T1		✓		✓
T2	✓	✓	✓	
T3	✓	✓	✓	✓
T4	✓	✓		✓
T5	✓	✓		✓

Table 2: Summary of different levels of information that each user has interacted with.

lead to uncommon or less-studied topics unreachable unless the accurate term has been searched. Another limitation is from the integration of multiple datasets and tools. Artifacts that are in the original data or generated after processing might persist in the final visualizations.

4 Related Work

With the emerging of various COVID-19 data resources, many tools have been developed to enable the visualization and exploration of the large amount of articles that are growing everyday.

Hope et al. (2020) developed SciSight[10], a tool that can be used to visualize co-mentions of biomedical concepts such as genes, proteins and cells that are found in the articles related to COVID-19. It focuses more on displaying purely the association between entities that are mined from articles. IBM COVID-19 Navigator[11] supports the semantic search by building queries with the combination of general terms, UMLS (Unified Medical Language System) concepts, authors and boolean operators. It only provides term-level search and no visualization functionality. COVID-SEE[12], proposed by Verspoor et al. (2020), supports the search from CORD-19 dataset and visualization of article topics and relational concepts. Most other visualizations, however, relate to epidemiological statistics and the effects of Covid-19 on social and health factors[13].

Recent work has been mining useful data from biomedical text. Kordjamshidi et al. (2015) explored the text structure of biomedical data and used information from different levels of the structure as the features to automatically extract bacteria names. Liu et al. (2015) proposed a text mining system for identifying relationships between biomedical entities. It supports template-based queries for structured search and also provides key sentences as the provenance of identified relations. Fabregat et al. (2018) proposed a knowledge base of human pathways and reactions. It supports visualization of event hierarchy and pathway networks.

Linguistic visualization research in general is an emerging field of visual analytics for linguistics (Butt et al., 2020). Previous research in this field covers thematic text cluster analysis (Gold et al., 2015), NER-based document content analysis (El-Assady et al., 2017b), multi-party discourse analysis (El-Assady et al., 2017a) and topic modeling visualization (El-Assady et al., 2018). Butt et al. (2020) propose a web framework that consists of various linguistic visualization techniques. However, existing work in this field focuses on the analysis of corpora of conversational text and transcripts, and does not include approaches for analyzing and visualizing semantics of relations.

5 Conclusion

We have proposed *semantic visualization*, a linguistic visual analytic method of multiple steps involving data extraction, parameter reduction, hierarchical structure building and visualization design. It can facilitate the exploration over large and complex datasets by exploiting the semantics of the relations in them. We have also presented COVID-SEMVIZ, a working prototype for the visualization and exploration of three COVID-19-related datasets. Our user studies indicate that COVID-SEMVIZ is helpful to the biomedical community and the utility of *semantic visualization* techniques. Although we only demonstrated how to apply semantic visualization to COVID-related articles, our proposed method is generalizable enough to be applied to other text corpora. Future work includes addressing current limitations, applying to data from other domains and incorporating more and useful information extraction models in the pipeline. It is our hope that this semantic visualization environment will enable the discovery of novel inferences over relations in complex data that otherwise would go unnoticed.

Acknowledgments

Thanks to the NAACL SRW mentor Roy Schwartz and two anonymous reviewers for providing feedback on this paper. Thank you to Kyeongmin Rim and Kelley Lynch for providing various help on this project.

[10] https://scisight.apps.allenai.org/jnlpba/

[11] https://covid-19-navigator.mybluemix.net/search

[12] https://covid-see.com/

[13] https://www.cdc.gov/coronavirus/2019-ncov/covid-data/data-visualization.htm

References

Giuseppe Agapito, Pietro Hiram Guzzi, and Mario Cannataro. 2013. Visualization of protein interaction networks: problems and solutions. *BMC bioinformatics*, 14(S1):S1.

Anastasia Baryshnikova. 2016. Systematic functional annotation and visualization of biological networks. *Cell systems*, 2(6):412–421.

M. Butt, A. Hautli-Janisz, and V. Lyding. 2020. *LingVis: Visual Analytics for Linguistics*. CSLI lecture notes. CSLI Publications/Center for the Study of Language & Information.

Q. Chen, A. Allot, and Z. Lu. 2020. Keep up with the latest coronavirus research. *Nature*, 579(7798):193.

Mennatallah El-Assady, Annette Hautli-Janisz, Valentin Gold, Miriam Butt, Katharina Holzinger, and Daniel Keim. 2017a. Interactive visual analysis of transcribed multi-party discourse. In *Proceedings of ACL 2017, System Demonstrations*, pages 49–54, Vancouver, Canada. Association for Computational Linguistics.

Mennatallah El-Assady, Rita Sevastjanova, Bela Gipp, D. Keim, and C. Collins. 2017b. Nerex: Named-entity relationship exploration in multi-party conversations. *Computer Graphics Forum*, 36.

Mennatallah El-Assady, Fabian Sperrle, Rita Sevastjanova, M. Sedlmair, and D. Keim. 2018. Ltma: Layered topic matching for the comparative exploration, evaluation, and refinement of topic modeling results. *2018 International Symposium on Big Data Visual and Immersive Analytics (BDVA)*, pages 1–10.

A. Fabregat, S. Jupe, L. Matthews, Konstantinos Sidiropoulos, M. Gillespie, P. Garapati, R. Haw, B. Jassal, Florian Korninger, Bruce May, M. Milacic, C. Duenas, K. Rothfels, C. Sevilla, V. Shamovsky, Solomon Shorser, Thawfeek M. Varusai, G. Viteri, J. Weiser, Guanming Wu, L. Stein, H. Hermjakob, and P. D'Eustachio. 2018. The reactome pathway knowledgebase. *Nucleic Acids Research*, 42:D472 – D477.

A. Glaws, P. Constantine, and R. Cook. 2020. Inverse regression for ridge recovery: a data-driven approach for parameter reduction in computer experiments. *Statistics and Computing*, 30:237–253.

Valentin Gold, Christian Rohrdantz, and Mennatallah El-Assady. 2015. Exploratory text analysis using lexical episode plots. In *EuroVis*.

Benjamin M. Gyori, John A. Bachman, Kartik Subramanian, Jeremy L. Muhlich, Lucian Galescu, and Peter K. Sorger. 2017. From word models to executable models of signaling networks using automated assembly. *Molecular Systems Biology*, 13.

Tom Hope, Jason Portenoy, Kishore Vasan, Jonathan Borchardt, Eric Horvitz, Daniel S Weld, Marti A Hearst, and Jevin West. 2020. Scisight: Combining faceted navigation and research group detection for covid-19 exploratory scientific search. *arXiv preprint arXiv:2005.12668*.

Rob Johnson, Anthony Watkinson, and Michael Mabe. 2018. *The STM report*. International Association of Scientific, Technical and Medical Publishers.

Juyong Kim, Yookoon Park, Gunhee Kim, and Sung Ju Hwang. 2017. Splitnet: Learning to semantically split deep networks for parameter reduction and model parallelization. In *ICML*.

Parisa Kordjamshidi, D. Roth, and Marie-Francine Moens. 2015. Structured learning for spatial information extraction from biomedical text: bacteria biotopes. *BMC Bioinformatics*, 16.

Ying Lin, Heng Ji, Fei Huang, and Lingfei Wu. 2020. A joint neural model for information extraction with global features. In *Proceedings of the 58th Annual Meeting of the Association for Computational Linguistics*, pages 7999–8009.

Y. Liu, Yongjie Liang, and D. Wishart. 2015. Polysearch2: a significantly improved text-mining system for discovering associations between human diseases, genes, drugs, metabolites, toxins and more. *Nucleic Acids Research*, 43:W535 – W542.

David Mcdonald. 1992. An efficient chart-based algorithm for partial-parsing of unrestricted texts. In *Proceedings of the 3d Conference on Applied Natural Language Processing*, pages 193–200.

Daniele Mercatelli, Laura Scalambra, Luca Triboli, Forest Ray, and Federico M Giorgi. 2020. Gene regulatory network inference resources: A practical overview. *Biochimica et Biophysica Acta (BBA)-Gene Regulatory Mechanisms*, 1863(6):194430.

Walter Nelson, Marinka Zitnik, Bo Wang, Jure Leskovec, Anna Goldenberg, and Roded Sharan. 2019. To embed or not: network embedding as a paradigm in computational biology. *Frontiers in genetics*, 10:381.

Mark Neumann, Daniel King, Iz Beltagy, and Waleed Ammar. 2019. ScispaCy: Fast and Robust Models for Biomedical Natural Language Processing. In *Proceedings of the 18th BioNLP Workshop and Shared Task*, pages 319–327, Florence, Italy. Association for Computational Linguistics.

Sampo Pyysalo, Tomoko Ohta, and Sophia Ananiadou. 2013. Overview of the cancer genetics (cg) task of bionlp shared task 2013. In *BioNLP@ACL*.

Gustavo A Salazar, Ayton Meintjes, and Nicola Mulder. 2014. Ppi layouts: Biojs components for the display of protein-protein interactions. *F1000Research*, 3.

Marco A Valenzuela-Escárcega, Özgün Babur, Gus Hahn-Powell, Dane Bell, Thomas Hicks, Enrique Noriega-Atala, Xia Wang, Mihai Surdeanu, Emek Demir, and Clayton T Morrison. 2018. Large-scale automated machine reading discovers new cancer driving mechanisms. *Database: The Journal of Biological Databases and Curation*.

K. Verspoor, Simon vSuster, Yulia Otmakhova, Shevon Mendis, Zenan Zhai, Biaoyan Fang, Jey Han Lau, Timothy Baldwin, A. J. Yepes, and D. Martínez. 2020. Covid-see: Scientific evidence explorer for covid-19 related research. *ArXiv*, abs/2008.07880.

Lucy Lu Wang, Kyle Lo, Yoganand Chandrasekhar, Russell Reas, Jiangjiang Yang, Darrin Eide, Kathryn Funk, Rodney Michael Kinney, Ziyang Liu, William. Merrill, Paul Mooney, Dewey A. Murdick, Devvret Rishi, Jerry Sheehan, Zhihong Shen, Brandon Stilson, Alex D. Wade, Kuansan Wang, Christopher Wilhelm, Boya Xie, Douglas M. Raymond, Daniel S. Weld, Oren Etzioni, and Sebastian Kohlmeier. 2020. Cord-19: The covid-19 open research dataset. *ArXiv*.

Ryen W. White and Resa A. Roth. 2009. Exploratory search: Beyond the query-response paradigm. *Synthesis Lectures on Information Concepts, Retrieval, and Services*, 1:98.

A COVID-SemViz Overview

Figure 5 shows the various visualization techniques that have been applied in COVID-SemViz.

Technical Detail We store the processed hierarchical structured data as the JSON format, and store the generated COVID graph data into neo4j[14] database. The back-end text-based search functionality of COVID-SemViz is built using Elasticsearch[15], and the back-end graph-based retrieval is supported by querying neo4j database. The front-end visualizations are build using Kibana[16] and D3.js[17]. Kibana supports a collection of visualization types. It can be directly applied on the data that has been indexed for Elasticsearch. Elements built from Kibana can be arranged as desired and visualizations will be updated in real-time when a search is performed. It can also provide quick insights into subset of data and enable users to drill down into details through a few clicks. We think our hierarchical indexed data can largely benefit from these features for interaction. D3.js is a JavaScript library that can be used to build customized interactive visualizations. We primarily used it to build graph-based visualizations.

Navigation The navigation of a dashboard from COVID-SemViz is through clicking and searching. By clicking the functional type `CASP3 Activator` in the word cloud named "Regulatory Processes" (Figure 5), a constraint on the type and regulators of proteins is added. Correspondingly, all the other visualizations will be changed. For example, the "Subject Proteins" word will only contains protein entities that can activate CASP3; the "Evidence Sentences and PubMed URL" tabular form will display evidencing sentences that involve proteins that can activate CASP3 in the relations. The "Abstract Keyword - Journal Relations" heat map will form new color shade clusters based on the new set of articles that mentioned CASP3 or its regulators. One can also put a query into the search box to navigate the dashboard. Navigation through the Covid Graphs is similar. One can use searching and clicking to retrieve relevant sub-graphs and examine the context information of a node such as the relations it belongs to and its provenance. In addition, COVID-SemViz supports abstracting graphs by reducing nodes to functional types and expanding node neighbors that are specifically for graphs.

The Covid Causal Assertions Visualization The Covid Causal Assertions (CA) dashboard contains a set of visualizations that are designed to enable users to discover novel inferences of protein-protein interactions and associated context information. Users can type in a query to search for relevant CA and context information. We include several kinds of visualizations: (1) tabular forms for tracing evidence associated with relations, (2) indicator panes to display the count of evidences and of unique articles, (3) word clouds and heat maps for some metadata, (4) type-level and phrase-level visualizations that enable users to drill down into the elements in the relations, (5) dense visualizations for functional types, and (6) visualizations of upstream regulators. We now elaborate on the last three of these.

Type-level and phrase-level visualizations. Each CA contains three elements: protein-A, relation type, and protein-B. We group the 24 relation types into two "metatypes": `RegulateActivity` and `Modification`. Furthermore, protein-A and protein-B involved in RegulateActivity relations are categorized into `Subject` and `Object`. Protein-A and protein-B involved in Modification relations are categorized into `Enzyme` and `Substrate`. We believe this categorization allows our visualizations to conform to biological convention. On the dashboard, we create words clouds for these categories. We also create a subject-object interaction heat map to show regulatory relationships, an enzyme-substrate interaction heat map to show protein modification relationships, and heat maps for some common relation types such as `Activation` and `Inhibition`. Finally, we include word clouds for entity types extracted with the NER model.

Visualizations for functional types. We also enable the visualization of CAs by applying parameter reduction, which is a critical step in semantic visualization. Given two CA tuples *(Protein-A, Activation, Protein-B)* and *(Protein-B, Activation, Protein-C)*, we create the functional type *Protein-C-Activator* with members *Protein-A* and *Protein-B*. We now have a word cloud for all functional types (see Figure 6) and a separate word cloud for the subject proteins associated with them. Clicking one of the functional types restricts the subject pro-

[14] `https://neo4j.com/`

[15] `https://www.elastic.co/elasticsearch/`

[16] `https://www.elastic.co/kibana`

[17] `https://d3js.org/`

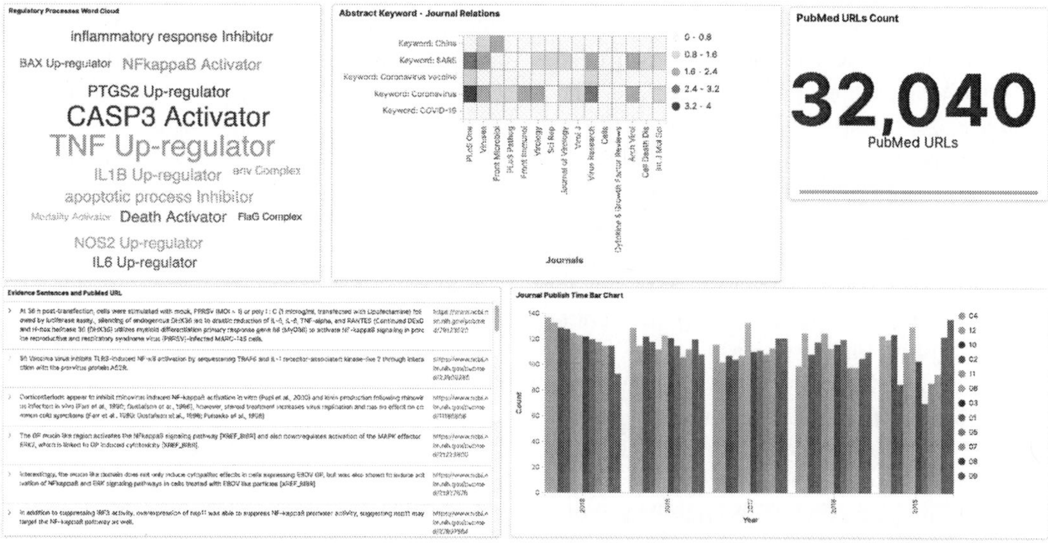

Figure 5: Visualization techniques from COVID-SEMVIZ. First row: (1) Word cloud of functional types as regulatory processes; (2) Heat map represents the relations between article keywords and journal names; (3) Indicator of total number of articles. Second row: (4) Tabular form of evidencing sentences and provenance URL; (5) Bar chart shows the number of articles that are published in each month from year 2015 to 2019.

Figure 6: Sample regulators.

teins to just the ones involved in the functional type selected.

Visualizations for upstream regulators. One advantage of parameter reduction is that it can represent higher order relations so that those relations can be easily visualized with word clouds and heat maps . In the Covid CA dashboard, We present two types of second order CAs: one that has the same relation type as the functional type, and one that has the opposite relation type. In the dashboard, we add the "Upstream Regulators" word cloud and the "Opposite Upstream Regulators" word cloud to display second order relations. For example, with a functional type *Interferon-Activator* the "Upstream Regulators" word cloud would include all proteins X that activate one of the Interferon activators, thereby generating a novel inference from *X* to *Interferon*. Through navigation over the keywords in each word cloud, one can easily check the evidencing sentences of deeper CAs that are inferred through parameter reduction.

Formally, if we have identified `Protein-2 Activator` and have the opposite relation pair `Activation` and `Inhibition` in our dataset, we are interested in a set of `X` that `X` activate `Protein-2 Activator` or inhibit `Protein-2 Activator`. Thereby we are able to generate novel inference from `X` to `Protein-2`. `X` is also called the second order containers in our case. We pair the opposite relation types in our dataset and leave the others unchanged that can only have the same second order relations.

The Covid KGs Visualization The Covid KG dashboard contains a collection of visualizations that enable the discovery of the relationships among genes, chemicals and diseases that are related to COVID-19. This includes chemical-gene, chemical-disease and gene-disease relations, which are supported by the evidencing sentences not only from COVID-19 articles but also from various other medical articles. Thus, the most challenging part in the visualization is to simplify and unify the complex relations while displaying the information in breadth and depth.

We start by making the connections between chemical-gene and gene-disease relations using the same gene entries that appear in both sides. Then we index the new chemical-gene-disease relations and visualize them via chemical-gene sub-relation heat map and gen-disease sub-relation heat map. These two heat maps are designed to be interactive with each other to show the full chemical-gene-disease triplet relations, as well as to be flexible enough to be controlled by enabling or disabling arguments of the triplet relations.

Similar to the Covid CA dashboard, we build a tabular form that displays evidencing sentences and PubMed URLs, as well as word clouds of chemicals, genes and diseases from the relations. Users can navigate the dashboard to find relevant context information by filtering on entities from the word clouds. we also create a word cloud of gene functional types by grounding chemical-gene relations. For example, given a chemical-gene tuple (D014013, Decrease Reaction, CASP3), the functional type `-CASP3 Regulator` is generated.

The Covid Graph Visualization Covid Graph dashboard contains two graph-based visualizations: the all-connected knowledge graph and protein pathways. Figure 7 shows the knowledge graph visualization. The main window shows a color-coded graph of predefined nodes such as proteins, evidence and PPIs. Nodes are connected by different relationships based on the labels of nodes. The sidebar on the right displays the information of clicked node. For example, if an evidence node is clicked, it shows the content of the evidence and the article URL that contains this evidencing sentence. An input box on the bottom takes a Cypher query and generates the corresponding graph. The knowledge graph enables the visualization of data of different granularity in one place. It can also be context-aware by dynamically generating neighbors of a right-clicked node.

Figure 8 shows the interface of protein pathways visualization. A variable-length pathway can be retrieved by specifying the starting and ending proteins as well as the number of hops. We also apply parameter reduction operations on sub-paths of the whole pathway, compressing the graph without any semantic information loss, and provides the clear and dense visualization over complex graph. Specifically, given a sub-path of length 3 (e.g. SP-[decreseAmount]→ACE2-[Activates]→COVID-19), it can be compressed into a binary relation containing a functional type and an entity (e.g. ACE2 down-regulator-[Activates]→COVID-19). Each functional type like "ACE2 downRegulator" represents a set that can contain any protein down-regulating ACE2.

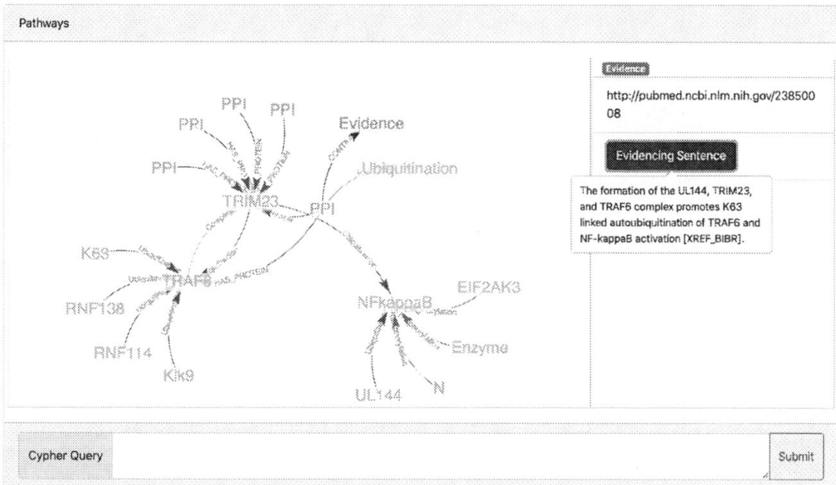

Figure 7: Interface of Covid knowledge graph visualization.

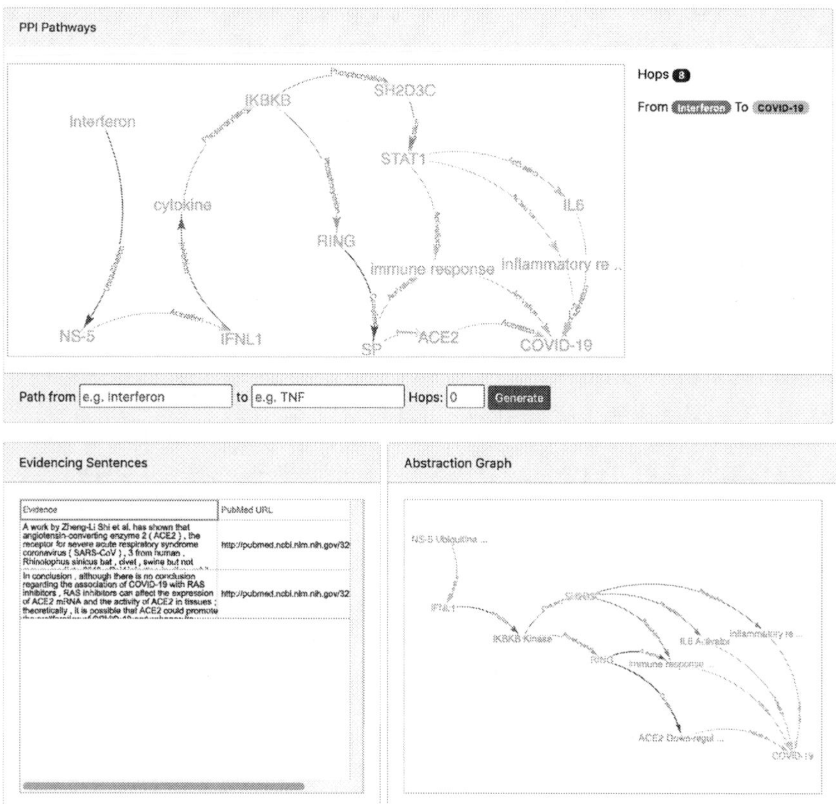

Figure 8: Interface of protein pathways visualization.

Shuffled-token Detection for Refining Pre-trained RoBERTa

Subhadarshi Panda
Graduate Center
CUNY
spanda@gc.cuny.edu

Anjali Agrawal
New York University
aa7513@nyu.edu

Jeewon Ha
New York University
jh6926@nyu.edu

Benjamin Bloch
New York University
bb1976@nyu.edu

Abstract

State-of-the-art transformer models have achieved robust performance on a variety of NLP tasks. Many of these approaches have employed domain agnostic pre-training tasks to train models that yield highly generalized sentence representations that can be fine-tuned for specific downstream tasks. We propose refining a pre-trained NLP model using the objective of detecting shuffled tokens. We use a sequential approach by starting with the pre-trained RoBERTa model and training it using our approach. Applying random shuffling strategy on the word-level, we found that our approach enables the RoBERTa model achieve better performance on 4 out of 7 GLUE tasks. Our results indicate that learning to detect shuffled tokens is a promising approach to learn more coherent sentence representations.[1]

1 Introduction

The method of pre-training natural language models has been shown to greatly improve model performance on a wide range of NLP tasks (Peters et al., 2018; Radford et al., 2018; Howard and Ruder, 2018). State-of-the-art models that utilize transformers and deep bi-directional representations of text such as BERT, RoBERTa, and ALBERT (Devlin et al., 2019; Liu et al., 2019; Lan et al., 2020) have achieved superior results by pre-training on general, large corpora to learn rich representations from unlabeled data. Particularly helpful in low training data resource scenarios, unsupervised pre-training has become the first step for many language models to build powerful linguistic representations before fine tuning for downstream target tasks.

BERT style models use masked language modeling (MLM) and sometimes next sentence prediction, as pre-training tasks. While these tasks have been shown to produce transferable sentence representations for many NLP tasks, using additional domain-agnostic pre-training tasks such as sentence shuffling may improve model performance. In a seminal cognitive psychology study it has been demonstrated that humans have a well trained ability to parse shuffled sentences (McCusker et al., 1981). Moreover, it has been shown that pre-trained models sometimes overlook word order while making predictions (Pham et al., 2020), and encouraging models to capture word order improves the classification performance. Shuffling as a pre-training task may therefore help expand transformer models to achieve even better performance on NLP tasks.

Drawing inspiration from recent work in reconstructing shuffled text (Lewis et al., 2020; Raffel et al., 2020), we propose that pre-training the RoBERTa model with a token modification discrimination head on randomly shuffled sentences provides constructive learning objective, which helps the model learn coherent representations and facilitate model recognition of the key pieces of a sentence and their association. To substantiate the argument, we design experiments to examine the model performance of RoBERTa with the proposed approach. The results demonstrate that pre-training the model with shuffled sentences enhances the scores of a majority of GLUE tasks.

2 Related Work

Shuffling sentences and words has often been used as a downstream task to evaluate model performance. One relevant example is the work by Sakaguchi et al. (2017) to develop a semi-character RNN model that surpasses previous spell-check methodologies on the *Cmadbrigde Uinervtisy* effect, where humans can easily reconstruct the shuffled token. Yang and Gao (2019) explored the performance of BERT on a shuffled sentence downstream task and highlighted some induced bias in the model that is the cause of incorrect predictions

[1]The code is available at `https://github.com/subhadarship/learning-to-unjumble`.

Proceedings of NAACL-HLT 2021: Student Research Workshop, pages 88–93

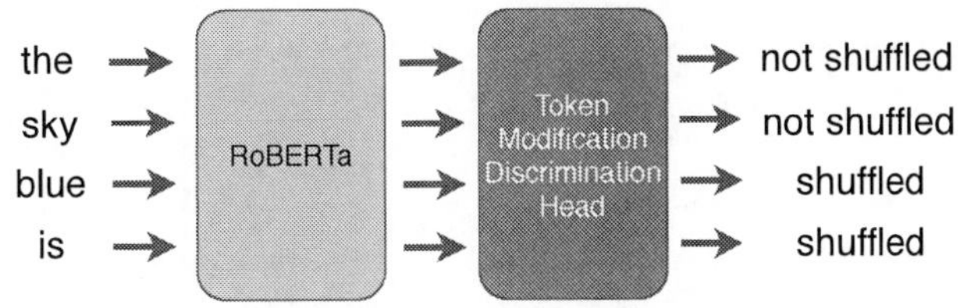

Figure 1: Illustration of our model for detecting shuffled tokens. The original sentence is "the sky is blue".

for noisy inputs. While the authors propose removing the induced bias from the representations to improve results, they do not consider the possibility of pre-training the model with shuffled sentences.

The use of un-ordered or noisy data in model training itself has proven effective. A number of studies have focused on using shuffled input to create useful sentence representation vectors for language models. Kiros et al. (2015) developed the skip-thoughts method to accomplish the task of reconstructing sentence order from a shuffled input. The authors used an encoder-decoder RNN model at the sentence level that allows a sentence to predict the adjacent sentences. Logeswaran et al. (2016) explored how sentence ordering tasks can help models learn text coherence. Using an RNN based approach, they train models to identify the correct ordering of sentences and show that models learn both document structure and useful sentence representations during this task. Jernite et al. (2017) employed discourse based learning objectives to help models understand discourse coherence. Specifically, given some sentences, they ask the model to predict if the sentences are in order, or if one sentence comes next to a set of sentences, or to predict the conjunction that joins the sentences. They showed that using these objectives to train models achieves significant reduction in computational training costs and is also effective when using unlabeled data.

There are a number of papers that focus on word-level shuffling, as opposed to sentence-level shuffling. Hill et al. (2016) developed the Sequential Denoising Autoencoder (SDAE) method, where a sentence is corrupted using a noise function determined by free parameters. After a certain percentage of words have been corrupted, an LSTM encoder-decoder model is tasked with predicting the original sentence from the corrupted version. The authors demonstrate training with noisy inputs allowed SDAE to significantly outperform regular SAE models, which did not introduce word-level-noise factors.

One closely related paper in the field of computer vision leverages the use of shuffled input in model training. Noroozi and Favaro (2016) employ a CNN model that is trained to solve jigsaw puzzles to determine correct spatial representation. Their results show that using shuffled input helps models learn that images are made up of different parts, and their relationship to the whole.

Finally, a variety of studies demonstrate that further pre-training performed after the general purpose BERT pre-training leads to better model results instead of simply fine-tuning downstream. Domain specific pre-training, such as BioBERT (Lee et al., 2019), story ending prediction by TransBERT (Li et al., 2019), and video caption classification by videoBERT (Sun et al., 2019) are all examples where expanding the pre-training tasks for BERT has achieved enhancement in model performance. TransBERT in particular demonstrates that further pre-training using targeted supervised tasks achieves better results than relying only on the unsupervised pre-training in BERT.

3 Methodology

Consider a sequence of tokens x. We first obtain x^{shuffled} from x by shuffling a set of tokens of x. Given x^{shuffled}, we detect if tokens are shuffled or not by using a token modification discrimination head on top of the RoBERTa base model. Our choice of the discriminative head is motivated by the recent success of ELECTRA (Clark et al., 2019).

3.1 Creating Shuffled Tokens for Training

We permute text sequences at the word level based on a probability p. We consider shuffling on a word level rather than a sub-word level. One straightforward approach to achieve is to create the shuffled tokens from a sequence and then use `RobertaTokenizer` to tokenize the shuffled sequence. However, this approach is problematic since the number of sub-words after tokenization

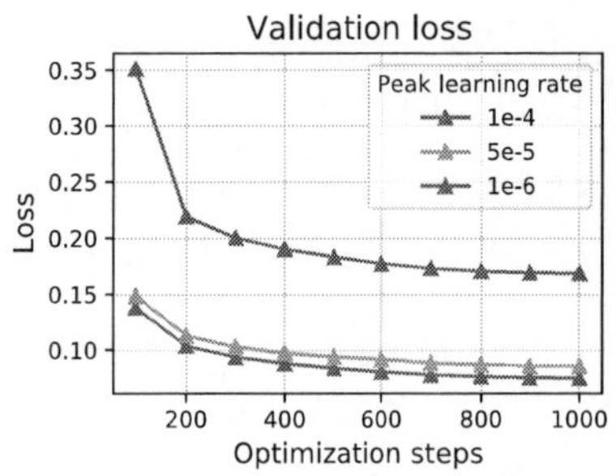

Figure 2: Validation loss as training progresses.

may differ between the original and the shuffled sentence. In order to ensure that the sub-words belonging to a word stay intact and are not shuffled away, we create a mapping, which maps each sub-word to the corresponding word. Then, we tokenize the original sequence and shuffle the tokens based on the mapping so that all the sub-words belonging to a word occur together. Further, we define the target tensor which has binary labels for each token that specifies whether the token was shuffled or not.

3.2 Shuffling Strategy

We randomly permute the words in a sequence based on a probability p for our experiments highlighted in Section 4. Note that fraction $\geq p$ of the input tokens would be shuffled since one or more input tokens (sub-words) belong to a single word.

3.3 RoBERTa Model with Token Modification Discrimination Head

Figure 1 shows an overview of our complete model. We use the RoBERTa model to map a sequence of input tokens $\boldsymbol{x}^{\text{shuffled}} = [x_1, \ldots, x_n]$ into a sequence of contexualized vectors $h(\boldsymbol{x}) = [h_1, \ldots, h_n]$. We add a token modification discriminator head to classify each hidden representation h_i to 0 (if the token at i-th place is not shuffled) or 1 (if the token at the i-th place is shuffled). Specifically, the head contains two linear layers with parameters $\{W_A\}$ and $\{W_B\}$. First, for every hidden vector h_i, we compute $h_i^{'} = \text{GELU}(W_A^T h_i)$ where the GELU activation function (Hendrycks and Gimpel, 2016) is used. Then, we compute the output of the model $D(\boldsymbol{x}^{\text{shuffled}}, i) = \sigma(W_B^T h_i^{'})$. During training, we minimize the sum of the binary cross entropy loss for every token.

$$\mathcal{L}(\boldsymbol{x}, \theta) = \mathbb{E}\Bigg(\sum_{i=1}^{n} -\mathbb{1}\Big(x_i^{\text{shuffled}} = x_i\Big) \log D\Big(\boldsymbol{x}^{\text{shuffled}}, i\Big) - \mathbb{1}\Big(x_i^{\text{shuffled}} \neq x_i\Big) \log\Big(1 - D(\boldsymbol{x}^{\text{shuffled}}, i)\Big)\Bigg)$$

4 Experiments

4.1 Baseline

As our baseline approach, we trained the RoBERTa base model with the token modification discrimination head for detecting masked tokens instead of detecting shuffled tokens. The baseline training was done for the same number of optimization steps as the proposed approach for a fair comparison.

4.2 Dataset for Shuffled-Token Detection

We extracted 133K articles from Wikidump.[2] We used each paragraph in the extracted text as a data sample for our model. We filtered out samples that were either spaces-only or had more than 512 tokens after tokenizing with the pretrained `RobertaTokenizer` of the `roberta-base` model. We finally randomly split the samples into 1.3M for training and 14K for validation.

Dataset for masked token detection We used the same Wikidump dataset for the baseline approach as well, where we continue training pretrained RoBERTa on the objective of detecting masked tokens.

4.3 Implementation

We built our model using HuggingFace transformers (Wolf et al., 2020). All experiments have been performed using the RoBERTa base model with the token modification discrimination head described in Section 3.3.

The hyperparameters used in our experiments follow the hyperparameters of the RoBERTa base model except for the warmup steps, batch size, peak learning rate, and the maximum training steps. For our experiments, we use 100 linear warmup steps followed by linear decay of the learning rate outlined in Figure 3.

To find the optimal peak learning rate and the maximum steps, we performed a hyperparameter search over the learning rates {1e-4, 5e-5, 1e-6}

[2]Timestamp May 9th, 2020. We used the scripts from `https://github.com/NVIDIA/DeepLearningExamples/tree/master/PyTorch/LanguageModeling/BERT#getting-the-data` to extract the data.

Task →	CoLA	SST-2	MRPC	STS-B	QNLI	RTE	WNLI
Metric →	Matthew's corr.	Accuracy	F1 score	Spearman corr	Accuracy	Accuracy	Accuracy
Plain pre-trained RoBERTa	0.557	0.946	0.901	**0.896**	**0.928**	0.661	0.423
Masked-token detection (Baseline)	0.508	**0.950**	0.869	0.888	0.924	0.631	**0.563**
Shuffled-token detection	**0.621**	0.92	**0.905**	0.886	**0.928**	**0.704**	0.437

Table 1: Results on GLUE tasks.

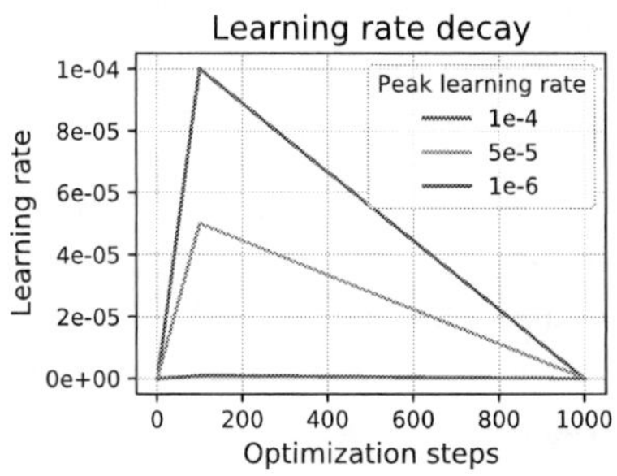

Figure 3: Learning rate as training progresses.

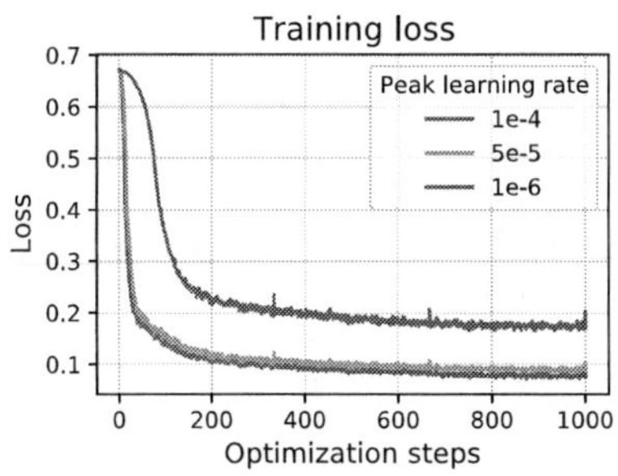

Figure 4: Training loss logged after every training step.

and over the maximum steps from [100, 1000] with a step size of 100. Changes in learning rate with the increase in optimization steps for different peak learning rates are shown in Figure 3. The results for the validation loss with an increasing number of optimization steps for the different learning rates is illustrated in Figure 2. The training loss is outlined in Figure 4. We observe that the minimum training loss, as well as validation loss, are achieved with the peak learning rate of 1e-4. Moreover, the training loss and the validation loss keep on decreasing with the number of optimization steps continuously till 1000 steps which shows that training the model for more number of steps could be beneficial. The optimal maximum steps as shown in Figure 4 and 2 is 1000.[3] For training our baseline approach of detecting mask tokens, we set the learning rate to 1e-4.

The probability of masking tokens (sub-words) in the baseline approach was fixed to 0.15 as done in previous work (Devlin et al., 2019; Liu et al., 2019). For the proposed approach, we also set the probability p of shuffling tokens (words) to 0.15.

On using large batch sizes Pre-training procedures have been shown to be effective when using large batch sizes (Liu et al., 2019). Training our model directly on a very large batch size required computation power beyond what was available. To alleviate this problem, we used gradient accumulation for 64 steps with a per GPU batch size of 16. We used distributed training on 4 Nvidia K80 GPUs to train our models. The effective batch size during training was 4096.

4.4 Downstream Evaluation

We evaluate our approach on 7 GLUE tasks using the metrics outlined in Table 1. We use the same set of hyperparameters for fine-tuning for downstream tasks for each approach for a fair comparison. Methods for comparison to our approach include (a) the baseline approach where the training objective is detecting masked tokens, and (b) the plain pre-trained RoBERTa base model. The values of hyperparameters used for GLUE fine-tuning are outlined in Table 2. The rest of the hyperparameters are set to default values.[4]

Hyperparameter	Value
Maximum Sequence Length	128
Batch Size	64
Learning Rate	2e-5
Number of epochs	3

Table 2: Hyperparameters for fine-tuning RoBERTa model.

4.5 Results and Analysis

Table 1 presents the results for the 7 GLUE tasks. Our model trained to detect randomly shuffled to-

[3] An actual optimum number of steps could be more than 1000 and training further would give us the best value for the maximum steps.

[4] The default hyperparameters are as in `https://github.com/huggingface/transformers/blob/v2.8.0/examples/run_glue.py`.

kens performs the best in 4 of the 7 downstream tasks, namely CoLA, MRPC, QNLI and RTE. The scores for the baseline, where the objective is to detect masked tokens, are interestingly sometimes worse than the plain pre-trained RoBERTa's scores. For example, the CoLA score using plain pre-trained RoBERTa is 0.557 whereas the score obtained by the baseline is 0.508.

The model performance based on the proposed approach on individual tasks gives us insights about what aspects of natural language our model improved in learning. Our model's performance on CoLA, which predicts grammatical correctness of a sentence, is better, indicating that the pre-training task may have enhanced the model's ability to learn grammatical information. Moreover, better performance on RTE, MRPC and QNLI shows that with the proposed approach, the model better understands the semantic relationships such as similarity and entailment.

However, random shuffling hurts the performance of the model on WNLI significantly in comparison to the baseline. This may be due to the fact that WNLI forms a pair of sentences by replacing the ambiguous pronouns with their referents. Since we are shuffling the words, it is likely that the nouns will be shuffled, resulting in misleading replacement of the ambiguous pronoun.

Our baseline model outperforms the shuffled-token detection approach on SST-2 task which predicts the sentiment polarity of the movie reviews. One possible explanation is that shuffling negations in presence of contrasting conjunctions can significantly change the sentiment associated with the sentence.[5]

5 Conclusion and Future Work

In this paper, we examine the performance of RoBERTa model with token modification discrimination head on detecting randomly shuffled tokens. We have demonstrated that detecting shuffled tokens is indeed a challenging yet advantageous task, which allows the model to learn coherent representations of the sentences. In this work, we start with pre-trained RoBERTa base model and train it further on the shuffled token detection task.

For future work, the model can be further explored by expanding the shuffling strategy. One possible strategy is part of speech (POS) shuffling, which randomly permutes specific POS tokens such as nouns or verbs. Instead of detecting shuffled tokens, another objective would be to predict the original positions of the shuffled tokens. Yet another objective that can be explored is combining our proposed loss with the masked language modeling loss. We would also like to study our approach when applied to other pre-trained models such as ALBERT and ELECTRA.

[5]For instance, consider the sentence "That movie was good but I did not watch it." A random shuffled sentence can be "The movie was not good but I did watch it."

Acknowledgments

We thank Sam Bowman for friendly discussions. We also thank the anonymous reviewers for the useful comments and suggestions.

References

Kevin Clark, Minh-Thang Luong, Quoc V Le, and Christopher D Manning. 2019. Electra: Pre-training text encoders as discriminators rather than generators. In *International Conference on Learning Representations*.

Jacob Devlin, Ming-Wei Chang, Kenton Lee, and Kristina Toutanova. 2019. BERT: Pre-training of deep bidirectional transformers for language understanding. In *Proceedings of the 2019 Conference of the North American Chapter of the Association for Computational Linguistics: Human Language Technologies, Volume 1 (Long and Short Papers)*, pages 4171–4186, Minneapolis, Minnesota. Association for Computational Linguistics.

Dan Hendrycks and Kevin Gimpel. 2016. Gaussian error linear units (gelus). *arXiv preprint arXiv:1606.08415*.

Felix Hill, Kyunghyun Cho, and Anna Korhonen. 2016. Learning distributed representations of sentences from unlabelled data. In *Proceedings of the 2016 Conference of the North American Chapter of the Association for Computational Linguistics: Human Language Technologies*, pages 1367–1377, San Diego, California. Association for Computational Linguistics.

Jeremy Howard and Sebastian Ruder. 2018. Universal language model fine-tuning for text classification. In *Proceedings of the 56th Annual Meeting of the Association for Computational Linguistics (Volume 1: Long Papers)*, pages 328–339, Melbourne, Australia. Association for Computational Linguistics.

Yacine Jernite, Samuel R. Bowman, and David A. Sontag. 2017. Discourse-based objectives for fast unsupervised sentence representation learning. *CoRR*, abs/1705.00557.

Ryan Kiros, Yukun Zhu, Russ R Salakhutdinov, Richard Zemel, Raquel Urtasun, Antonio Torralba, and Sanja Fidler. 2015. Skip-thought vectors. In C. Cortes, N. D. Lawrence, D. D. Lee, M. Sugiyama, and R. Garnett, editors, *Advances in Neural Information Processing Systems 28*, pages 3294–3302. Curran Associates, Inc.

Zhenzhong Lan, Mingda Chen, Sebastian Goodman, Kevin Gimpel, Piyush Sharma, and Radu Soricut. 2020. Albert: A lite bert for self-supervised learning of language representations. In *International Conference on Learning Representations*.

Jinhyuk Lee, Wonjin Yoon, Sungdong Kim, Donghyeon Kim, Sunkyu Kim, Chan Ho So, and Jaewoo Kang. 2019. BioBERT: a pre-trained biomedical language representation model for biomedical text mining. *Bioinformatics*, 36(4):1234–1240.

Mike Lewis, Yinhan Liu, Naman Goyal, Marjan Ghazvininejad, Abdelrahman Mohamed, Omer Levy, Veselin Stoyanov, and Luke Zettlemoyer. 2020. BART: Denoising sequence-to-sequence pre-training for natural language generation, translation, and comprehension. In *Proceedings of the 58th Annual Meeting of the Association for Computational Linguistics*, pages 7871–7880, Online. Association for Computational Linguistics.

Zhongyang Li, Xiao Ding, and Ting Liu. 2019. Story ending prediction by transferable bert. In *Proceedings of the Twenty-Eighth International Joint Conference on Artificial Intelligence, IJCAI-19*, pages 1800–1806. International Joint Conferences on Artificial Intelligence Organization.

Yinhan Liu, Myle Ott, Naman Goyal, Jingfei Du, Mandar Joshi, Danqi Chen, Omer Levy, Mike Lewis, Luke Zettlemoyer, and Veselin Stoyanov. 2019. Roberta: A robustly optimized BERT pretraining approach. *CoRR*, abs/1907.11692.

Lajanugen Logeswaran, Honglak Lee, and Dragomir R. Radev. 2016. Sentence ordering using recurrent neural networks. *CoRR*, abs/1611.02654.

Leo McCusker, Philip Gough, and Randolph Bias. 1981. Word recognition inside out and outside in. journal of experimental psychology: Human perception and performance. *7(3):538–551*.

Mehdi Noroozi and Paolo Favaro. 2016. Unsupervised learning of visual representations by solving jigsaw puzzles. In *Computer Vision – ECCV 2016*, pages 69–84, Cham. Springer International Publishing.

Matthew Peters, Mark Neumann, Mohit Iyyer, Matt Gardner, Christopher Clark, Kenton Lee, and Luke Zettlemoyer. 2018. Deep contextualized word representations. In *Proceedings of the 2018 Conference of the North American Chapter of the Association for Computational Linguistics: Human Language Technologies, Volume 1 (Long Papers)*, pages 2227–2237, New Orleans, Louisiana. Association for Computational Linguistics.

Thang M. Pham, Trung Bui, Long Mai, and Anh Nguyen. 2020. Out of order: How important is the sequential order of words in a sentence in natural language understanding tasks?

Alec Radford, Karthik Narasimhan, Tim Salimans, and Ilya Sutskever. 2018. Improving language understanding by generative pre-training.

Colin Raffel, Noam Shazeer, Adam Roberts, Katherine Lee, Sharan Narang, Michael Matena, Yanqi Zhou, Wei Li, and Peter J. Liu. 2020. Exploring the limits of transfer learning with a unified text-to-text transformer. *Journal of Machine Learning Research*, 21(140):1–67.

Keisuke Sakaguchi, Kevin Duh, Matt Post, and Benjamin Van Durme. 2017. Robsut wrod reocginiton via semi-character recurrent neural network. In *Proceedings of the Thirty-First AAAI Conference on Artificial Intelligence*, AAAI'17, page 3281–3287. AAAI Press.

Chen Sun, Austin Myers, Carl Vondrick, Kevin Murphy, and Cordelia Schmid. 2019. Videobert: A joint model for video and language representation learning. In *Proceedings of the IEEE/CVF International Conference on Computer Vision (ICCV)*.

Thomas Wolf, Lysandre Debut, Victor Sanh, Julien Chaumond, Clement Delangue, Anthony Moi, Pierric Cistac, Tim Rault, Rémi Louf, Morgan Funtowicz, Joe Davison, Sam Shleifer, Patrick von Platen, Clara Ma, Yacine Jernite, Julien Plu, Canwen Xu, Teven Le Scao, Sylvain Gugger, Mariama Drame, Quentin Lhoest, and Alexander M. Rush. 2020. Transformers: State-of-the-art natural language processing. In *Proceedings of the 2020 Conference on Empirical Methods in Natural Language Processing: System Demonstrations*, pages 38–45, Online. Association for Computational Linguistics.

Runzhe Yang and Zhongqiao Gao. 2019. Can machines read jmulbed senetcnes?

Morphology-Aware Meta-Embeddings for Tamil

Arjun Krishnan*
Princeton University
ak36@princeton.edu

Seyoon Ragavan*
Princeton University
sragavan@princeton.edu

Abstract

In this work, we explore generating morphologically enhanced word embeddings for Tamil, a highly agglutinative South Indian language with rich morphology that remains low-resource with regards to NLP tasks. We present here the first-ever word analogy dataset for Tamil, consisting of 4499 hand-curated word tetrads across 10 semantic and 13 morphological relation types. Using a rules-based morphological segmenter and meta-embedding techniques, we train meta-embeddings that outperform existing baselines by 16% on our analogy task and appear to mitigate a previously observed trade-off between semantic and morphological accuracy.

1 Introduction

Continuous-space word embedding methods such as word2vec (Mikolov et al., 2013) have proven to be very useful for a wide range of NLP tasks. However, it has been observed that representations that treat each word holistically face inherent limitations when working with morphologically rich languages, and methods have accordingly been designed to incorporate subword information (Cotterell and Schütze, 2015; Luong et al., 2013). Among these, the fastText embeddings remain one of the best-known (Bojanowski et al., 2017; Grave et al., 2018), using character n-grams to approximate word-internal structural features.

In this work, we focus on producing morphology-aware embeddings for Tamil, a Dravidian language with over 68 million speakers across India, Sri Lanka, Malaysia, and Singapore (Wikipedia, 2020). Tamil remains a low-resource language for NLP tasks despite its large speaker base, and traditional methods of evaluating word embeddings, for instance the word analogy task (Mikolov et al., 2013), are almost entirely lacking. Thus, to facilitate our work, we present here a novel, human-curated analogy dataset consisting of 4499 analogy tetrads.

With regard to morphology, Tamil is highly agglutinative, encoding grammatical features such as gender, number, and case in single words comprising large sequences of compounded morphemes. Approaches such as character n-grams that generically incorporate subword information may be too coarse when working with Tamil, due to short morpheme lengths paired with high similarity between morphemes and sandhi across morpheme boundaries. The high frequency of 'false morphemes' or character sequences resembling morphemes in non-productive situations compounds this further. In our work, we attempt to tailor embeddings to Tamil morphology with the incorporation of a rules-based morphological segmenter.

We present three primary contributions:

(1) We present the first-ever human-generated analogy dataset for Tamil, capturing both semantic and morphological analogies.

(2) We construct a set of novel word embeddings for Tamil that incorporates morphological segmentation and outperforms existing baselines trained on the same corpus.

(3) Finally, we show that meta-embedding methods used in conjunction with linear dimension reduction can mitigate previously observed trade-offs between capturing semantic and morphological/syntactic information in embeddings (Avraham and Goldberg, 2017; Qiu et al., 2014).

Our dataset, embeddings, and experiments are all publicly available with documentation at our GitHub repository.

2 Related Work

Explicit morphology in word representations. Explicit incorporation of morphology is limited

*Equal contribution.

Proceedings of NAACL-HLT 2021: Student Research Workshop, pages 94–111
June 6–11, 2021. ©2021 Association for Computational Linguistics

by the need for accurate morphological annotation – Luong et al. (2013) used a recursive neural network to combine learned representations of individual morphemes, using the toolkit Morfessor (Creutz and Lagus, 2007) for unsupervised morphological segmentation. Cotterell and Schütze (2015) utilized a hand-annotated, morphologically-labelled corpus to train embeddings to predict morphological tags and thereby encode morphology.

Morphology for low-resource languages. There has been some recent work focusing on morphological incorporation for low-resource agglutinative languages such as Turkish and Uyghur (Pan et al., 2020). Kumar et al. (2017) focused entirely on Dravidian languages, creating a corpus partially annotated for morphological segmentation and POS tagging.

Meta-embeddings. It has been observed that various methods of combining word embeddings into *meta-embeddings* can combine the strengths of individual embeddings to improve performance. Such methods include concatenation (Yin and Schütze, 2016), averaging or summing (Coates and Bollegala, 2018), and constructing a vector of complex numbers (Wittek et al., 2013).

Dimension reduction for word representations. Yin and Schütze (2016) also observed that PCA could reduce the dimension of meta-embeddings without significantly hurting performance. In a similar vein, Mu and Viswanath (2018) found that removing the top few principal components improved performance. Raunak et al. (2019) found that composing these two methods improved dimension reduction, often producing embeddings that even outperformed the original embeddings.

Tamil word embeddings. Tamil word embeddings remain a relatively under-explored space in the literature. The well-known fastText embeddings contain Tamil embeddings in both iterations (Bojanowski et al., 2017; Grave et al., 2018), and represent the state-of-the-art. Kumar et al. (2020) produced a range of embeddings using conventional methods on corpora they produced for 14 Indian languages including Tamil.

Word analogy datasets. The state-of-the-art word analogy dataset in English remains the Google analogy test set developed by Mikolov et al. (2013). Similar datasets have been produced for Spanish (Cardellino, 2016), Russian and Arabic (Abdou et al., 2018), and Chinese (Jin and Wu, 2012), among others. Hindi is the only South Asian language with a high-quality word analogy dataset to date (Grave et al., 2018), which incorporates particular forms of culturally-linked analogies such as kinship terms. In our work, we attempt to similarly capture language-specific analogies for Tamil.

3 Model

3.1 Atomization

Given that we are considering methods that decompose a word into either character n-grams or morphemes, we consider both of these as special cases of decomposing a word into constituent 'atoms', a process we call 'atomization'. An atomizer takes in a word w and outputs a sequence $S(w)$ of atoms. We detail the two main atomizers used in generating our models here:

(1) The first, henceforth called *character 5-grams*, follows the original fastText papers (Bojanowski et al., 2017; Grave et al., 2018), in which a word's atoms are its character 5-grams, as well as the entire word itself.

(2) In our second method, which we designate *morphemes + stem (1-3)-grams*, we modify a pre-existing Tamil stemmer [1] into a rules-based morphological segmenter using `sbl2py` [2]. The segmenter's role is to map each word to its stem and its sequence of morphemes. A word's atoms are then its stem, constituent morphemes, and character (1-3)-grams of the stem. We will closely examine the segmenter's behavior in section 3.4.

3.2 Training

Our setup slightly extends that of Bojanowski et al. (2017), allowing atoms produced by any atomization method to fulfil the role played by character n-grams in the original paper. The model's trainable parameters are the embeddings z_a for the individual atoms and the output vectors v'_w. Following Bojanowski et al. (2017), we sum the atom vectors to obtain the input vector for the word:

$$v_w = \sum_{a \in S(w)} z_a$$

[1] https://github.com/rdamodharan/tamil-stemmer
[2] https://github.com/torfsen/sbl2py

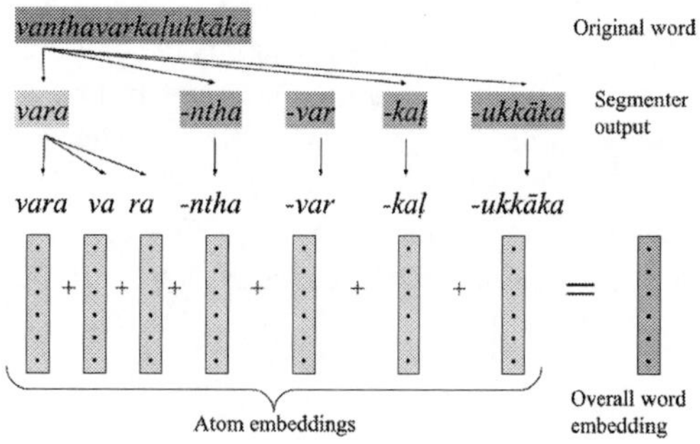

Figure 1: A visualization of a single word's embedding with morphemes + stem (1-3)-grams atomization. The segmenter breaks the word down into morphemes, which together with (1-3)-grams of the stem are our final atoms. The sum of the atom embeddings (which are updated throughout training) is the overall embedding.

The relationship between atom embeddings and the overall word embeddings in training are visualized in Figure 1. Each word has its own output vector that does not depend on the atoms. Using a large text corpus (in this case Wikipedia), we train these embeddings with the skip-gram objective and negative sampling applied to the input and output vectors v_w, v'_w as in (Mikolov et al., 2013).

3.3 Constructing meta-embeddings

Our key primitive for constructing meta-embeddings is a merging operation (Algorithm 1) that takes two separate sets of d-dimensional word embeddings as input and outputs another set of d-dimensional embeddings. It does this by concatenating the two sets of embeddings, then applying PCA to obtain the desired dimensionality. This procedure is visualized in Figure 2.

Algorithm 1: Merge(X_1, X_2)

Data: Embedding matrices
$X_1, X_2 \in \mathbb{R}^{n \times d}$
Result: A new meta-embedding $X \in \mathbb{R}^{n \times d}$
`// Rescale to norm 1`
$X_1 = \text{NormaliseToUnitNorm}(X_1)$;
$X_2 = \text{NormaliseToUnitNorm}(X_2)$;
`// Concatenate and apply PCA`
$X_{\text{concat}} = \text{Concat}(X_1, X_2) \in \mathbb{R}^{n \times 2d}$;
$X = \text{PCA}(X_{\text{concat}}, d)$;

With this, we define a procedure (Algorithm 2) to combine four sets of embeddings by merging them in pairs first then merging the two results.

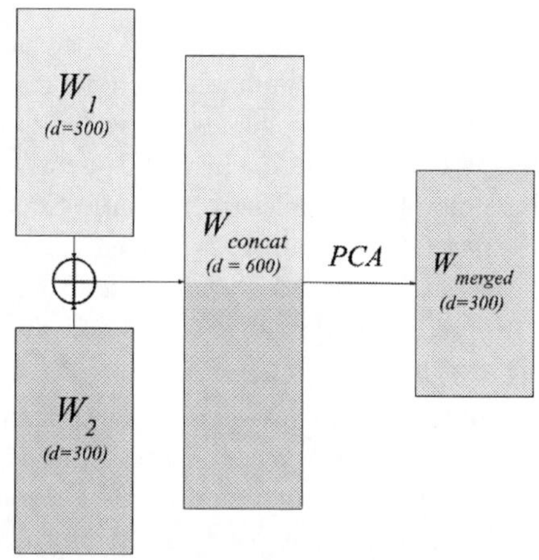

Figure 2: A visualization of the Merge procedure for obtaining a set of meta-embeddings from two separate sets of word embeddings. As detailed in algorithm 1, first the individual embeddings are concatenated and then dimension reduction via PCA is applied.

Algorithm 2: TripleMerge(X_i, X_o, Y_i, Y_o)

Data: Embedding matrices
$X_i, X_o, Y_i, Y_o \in \mathbb{R}^{n \times d}$
Result: A new meta-embedding $Z \in \mathbb{R}^{n \times d}$
$X_{\text{merged}} = \text{Merge}(X_i, X_o)$;
$Y_{\text{merged}} = \text{Merge}(Y_i, Y_o)$;
$Z = \text{Merge}(X_{\text{merged}}, Y_{\text{merged}})$;

Our final embeddings are defined as follows. We train one set of embeddings from the character 5-grams atomization. Hereby we refer to this model as "fastText" [3] and call its input and output embedding matrices FT_i, FT_o respectively. We then train another set of embeddings with the morphemes + stem (1-3)-grams atomization, which we refer to as "MorphoSeg". We label its input and output embedding matrices by MS_i, MS_o. Our final embeddings are the columns of the matrix $\text{TripleMerge}(\text{FT}_i, \text{FT}_o, \text{MS}_i, \text{MS}_o)$.

3.4 Analysis of rules-based segmenter

Here we discuss the strengths and weaknesses of the segmenter (introduced in section 3.1) as a core part of our methodology.

Strengths. We find that the segmenter performs well on and correctly identifies a wide range of

[3] This is similar but not identical to fastText, since we used another Wikipedia dump and used only character 5-grams and not (3-6)-grams due to computational constraints. However, we note that Grave et al. (2018) also changed the range from (3-6) to 5 and found it minimally impacted accuracy.

morphemes. In particular, it almost always correctly breaks down inflectional increments across morpheme boundaries, for instance with *marattai* 'tree(ACC)' $\longrightarrow$ *maram* 'tree' + *ai* (accusative suffix). Additionally, long agglutinative compounds are often broken up correctly, for instance *ezudappaṭukiṛadu* $\longrightarrow$ *ezuda* + *paṭu* + *kiṛa*+ *du*.

Weaknesses. However, we also find a number of distinct failure modes of the segmenter. We find undersegmentation of morphemes (e.g. inability to separate multiple stems in one word), oversegmentation of 'false' morphemes (in words that contain homophones of morphemes, e.g. *paccai* 'green' which happens to end in *ai*, the accusative suffix), ellision of certain morphemes, and difficulty with irregular forms. While it is beyond the scope of this paper to thoroughly analyze the segmenter, we anticipate that our gains on morphological tasks could be vastly improved with a better segmenter. More details are provided in our code.

4 Dataset

One of the primary contributions of this work is our novel Tamil analogy dataset, the first available for the language. The dataset is a hand-crafted set of 426 paired relations between words, and was produced by the authors. These word pairs are split into 10 semantic and 13 morphological relation types (see Appendix A). Analogy tetrads are then generated in a combinatorial fashion by combining pairs from the same class.

Given that Tamil is a low-resource language, automated construction of analogy dataset is relatively infeasible; lexicons rarely list fully inflected or complex morphological forms, and the use of a segmenter would subject the dataset to limitations similar to those discussed in section 3.4. As such, the decision to produce a human-curated analogy dataset was motivated by the desire to produce a gold-standard analogy task resource.

As a result of Tamil's morphological richness, even semantic relations often contain pairs with similar morphology. As such, we clustered word pairs within each relation type that shared identical morphology into labelled sub-classes. Analogies produced from morphologically identical pairs, along with analogies from morphological relations, were sorted into the **Subword** category of analogies, and semantic tetrads that were produced from morphologically non-identical pairs were placed in the **Non-subword** category.

Table 3 shows 4 examples of word tetrads for the semantic and morphological categories respectively, with two word pairs given per relation. The full dataset contains 4499 analogy tetrads, with 3487 analogy tetrads across 19 relation types in the **Subword** category and 1012 tetrads across 10 relation types in the **Non-subword** category. A complete list of relation types with examples (and numerical distributions across the full dataset, development, and test sets) can be found in Appendix A.

We note that our segmenter does not correctly identify all morphological relations. Therefore, MorphoSeg may not improve overall performance even in the subword category. However, we will see in Section 6 that it significantly improves performance on certain morphological relations, and that our final meta-embedding absorbs these strengths to substantially improve overall performance (across relations and categories).

5 Experimental setup

5.1 Training corpus and analogy task

We extracted [4] a corpus from the Tamil Wikipedia dump [5] (comprising 133732 articles) on April 20, 2020 and shuffled the sentences to obtain our final training corpus. A copy of the dump is available at our GitHub repository. We note that while Wikipedia may not capture the full range of Tamil inflectional morphology (having predominantly present/past tense and third-person conjugations), it captures rich derivational morphology that provides a good source of productive morphological diversity for our embeddings.

Our evaluation task measured performance on a word-analogy task performed by 'guessing' a missing word in our set of tetrads, which was computed by the gensim `most_similar` function (Řehůřek and Sojka, 2010). Correctness on each analogy tetrad was measured by top-k accuracy for each $k \in \{1, 5, 10\}$. From this, top-k accuracies were computed for each relation type. These accuracies were averaged within subword and non-subword categories, and overall model performance was measured by averaging the two figures. For brevity, we only present top-10 results here but we observe qualitatively similar behavior for top-1 and top-5 accuracy. Details are provided in Appendix C. We used a 75/25 dev/test split.

[4]https://github.com/attardi/wikiextractor

[5]https://dumps.wikimedia.org/

Type of relationship	Word Pair 1		Word Pair 2	
male- female	*āṇ* 'male'	*peṇ* 'female'	*rājā* 'king'	*rāṇi* 'queen'
profession- product	*kuyavar* 'potter'	*pānai* 'pot'	*necavāḷar* 'weaver'	*thuṇi* 'cloth'
animal- young	*nāi* 'dog'	*nāikkuṭṭi* 'dog-pup'	*pacu* 'cow'	*kanṛu* 'calf'
elder female kin- young male kin	*pāṭṭi* 'grandma'	*pēran* 'grandson'	*tāy* 'mother'	*makan* 'son'
nominative- accusative	*avan* 'he'	*avanai* 'him'	*kai* 'hand(nom)'	*kaiyai* 'hand(acc)'
adjective- adverb	*makizcciyāna* 'happy'	*makizcciyāka* 'happily'	*kopamāna* 'angry'	*kopamāka* 'angrily'
verb- for those who verb-ed	*vara* 'to come'	*vandavarkaḷukkāka* 'for those who came'	*pēca* 'to speak'	*pēciyavarkaḷukkāka* 'for those who spoke'
past- past completive COS	*keṭṭadu* 'it spoiled'	*keṭṭupōnadu* 'it spoiled'	*kuraindadu* 'it reduced'	*kuraindupōnadu* 'it reduced'

Figure 3: The table above shows four examples of tetrads from our **Non-Subword** analogy category, and four examples from our **Subword** category (in that vertical order). The table captures some of the variation inherent in Tamil verbal and noun forms even morphologically identical forms can vary in the way they append to a verbal/noun root (as in rows 7 and 8), and multiple morphemes often exist for a given meaning.

5.2 Implementation details

We used our training corpus to produce 300-dimensional embeddings. We based our training code on Tzu-Ray Su's PyTorch implementation of word2vec[6]. More hyperparameters are provided in Appendix B.

In our evaluation of our models, we were unable to utilize the full set of 4499 analogy tetrads, as many tetrads contained out-of-vocabulary (OOV) words due to the limitations of the Wikipedia training corpus. As our model was unable to did handle OOV tokens, we had to filter our dataset for applicable tetrads. After filtering for OOV tokens, there remained 1576 analogies (45.2%) across 13 relation types in the **Subword** category, and 794 analogies (78.5%) across 9 relation types in the **Non-subword** category.

We also trained a standard word2vec skip-gram model (Mikolov et al., 2013) as a baseline.

6 Results and Analysis

Results on the test set are shown in Figure 4. Our model was the strongest among those evaluated in both the subword and non-subword categories. First, we examine individual sets of word embeddings in section 6.1 and observe that they differ substantially in their success modes. In particular, we show that the incorporation of the morphological segmenter appears to significantly boost performance on certain morphological relations. Secondly, we turn to analyzing our meta-embeddings in section 6.2. Counterintuitively, we find that meta-embeddings in fact improve their performance when reduced to the same dimension as our original embeddings, seemingly combining the strengths of different representations.

6.1 Comparing individual models

'fastText, input' was the strongest individual model in both categories by a substantial margin. However, there are some relations in the dataset where it fell short and some of the other individual models performed better. As expected, 'MorphoSeg, input' was very effective on morphological relations that our segmenter correctly identified. More interestingly, both 'MorphoSeg, output' and 'fastText, output' performed better than 'fastText, input' across the kinship relations in the non-subword category. We hypothesize that kinship relations contain word pairs that rarely share subword information, so output vectors were more successful as they did not explicitly use subword-based atomization. Results on some such relations are shown in Figure 5.

[6]https://github.com/ray1007/pytorch-word2vec

Model	Subword	Non-subword	Average
Skip-gram, input	15.87	23.57	19.72
MS_i (MorphoSeg, input)	62.99	16.75	39.87
MS_o (MorphoSeg, output)	15.91	22.95	19.43
FT_i (fastText, input)	72.22	34.04	53.13
FT_o (fastText, output)	17.89	25.89	21.89
$\text{Concat}(MS_i, MS_o)^\dagger$	75.81	24.79	50.30
$\text{Merge}(MS_i, MS_o)$	83.07	29.99	56.53
$\text{Concat}(FT_i, FT_o)^\dagger$	72.69	42.68	57.68
$\text{Merge}(FT_i, FT_o)$	78.85	47.48	63.17
$\text{TripleMerge}(FT_i, FT_o, MS_i, MS_o)$	**90.24**	**48.52**	**69.38**

Figure 4: Top-10 accuracies of various models on our test set. The top row shows the standard skip-gram word2vec baseline. The next sub-table comprises the uncombined models arising from our atomization methods. The final sub-table consists of our final meta-embedding in the bottom row, as well as the intermediate meta-embeddings used to construct it (as described in algorithm 2). Models marked by † have 600 dimensions rather than 300 since they have only been concatenated.

Model	Nom-acc	Prof-prod	Kinship
MS_i	**80.15**	3.57	0.00
MS_o	20.59	17.86	17.86
FT_i	63.24	**35.71**	14.29
FT_o	21.32	25.00	**32.14**
TripleMerge	**88.97**	**64.29**	28.57

Figure 5: Top-10 accuracies of our four individual models and final meta-embeddings on a subset of relations. The final meta-embedding draws on complementary strengths of individual models to mitigate trade-offs between them.

This illustrates that the four individual embeddings had complementary success modes, suggesting the applicability of meta-embedding methods. Furthermore, the complementary strengths of models across relations appeared to occur along the lines of previously observed semantic-morphological trade-offs (Avraham and Goldberg, 2017), which warrants further investigation.

6.2 Improvements from meta-embeddings

The results highlight that both concatenation and PCA were highly effective in increasing performance. Each of $\text{Concat}(MS_i, MS_o)$ and $\text{Concat}(FT_i, FT_o)$ performed at least as well as each of their constituent individual models in both categories. Moreover, the PCA step (between Concat and Merge) consistently improved upon the Concat models by around 5% in both categories.

Examining the results of our final meta-embedding on each relation as in Figure 5 revealed that it drew on the complementary success modes of the individual models, thus mitigating the semantic-morphological trade-offs between them. In most relations, the meta-embedding performed at least as well as the best individual model, if not substantially better.

7 Conclusion and Future Work

In this paper, we investigated directly incorporating morphology into Tamil word embeddings using a morphological segmenter, following Bojanowski et al. (2017) in computing representations for subword units. We constructed a word analogy dataset for Tamil consisting of 13 types of morphological relations and 10 types of semantic relations to evaluate performance. We combine individual models to obtain more versatile meta-embeddings that seem to overcome previously observed trade-offs.

It remains for future work to investigate the performance of our techniques on OOV words, and the improvements better morphological segmentation might bring. Evaluating our embeddings on other tasks for Indian languages, such as Akhtar et al. (2017)'s Tamil word similarity dataset, remains an important direction, as does studying the importance of incorporating morphology for downstream tasks such as POS tagging and NMT (Kumar et al., 2020). Exploring the applicability of our pipeline of morphological segmentation and meta-embeddings to other morphology-rich languages is another avenue for future work.

References

Mostafa Abdou, Artur Kulmizev, and Vinit Ravishankar. 2018. Mgad: Multilingual generation of analogy datasets. In *Proceedings of the Eleventh International Conference on Language Resources and Evaluation (LREC 2018)*.

Syed Sarfaraz Akhtar, Arihant Gupta, Avijit Vajpayee, Arjit Srivastava, and Manish Shrivastava. 2017. Word similarity datasets for Indian languages: Annotation and baseline systems. In *Proceedings of the 11th Linguistic Annotation Workshop*, pages 91–94, Valencia, Spain. Association for Computational Linguistics.

Oded Avraham and Yoav Goldberg. 2017. The interplay of semantics and morphology in word embeddings. In *Proceedings of the 15th Conference of the European Chapter of the Association for Computational Linguistics: Volume 2, Short Papers*, pages 422–426, Valencia, Spain. Association for Computational Linguistics.

Piotr Bojanowski, Edouard Grave, Armand Joulin, and Tomas Mikolov. 2017. Enriching word vectors with subword information. *Transactions of the Association for Computational Linguistics*, 5:135–146.

Cristian Cardellino. 2016. Spanish billion words corpus and embeddings (march 2016). *URL http://crscardellino. me/SBWCE.*

Joshua Coates and Danushka Bollegala. 2018. Frustratingly easy meta-embedding – computing meta-embeddings by averaging source word embeddings. In *Proceedings of the 2018 Conference of the North American Chapter of the Association for Computational Linguistics: Human Language Technologies, Volume 2 (Short Papers)*, pages 194–198, New Orleans, Louisiana. Association for Computational Linguistics.

Ryan Cotterell and Hinrich Schütze. 2015. Morphological word-embeddings. In *Proceedings of the 2015 Conference of the North American Chapter of the Association for Computational Linguistics: Human Language Technologies*, pages 1287–1292, Denver, Colorado. Association for Computational Linguistics.

Mathias Creutz and Krista Lagus. 2007. Unsupervised models for morpheme segmentation and morphology learning. *ACM Transactions on Speech and Language Processing*, 4(1).

Edouard Grave, Piotr Bojanowski, Prakhar Gupta, Armand Joulin, and Tomas Mikolov. 2018. Learning word vectors for 157 languages. In *Proceedings of the Eleventh International Conference on Language Resources and Evaluation, LREC 2018, Miyazaki, Japan, May 7-12, 2018*. European Language Resources Association (ELRA).

Peng Jin and Yunfang Wu. 2012. Semeval-2012 task 4: evaluating chinese word similarity. In ** SEM 2012: The First Joint Conference on Lexical and Computational Semantics–Volume 1: Proceedings of the main conference and the shared task, and Volume 2: Proceedings of the Sixth International Workshop on Semantic Evaluation (SemEval 2012)*, pages 374–377.

Arun Kumar, Ryan Cotterell, Lluís Padró, and Antoni Oliver. 2017. Morphological analysis of the Dravidian language family. In *Proceedings of the 15th Conference of the European Chapter of the Association for Computational Linguistics: Volume 2, Short Papers*, pages 217–222, Valencia, Spain. Association for Computational Linguistics.

Saurav Kumar, Saunack Kumar, Diptesh Kanojia, and Pushpak Bhattacharyya. 2020. "a passage to India": Pre-trained word embeddings for Indian languages. In *Proceedings of the 1st Joint Workshop on Spoken Language Technologies for Under-resourced languages (SLTU) and Collaboration and Computing for Under-Resourced Languages (CCURL)*, pages 352–357, Marseille, France. European Language Resources association.

Thang Luong, Richard Socher, and Christopher Manning. 2013. Better word representations with recursive neural networks for morphology. In *Proceedings of the Seventeenth Conference on Computational Natural Language Learning*, pages 104–113, Sofia, Bulgaria. Association for Computational Linguistics.

Tomas Mikolov, Ilya Sutskever, Kai Chen, Greg S Corrado, and Jeff Dean. 2013. Distributed representations of words and phrases and their compositionality. In C. J. C. Burges, L. Bottou, M. Welling, Z. Ghahramani, and K. Q. Weinberger, editors, *Advances in Neural Information Processing Systems 26*, pages 3111–3119. Curran Associates, Inc.

Jiaqi Mu and Pramod Viswanath. 2018. All-but-the-top: Simple and effective postprocessing for word representations. In *6th International Conference on Learning Representations, ICLR 2018, Vancouver, BC, Canada, April 30 - May 3, 2018, Conference Track Proceedings*. OpenReview.net.

Yirong Pan, Xiao Li, Yating Yang, and Rui Dong. 2020. Morphological word segmentation on agglutinative languages for neural machine translation. *CoRR*, abs/2001.01589.

Siyu Qiu, Qing Cui, Jiang Bian, Bin Gao, and Tie-Yan Liu. 2014. Co-learning of word representations and morpheme representations. pages 141–150.

Vikas Raunak, Vivek Gupta, and Florian Metze. 2019. Effective dimensionality reduction for word embeddings. In *Proceedings of the 4th Workshop on Representation Learning for NLP, RepL4NLP@ACL 2019, Florence, Italy, August 2, 2019*, pages 235–243. Association for Computational Linguistics.

Radim Řehůřek and Petr Sojka. 2010. Software Framework for Topic Modelling with Large Corpora. In *Proceedings of the LREC 2010 Workshop on New Challenges for NLP Frameworks*, pages 45–50, Valletta, Malta. ELRA.

Wikipedia. 2020. Tamil language — Wikipedia, the free encyclopedia. [Online; accessed 12-May-2020].

Peter Wittek, Bevan Koopman, Guido Zuccon, and Sándor Darányi. 2013. Combining word semantics within complex hilbert space for information retrieval. In *Quantum Interaction - 7th International Conference, QI 2013, Leicester, UK, July 25-27, 2013. Selected Papers*, volume 8369 of *Lecture Notes in Computer Science*, pages 160–171. Springer.

Wenpeng Yin and Hinrich Schütze. 2016. Learning word meta-embeddings. In *Proceedings of the 54th Annual Meeting of the Association for Computational Linguistics (Volume 1: Long Papers)*, pages 1351–1360, Berlin, Germany. Association for Computational Linguistics.

A Dataset Details

In this section of the Appendix, we provide details of our word analogy dataset and its construction. Essentially, as mentioned in the main work, we present a set of 4499 word tetrads split across 10 semantic and 13 morphological categories.

A.1 Relation types

In our first section here, we provide examples of each relation type we generated words for, with illustrative examples provided in Tamil text, Roman transliteration, and translations. Tables 1 and 2 show semantic and morphological word pair categories respectively.

A.2 Distribution of pairs across relation types

In Tables 3 and 4, we show the numerical distribution of pairs across categories in the full dataset and the dataset used in the paper for evaluation after filtering of OOV tokens. We attempt to attain as even a spread as possible over analogy categories (and furnish a range of morphology over the language).

A.3 Distribution of tetrads across relation types

In Tables 5 and 6, we show the numerical distributions of analogy tetrads over our distinct relation types. We also provide here the final train/test split of our data to show that the relative distributions over relation types were largely maintained, and also seek to show the breakdown of analogies across relation types in the original, unfiltered dataset. We review here briefly the process by which analogy tetrads are constructed. Within our 10 semantic and 13 morphological relation types, we assign pairs with similar morphology to a class. Following this, word pairs are combinatorially paired to produce tetrads; pairs of the same class and the same relation type, that is, pairs that share identical/highly similar morphology get assigned to the **Subword** class of analogies, and tetrads consisting of two divergent pairs get assigned to the **Non-subword** class. The idea here is that we want to differentiate analogies that can be solved with use of subword information from those that cannot as such, we notate this in our results, and capture this distinction across our different relation types in Tables 5 and 6.

B Implementation Details

B.1 Atomization

There is a subtle difference between the n-grams we take of the entire word in the character 5-grams atomization and the n-grams we take of the stem in the morphemes + stem (1-3)-grams atomization. Specifically, Tamil is an abugida script, which means vowel values attached to consonants are expressed as a series of diacritics.

The original fastText paper and the character 5-grams method we implemented separate diacritics from their stem consonants since they are given distinct Unicode characters. However, for the morphemes + stem (1-3)-grams, we tried taking n-grams with and without separate diacritics and stems, and ultimately chose not to separate them. We used a smaller n-gram window of 1-3 to account for this.

B.2 Training Hyperparameters

We tabulate all hyperparameters in Table 7. These were mostly unchanged from the defaults used in Tzu-Ray Su's original GitHub repository. The only change was that we used 5 negative samples, following the original fastText setup (Bojanowski et al., 2017).

B.3 Alternative Dimension Reduction Methods

We briefly note that we tried incorporating the dimension reduction method proposed by Raunak et al. (2019), which combines removing the top few principal components of the embeddings with PCA. We found that this was less effective than simple PCA for our embeddings. We hypothesize that this was because our embeddings did not have disproportionately high top singular values, contrasting the observations made by Raunak et al. (2019) for the embeddings that they considered.

C Detailed Results

This section expands on the results presented in the body of this paper in two ways: we show top-k results for each $k \in \{1, 5, 10\}$, and we show these results for each individual relation in our dataset.

We note that we attempted to compare our models against other existing baselines trained on slightly different corpora such as those released by Kumar et al. (2020). However, due to the different corpora, these models had additional OOV tokens in our analogy dataset that we would have had to remove to evaluate them together with our models. Running methods such as ours alongside many standard baselines on a fixed corpus and comparing the resulting models is an important area for future work.

C.1 Results in subword categories

Results for top-1, top-5, and top-10 accuracies are shown in Tables 8, 9, and 10 respectively. Categories are numbered according to the numbering convention established in Tables 1 and 2.

The TripleMerged model (our final set of meta-embeddings) generally outperforms all other models in these categories by margins of $\approx 10\%$, although this is not uniformly true across all categories. This is to be expected since this is the only meta-embedding incorporating both the FT_i and MS_i embeddings, which are the two individual embeddings that incorporate subword information. This explanation is also supported by the strong performances of these two individual embeddings in the Subword categories.

C.2 Results in non-subword categories

Results for top-1, top-5, and top-10 accuracies are shown in Tables 11, 12, and 13 respectively. The strongest performing models here are TripleMerged, $\text{FT}_{\text{concat}}$, and $\text{FT}_{\text{merged}}$. While TripleMerged generally outperforms $\text{FT}_{\text{concat}}$, $\text{FT}_{\text{merged}}$ is in general slightly better than TripleMerged in these categories. This is once again to be expected since the FT_i and FT_o models are the best-performing individual embeddings in the Non-subword categories. Still, it is remarkable that TripleMerged is only slightly worse in general than $\text{FT}_{\text{merged}}$, given that it was the result of merging $\text{FT}_{\text{merged}}$ with $\text{MS}_{\text{merged}}$, which was significantly weaker in the Non-subword categories.

C.3 Overall results

Overall results averaged across categories are shown in Table 14. TripleMerged exhibits the strongest performance overall, compensating for its slight weakness in the Non-subword category with significant improvements in the Subword category on all other models.

No.	Category	Example	Transliteration	Meaning
0	male-female	ராஜா ராணி	*rājā rāṇi*	'king/queen'
1	me-my	அவன் அவனுடைய	*avan avanuḍaiya*	'he/his'
2	profession-product	நெசவாளர் துணி	*necavāḷar thuṇi*	'weaver/cloth'
3	fruit_A-tree_A	கொய்யா கொய்யாமரம்	*koyyā koyyāmaram*	'guava/guava-tree'
4	verb_form-noun_form	யோசிக்க யோசனை	*yōcikka yōcanai*	'to think/thought'
5	animal-young	மாடு கன்று	*pacu kanṛu*	'cow/calf'
6	kin_elder-kin_young[1]	மாமா மருமகன்	*māmā marumakan*	'maternal uncle/nephew'
7	kin_elder-kin_young[2]	தந்தை மகள்	*thanthai makaḷ*	'father/daughter'
8	kin_elder-kin_young[3]	பாட்டி பேரன்	*pāṭṭi pēran*	'grandmother/grandson'
9	positive-negative	வெற்றி தோல்வி	*veṛṛi thōlvi*	'victory/loss'

Table 1: This table shows our numbered relation types for semantic word pairs, consisting of 10 types. We provide Tamil text, transliteration, and translations.

No.	Category	Example	Transliteration	Meaning
10	nom-acc	அவன் அவனை	*avan avanai*	'he/him'
11	nom-dat	அவள் அவளுக்கு	*avaḷ avaḷukku*	'she/to her'
12	adjective-adverb	மகிழ்ச்சியான மகிழ்ச்சியாக	*makizcciyāna makizcciyāka*	'happy/happily'
13	verb-past_respect	பறக்க பறந்தார்	*paṛakka paṛanthār*	'fly/they flew'
14	past-past_cmp1_inan	மாறியது மாறிபோனது	*māṛiyathu māṛipōnathu*	'changed/changed(completive)'
15	verb-verb_doer_dat	பார்க்க பார்த்தவர்களுக்காக	*pr̄kka pr̄tthavarkaḷukkāka*	'to see/for the sake of those who saw'
16	past-past_cmp2_male	பண்ணான் பண்ணிவிட்டான்	*paṇṇān paṇṇiviṭṭān*	'he did/he did(completive)'
17	past-past_cmp2_female	பண்ணாள் பண்ணிவிட்டாள்	*paṇṇāḷ paṇṇiviṭṭāḷ*	'she did/he did(completive)'
18	male_past-female_past	பண்ணான் பண்ணாள்	*paṇṇān paṇṇāḷ*	'he did/she did'
19	verb-doer_female	பாட பாடியவள்		'to sing/the female who sang'
20	verb-doer_male	பாட பாடியவன்	*pāṭa pāṭiyavan*	'to sing/the male who sang'
21	verb-passive_pl_inan	காண காணப்பட்டன	*kāṇa kāṇappaṭṭana*	'to see/they were seen'
22	verb-past_inan	சொல்ல சொன்னது	*colla connadu*	'to say/that which was said'

Table 2: This table shows our numbered relation types for morphological word pairs, consisting of 13 types. We provide Tamil text, transliteration, and translations.

Dataset	Semantic relation type										Total
	0	1	2	3	4	5	6	7	8	9	
Full dataset	29	30	9	9	23	5	8	4	4	24	145
OOV Removed	22	30	8	6	22	5	8	4	4	22	131

Table 3: Numerical distribution of analogy pairs across the different semantic relation types (see Figure for individual relation type meanings/examples

Dataset	Morphological relation type													Total
	10	11	12	13	14	15	16	17	18	19	20	21	22	
Full dataset	19	19	22	30	22	15	20	20	30	19	19	23	23	281
OOV Removed	17	19	20	27	0	0	0	1	10	0	1	16	17	128

Table 4: Numerical distribution of analogy pairs across the different morphological relation types (see Figure for individual relation type meanings/examples

Dataset		Semantic relation type										Total
		0	1	2	3	4	5	6	7	8	9	
Full dataset	Subword	43	354	1	12	62	3	0	0	0	5	480
	Non-subword	363	81	35	24	191	7	28	6	6	271	1012
Development set	Subword	5	265	0	4	39	2	0	0	0	3	318
	Non-subword	168	60	21	6	134	5	21	4	4	169	592
Test set	Subword	2	89	0	2	13	1	0	0	0	2	109
	Non-subword	56	21	7	3	45	2	7	2	2	57	202

Table 5: Numerical distribution of analogy tetrads across the different semantic relation types (see Figure for individual relation type meanings/examples

Dataset		Morphological relation type													Total
		10	11	12	13	14	15	16	17	18	19	20	21	22	
Full dataset	Subword	171	171	231	435	231	105	190	190	435	171	171	253	253	3007
Development set	Subword	102	128	142	263	0	0	0	0	33	0	0	90	102	860
Test set	Subword	34	43	48	88	0	0	0	0	12	0	0	30	34	289

Table 6: Numerical distribution of analogy tetrads across the different morphological relation types (see Figure for individual relation type meanings/examples

Epochs	Initial LR	LR schedule	Momentum	Batch size	Context window	Negative samples
5	0.025	Linear annealing	0.0	100	5	5

Table 7: Training hyperparameters that we used.

Model	sub_0	sub_1	sub_3	sub_4	sub_5	sub_9	sub_10	sub_11	sub_12	sub_13	sub_18	sub_21	sub_22	sub_mean
skipgram_input	12.50	12.36	0.00	1.92	0.00	0.00	13.97	12.79	14.06	6.25	2.08	1.67	3.68	6.25
MS_input	0.00	**71.07**	**50.00**	19.23	25.00	12.50	32.35	37.79	58.33	21.31	22.92	30.00	20.59	30.85
MS_output	37.50	11.52	0.00	0.00	0.00	0.00	8.82	12.79	9.38	5.97	0.00	2.50	0.74	6.86
FT_input	25.00	6.18	25.00	30.77	50.00	25.00	11.76	17.44	48.44	22.44	85.42	**74.17**	8.09	33.05
FT_output	25.00	14.04	0.00	0.00	25.00	0.00	10.29	11.63	6.77	6.82	2.08	4.17	4.41	8.48
MS_concat	12.50	53.09	12.50	7.69	0.00	25.00	36.76	38.37	66.15	32.67	25.00	30.83	25.74	28.18
MS_merged	25.00	64.61	0.00	9.62	50.00	37.50	**54.41**	49.42	76.56	41.19	31.25	47.50	38.24	40.41
FT_concat	**50.00**	28.37	12.50	21.15	0.00	37.50	19.85	23.84	47.40	25.57	**89.58**	60.00	8.09	32.60
FT_merged	**50.00**	28.09	12.50	30.77	25.00	**87.50**	22.79	34.30	60.42	32.95	**89.58**	69.17	17.65	43.13
TripleMerged	**50.00**	62.36	0.00	**32.69**	**75.00**	62.50	44.85	**52.91**	**80.73**	**57.95**	66.67	72.50	**58.09**	**55.10**

Table 8: Detailed per-category top-1 accuracies in the Subword category for all models we considered.

Model	sub_0	sub_1	sub_3	sub_4	sub_5	sub_9	sub_10	sub_11	sub_12	sub_13	sub_18	sub_21	sub_22	sub_mean
skipgram_input	12.50	28.37	0.00	5.77	0.00	0.00	27.21	24.42	22.92	16.19	6.25	5.00	11.03	12.28
MS_input	25.00	80.90	**62.50**	53.85	25.00	37.50	64.71	58.72	96.88	44.60	54.17	55.83	58.82	55.27
MS_output	37.50	21.63	0.00	0.00	0.00	0.00	18.38	25.58	15.62	14.77	2.08	3.33	5.15	11.08
FT_input	**75.00**	37.08	**62.50**	46.15	75.00	**87.50**	35.29	44.19	84.38	43.47	**97.92**	83.33	22.79	61.12
FT_output	37.50	31.18	0.00	1.92	25.00	12.50	19.12	25.00	12.50	12.22	10.42	5.83	5.88	15.31
MS_concat	62.50	80.06	50.00	44.23	75.00	25.00	69.85	62.79	92.71	61.36	50.00	65.00	60.29	61.45
MS_merged	62.50	83.43	50.00	63.46	75.00	75.00	77.21	68.02	96.88	70.17	50.00	83.33	70.59	71.20
FT_concat	62.50	58.99	25.00	38.46	**100.00**	**87.50**	49.26	54.65	80.73	53.98	**97.92**	80.83	26.47	62.79
FT_merged	**75.00**	62.64	37.50	50.00	**100.00**	**87.50**	54.41	61.05	92.71	64.77	**97.92**	90.00	52.94	71.26
TripleMerged	**75.00**	**87.08**	50.00	**75.00**	**100.00**	62.50	**81.62**	**74.42**	**98.44**	**87.22**	85.42	**95.83**	**80.88**	**81.03**

Table 9: Detailed per-category top-5 accuracies in the Subword category for all models we considered.

Model	sub_0	sub_1	sub_3	sub_4	sub_5	sub_9	sub_10	sub_11	sub_12	sub_13	sub_18	sub_21	sub_22	sub_mean
skipgram_input	12.50	35.39	0.00	7.69	0.00	12.50	32.35	30.23	25.52	21.31	8.33	5.00	15.44	15.87
MS_input	37.50	85.67	62.50	61.54	25.00	50.00	80.15	70.35	97.92	51.70	56.25	74.17	66.18	62.99
MS_output	37.50	27.25	0.00	1.92	25.00	12.50	20.59	30.23	19.79	18.47	2.08	4.17	7.35	15.91
FT_input	75.00	61.80	**75.00**	51.92	75.00	**100.00**	63.24	58.14	95.31	58.52	**97.92**	85.83	41.18	72.22
FT_output	37.50	37.36	0.00	3.85	25.00	12.50	21.32	28.49	17.71	17.61	12.50	9.17	9.56	17.89
MS_concat	75.00	85.39	**75.00**	67.31	75.00	75.00	82.35	75.58	98.44	75.85	56.25	76.67	67.65	75.81
MS_merged	**87.50**	87.92	62.50	76.92	**100.00**	75.00	**88.97**	**81.98**	99.48	85.23	56.25	95.83	82.35	83.07
FT_concat	62.50	69.38	50.00	46.15	**100.00**	87.50	62.50	66.86	95.31	66.48	**97.92**	86.67	53.68	72.69
FT_merged	**87.50**	75.56	37.50	59.62	**100.00**	87.50	72.79	69.19	98.44	74.43	**97.92**	93.33	71.32	78.85
TripleMerged	**87.50**	**91.29**	**75.00**	**88.46**	**100.00**	87.50	**88.97**	79.65	**100.00**	**92.05**	91.67	**99.17**	**91.91**	**90.24**

Table 10: Detailed per-category top-10 accuracies in the Subword category for all models we considered.

Model	nonsub_0	nonsub_1	nonsub_2	nonsub_3	nonsub_4	nonsub_5	nonsub_6	nonsub_7	nonsub_8	nonsub_9	nonsub_mean
skipgram_input	25.00	7.14	14.29	0.00	1.67	0.00	**14.29**	0.00	0.00	10.09	7.25
MS_input	0.00	25.00	3.57	**8.33**	2.78	0.00	0.00	0.00	0.00	0.00	3.97
MS_output	26.34	10.71	7.14	0.00	1.11	0.00	7.14	0.00	25.00	10.53	8.80
FT_input	12.95	2.38	0.00	**8.33**	8.33	0.00	0.00	**12.50**	12.50	9.65	6.66
FT_output	24.55	11.90	3.57	0.00	2.22	0.00	7.14	0.00	25.00	10.09	8.45
MS_concat	12.50	30.95	7.14	0.00	6.67	0.00	0.00	0.00	0.00	7.89	6.52
MS_merged	13.84	34.52	10.71	0.00	11.11	12.50	0.00	0.00	0.00	8.33	9.10
FT_concat	30.80	9.52	14.29	0.00	7.22	12.50	7.14	0.00	**37.50**	14.47	13.35
FT_merged	**33.93**	9.52	**28.57**	0.00	11.11	12.50	7.14	**12.50**	**37.50**	**20.61**	**17.34**
TripleMerged	21.88	**36.90**	25.00	0.00	**19.44**	**25.00**	3.57	**12.50**	0.00	17.11	16.14

Table 11: Detailed per-category top-1 accuracies in the Non-subword category for all models we considered.

Model	nonsub_0	nonsub_1	nonsub_2	nonsub_3	nonsub_4	nonsub_5	nonsub_6	nonsub_7	nonsub_8	nonsub_9	nonsub_mean
skipgram_input	35.71	27.38	17.86	0.00	3.89	0.00	21.43	25.00	37.50	16.23	18.50
MS_input	4.02	64.29	3.57	16.67	16.67	12.50	0.00	0.00	0.00	2.63	12.03
MS_output	34.82	20.24	14.29	0.00	3.33	0.00	7.14	25.00	**50.00**	12.72	16.75
FT_input	28.12	13.10	28.57	**33.33**	23.33	**25.00**	0.00	12.50	37.50	18.86	22.03
FT_output	35.71	33.33	14.29	0.00	8.33	12.50	**28.57**	25.00	37.50	13.60	20.88
MS_concat	22.77	72.62	14.29	8.33	20.56	12.50	0.00	0.00	12.50	14.91	17.85
MS_merged	23.66	**77.38**	17.86	8.33	30.00	**25.00**	3.57	12.50	12.50	18.86	22.97
FT_concat	45.09	35.71	35.71	25.00	21.11	**25.00**	25.00	37.50	**50.00**	28.07	32.82
FT_merged	**46.43**	38.10	**53.57**	25.00	27.22	**25.00**	21.43	**50.00**	**50.00**	**30.26**	**36.70**
TripleMerged	41.52	75.00	**53.57**	0.00	**39.44**	**25.00**	21.43	37.50	25.00	26.75	34.52

Table 12: Detailed per-category top-5 accuracies in the Non-subword category for all models we considered.

Model	nonsub_0	nonsub_1	nonsub_2	nonsub_3	nonsub_4	nonsub_5	nonsub_6	nonsub_7	nonsub_8	nonsub_9	nonsub_mean
skipgram_input	43.30	40.48	25.00	0.00	4.44	0.00	28.57	37.50	37.50	18.86	23.57
MS_input	7.59	82.14	3.57	25.00	30.56	12.50	0.00	0.00	0.00	6.14	16.75
MS_output	40.62	34.52	17.86	0.00	5.00	12.50	17.86	25.00	**62.50**	13.60	22.95
FT_input	40.62	39.29	35.71	**41.67**	27.78	**50.00**	14.29	25.00	37.50	28.51	34.04
FT_output	37.95	38.10	25.00	0.00	11.67	12.50	32.14	37.50	50.00	14.04	25.89
MS_concat	30.36	86.90	17.86	16.67	36.67	12.50	3.57	12.50	12.50	18.42	24.79
MS_merged	32.59	90.48	39.29	8.33	42.22	25.00	10.71	12.50	12.50	26.32	29.99
FT_concat	50.00	46.43	46.43	**41.67**	29.44	25.00	32.14	**75.00**	50.00	30.70	42.68
FT_merged	**56.25**	50.00	57.14	33.33	41.67	25.00	**39.29**	**75.00**	**62.50**	**34.65**	47.48
TripleMerged	51.34	**91.67**	**64.29**	25.00	**52.22**	**50.00**	28.57	62.50	25.00	**34.65**	**48.52**

Table 13: Detailed per-category top-10 accuracies in the Non-subword category for all models we considered.

Model	Top-1			Top-5			Top-10		
	Subword	Non-subword	Overall	Subword	Non-subword	Overall	Subword	Non-subword	Overall
skipgram_input	6.25	7.25	6.75	12.28	18.50	15.39	15.87	23.57	19.72
MS_input	30.85	3.97	17.41	55.27	12.03	33.65	62.99	16.75	39.87
MS_output	6.86	8.80	7.83	11.08	16.75	13.92	15.91	22.95	19.43
FT_input	33.05	6.66	19.86	61.12	22.03	41.58	72.22	34.04	53.13
FT_output	8.48	8.45	8.46	15.31	20.88	18.10	17.89	25.89	21.89
MS_concat	28.18	6.52	17.35	61.45	17.85	39.65	75.81	24.79	50.30
MS_merged	40.41	9.10	24.75	71.20	22.97	47.08	83.07	29.99	56.53
FT_concat	32.60	13.35	22.97	62.79	32.82	47.81	72.69	42.68	57.68
FT_merged	43.13	**17.34**	30.24	71.26	**36.70**	53.98	78.85	47.48	63.17
TripleMerged	**55.10**	16.14	**35.62**	**81.03**	34.52	**57.78**	**90.24**	**48.52**	**69.38**

Table 14: Average top-1, top-5, and top-10 accuracies for all models in the Sub-word and Non-subword categories, as well as overall accuracies (taken to be the average of Sub-word and Non-subword scores).

Seed Word Selection for Weakly-Supervised Text Classification with Unsupervised Error Estimation

Yiping Jin[1,2], **Akshay Bhatia**[2], **Dittaya Wanvarie**[1]
[1]Department of Mathematics & Computer Science, Chulalongkorn University, Thailand
[2]Knorex, 140 Robinson Road, 14-16 Crown @ Robinson, Singapore
{jinyiping, akshay.bhatia}@knorex.com
Dittaya.W@chula.ac.th

Abstract

Weakly-supervised text classification aims to induce text classifiers from only a few user-provided seed words. The vast majority of previous work assumes high-quality seed words are given. However, the expert-annotated seed words are sometimes non-trivial to come up with. Furthermore, in the weakly-supervised learning setting, we do not have any labeled document to measure the seed words' efficacy, making the seed word selection process "a walk in the dark". In this work, we remove the need for expert-curated seed words by first mining (noisy) candidate seed words associated with the category names. We then train interim models with individual candidate seed words. Lastly, we estimate the interim models' error rate in an unsupervised manner. The seed words that yield the lowest estimated error rates are added to the final seed word set. A comprehensive evaluation of six binary classification tasks on four popular datasets demonstrates that the proposed method outperforms a baseline using only category name seed words and obtained comparable performance as a counterpart using expert-annotated seed words [1].

1 Introduction

Weakly-supervised text classification eliminates the need for any labeled document and induces classifiers with only a handful of carefully chosen seed words. However, some researchers pointed out that the choice of seed words has a significant impact on the performance of weakly-supervised models (Li et al., 2018; Jin et al., 2020). The vast majority of previous work assumed high-quality seed words are given. However, many seed words reported in previous work are not intuitive to come up with. For example, in Meng et al. (2019), the seed words used for the category "Soccer" are {cup, champions, united} instead of more intuitive keywords like "soccer" or "football". We conjecture the authors might have tried these more general keywords but avoided them because they do not perform well.

While it is common to use labeled corpora to evaluate weakly-supervised text classifiers in the literature, we do not have access to any labeled document for new categories in the real-world setting. Therefore, there is no way to measure the model's performance and select the seed words that yield the best accuracy. A similar concern on assessing active learning performance at runtime has been raised by Kottke et al. (2019).

In this work, we device *OptimSeed*, a novel framework to automatically compose and select seed words for weakly-supervised text classification. We firstly mine (noisy) candidate seed words associated with the category names. We then train interim models with individual candidate seed words in an iterative manner. Lastly, we use an unsupervised error estimation method to estimate the interim models' error rates. The keywords that yield the lowest estimated error rates are selected as the final seed word set. A comprehensive evaluation of six classification tasks on four popular datasets demonstrates the effectiveness of the proposed method. The proposed method outperforms a baseline using only the category name as seed word and obtained comparable performance as a counterpart using expert-annotated seed words. We use binary classification as a case study in this work, while the idea can be generalized to multi-class classification using one-vs.-rest strategy.

The contributions of this work are three-fold:

1. We propose a novel combination of unsupervised error estimation and weakly-supervised text classification to improve the classification performance and robustness.
2. We conduct an in-depth study on the impact of different seed words on weakly-supervised text classification, supported by experiments

[1] Source code can be found at `https://github.com/YipingNUS/OptimSeed`.

Proceedings of NAACL-HLT 2021: Student Research Workshop, pages 112–118
June 6–11, 2021.

with various models and classification tasks.

3. The proposed method generates keyword sets that yield consistent and competitive performance against expert-curated seed words.

2 Related Work

We review the literature in three related fields: (1) weakly-supervised text classification, (2) unsupervised error estimation, and (3) keyword mining.

2.1 Weakly-Supervised Text Classification

Weakly-supervised text classification (Druck et al., 2008; Meng et al., 2018, 2019) aims to use a handful of labeled seed words to induce text classifiers instead of relying on labeled documents.

Druck et al. (2008) proposed generalized expectation (GE), which specifies the expected posterior probability of labeled seed words appearing in each category. GE is trained by optimizing towards satisfying the posterior constraints without making use of pseudo-labeled documents.

Chang et al. (2008) introduced the first embedding based weakly-supervised text classification method. They mapped category names and documents into the same semantic space. Document classification is then performed by searching for the nearest category embedding given an input document.

Meng et al. (2018) proposed weakly-supervised neural text classification. They generate unambiguous pseudo-documents, which are used to induce text classifiers with different architectures such as convolutional neural networks (Kim, 2014) or Hierarchical Attention Network (Yang et al., 2016).

Recently, Mekala and Shang (Mekala and Shang, 2020) disambiguate the seed words by explicitly learning different senses of each word with contextualized word embeddings. They first performed k-means clustering for each word in the vocabulary to identify potentially different senses, then eliminated the ambiguous keyword senses.

Two most recent works developed concurrently but independently from our work (Meng et al., 2020; Wang et al., 2020) addressed the same task we are tackling: weakly-supervised text classification from only the category name. They both tap on the category names' contextualized representation and expand the seed word list by finding other words that would fit into the same context.

2.2 Unsupervised Error Estimation

Unsupervised error estimation aims to estimate the error rate of a list of classifiers *without a labeled evaluation dataset.* It is widely relevant to machine learning models in production, such as when a pre-trained model is applied to a new domain or when labeled dataset is costly to obtain. To our best knowledge, no previous work in weakly-supervised classification applied unsupervised error estimation. Instead, they trained classifiers without labeled *training* datasets but evaluated their models used labeled *evaluation* datasets.

Most work in unsupervised error estimation derive the error rate analytically by making simplifying assumptions. Donmez et al. (2010) and Jaffe et al. (2015) assumed the marginal probability of the category $p(y)$ is known. Platanios et al. (2014) assumed classifiers make conditionally independent errors. While these approaches laid an important theoretical foundation, most assumptions cannot be met for real-world datasets and classifiers.

Platanios et al. (2016) proposed a Bayesian approach for error estimation. The model infers the true category and the error rates jointly using Gibbs sampling. The approach was benchmarked with various baselines such as majority vote and Platanios et al. (2014) and achieved superior performance. The estimated accuracy is usually within a few percents from the true accuracy. Notably, the only mild assumption it makes is that more than half of the classifiers have an error rate lower than 50%.

2.3 Keyword Mining

Keyword mining aims to bootstrap high-quality keyword lexicons from a small set of seed words, and it has been widely used in mining opinion lexicons (Hu and Liu, 2004; Hai et al., 2012) and technical glossaries (Elhadad and Sutaria, 2007). We want to draw the association between keyword mining and weakly-supervised text classification. Both tasks take a small list of seed words and unlabeled corpus as input, aiming to "expand" the knowledge about the target semantic category. Having more high-quality keywords will improve classification accuracy, while an accurate classifier will make the keyword mining task much easier by eliminating irrelevant/noisy documents.

3 Method

Figure 1 overviews OptimSeed, a framework to select seed words for weakly-supervised text classification involving the following steps: (1) expanding candidate keywords from a single seed word, (2) training interim classifiers with individual candidate seed keywords using weakly supervision, (3) select the final seed words with the feedback from unsupervised error estimation. We discuss the proposed framework in detail in the following sections. To make our paper self-contained, we also brief the weakly-supervised classification and unsupervised error estimation model we use.

3.1 Expanding Candidate Keywords from a Single Seed

We use either the category name or trivial keywords (e.g., "good" and "bad" for sentiment classification tasks) as the only input seed word and use a keyword expansion algorithm to mine more candidate keywords. We apply $pmi\text{-}freq$ (Equation 1) following Jin et al. (2020). It is a product of the logarithm of the candidate keyword w's document frequency and the point-wise mutual information between w and the seed word s. The higher the $pmi\text{-}freq$ score, the more strongly the candidate keyword is associated with the seed word s. Additionally, we filter the mined keywords based on their part-of-speech tag depending on the classification task. We keep only noun candidates for topic classification and adjective candidates for sentiment classification.

$$pmi\text{-}freq(w; s) \equiv log\, df(w) log \frac{p(w, s)}{p(w)p(s)} \quad (1)$$

3.2 Training interim classifiers

The candidate keywords and unlabeled dataset are used to induce *interim classifiers*. Interim classifiers' purpose is to isolate the impact of individual seed words so that we can rank them. Specifically, iteration A in Figure 1 tries to rank candidate seed words for Category A (Movies) in the classification task Movies-Television. The initial seed word "television" for Category B is fixed, and it forms seed word tuples with each candidate word in Category A. We use each such seed word tuple as input to train an interim classifier. We then use each interim classifier's predictions to perform unsupervised error estimation.

We use Generalized Expectation (GE) (Druck et al., 2008) to train both interim classifiers and the final classifier because of its competitive performance and fast training speed [2]. GE translates labeled keywords to constraint functions. For example, the first keyword tuple (hollywood, television) in Figure 1 translates to two constraint functions: $hollywood \rightarrow A : 0.9, B : 0.1$ and $television \rightarrow A : 0.1, B : 0.9$, which means "hollywood" is expected to occur 90% in a document of category A while 10% in a document of category B, vice versa for the keyword "television".

Each constraint function on a labeled word w_k contributes to a term in the objective function in Equation 2 and the underlying logistic regression model is trained by minimizing the L2 distance between the reference distribution $\hat{p}(y|w_k > 0)$ (specified by the constraint function) and the empirical distribution $\tilde{p}(y|w_k > 0)$ (predicted by the model) of the category y when word w_k is present.

$$\mathcal{O} = -\sum_{k \in K} dist(\hat{p}(y|w_k > 0)||\tilde{p}(y|w_k > 0)) \quad (2)$$

3.3 Keyword Evaluation with Bayesian Error Estimation

We apply unsupervised error estimation on the interim classifiers' predictions to estimate their accuracy and select the best seed words for the final classifier. As shown in Figure 1 iteration A, the three keywords "hollywood", "filmmaker", and "theaters" are added to the final seed word set of Category A (Movies) because their corresponding interim classifiers have estimated accuracy above the threshold. The process is repeated in iteration B to select seed words for Category B.

We use the Bayesian error estimation (BEE) model (Platanios et al., 2016) to perform this step. In BEE, each instance's true label is latent, while each model's predictions are observed. The accuracy/error rate can be derived from the predictions and the latent true labels. The assumption that half of the classifiers have an error rate below 50% implicitly uses inter-classifier agreement.

BEE uses Gibbs sampling to infer the error rates of individual classifiers e_j and the true label l_i jointly. We refer the readers to Section 4.1 in Platanios et al. (2016) for the exact conditional probabilities used in Gibbs sampling.

[2] All GE models in this work can be trained within a few seconds using a single CPU core.

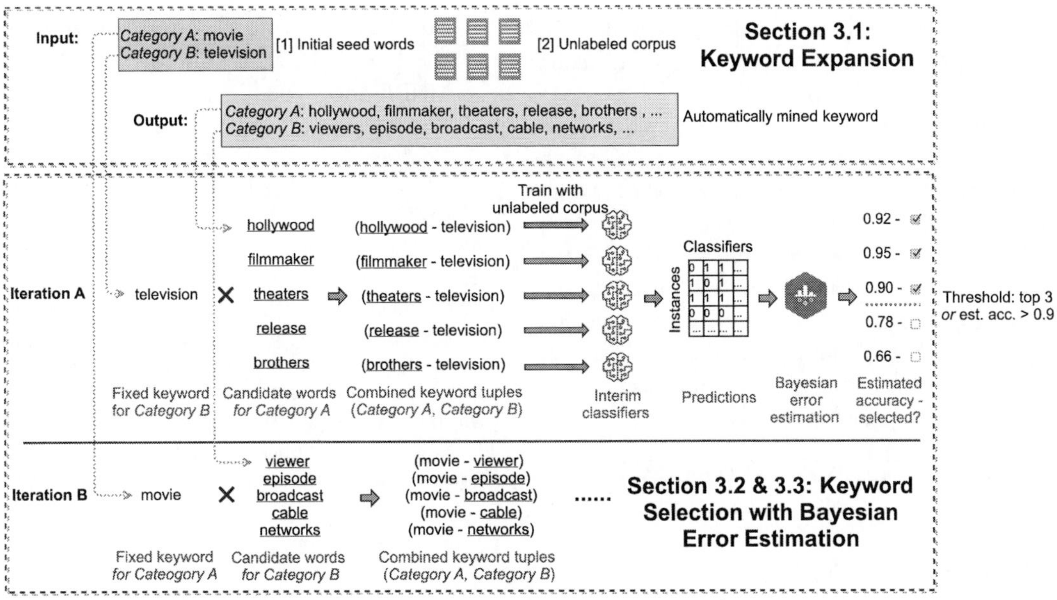

Figure 1: OptimSeed, a method to select seed words for weakly-supervised text classification. We first mine noisy keywords associated with the category name (the initial seed word). We use one iteration to refine the keywords for each category. In each iteration, We fix the seed word for one category and combine it with each mined keyword in the other category. The resultant keyword tuples are used to train separate interim classifiers. Finally, we use Bayesian error estimation to estimate the accuracy of classifiers induced from each keyword tuple and select the keywords with the highest estimated accuracy.

4 Experimental Setup

We use six binary classification tasks from four datasets to evaluate our framework. We choose the evaluation tasks so that they cover different granularities and domains. The details are as follows:

- **AG's News Dataset:** contains 120,000 documents evenly distributed into 4 coarse categories. We randomly choose two binary classification tasks: "Politics" vs. "Technology" and "Business" vs. "Sports".
- **The New York Times (NYT) Dataset:** contains 13,081 news articles covering 5 coarse and 25 fine-grained categories. We choose two fine-grained binary classification tasks involving categories with similar semantics: "International Business" (InterBiz) vs. "Economy" and "Movies" vs. "Television".
- **Yelp Restaurant Review Dataset:** contains 38,000 reviews evenly distributed into 2 categories: "Positive" vs. "Negative".
- **IMDB Movie Review Dataset:** contains 50,000 reviews evenly distributed into 2 categories: "Positive" vs. "Negative".

We report the performance of the following weakly-supervised models besides Generalized Expectation (GE):

- **Dataless (Chang et al., 2008):** maps both input documents and category seed words into a semantic space using Explicit Semantic Analysis (ESA) (Gabrilovich et al., 2007) over Wikipedia concepts and assigns the category nearest to the input document's embedding.
- **MNB/Priors (Settles, 2011):** increases priors for labeled keywords in a Naïve Bayes model and learns from an unlabeled corpus using EM algorithm.
- **WeSTClass (Meng et al., 2018):** weakly-supervised neural text classifier trained using pseudo documents. We use the CNN architecture because Meng et al. (2018) showed that it outperformed other architectures such as RNNs and Hierarchical Attention Network.
- **ConWea (Mekala and Shang, 2020):** leverages contextualized word representations to differentiate multiple senses. It also trains classifiers and expands seed words in an iterative manner.

We also report the performance of **LR**, a supervised logistic regression model trained using all the documents in the training set [3].

In all experiments, we mine 16 candidate seed words with the highest *pmi-freq* score for each category. We select a candidate keyword for the final classifier if its estimated accuracy is among the top three or is higher than 0.9 [4]. For GE, we use a reference distribution of 0.9 (meaning a labeled keyword is expected to appear in its specified categories 90% of the time) following Druck et al. (2008). Table 1 shows the initial seed words used in our work and in previous work [5].

Class	Our Work	Previous Work
Politics	political;	democracy religion liberal;
Tech	technology	scientists biological computing
Business	business;	economy industry investment;
Sports	sports	hockey tennis basketball
InterBiz	international;	china union euro;
Economy	economy	fed economists economist
Movies	movie;	hollywood directed oscar;
Television	television	episode viewers episodes
Yelp & IMDB	good;	terrific great awesome;
	bad	horrible subpar disappointing

Table 1: Initial seed words for each task.

5 Classification Performance

Table 2 presents each model's average accuracy across six datasets.

We can see that OptimSeed seed words yield better performance than using the category name alone by a large margin for all weakly-supervised models, validating the effectiveness of our seed word expansion and selection method. It also achieved better or similar performance as expert-curated seed words for three out of five models.

Method	cate	ours	gold
Dataless	54.7	**60.4***	56.7
MNB/Priors	68.5	71.7	**74.4**
WeSTClass	75.7	**77.2**	77.0
ConWea	60.0	66.0	**70.7**
GE	80.4	84.8*	**85.1**
LR		91.8	

Table 2: Average accuracy scores in percentage for all methods on all six classification tasks. **cate**, **ours**, **gold** indicates the result using the category name, keywords selected by OptimSeed and expert-composed keywords used in previous work. For each model, the best-performing keyword set is highlighted in bold. * indicates statistical significance from the same model using "cate" seed word with p-value of 0.05 using paired t-test.

Among the learning algorithms, GE obtained the best average performance for all seed word sets. The average accuracy of GE using OptimSeed seed words (84.8%) is only 0.3% lower than using expert-curated seed words, virtually eliminating human experts from the loop. GE+OptimSeed's accuracy is 7% below a fully-supervised logistic regression model trained on hundreds to tens of thousands of labeled documents.

Table 3 shows each model's classification accuracy on topic classification tasks. Summing over all models and datasets, OptimSeed achieved better or equal performance than the category name baseline 80% of the time (16/20) and better or equal performance than the gold seed words 65% of the time. It demonstrates the robustness of our seed word selection method across different tasks.

While ConWea claimed to resolve ambiguity through contextualized embeddings, we observed that it works well only when the input seed words are unambiguous ("ours" or "gold" column). On the Business-Sports classification task, its accuracy was only 39.1% while other baselines could achieve over 90%. We inspected the model and found the keywords expanded by ConWea are much noisier than OptimSeed, which caused the poor performance.

We can make similar observations on the performance of sentiment classification tasks (Table 4). However, the gap between weakly-supervised mod-

[3] We use the logistic regression implementation in scikit-learn with default parameters and tf-idf features.

[4] Mekala and Shang (2020) observed that three seed words per class are needed for reasonable performance while more high-quality keywords help. Therefore, we use the accuracy threshold of 0.9 to include additional keywords.

[5] The seed words for NYT corpus were reported in Meng et al. (2019) and the rest are from Meng et al. (2018). No previous work in weakly supervision used IMDB dataset, so we use the same manual seed words as Yelp dataset.

Method	Poli-Tech			Biz-Sport			IB-Econ			Movie-TV		
	cate	ours	gold	cate	ours	gold	cate	ours	gold	cate	ours	gold
Dataless	50.1	**51.4**	50.2	50.0	50.2	**50.4**	59.1	**75.0**	67.1	67.8	**70.0**	67.8
MNB/Priors	87.3	**88.9**	**88.9**	**95.6**	93.9	92.9	58.5	54.3	**93.9**	67.8	67.8	**68.9**
WeSTClass	87.4	**89.5**	88.8	92.7	**94.8**	94.3	77.7	**83.0**	75.1	50.4	**76.6**	62.1
ConWea	71.5	**73.7**	71.4	39.1	67.0	**82.0**	75.1	71.2	**84.3**	66.9	**77.0**	76.4
GE	86.9	87.8	**88.5**	**93.0**	**93.0**	79.4	70.7	81.7	**91.5**	94.4	**98.9**	97.8
LR		96.3			98.6			90.2			85.5	

Table 3: Accuracy on topic classification tasks. For each model-dataset combination, we highlight the best performance in bold.

els and the supervised baseline is much larger topic classification tasks, suggesting that some reviews' sentiment might be expressed implicitly and requires more than word-level understanding. Meng et al. (2020) also made a similar remark based on their experiment.

Method	Yelp		
	cate	ours	gold
Dataless	51.0	**55.5**	52.2
MNB/Priors	50.9	**71.5**	51.7
WeSTClass	78.3	58.8	**81.5**
ConWea	51.0	**51.3**	50.7
GE	68.0	75.2	**79.3**
LR		92.2	
Method	**IMDB**		
	cate	**ours**	**gold**
Dataless	50.1	**60.4**	52.2
MNB/Priors	51.1	**54.0**	50.3
WeSTClass	**67.7**	60.6	60.5
ConWea	56.5	55.7	**59.1**
GE	69.6	72.2	**74.0**
LR		88.3	

Table 4: Accuracy on sentiment classification tasks. For each model-dataset combination, we highlight the best performance in bold.

6 Case Study

To demonstrate the working of our proposed framework, we present a case study on the classification task "International Business" vs. "Economy" in Table 5 and show different seed word sets for the category "economy" and their corresponding performance.

Keyword expansion alone improved the accuracy significantly from the category name baseline. However, it may introduce some ambiguous keywords in the meantime. The unsupervised error estimator successfully identified top keywords such as "economist" and "economists" and eliminated poor keywords like "purchases" and "growth", which further improved the accuracy by 2.4%.

Stage:Acc	Seed Words for "Economy"
Init: 70.7	economy
Keyword Expansion: 79.3	purchases pace index borrowing unemployment economists economy stimulus rates recovery economist rate fed reserve inflation growth
Final: 81.7	economist economists rate recovery index

Table 5: Seed words for "Economy" at different stages of the OptimSeed framework.

7 Conclusion

Weakly-supervised text classification can induce classifiers with a handful of carefully-chosen seed words instead of labeled documents. However, the choice of seed words has a significant impact on classification performance. We proposed *OptimSeed*, a novel framework to compose the seed words automatically. It first mines keywords associated with the category name and then estimates each seed word's impact directly using unsupervised error estimation. The framework outputs seed words yielding a comparable performance as expert-curated seed words, virtually eliminating human experts from the loop.

8 Acknowledgements

YJ was supported by the scholarship from 'The 100th Anniversary Chulalongkorn University Fund for Doctoral Scholarship'. We thank anonymous reviewers for their valuable feedback.

References

Ming-Wei Chang, Lev-Arie Ratinov, Dan Roth, and Vivek Srikumar. 2008. Importance of semantic representation: Dataless classification. In *Proceedings of the AAAI Conference on Artificial Intelligence*, volume 2, pages 830–835.

Pinar Donmez, Guy Lebanon, and Krishnakumar Balasubramanian. 2010. Unsupervised supervised learning i: Estimating classification and regression errors without labels. *Journal of Machine Learning Research*, 11(4).

Gregory Druck, Gideon Mann, and Andrew McCallum. 2008. Learning from labeled features using generalized expectation criteria. In *Proceedings of the 31st Annual International ACM SIGIR Conference on Research and Development in Information Retrieval*, pages 595–602. ACM.

Noemie Elhadad and Komal Sutaria. 2007. Mining a lexicon of technical terms and lay equivalents. In *Proceedings of Biological, Translational, and Clinical Language Processing*, pages 49–56, Prague, Czech Republic. Association for Computational Linguistics.

Evgeniy Gabrilovich, Shaul Markovitch, et al. 2007. Computing semantic relatedness using wikipedia-based explicit semantic analysis. In *Proceedings of the Twentieth International Joint Conference on Artificial Intelligence*, volume 7, pages 1606–1611.

Zhen Hai, Kuiyu Chang, and Gao Cong. 2012. One seed to find them all: mining opinion features via association. In *Proceedings of the 21st ACM International Conference on Information and Knowledge Management*, pages 255–264.

Minqing Hu and Bing Liu. 2004. Mining opinion features in customer reviews. In *Proceedings of the 19th National Conference on Artifical Intelligence*, pages 755–760.

Ariel Jaffe, Boaz Nadler, and Yuval Kluger. 2015. Estimating the accuracies of multiple classifiers without labeled data. In *Proceedings of the International Conference on Artificial Intelligence and Statistics*, pages 407–415.

Yiping Jin, Dittaya Wanvarie, and Phu TV Le. 2020. Learning from noisy out-of-domain corpus using dataless classification. *Natural Language Engineering*, In press:1–35.

Yoon Kim. 2014. Convolutional neural networks for sentence classification. In *Proceedings of the 2014 Conference on Empirical Methods in Natural Language Processing (EMNLP)*, pages 1746–1751.

Daniel Kottke, Jim Schellinger, Denis Huseljic, and Bernhard Sick. 2019. Limitations of assessing active learning performance at runtime. *arXiv preprint arXiv:1901.10338*.

Chenliang Li, Shiqian Chen, Jian Xing, Aixin Sun, and Zongyang Ma. 2018. Seed-guided topic model for document filtering and classification. *ACM Transactions on Information Systems (TOIS)*, 37(1):1–37.

Dheeraj Mekala and Jingbo Shang. 2020. Contextualized weak supervision for text classification. In *Proceedings of the 58th Annual Meeting of the Association for Computational Linguistics*, pages 323–333.

Yu Meng, Jiaming Shen, Chao Zhang, and Jiawei Han. 2018. Weakly-supervised neural text classification. In *Proceedings of the 27th ACM International Conference on Information and Knowledge Management*, pages 983–992.

Yu Meng, Jiaming Shen, Chao Zhang, and Jiawei Han. 2019. Weakly-supervised hierarchical text classification. In *Proceedings of the AAAI Conference on Artificial Intelligence*, volume 33, pages 6826–6833.

Yu Meng, Yunyi Zhang, Jiaxin Huang, Chenyan Xiong, Heng Ji, Chao Zhang, and Jiawei Han. 2020. Text classification using label names only: A language model self-training approach. In *Proceedings of the 2020 Conference on Empirical Methods in Natural Language Processing*.

Emmanouil Antonios Platanios, Avrim Blum, and Tom Mitchell. 2014. Estimating accuracy from unlabeled data. In *Proceedings of the Thirtieth Conference on Uncertainty in Artificial Intelligence*, pages 682–691, Arlington, Virginia, USA. AUAI Press.

Emmanouil Antonios Platanios, Avinava Dubey, and Tom Mitchell. 2016. Estimating accuracy from unlabeled data: A bayesian approach. In *Proceedings of the International Conference on Machine Learning*, pages 1416–1425.

Burr Settles. 2011. Closing the loop: Fast, interactive semi-supervised annotation with queries on features and instances. In *Proceedings of the Conference on Empirical Methods in Natural Language Processing*, pages 1467–1478. Association for Computational Linguistics.

Zihan Wang, Dheeraj Mekala, and Jingbo Shang. 2020. X-class: Text classification with extremely weak supervision.

Zichao Yang, Diyi Yang, Chris Dyer, Xiaodong He, Alex Smola, and Eduard Hovy. 2016. Hierarchical attention networks for document classification. In *Proceedings of the 2016 Conference of the North American Chapter of the Association for Computational Linguistics: Human Language Technologies*, pages 1480–1489.

Multi-Task Learning of Generation and Classification for Emotion-Aware Dialogue Response Generation

Tatsuya Ide and **Daisuke Kawahara**
Waseda University
{t-ide@toki., dkw@}waseda.jp

Abstract

For a computer to naturally interact with a human, it needs to be human-like. In this paper, we propose a neural response generation model with multi-task learning of generation and classification, focusing on emotion. Our model based on BART (Lewis et al., 2020), a pre-trained transformer encoder-decoder model, is trained to generate responses and recognize emotions simultaneously. Furthermore, we weight the losses for the tasks to control the update of parameters. Automatic evaluations and crowdsourced manual evaluations show that the proposed model makes generated responses more emotionally aware.

1 Introduction

The performance of machine translation and summarization has been approaching a near-human level in virtue of pre-trained encoder-decoder models, such as BART (Lewis et al., 2020) and T5 (Raffel et al., 2020). The same technology has been applied to dialogue systems, which are now expected to be put to practical use.

To interact naturally with a human, the computer needs to be human-like. Several methods have been proposed to build such dialogue systems. They include a system interacting based on knowledge and common sense (Dinan et al., 2019) and that interacting by considering one's own and the other's personality (Zhang et al., 2018). In particular, we focus on the viewpoint of emotion as targeted in Rashkin et al. (2019).

In this paper, we propose a multi-task learning method for building a dialogue system that takes the speaker's emotions into account. Also, we focus on the hierarchy of emotions (Kumar et al., 2019) and simultaneously train multiple emotion recognition tasks with different granularity. Our multi-task learning model is not expected to share complementary information among similar tasks as previous work (Liu et al., 2019), and we do not aim at improving the accuracy of emotion recognition. Instead, we focus on generating emotion-aware responses. Also, concerned that the ratio of emotion recognition in multi-task learning is too large, we explore further quality improvement by weighting each loss. We build a model based on BART (Lewis et al., 2020), a pre-trained Transformer (Vaswani et al., 2017) model, to implement multi-task learning of response generation and emotion recognition.

Experiments are performed using a dialogue corpus without context. The effectiveness of the proposed method in generating responses is confirmed by automatic and manual evaluations. Multi-task learning of response generation and emotion recognition makes generated responses more emotionally aware of utterances. The improvement is not only on the emotional aspect but also on the quality of fluency, informativeness, and relevance. We also found that controlling the parameters by weighting the losses improved the performance of the model.

2 Related Work

One of the previous studies on emotion-based response generation is the Emotional Chatting Machine (ECM) (Zhou et al., 2018). ECM is used together with an emotion classifier to generate a response based on a given emotion. EmpTransfo (Zandie and Mahoor, 2020) is a similar model to ours. Given an utterance, a model based on GPT (Radford et al., 2018) learns an emotion and an action simultaneously in addition to a response, which improves the quality of generated responses. These models focus on the emotion of a response so that they do not generate a response based on the emotion of an utterance.

Lubis et al. (2018) incorporate an emotion encoder into a hierarchical seq2seq architecture, enabling a system to understand the emotional context on a user. TG-EACM (Wei et al., 2020), the suc-

Proceedings of NAACL-HLT 2021: Student Research Workshop, pages 119–125
June 6–11, 2021.

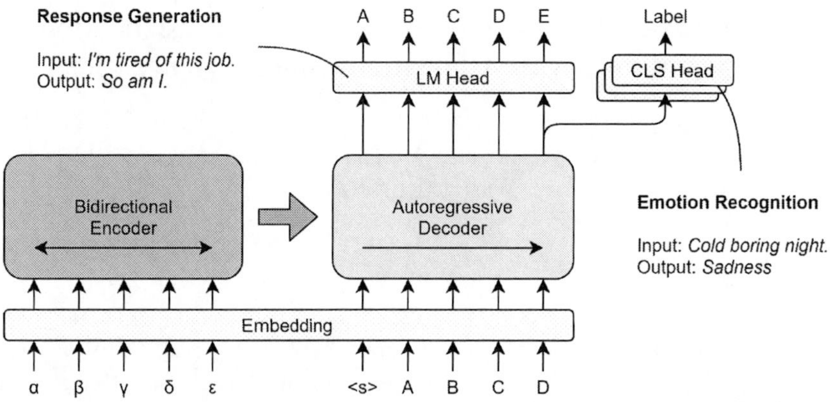

Figure 1: The architecture of our model, based on BART (Lewis et al., 2020). It contains one LM head and several CLS heads, which solve generation and classification, respectively. In our experiments, three CLS heads are used for the emotion recognition tasks with different granularity.

cessor of EACM (Wei et al., 2019), is a model that considers not only the emotion in an utterance but also the emotion that a response should have. The model learns a distribution to infer both the emotion of the utterance and the response from a given utterance. CARE (Zhong et al., 2021) uses some commonsense to generate a response with both rationality and emotion. Through latent concepts obtained from an emotionally aware knowledge graph, predicted responses can be emotional and rational.

Actually, the above models require separate units or special architecture for understanding emotion in a dialogue. In contrast, our proposed model achieves that with a single structure, inherited from Transformer (Vaswani et al., 2017) and BART (Lewis et al., 2020). In other words, our model does not need an extra unit. Therefore, the proposed method consequently reduces the redundancy of Transformer parameters (Kovaleva et al., 2019) and realizes more efficient understanding of emotion to generate a response.

3 Emotion-Aware Response Generation by Multi-Task Learning

3.1 Overview

Our model learns response generation as a generation task and emotion recognition as a classification task. By learning response generation and emotion recognition simultaneously through multi-task learning, it is possible to generate a response by considering the emotion of a given utterance.

Multi-task learning often involves several similar tasks because they can share information and thus the performance of each task can be improved. However, the purpose of our multi-task learning method is to improve the quality of response generation, not to improve the performance of emotion recognition. This is different from general multi-task learning.

Our model is based on BART (Lewis et al., 2020). Its architecture is shown in Figure 1. The model has several output layers, or heads, for the tasks to be trained, which include an LM head for generating words in response generation and CLS heads for solving classification tasks. Given a sentence, the CLS head predicts its label such as `positive` or `negative`. One CLS head is set for each classification task.

The input/output format of each task is the same as that in BART. In the generation task, we put an utterance and a right-shifted response into the encoder and decoder, respectively. In the classification task, we put an utterance and a right-shifted utterance into the encoder and decoder, respectively. Following the learning algorithm of MT-DNN (Liu et al., 2019), each task that the model learns is selected for each mini-batch. A different loss is calculated for each task, and the parameters are updated for each mini-batch.

3.2 Losses of Generation and Classification Tasks

Let $\boldsymbol{x} = (x_1, \ldots, x_M)$ be the given utterance and $\boldsymbol{\theta}$ be the parameters of the model. Our model is trained by updating $\boldsymbol{\theta}$ based on the loss for each task.

Dataset	Train	Validation	Test
DailyDialog	76,052	7,069	6,740
TEC	16,841	2,105	2,105
SST-2	16,837	872	1,822
CrowdFlower	15,670	1,958	1,958

Table 1: The statistics of the datasets for our experiments, where TEC stands for Twitter Emotion Corpus. Because TEC and CrowdFlower have no split of train, validation, and test, we split them into three at 8:1:1.

Generation The response to $\boldsymbol{x}$ is defined as $\boldsymbol{y} = (y_1, \ldots, y_N)$. The model infers an appropriate $\boldsymbol{y}$ from $\boldsymbol{x}$. The generation loss $\mathcal{L}_{\text{gen}}$ is calculated as the negative log-likelihood loss.

$$\mathcal{L}_{\text{gen}} = -\sum_{j=1}^{N} \log p(y_j | \boldsymbol{x}, y_1, \ldots, y_{j-1}; \boldsymbol{\theta}) \quad (1)$$

Classification If the correct label of $\boldsymbol{x}$ is c, the model infers c from $\boldsymbol{x}$. The negative log-likelihood loss is also used for the classification loss $\mathcal{L}_{\text{cls}}$.

$$\mathcal{L}_{\text{cls}} = -\log p(c | \boldsymbol{x}; \boldsymbol{\theta}) \quad (2)$$

3.3 Loss Weighting

Although the proposed multi-task learning model learns the generation and classification tasks simultaneously, there is a possibility that the ratio of learning for the classification task is too large. When solving a general classification task, the end of learning is often determined by the convergence of the loss in the validation data. On the other hand, the target of our model is a generation task, and the number of epochs required for generation is larger than that of the classification task.

Therefore, we consider weighting the loss functions. While the weight for response generation is fixed at 1, the weight for emotion recognition is varied between 0 and 1. This makes the contribution of the classification task reduced in updating the parameters.

4 Experiments

4.1 Datasets

We train a model with three tasks of emotion recognition in addition to response generation using multi-task learning. Each emotion recognition task is a classification task with 6, 2, and 12 labels, and we call them emotion recognition, coarse-grained emotion recognition, and fine-grained emotion recognition, respectively. The datasets for such emotion recognition were selected according to Bostan and Klinger (2018). The numbers of instances are summarized in Table 1.

Response Generation DailyDialog (Li et al., 2017) is used for response generation. The dataset is a multi-turn dialogue corpus, and we obtain pairs of an utterance and a response by extracting two turns at a time. Each utterance in the corpus has an emotion label, but we do not use these labels in the experiment. This is because almost all of the emotion labels are `other`, which is not suitable for our method.

Emotion Recognition For the core emotion recognition dataset, we use the Twitter Emotion Corpus (Mohammad, 2012). It was constructed based on Twitter hashtags and consists of six labels: {`anger`, `disgust`, `fear`, `joy`, `sadness`, `surprise`}. Because there is no distinction between train, validation, and test in the dataset, 80% of the total samples is assigned to train, and the remaining 10% each is assigned to validation and test.

Coarse-Grained Emotion Recognition For coarse-grained emotion recognition, we use SST-2 (Socher et al., 2013). This is a dataset of movie comments labeled with {`positive`, `negative`}. To maintain a balance with the number of instances for the other emotion recognition tasks, we reduce the number of instances for training to 25%.

Fine-Grained Emotion Recognition For fine-grained emotion recognition, we use the emotionally-tagged corpus provided by CrowdFlower.[1] We exclude the label `empty` and adopt this corpus for a classification task with 12 labels: {`anger`, `boredom`, `enthusiasm`, `fun`, `happiness`, `hate`, `love`, `neutral`, `relief`, `sadness`, `surprise`, `worry`}. As with the Twitter Emotion Corpus, this corpus does not have a split of train, validation, and test, and thus the whole data is divided into 8:1:1. Furthermore, for the same reason as in SST-2, only 50% of the total data is used.

4.2 Training

The hyperparameters are set based on BART (Lewis et al., 2020) and the Fairseq

[1]The original link is no longer available. An alternative is `https://data.world/crowdflower/sentiment-analysis-in-text`.

Model	Auto Eval				Manual Eval			
	BLEU	*dist*-1	*dist*-2	Avg Len	*Emo*	*Flu*	*Info*	*Relv*
R	32.35	5.87	30.48	14.12	3.44	3.48	3.63	3.55
R+E6	32.29	5.93	30.48	14.12	**3.59**	**3.82**	3.62	**3.96**
R+E6+E2	32.39	**6.00**	**30.77**	14.11	3.58	3.75	**3.74**	3.70
R+E6+E12	**32.55**	5.89	30.57	**14.14**	3.52	3.48	3.55	3.58
R+E6+E2+E12	32.29	5.91	30.47	14.12	**3.59**	3.75	3.57	3.64

Table 2: Evaluation results of our models by multi-task learning. R stands for response generation, and E• is emotion recognition with • labels. *Emo*, *flu*, *info*, and *relv* are the four aspects for the manual evaluation by crowdsourcing.

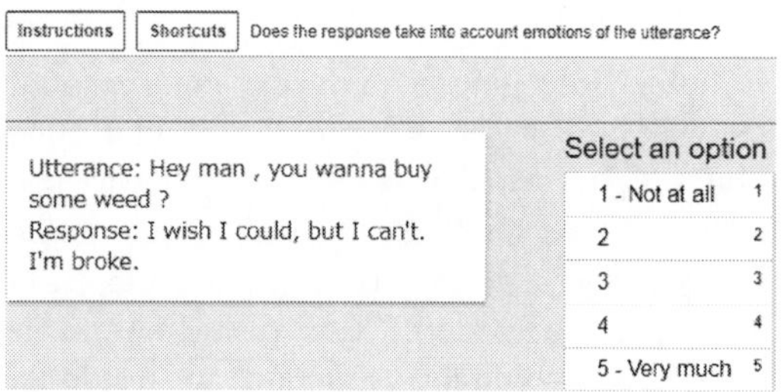

Figure 2: An example of the manual evaluation by crowdsourcing on Amazon Mechanical Turk. Workers are supposed to answer such questions by rating the given dialogue on a five-point scale.

example.[2] The learning rate is set to 3e-5, and the parameters are optimized by Adam with weight decay. For response generation, we apply label smoothing of 0.1 to the negative log-likelihood loss. The number of input and output tokens is set to 64, and training is performed for 64 epochs. We use beam search with 5 beams to select words and eliminate cases where there are more than three repeated n-grams. Training and generation are performed on NVIDIA Tesla V100.

4.3 Evaluation Metrics

We evaluate the trained models automatically and manually.

Automatic Evaluation First, we evaluate how much the output responses are related to the correct response using BLEU (Papineni et al., 2002). Second, we evaluate whether the output responses are lexically diverse using *distinct* (Li et al., 2016). For *distinct*, *distinct*-1 and *distinct*-2 are calculated, which focus on unigrams and bigrams, respectively. We also compare the average number of words in output responses, which is based on the assumption that the longer a response is, the less common it is. The large average number indicates that generated responses tend to be not dull.

Manual Evaluation Actually, the lack of correlation between automatic and manual evaluation (Liu et al., 2016) has been indicated especially in regards to generation tasks. Thus, we perform manual evaluation by crowdsourcing, where Amazon Mechanical Turk is used as the platform. We use four metrics mainly following Rashkin et al. (2019): *emotion*, *fluency*, *informativeness*, and *relevance*. Each of the questions asks whether the generated response takes into account the emotion of the utterance, whether the generated response is syntactically correct, whether a generated response provides some information for the utterance, and whether the content of the response is appropriately related to the utterance. A total of 100 randomly selected responses for the test data are asked to rate the above four metrics on a five-point scale. US residents are designated as workers, and seven workers are requested for each metric of each sample. The final score is obtained as the average of the values obtained from the seven workers. An example of the questions asked to the workers is shown in Figure 2.

4.4 Results

Multi-Task Learning The evaluation results are shown in Table 2. The response generation is denoted by R, and the emotion recognition for the Twitter Emotion Corpus, SST-2, and CrowdFlower datasets is denoted by E6, E2, and E12, respectively. In terms of automatic evaluation, R+E6+E2 and R+E6+E12 maximized the *distinct* and BLEU, respectively. In the proposed multi-task learning model, therefore, emotion recognition of different granularity is effective in relevance and diversity. For manual evaluation, all models that include emo-

[2] https://github.com/pytorch/fairseq/blob/master/examples/bart/README.summarization.md.

Utterance	Gold Response	R	R+E6
Yes, my parents, and soon my brother as well.	I didn't know you had a brother.	I see. In a few months, you'll be moving to a new place.	I hope I get to meet you soon.
It falls on the fifth day of the fifth lunar month.	Could you tell me the origin of the two festivals?	Oh, then on that day?	Oh? Why is that day?
How smart of you to book the tickets before hand!	Oh, do you really think so?	Sorry, I didn't think of it that way.	Yeah, yeah, I know. It was the last thing I wanted to do.
I can't. I'm waiting for Paul, but he's late.	I'll say the movie's starting in the minute.	Would you like me to call him?	Where is he?
thank you. I think I should also have a look at the Internet to see if anyone's got a sublet.	how much do are you looking to spend?	if you need a flat, you can always look online. Do you have any questions?	good idea. You can ask around at the office. If you need a flat, they'll probably have one.

Table 3: Examples generated by the baseline model (R) and the proposed model (R+E6). We chose examples where the *emotion* score in manual evaluation is quite improved by adding E6 to R.

Model	Acc [%]	F1 [%]
R	17.29	12.25
R+E6	64.32	56.53
R+E6+E2	63.23	54.88
R+E6+E12	66.27	57.86
R+E6+E2+E12	64.85	56.09

Table 4: Emotion recognition (E6) performance of our models in Table 2. The values for R, trained only on response generation, are very low, while R+E6+E12 marks the best score among these models.

tion recognition outperformed the model with only response generation. Moreover, R+E6 scores were particularly high for all four metrics. The proposed multi-task learning model not only makes the generated responses more emotionally aware but can also improve the quality of other metrics, such as fluency and informativeness.

Several examples of responses generated by the obtained model are shown in Table 3. We compare the given utterances and their responses of R and R+E6. We can see that R+E6 generated more emotion-sensitive sentences, such as "Yeah, yeah, I know" and "good idea."

In addition, we show the results of emotion recognition in Table 4, which is especially on a six-label classification task. We calculate accuracy and F1-score as metrics for evaluation. The result shows that, on emotion recognition, increasing the number of tasks to train does not necessarily lead to improvement of the scores. We can see that models with training of emotion recognition on fine-grained labels tend to outperform the other models. However, the goal of our model is not improvement of classification but that of generation, so that those score variation is not essential in this work.

Loss Weighting The evaluation results for different loss weighting are shown in Table 5. The weight for the loss of E• is denoted as $\lambda_{E\bullet}$. In automatic evaluation, we can see the improvement of the scores by weighting, especially in the model with E12. On the other hand, the manual evaluation shows that weighting improves some scores, with the case (.5, .5, 0) producing the highest score. Therefore, weighting each loss can improve the quality of generated responses, and in the condition of our experiment, it is most effective to reduce the weights of E6 and E2 by half.

5 Conclusion

We worked on improving the quality of neural network-based response generation. Focusing on the aspect of emotion, we proposed a multi-task learning response generation model that includes the tasks of generation and classification. Through automatic and manual evaluations, we confirmed that the proposed model improved several metrics of performance. Moreover, we further improved the quality of the model by weighting losses. As a result, we found that such weighting improved

$(\lambda_{E6}, \lambda_{E2}, \lambda_{E12})$	Auto Eval				Manual Eval			
	BLEU	*dist*-1	*dist*-2	Avg Len	*Emo*	*Flu*	*Info*	*Relv*
(1, 0, 0)	32.29	5.93	30.48	14.12	3.59	3.82	3.62	**3.96**
(.5, .5, 0)	32.48	5.86	30.54	**14.15**	**4.00**	**4.16**	**4.01**	**3.96**
(.5, 0, .5)	**32.52**	5.93	30.62	14.04	3.37	3.60	3.37	3.36
(.33, .33, .33)	32.43	**5.97**	**30.81**	14.01	3.63	3.37	3.49	3.66

Table 5: Evaluation results for differed loss. $\lambda_{E\bullet}$ indicates the weight for the loss of E•, and the metrics are the same as those of Table 2. The weight for the response generation loss (λ_R) is fixed at 1 throughout the experiments. Note that (1, 0, 0) is equivalent to R+E6 in Table 2.

several scores and the balance of parameter updates was also an important factor.

This paper focused on the emotion of the dialogue and generated responses that take into account the emotion of an utterance. On the other hand, we did not focus on the emotion of a response, which is a subject for our future work. We plan to work on estimating the emotions that a response should have and generating a response based on a specified emotion. In the experiments of this paper, we omitted the context of a dialogue. However, it is also necessary to consider past utterances and their effects on emotions for generating responses, which is also an issue to be addressed in the future.

Acknowledgements

This work was supported by JSPS KAKENHI Grant Number JP18H03286.

References

Laura-Ana-Maria Bostan and Roman Klinger. 2018. An analysis of annotated corpora for emotion classification in text. In *Proceedings of the 27th International Conference on Computational Linguistics*, pages 2104–2119, Santa Fe, New Mexico, USA. Association for Computational Linguistics.

Emily Dinan, Stephen Roller, Kurt Shuster, Angela Fan, Michael Auli, and Jason Weston. 2019. Wizard of wikipedia: Knowledge-powered conversational agents. *arXiv preprint arXiv:1811.01241*.

Olga Kovaleva, Alexey Romanov, Anna Rogers, and Anna Rumshisky. 2019. Revealing the dark secrets of BERT. In *Proceedings of the 2019 Conference on Empirical Methods in Natural Language Processing and the 9th International Joint Conference on Natural Language Processing (EMNLP-IJCNLP)*, pages 4365–4374, Hong Kong, China. Association for Computational Linguistics.

A. Kumar, A. Ekbal, D. Kawahra, and S. Kurohashi. 2019. Emotion helps sentiment: A multi-task model for sentiment and emotion analysis. In *2019 International Joint Conference on Neural Networks (IJCNN)*, pages 1–8.

Mike Lewis, Yinhan Liu, Naman Goyal, Marjan Ghazvininejad, Abdelrahman Mohamed, Omer Levy, Veselin Stoyanov, and Luke Zettlemoyer. 2020. BART: Denoising sequence-to-sequence pretraining for natural language generation, translation, and comprehension. In *Proceedings of the 58th Annual Meeting of the Association for Computational Linguistics*, pages 7871–7880, Online. Association for Computational Linguistics.

Jiwei Li, Michel Galley, Chris Brockett, Jianfeng Gao, and Bill Dolan. 2016. A diversity-promoting objective function for neural conversation models. In *Proceedings of the 2016 Conference of the North American Chapter of the Association for Computational Linguistics: Human Language Technologies*, pages 110–119, San Diego, California. Association for Computational Linguistics.

Yanran Li, Hui Su, Xiaoyu Shen, Wenjie Li, Ziqiang Cao, and Shuzi Niu. 2017. DailyDialog: A manually labelled multi-turn dialogue dataset. In *Proceedings of the Eighth International Joint Conference on Natural Language Processing (Volume 1: Long Papers)*, pages 986–995, Taipei, Taiwan. Asian Federation of Natural Language Processing.

Chia-Wei Liu, Ryan Lowe, Iulian Serban, Mike Noseworthy, Laurent Charlin, and Joelle Pineau. 2016. How NOT to evaluate your dialogue system: An empirical study of unsupervised evaluation metrics for dialogue response generation. In *Proceedings of the 2016 Conference on Empirical Methods in Natural Language Processing*, pages 2122–2132, Austin, Texas. Association for Computational Linguistics.

Xiaodong Liu, Pengcheng He, Weizhu Chen, and Jianfeng Gao. 2019. Multi-task deep neural networks for natural language understanding. In *Proceedings of the 57th Annual Meeting of the Association for Computational Linguistics*, pages 4487–4496, Florence, Italy. Association for Computational Linguistics.

Nurul Lubis, Sakriani Sakti, Koichiro Yoshino, and Satoshi Nakamura. 2018. Eliciting positive emotion through affect-sensitive dialogue response generation: A neural network approach. *Proceedings of the AAAI Conference on Artificial Intelligence*, 32(1).

Saif Mohammad. 2012. #emotional tweets. In **SEM 2012: The First Joint Conference on Lexical and Computational Semantics – Volume 1: Proceedings of the main conference and the shared task, and Volume 2: Proceedings of the Sixth International Workshop on Semantic Evaluation (SemEval 2012)*, pages 246–255, Montréal, Canada. Association for Computational Linguistics.

Kishore Papineni, Salim Roukos, Todd Ward, and Wei-Jing Zhu. 2002. Bleu: a method for automatic evaluation of machine translation. In *Proceedings of the 40th Annual Meeting of the Association for Computational Linguistics*, pages 311–318, Philadelphia, Pennsylvania, USA. Association for Computational Linguistics.

Alec Radford, Karthik Narasimhan, Tim Salimans, and Ilya Sutskever. 2018. Improving language understanding by generative pre-training.

Colin Raffel, Noam Shazeer, Adam Roberts, Katherine Lee, Sharan Narang, Michael Matena, Yanqi Zhou, Wei Li, and Peter J. Liu. 2020. Exploring the limits of transfer learning with a unified text-to-text transformer. *Journal of Machine Learning Research*, 21(140):1–67.

Hannah Rashkin, Eric Michael Smith, Margaret Li, and Y-Lan Boureau. 2019. Towards empathetic open-domain conversation models: A new benchmark and dataset. In *Proceedings of the 57th Annual Meeting of the Association for Computational Linguistics*, pages 5370–5381, Florence, Italy. Association for Computational Linguistics.

Richard Socher, Alex Perelygin, Jean Wu, Jason Chuang, Christopher D. Manning, Andrew Ng, and Christopher Potts. 2013. Recursive deep models for semantic compositionality over a sentiment treebank. In *Proceedings of the 2013 Conference on Empirical Methods in Natural Language Processing*, pages 1631–1642, Seattle, Washington, USA. Association for Computational Linguistics.

Ashish Vaswani, Noam Shazeer, Niki Parmar, Jakob Uszkoreit, Llion Jones, Aidan N. Gomez, Lukasz Kaiser, and Illia Polosukhin. 2017. Attention is all you need. *arXiv preprint arXiv:1706.03762*.

Wei Wei, Jiayi Liu, Xianling Mao, Guibin Guo, Feida Zhu, Pan Zhou, Yuchong Hu, and Shanshan Feng. 2020. Target guided emotion aware chat machine. *arXiv preprint arXiv:2011.07432*.

Wei Wei, Jiayi Liu, Xianling Mao, Guibing Guo, Feida Zhu, Pan Zhou, and Yuchong Hu. 2019. Emotion-aware chat machine: Automatic emotional response generation for human-like emotional interaction. In *Proceedings of the 28th ACM International Conference on Information and Knowledge Management*, CIKM '19, page 1401–1410, New York, NY, USA. Association for Computing Machinery.

Rohola Zandie and Mohammad H. Mahoor. 2020. Emptransfo: A multi-head transformer architecture for creating empathetic dialog systems. *arXiv preprint arXiv:2003.02958*.

Saizheng Zhang, Emily Dinan, Jack Urbanek, Arthur Szlam, Douwe Kiela, and Jason Weston. 2018. Personalizing dialogue agents: I have a dog, do you have pets too? In *Proceedings of the 56th Annual Meeting of the Association for Computational Linguistics (Volume 1: Long Papers)*, pages 2204–2213, Melbourne, Australia. Association for Computational Linguistics.

Peixiang Zhong, Di Wang, Pengfei Li, Chen Zhang, Hao Wang, and Chunyan Miao. 2021. Care: Commonsense-aware emotional response generation with latent concepts. *arXiv preprint arXiv:2012.08377*.

Hao Zhou, Minlie Huang, Tianyang Zhang, Xiaoyan Zhu, and Bing Liu. 2018. Emotional chatting machine: Emotional conversation generation with internal and external memory. *Proceedings of the AAAI Conference on Artificial Intelligence*, 32(1).

Comparison of Grammatical Error Correction Using Back-Translation Models

Aomi Koyama Kengo Hotate* Masahiro Kaneko† Mamoru Komachi
Tokyo Metropolitan University
koyama-aomi@ed.tmu.ac.jp, kengo_hotate@r.recruit.co.jp
masahiro.kaneko@nlp.c.titech.ac.jp, komachi@tmu.ac.jp

Abstract

Grammatical error correction (GEC) suffers from a lack of sufficient parallel data. Therefore, GEC studies have developed various methods to generate pseudo data, which comprise pairs of grammatical and artificially produced ungrammatical sentences. Currently, a mainstream approach to generate pseudo data is back-translation (BT). Most previous GEC studies using BT have employed the same architecture for both GEC and BT models. However, GEC models have different correction tendencies depending on their architectures. Thus, in this study, we compare the correction tendencies of the GEC models trained on pseudo data generated by different BT models, namely, Transformer, CNN, and LSTM. The results confirm that the correction tendencies for each error type are different for every BT model. Additionally, we examine the correction tendencies when using a combination of pseudo data generated by different BT models. As a result, we find that the combination of different BT models improves or interpolates the $F_{0.5}$ scores of each error type compared with that of single BT models with different seeds.

1 Introduction

Grammatical error correction (GEC) aims to automatically correct errors in text written by language learners. It is generally considered as a translation from ungrammatical sentences to grammatical sentences, and GEC studies use machine translation (MT) models as GEC models. After Yuan and Briscoe (2016) applied an encoder–decoder (EncDec) model (Sutskever et al., 2014; Bahdanau et al., 2015) to GEC, various EncDec-based GEC models have been proposed (Ji et al., 2017; Chollampatt and Ng, 2018; Junczys-Dowmunt et al., 2018; Zhao et al., 2019; Kaneko et al., 2020).

GEC models have different correction tendencies in each architecture. For example, a GEC model based on CNN (Gehring et al., 2017) tends to correct errors effectively using the local context (Chollampatt and Ng, 2018). Furthermore, some studies have combined multiple GEC models to exploit the difference in correction tendencies, thereby improving performance (Grundkiewicz and Junczys-Dowmunt, 2018; Kantor et al., 2019).

Despite their success, EncDec-based models require considerable amounts of parallel data for training (Koehn and Knowles, 2017). However, GEC suffers from a lack of sufficient parallel data. Accordingly, GEC studies have developed various pseudo data generation methods (Xie et al., 2018; Ge et al., 2018a; Zhao et al., 2019; Lichtarge et al., 2019; Xu et al., 2019; Choe et al., 2019; Qiu et al., 2019; Grundkiewicz et al., 2019; Kiyono et al., 2019; Grundkiewicz and Junczys-Dowmunt, 2019; Wang et al., 2020; Takahashi et al., 2020; Wang and Zheng, 2020; Zhou et al., 2020a; Wan et al., 2020). Moreover, Wan et al. (2020) showed that the correction tendencies of the GEC model are different when using (1) a pseudo data generation method by adding noise to latent representations and (2) a rule-based pseudo data generation method. Furthermore, they improved the GEC model by combining pseudo data generated by these methods. Therefore, the combination of pseudo data generated by multiple methods with different tendencies allows us to improve the GEC model further.

One of the most common methods to generate pseudo data is back-translation (BT) (Sennrich et al., 2016a). In BT, we train a BT model (i.e., the reverse model of the GEC model), which generates an ungrammatical sentence from a given grammatical sentence. Subsequently, a grammatical sentence is provided as an input to the BT model, generating a sentence containing pseudo errors. Finally, pairs of erroneous sentences and their input sentences are used as pseudo data to train a GEC model.

Kiyono et al. (2019) reported that a GEC model using BT achieved the best performance among

*Current affiliation: Recruit Co., Ltd.
†Current affiliation: Tokyo Institute of Technology

Proceedings of NAACL-HLT 2021: Student Research Workshop, pages 126–135
June 6–11, 2021. ©2021 Association for Computational Linguistics

other pseudo data generation methods. However, most previous GEC studies using BT have used the BT model with the same architecture as the GEC model (Xie et al., 2018; Ge et al., 2018a,b; Zhang et al., 2019; Kiyono et al., 2019, 2020). Thus, it is unclear whether the correction tendencies differ when using BT models with different architectures.

We investigated correction tendencies of the GEC model using pseudo data generated by different BT models. Specifically, we used three BT models: Transformer (Vaswani et al., 2017), CNN (Gehring et al., 2017), and LSTM (Luong et al., 2015). The results showed that correction tendencies of each error type are different for each BT model. In addition, we examined correction tendencies of the GEC model when using a combination of pseudo data generated by different BT models. As a result, we found that the combination of different BT models improves or interpolates the $F_{0.5}$ scores of each error type compared with that of single BT models with different seeds.

The main contributions of this study are as follows:

- We confirmed that correction tendencies of the GEC model are different for each BT model.
- We found that the combination of different BT models improves or interpolates the $F_{0.5}$ scores compared with that of single BT models with different seeds.

2 Related Works

2.1 Back-Translation in Grammatical Error Correction

Sennrich et al. (2016a) showed that BT can effectively improve neural machine translation. Therefore, many MT studies focused on BT (Poncelas et al., 2018; Fadaee and Monz, 2018; Edunov et al., 2018; Graça et al., 2019; Caswell et al., 2019; Edunov et al., 2020; Soto et al., 2020; Dou et al., 2020). Subsequently, BT was applied to GEC. For example, Xie et al. (2018) proposed noising beam search methods, and Ge et al. (2018a) proposed back-boost learning. Moreover, Rei et al. (2017) and Kasewa et al. (2018) applied BT to a grammatical error detection task.

Kiyono et al. (2019) compared pseudo data generation methods, including BT. They reported that (1) the GEC model using BT achieved the best performance and (2) using pseudo data for pre-training improves the GEC model more effectively than using a combination of pseudo data and genuine parallel data. This is because the amount of pseudo data is much larger than that of genuine parallel data. This usage of pseudo data in GEC contrasts with the usage of a combination of pseudo data and genuine parallel data in MT (Sennrich et al., 2016a; Edunov et al., 2018; Caswell et al., 2019).

Htut and Tetreault (2019) compared four GEC models—Transformer, CNN, PRPN (Shen et al., 2018), and ON-LSTM (Shen et al., 2019)—using pseudo data generated by different BT models. Specifically, they used Transformer and CNN as BT models. It was reported that the Transformer using pseudo data generated by CNN achieved the best $F_{0.5}$ score. However, the correction tendencies for each BT model were not reported. Moreover, although using pseudo data for pre-training is common in GEC (Zhao et al., 2019; Lichtarge et al., 2019; Grundkiewicz et al., 2019; Zhou et al., 2020a; Hotate et al., 2020), they used a less common method of utilizing pseudo data for re-training after training with genuine parallel data. Therefore, we used Transformer as the GEC model and investigated correction tendencies when using Transformer, CNN, and LSTM as BT models. Further, we used pseudo data to pre-train the GEC model.

2.2 Correction Tendencies When Using Each Pseudo Data Generation Method

White and Rozovskaya (2020) conducted a comparative study of two rule/probability-based pseudo data generation methods. The first method (Grundkiewicz et al., 2019) generates pseudo data using a confusion set based on a spell checker. The second method (Choe et al., 2019) generates pseudo data using human edits extracted from annotated GEC corpora or replacing prepositions/nouns/verbs with predefined rules. Based on the comparison results of these methods, it was reported that the former has better performance in correcting spelling errors, whereas the latter has better performance in correcting noun number and tense errors. In addition, Lichtarge et al. (2019) compared pseudo data extracted from Wikipedia edit histories with that generated by round-trip translation. They reported that the former enables better performance in correcting morphology and orthography errors, whereas the latter enables better performance in correcting preposition and pronoun errors. Similarly, we reported correction tendencies of the GEC model when using pseudo data generated by three

Dataset	Sents.	Refs.	Split
BEA-train	564,684	1	train
BEA-valid	4,384	1	valid
CoNLL-2014	1,312	2	test
JFLEG	747	4	test
BEA-test	4,477	5	test
Wikipedia	9,000,000	-	-

Table 1: Dataset used in the experiments.

BT models with different architectures.

Some studies have used a combination of pseudo data generated by different methods for training the GEC model (Lichtarge et al., 2019; Zhou et al., 2020a,b; Wan et al., 2020). For example, Zhou et al. (2020a) proposed a pseudo data generation method that pairs sentences translated by statistical machine translation and neural machine translation. Then, they combined pseudo data generated by it with pseudo data generated by BT to pre-train the GEC model. However, they did not report the correction tendencies of the GEC model when using combined pseudo data. Conversely, we reported correction tendencies when using a combination of pseudo data generated by different BT models.

3 Experimental Setup

3.1 Dataset

Table 1 shows the details of the dataset used in the experiments. We used the BEA-2019 workshop official shared task dataset (Bryant et al., 2019) as the training and validation data. This dataset consists of FCE (Yannakoudakis et al., 2011), Lang-8 (Mizumoto et al., 2011; Tajiri et al., 2012), NUCLE (Dahlmeier et al., 2013), and W&I+LOCNESS (Granger, 1998; Yannakoudakis et al., 2018). Following Chollampatt and Ng (2018), we removed sentence pairs with identical source and target sentences from the training data. Next, we applied byte pair encoding (Sennrich et al., 2016b) to both source and target sentences. Here, we acquired subwords from the target sentences in the training data and set the vocabulary size to 8,000. Hereinafter, we refer to the training and validation data as BEA-train and BEA-valid, respectively.

We used Wikipedia[1] as a seed corpus to generate pseudo data and removed possibly inappropriate sentences, such as URLs. In total, we extracted 9M sentences randomly.

[1]We used the 2020-07-06 dump file at `https://dumps.wikimedia.org/other/cirrussearch/`.

3.2 Evaluation

We evaluated the CoNLL-2014 test set (CoNLL-2014) (Ng et al., 2014), the JFLEG test set (JFLEG) (Heilman et al., 2014; Napoles et al., 2017), and the official test set of the BEA-2019 shared task (BEA-test). We reported M^2 (Dahlmeier and Ng, 2012) for the CoNLL-2014 and GLEU (Napoles et al., 2015, 2016) for the JFLEG. We also reported the scores measured by ERRANT (Felice et al., 2016; Bryant et al., 2017) for the BEA-valid and BEA-test. All the reported results, except for the ensemble model, are the average of three distinct trials using three different random seeds[2]. In the ensemble model, we reported the ensemble results of the three GEC models.

3.3 Grammatical Error Correction Model

Following Kiyono et al. (2019), we adopted Transformer, which is a representative EncDec-based model, using the fairseq toolkit (Ott et al., 2019). We used the "Transformer (base)" settings of Vaswani et al. (2017)[3], which has a 6-layer encoder and decoder with a dimensionality of 512 for both input and output and 2,048 for inner-layers, and 8 self-attention heads. We pre-trained GEC models on each 9M pseudo data generated by each BT model[4] and then fine-tuned them on BEA-train. We optimized the model by using Adam (Kingma and Ba, 2015) in pre-training and with Adafactor (Shazeer and Stern, 2018) in fine-tuning. Most of the hyperparameter settings were the same as those described in Kiyono et al. (2019). Additionally, we trained a GEC model using only the BEA-train without pre-training as a baseline model.

We investigated correction tendencies when using a combination of pseudo data generated by different BT models. Therefore, we pre-trained a GEC model on combined pseudo data and then fine-tuned it on the BEA-train. Notably, in this experiment, we combined pseudo data generated by the Transformer and CNN because they improved the GEC models compared with LSTM in most cases (Section 4.1). Specifically, we obtained 9M pseudo data from the Transformer and CNN and then created 18M pseudo data by combining them.

[2]To reduce the influence of the BT model's seed, we prepared BT models trained with the corresponding seed of each GEC model. Then, we pre-trained each GEC model using pseudo data generated by the corresponding BT models.

[3]Considering the limitation of computing resources, we used "Transformer (base)" instead of "Transformer (big)".

[4]See Section 3.4 for details of the BT models.

		CoNLL-2014			JFLEG	BEA-test		
Back-translation model	Pseudo data	Prec.	Rec.	$F_{0.5}$	GLEU	Prec.	Rec.	$F_{0.5}$
None (Baseline)	-	58.5/65.8	31.3/31.5	49.8/54.0	53.0/53.7	52.6/61.4	42.8/42.8	50.2/56.5
Transformer	9M	**65.0**/68.6	**37.6/37.7**	**56.7/59.0**	57.7/58.3	61.1/66.5	49.8/50.7	58.4/62.6
CNN	9M	64.0/68.1	37.4/37.4	56.0/58.5	**57.8/58.4**	**61.9/67.5**	**50.7/51.0**	**59.3/63.4**
LSTM	9M	64.7/**68.8**	36.2/36.4	55.9/58.4	57.0/57.4	61.3/67.1	49.5/49.9	58.5/62.8
Transformer & CNN	18M	65.2/**69.1**	**38.7/39.1**	**57.3/59.9**	**57.9**/58.5	**63.1/67.6**	51.1/51.1	**60.2/63.5**
Transformer & Transformer	18M	65.5/68.3	37.9/38.0	57.2/58.9	57.5/58.0	63.0/67.0	51.0/50.7	**60.2**/63.0
CNN & CNN	18M	**65.6/69.1**	38.2/38.7	**57.3**/59.8	**57.9/58.6**	61.9/67.1	**51.4/51.6**	59.5/63.3

Table 2: Results of each GEC model. The left and right scores represent single and ensemble model results, respectively. The top group delineates the performance of the GEC model using each BT model, and the bottom group delineates the performance of the GEC model when using combined pseudo data.

To eliminate the effect of increasing the pseudo data amount, we prepared GEC models that used a combination of pseudo data generated by single BT models with different seeds. We provided all BT models with the same target sentences to focus on the difference in the pseudo source sentences. Hence, in the combined pseudo data, the number of source sentence types increases; however, the number of target sentence types does not increase.

3.4 Back-Translation Model

Based on the GEC studies that used BT, we selected the Transformer (Vaswani et al., 2017), CNN (Gehring et al., 2017), and LSTM (Luong et al., 2015). For all BT models, we used implementations of the fairseq toolkit and its default settings, except for common settings[5].

Common settings. We used the Adam optimizer with $\beta_1 = 0.9$ and $\beta_2 = 0.98$. We used label smoothed cross-entropy (Szegedy et al., 2016) as a loss function and selected the model that achieved the smallest loss on the BEA-valid. We set the maximum number of epochs to 40. The learning rate schedule is the same as that described in Vaswani et al. (2017). We applied dropout (Srivastava et al., 2014) with a rate of 0.3. We set the beam size to 5 with length normalization. Moreover, to generate various errors, we used the noising beam search method proposed by Xie et al. (2018). In this method, we add $r\beta_{\text{random}}$ to the score of each hypothesis in the beam search. Here, r is randomly sampled from a uniform distribution of interval $[0, 1]$, and $\beta_{\text{random}} \in \mathbb{R}_{\geq 0}$ is a hyperparameter that adjusts the noise scale. In this experiment, β_{random} was set to 8, 10, and 12 for the Transformer, CNN, and LSTM, respectively[6].

Transformer. Our Transformer model was based on Vaswani et al. (2017), which is a 6-layer encoder and decoder with 512-dimensional embeddings, 2,048 for inner-layers, and 8 self-attention heads.

CNN. Our CNN model was based on Gehring et al. (2017), which is a 20-layer encoder and decoder with 512-dimensional embeddings, both using kernels of width 3 and hidden size 512.

LSTM. Our LSTM model was based on Luong et al. (2015), which is a 1-layer encoder and decoder with 512-dimensional embeddings and hidden size 512.

4 Results

4.1 Overall Results

Separate pseudo data. The top group in Table 2 depicts the results of the GEC model using each BT model; the best BT model was different for each test set. The GEC model using the Transformer achieved the best scores in the CoNLL-2014. In contrast, in the JFLEG and BEA-test, the GEC model using CNN achieved the best scores. Moreover, the GEC model using LSTM achieved a higher $F_{0.5}$ than that using the Transformer in the BEA-test. These results suggest that the Transformer, which is robust as the GEC model (Kiyono et al., 2019), is not necessarily a good BT model.

Combined pseudo data. The bottom group of Table 2 shows the results of the GEC model using combined pseudo data. As shown in Table 2, a combination of pseudo data generated by different BT models consistently improved the performance

[5] When training each BT model, the argument *–arch* in the fairseq toolkit was set to `transformer`, `fconv`, and `lstm` for the Transformer, CNN, and LSTM, respectively.

[6] Each β_{random} achieved the best $F_{0.5}$ score on the BEA-valid in the preliminary experiments.

Error type	Freq.	Baseline	Back-translation model					
			Transformer	CNN	LSTM	Transformer & CNN	Transformer & Transformer	CNN & CNN
OTHER	697	22.2±1.77	**31.8±0.71**	31.7±0.77	30.6±0.16	**34.2±1.03**	31.8±1.01	31.6±0.74
PUNCT	613	65.6±2.02	64.6±0.42	**67.8±0.83**	67.3±1.83	65.9±1.51	66.0±0.73	**67.8±0.93**
DET	607	53.8±0.71	64.8±1.62	65.0±0.41	**65.2±0.83**	64.8±0.64	**66.7±1.15**	64.7±0.75
PREP	417	48.2±0.55	58.1±0.76	**59.3±0.54**	55.2±1.74	**61.1±0.43**	60.3±0.76	60.3±1.06
ORTH	381	72.7±2.47	77.2±0.50	**78.7±1.50**	78.0±1.95	**79.2±1.25**	78.4±1.28	78.8±0.74
SPELL	315	58.3±3.49	71.0±1.71	71.1±1.45	**71.6±0.50**	**73.3±1.03**	72.5±0.40	71.1±0.49
NOUN:NUM	263	57.8±2.23	**64.4±1.09**	63.7±0.90	63.9±1.35	66.2±0.43	**66.3±0.61**	64.6±1.41
VERB:TENSE	256	43.9±2.35	52.1±1.58	**54.6±0.94**	52.6±0.50	53.7±1.71	54.6±0.64	**54.8±1.27**
VERB:FORM	213	62.0±2.26	66.7±2.63	**67.1±0.46**	66.0±1.60	66.3±0.34	**66.9±1.54**	66.6±1.01
VERB	196	32.5±3.41	36.0±1.18	36.3±0.91	**39.7±3.05**	**42.7±3.83**	39.0±0.76	38.2±0.98
VERB:SVA	157	66.1±1.38	73.7±3.00	**75.6±0.86**	73.8±2.51	75.1±1.04	**76.3±1.20**	74.3±0.44
MORPH	155	54.0±2.03	61.9±1.97	**63.8±1.23**	**63.8±0.53**	64.5±0.62	**66.3±1.26**	63.8±2.84
PRON	139	43.8±2.00	**53.0±2.79**	51.8±0.14	49.6±1.93	**53.3±1.10**	52.7±2.75	**53.3±0.46**
NOUN	129	19.7±2.04	**31.4±0.62**	30.2±2.39	30.5±2.17	**35.9±2.90**	34.5±1.48	32.8±2.80

Table 3: Each error type's $F_{0.5}$ of the single models on the BEA-test. We extracted error types with a frequency of 100 or more. The total frequency of all error types was 4,882. For details of error types, see Bryant et al. (2017).

compared with pseudo data from a single source (Transformer & CNN > Transformer, CNN). In contrast, in some of the items in Table 2, the performances of the GEC models using the single BT models with different seeds were lower than that using only a single BT model. For example, when using the Transformer as the BT model, the $F_{0.5}$ score of the ensemble model using a single BT model was 59.0 on the CoNLL-2014, whereas that using two homogeneous BT models was 58.9 (Transformer & Transformer: 58.9 < Transformer: 59.0). Similarly, for CNN, the $F_{0.5}$ score of the ensemble model using only a single BT model was 63.4 on the BEA-test, whereas that using two homogeneous BT models was 63.3 (CNN & CNN: 63.3 < CNN: 63.4). Hence, the combination of different BT models enables the construction of a more robust GEC model than the combination of single BT models with different seeds.

4.2 Results of Each Error Type

Separate pseudo data. The left side of Table 3 illustrates the $F_{0.5}$ scores of the single models on the BEA-test across various error types. When using the Transformer as the BT model, the performance of PRON was high. In contrast, the performance of PREP, VERB:TENSE, and VERB:SVA was high when using CNN, and the performance of VERB was high when using LSTM, to name a few. Therefore, it is considered that correction tendencies of each error type are different depending on the BT model.

In PUNCT, the performance of the GEC model using the Transformer was lower than that of the baseline model (Transformer: 64.6 < Baseline: 65.6). Moreover, when using CNN and LSTM as the BT model, the performance of PUNCT improved by only approximately 2 points in $F_{0.5}$ from the baseline model (CNN: 67.8, LSTM: 67.3 > Baseline: 65.6). It can be seen that this improvement of PUNCT is small compared with that of other error types. Therefore, when using pseudo data generated by BT, PUNCT is considered an error type that is difficult to improve.

Combined pseudo data. The right side of Table 3 shows the $F_{0.5}$ scores of the single models using combined pseudo data on the BEA-test across various error types. Except for 3 of the 14 error types shown in Table 3, the GEC model using Transformer & CNN yielded the higher $F_{0.5}$ scores than using at least either Transformer & Transformer or CNN & CNN. Therefore, it is considered that the combination of different BT models improves or interpolates performance compared with that of single BT models with different seeds.

In OTHER, the combination of single BT models with different seeds did not improve the performance of OTHER compared with a single BT model (Transformer & Transformer: 31.8 = Transformer: 31.8 and CNN & CNN: 31.6 < CNN: 31.7). Conversely, the combination of different BT models improved the performance of OTHER compared with a single BT model (Transformer & CNN: 34.2 > Transformer: 31.8, CNN: 31.7). Thus, by using different BT models, the GEC model is expected to correct more diverse error types.

Error type	Transformer Token	Transformer Type	Transformer $F_{0.5}$ w/ FT	Transformer $F_{0.5}$ w/o FT	CNN Token	CNN Type	CNN $F_{0.5}$ w/ FT	CNN $F_{0.5}$ w/o FT	LSTM Token	LSTM Type	LSTM $F_{0.5}$ w/ FT	LSTM $F_{0.5}$ w/o FT
Overall	64,733,183	12,364,575	58.4	**32.7**	77,784,638	17,711,223	**59.3**	31.4	**90,205,852**	**25,502,133**	58.5	25.2
OTHER	16,463,382	6,084,184	**31.8**	**10.0**	20,237,776	8,453,119	31.7	9.6	**29,286,403**	**13,844,773**	30.6	6.3
PUNCT	3,716,117	37,360	64.6	**47.1**	3,814,449	46,724	**67.8**	46.1	**4,082,594**	**53,739**	67.3	43.1
DET	8,074,615	**39,606**	64.8	**41.5**	**8,491,264**	39,402	65.0	39.2	8,217,106	33,389	**65.2**	33.0
PREP	6,832,627	19,521	58.1	**36.7**	7,935,894	23,564	**59.3**	35.8	**8,091,043**	**25,923**	55.2	30.3
ORTH	3,378,022	521,032	77.2	**62.7**	**3,973,439**	**646,475**	**78.7**	61.4	3,587,805	513,787	78.0	60.0
SPELL	6,620,395	2,795,425	71.0	**57.0**	11,224,522	4,737,493	71.1	56.3	**11,342,223**	**5,643,091**	**71.6**	50.8
NOUN:NUM	**2,241,413**	**31,939**	**64.4**	**45.2**	2,149,748	30,205	63.7	43.9	2,177,546	28,226	63.9	41.3
VERB:TENSE	2,585,017	58,935	52.1	**27.2**	**2,599,663**	**60,266**	**54.6**	26.6	2,418,040	59,207	52.6	22.6
VERB:FORM	1,287,912	47,071	66.7	45.5	1,421,381	**48,776**	**67.1**	**46.2**	**1,517,365**	48,117	66.0	41.1
VERB	1,821,117	328,147	36.0	**18.5**	2,201,360	453,181	36.3	17.2	**2,704,117**	**647,785**	**39.7**	12.9
VERB:SVA	761,768	**6,564**	73.7	52.5	784,762	6,136	**75.6**	**52.8**	**824,241**	6,019	73.8	45.5
MORPH	2,306,204	148,506	61.9	32.5	2,308,793	147,657	**63.8**	**32.6**	**2,613,870**	**167,440**	**63.8**	29.2
PRON	810,875	3,642	**53.0**	**14.7**	995,686	4,013	51.8	12.7	**1,248,554**	**5,267**	49.6	10.9
NOUN	4,402,909	1,888,994	**31.4**	**14.8**	6,155,680	2,697,991	30.2	14.4	**8,196,758**	**4,032,482**	30.5	9.8

Table 4: Number of edit pair tokens and types in pseudo data generated by each BT model and each error type's $F_{0.5}$ of the single models with and without fine-tuning on the BEA-test. As with Table 3, we extracted error types with a frequency of 100 or more in the BEA-test. FT denotes fine-tuning.

Effects of different seeds. Here, we consider the effect of different seeds in the BT model. In some error types in Table 3, the GEC model using single BT models with different seeds has the higher $F_{0.5}$ score than that using different BT models. One of the reasons for this is that there exists some variation (i.e., high standard deviation) in the $F_{0.5}$ score of each error type, even when changing merely the seed of the BT model. For example, in the GEC model using the Transformer, the standard deviation of DET was 1.62, which is relatively high. Then, the $F_{0.5}$ score of DET using Transformer & Transformer was higher than that using Transformer & CNN. Thus, in error types with some variation, using single BT models with different seeds may improve performance compared with using different BT models.

5 Discussion

We examined the number of edit pairs in pseudo data generated by each BT model. We annotated pseudo data using ERRANT and extracted edit pairs from the pseudo source sentences and target sentences. Table 4 shows the number of edit pair tokens and types in the pseudo data generated by each BT model. We expected that the higher the number of errors in each error type, the better the $F_{0.5}$ score of the GEC model for each error type. However, the results did not show such a tendency. Specifically, when the number of edit pair tokens and types was the highest in each error type, only 6 of the 14 error types had the highest $F_{0.5}$ score (ORTH, SPELL, NOUN:NUM, VERB:TENSE, VERB, and MORPH). This fact implies that simply increasing the number of tokens or types in each error type may not improve each error type's performance in the GEC model.

Moreover, we investigated the performance of the GEC model with and without fine-tuning. As shown in Table 4, when fine-tuning was not carried out (i.e., pre-training only), the GEC model using the Transformer had the highest $F_{0.5}$ score, and there was a 7.5 point difference in $F_{0.5}$ between the Transformer and the LSTM (Transformer: 32.7 > LSTM: 25.2). However, interestingly, when fine-tuning was performed, the GEC model using LSTM achieved a better $F_{0.5}$ score than that using the Transformer (Transformer: 58.4 < LSTM: 58.5). This result suggests that even if the performance of the GEC model is low in pre-training, it may become high after fine-tuning.

6 Conclusions

In this study, we investigated correction tendencies based on each BT model. The results showed that the correction tendencies of each error type varied depending on the BT models. In addition, we found that the combination of different BT models improves or interpolates the $F_{0.5}$ score compared with that of single BT models with different seeds.

Acknowledgments

We would like to thank Lang-8, Inc. for providing the text data. We would also like to thank the anonymous reviewers for their valuable comments. This work was partly supported by JSPS KAKENHI Grant Number 19KK0286.

References

Dzmitry Bahdanau, Kyunghyun Cho, and Yoshua Bengio. 2015. Neural Machine Translation by Jointly Learning to Align and Translate. In *Proceedings of the 3rd International Conference on Learning Representations*, San Diego, California.

Christopher Bryant, Mariano Felice, Øistein E. Andersen, and Ted Briscoe. 2019. The BEA-2019 Shared Task on Grammatical Error Correction. In *Proceedings of the Fourteenth Workshop on Innovative Use of NLP for Building Educational Applications*, pages 52–75, Florence, Italy. Association for Computational Linguistics.

Christopher Bryant, Mariano Felice, and Ted Briscoe. 2017. Automatic Annotation and Evaluation of Error Types for Grammatical Error Correction. In *Proceedings of the 55th Annual Meeting of the Association for Computational Linguistics*, pages 793–805, Vancouver, Canada. Association for Computational Linguistics.

Isaac Caswell, Ciprian Chelba, and David Grangier. 2019. Tagged Back-Translation. In *Proceedings of the Fourth Conference on Machine Translation*, pages 53–63, Florence, Italy. Association for Computational Linguistics.

Yo Joong Choe, Jiyeon Ham, Kyubyong Park, and Yeoil Yoon. 2019. A Neural Grammatical Error Correction System Built On Better Pre-training and Sequential Transfer Learning. In *Proceedings of the Fourteenth Workshop on Innovative Use of NLP for Building Educational Applications*, pages 213–227, Florence, Italy. Association for Computational Linguistics.

Shamil Chollampatt and Hwee Tou Ng. 2018. A Multilayer Convolutional Encoder-Decoder Neural Network for Grammatical Error Correction. In *Proceedings of the Thirty-Second AAAI Conference on Artificial Intelligence*, pages 5755–5762, New Orleans, Louisiana. Association for the Advancement of Artificial Intelligence.

Daniel Dahlmeier and Hwee Tou Ng. 2012. Better Evaluation for Grammatical Error Correction. In *Proceedings of the 2012 Conference of the North American Chapter of the Association for Computational Linguistics: Human Language Technologies*, pages 568–572, Montréal, Canada. Association for Computational Linguistics.

Daniel Dahlmeier, Hwee Tou Ng, and Siew Mei Wu. 2013. Building a Large Annotated Corpus of Learner English: The NUS Corpus of Learner English. In *Proceedings of the Eighth Workshop on Innovative Use of NLP for Building Educational Applications*, pages 22–31, Atlanta, Georgia. Association for Computational Linguistics.

Zi-Yi Dou, Antonios Anastasopoulos, and Graham Neubig. 2020. Dynamic Data Selection and Weighting for Iterative Back-Translation. In *Proceedings of the 2020 Conference on Empirical Methods in Natural Language Processing*, pages 5894–5904, Online. Association for Computational Linguistics.

Sergey Edunov, Myle Ott, Michael Auli, and David Grangier. 2018. Understanding Back-Translation at Scale. In *Proceedings of the 2018 Conference on Empirical Methods in Natural Language Processing*, pages 489–500, Brussels, Belgium. Association for Computational Linguistics.

Sergey Edunov, Myle Ott, Marc'Aurelio Ranzato, and Michael Auli. 2020. On The Evaluation of Machine Translation Systems Trained With Back-Translation. In *Proceedings of the 58th Annual Meeting of the Association for Computational Linguistics*, pages 2836–2846, Online. Association for Computational Linguistics.

Marzieh Fadaee and Christof Monz. 2018. Back-Translation Sampling by Targeting Difficult Words in Neural Machine Translation. In *Proceedings of the 2018 Conference on Empirical Methods in Natural Language Processing*, pages 436–446, Brussels, Belgium. Association for Computational Linguistics.

Mariano Felice, Christopher Bryant, and Ted Briscoe. 2016. Automatic Extraction of Learner Errors in ESL Sentences Using Linguistically Enhanced Alignments. In *Proceedings of the 26th International Conference on Computational Linguistics: Technical Papers*, pages 825–835, Osaka, Japan. The COLING 2016 Organizing Committee.

Tao Ge, Furu Wei, and Ming Zhou. 2018a. Fluency Boost Learning and Inference for Neural Grammatical Error Correction. In *Proceedings of the 56th Annual Meeting of the Association for Computational Linguistics*, pages 1055–1065, Melbourne, Australia. Association for Computational Linguistics.

Tao Ge, Furu Wei, and Ming Zhou. 2018b. Reaching Human-level Performance in Automatic Grammatical Error Correction: An Empirical Study. *arXiv preprint arXiv:1807.01270v5 [cs.CL].*

Jonas Gehring, Michael Auli, David Grangier, Denis Yarats, and Yann N. Dauphin. 2017. Convolutional Sequence to Sequence Learning. In *Proceedings of the 34th International Conference on Machine Learning*, pages 1243–1252, Sydney, Australia. PMLR.

Miguel Graça, Yunsu Kim, Julian Schamper, Shahram Khadivi, and Hermann Ney. 2019. Generalizing Back-Translation in Neural Machine Translation. In *Proceedings of the Fourth Conference on Machine Translation*, pages 45–52, Florence, Italy. Association for Computational Linguistics.

Sylviane Granger. 1998. The computerized learner corpus: a versatile new source of data for SLA research. In *Learner English on Computer*, pages 3–18. Addison Wesley Longman, London and New York.

Roman Grundkiewicz and Marcin Junczys-Dowmunt. 2018. Near Human-Level Performance in Grammatical Error Correction with Hybrid Machine Translation. In *Proceedings of the 2018 Conference of the North American Chapter of the Association for Computational Linguistics: Human Language Technologies*, pages 284–290, New Orleans, Louisiana. Association for Computational Linguistics.

Roman Grundkiewicz and Marcin Junczys-Dowmunt. 2019. Minimally-Augmented Grammatical Error Correction. In *Proceedings of the 5th Workshop on Noisy User-generated Text*, pages 357–363, Hong Kong, China. Association for Computational Linguistics.

Roman Grundkiewicz, Marcin Junczys-Dowmunt, and Kenneth Heafield. 2019. Neural Grammatical Error Correction Systems with Unsupervised Pre-training on Synthetic Data. In *Proceedings of the Fourteenth Workshop on Innovative Use of NLP for Building Educational Applications*, pages 252–263, Florence, Italy. Association for Computational Linguistics.

Michael Heilman, Aoife Cahill, Nitin Madnani, Melissa Lopez, Matthew Mulholland, and Joel Tetreault. 2014. Predicting Grammaticality on an Ordinal Scale. In *Proceedings of the 52nd Annual Meeting of the Association for Computational Linguistics*, pages 174–180, Baltimore, Maryland. Association for Computational Linguistics.

Kengo Hotate, Masahiro Kaneko, and Mamoru Komachi. 2020. Generating Diverse Corrections with Local Beam Search for Grammatical Error Correction. In *Proceedings of the 28th International Conference on Computational Linguistics*, pages 2132–2137, Barcelona, Spain (Online). International Committee on Computational Linguistics.

Phu Mon Htut and Joel Tetreault. 2019. The Unbearable Weight of Generating Artificial Errors for Grammatical Error Correction. In *Proceedings of the Fourteenth Workshop on Innovative Use of NLP for Building Educational Applications*, pages 478–483, Florence, Italy. Association for Computational Linguistics.

Jianshu Ji, Qinlong Wang, Kristina Toutanova, Yongen Gong, Steven Truong, and Jianfeng Gao. 2017. A Nested Attention Neural Hybrid Model for Grammatical Error Correction. In *Proceedings of the 55th Annual Meeting of the Association for Computational Linguistics*, pages 753–762, Vancouver, Canada. Association for Computational Linguistics.

Marcin Junczys-Dowmunt, Roman Grundkiewicz, Shubha Guha, and Kenneth Heafield. 2018. Approaching Neural Grammatical Error Correction as a Low-Resource Machine Translation Task. In *Proceedings of the 2018 Conference of the North American Chapter of the Association for Computational Linguistics: Human Language Technologies*, pages 595–606, New Orleans, Louisiana. Association for Computational Linguistics.

Masahiro Kaneko, Masato Mita, Shun Kiyono, Jun Suzuki, and Kentaro Inui. 2020. Encoder-Decoder Models Can Benefit from Pre-trained Masked Language Models in Grammatical Error Correction. In *Proceedings of the 58th Annual Meeting of the Association for Computational Linguistics*, pages 4248–4254, Online. Association for Computational Linguistics.

Yoav Kantor, Yoav Katz, Leshem Choshen, Edo Cohen-Karlik, Naftali Liberman, Assaf Toledo, Amir Menczel, and Noam Slonim. 2019. Learning to combine Grammatical Error Corrections. In *Proceedings of the Fourteenth Workshop on Innovative Use of NLP for Building Educational Applications*, pages 139–148, Florence, Italy. Association for Computational Linguistics.

Sudhanshu Kasewa, Pontus Stenetorp, and Sebastian Riedel. 2018. Wronging a Right: Generating Better Errors to Improve Grammatical Error Detection. In *Proceedings of the 2018 Conference on Empirical Methods in Natural Language Processing*, pages 4977–4983, Brussels, Belgium. Association for Computational Linguistics.

Diederik P. Kingma and Jimmy Ba. 2015. Adam: A Method for Stochastic Optimization. In *Proceedings of the 3rd International Conference on Learning Representations*, San Diego, California.

Shun Kiyono, Jun Suzuki, Masato Mita, Tomoya Mizumoto, and Kentaro Inui. 2019. An Empirical Study of Incorporating Pseudo Data into Grammatical Error Correction. In *Proceedings of the 2019 Conference on Empirical Methods in Natural Language Processing and the 9th International Joint Conference on Natural Language Processing*, pages 1236–1242, Hong Kong, China. Association for Computational Linguistics.

Shun Kiyono, Jun Suzuki, Tomoya Mizumoto, and Kentaro Inui. 2020. Massive Exploration of Pseudo Data for Grammatical Error Correction. *IEEE/ACM Transactions on Audio, Speech, and Language Processing*, 28:2134–2145.

Philipp Koehn and Rebecca Knowles. 2017. Six Challenges for Neural Machine Translation. In *Proceedings of the First Workshop on Neural Machine Translation*, pages 28–39, Vancouver, Canada. Association for Computational Linguistics.

Jared Lichtarge, Chris Alberti, Shankar Kumar, Noam Shazeer, Niki Parmar, and Simon Tong. 2019. Corpora Generation for Grammatical Error Correction. In *Proceedings of the 2019 Conference of the North American Chapter of the Association for Computational Linguistics: Human Language Technologies*, pages 3291–3301, Minneapolis, Minnesota. Association for Computational Linguistics.

Thang Luong, Hieu Pham, and Christopher D. Manning. 2015. Effective Approaches to Attention-based Neural Machine Translation. In *Proceed-*

ings of the 2015 Conference on Empirical Methods in Natural Language Processing, pages 1412–1421, Lisbon, Portugal. Association for Computational Linguistics.

Tomoya Mizumoto, Mamoru Komachi, Masaaki Nagata, and Yuji Matsumoto. 2011. Mining Revision Log of Language Learning SNS for Automated Japanese Error Correction of Second Language Learners. In *Proceedings of 5th International Joint Conference on Natural Language Processing*, pages 147–155, Chiang Mai, Thailand. Asian Federation of Natural Language Processing.

Courtney Napoles, Keisuke Sakaguchi, Matt Post, and Joel Tetreault. 2015. Ground Truth for Grammatical Error Correction Metrics. In *Proceedings of the 53rd Annual Meeting of the Association for Computational Linguistics and the 7th International Joint Conference on Natural Language Processing*, pages 588–593, Beijing, China. Association for Computational Linguistics.

Courtney Napoles, Keisuke Sakaguchi, Matt Post, and Joel Tetreault. 2016. GLEU Without Tuning. *arXiv preprint arXiv:1605.02592v1 [cs.CL].*

Courtney Napoles, Keisuke Sakaguchi, and Joel Tetreault. 2017. JFLEG: A Fluency Corpus and Benchmark for Grammatical Error Correction. In *Proceedings of the 15th Conference of the European Chapter of the Association for Computational Linguistics*, pages 229–234, Valencia, Spain. Association for Computational Linguistics.

Hwee Tou Ng, Siew Mei Wu, Ted Briscoe, Christian Hadiwinoto, Raymond Hendy Susanto, and Christopher Bryant. 2014. The CoNLL-2014 Shared Task on Grammatical Error Correction. In *Proceedings of the Eighteenth Conference on Computational Natural Language Learning: Shared Task*, pages 1–14, Baltimore, Maryland. Association for Computational Linguistics.

Myle Ott, Sergey Edunov, Alexei Baevski, Angela Fan, Sam Gross, Nathan Ng, David Grangier, and Michael Auli. 2019. fairseq: A Fast, Extensible Toolkit for Sequence Modeling. In *Proceedings of the 2019 Conference of the North American Chapter of the Association for Computational Linguistics (Demonstrations)*, pages 48–53, Minneapolis, Minnesota. Association for Computational Linguistics.

Alberto Poncelas, Dimitar Shterionov, Andy Way, Gideon Maillette De Buy Wenniger, and Peyman Passban. 2018. Investigating Backtranslation in Neural Machine Translation. In *Proceedings of the 21st Annual Conference of the European Association for Machine Translation*, pages 249–258, Alacant, Spain. European Association for Machine Translation.

Mengyang Qiu, Xuejiao Chen, Maggie Liu, Krishna Parvathala, Apurva Patil, and Jungyeul Park. 2019. Improving Precision of Grammatical Error Correction with a Cheat Sheet. In *Proceedings of the Fourteenth Workshop on Innovative Use of NLP for Building Educational Applications*, pages 240–245, Florence, Italy. Association for Computational Linguistics.

Marek Rei, Mariano Felice, Zheng Yuan, and Ted Briscoe. 2017. Artificial Error Generation with Machine Translation and Syntactic Patterns. In *Proceedings of the 12th Workshop on Innovative Use of NLP for Building Educational Applications*, pages 287–292, Copenhagen, Denmark. Association for Computational Linguistics.

Rico Sennrich, Barry Haddow, and Alexandra Birch. 2016a. Improving Neural Machine Translation Models with Monolingual Data. In *Proceedings of the 54th Annual Meeting of the Association for Computational Linguistics*, pages 86–96, Berlin, Germany. Association for Computational Linguistics.

Rico Sennrich, Barry Haddow, and Alexandra Birch. 2016b. Neural Machine Translation of Rare Words with Subword Units. In *Proceedings of the 54th Annual Meeting of the Association for Computational Linguistics*, pages 1715–1725, Berlin, Germany. Association for Computational Linguistics.

Noam Shazeer and Mitchell Stern. 2018. Adafactor: Adaptive Learning Rates with Sublinear Memory Cost. In *Proceedings of the 35th International Conference on Machine Learning*, pages 4596–4604, Stockholm, Sweden. PMLR.

Yikang Shen, Zhouhan Lin, Chin-Wei Huang, and Aaron C. Courville. 2018. Neural Language Modeling by Jointly Learning Syntax and Lexicon. In *Proceedings of the 6th International Conference on Learning Representations*, Vancouver, Canada. OpenReview.net.

Yikang Shen, Shawn Tan, Alessandro Sordoni, and Aaron C. Courville. 2019. Ordered Neurons: Integrating Tree Structures into Recurrent Neural Networks. In *Proceedings of the 7th International Conference on Learning Representations*, New Orleans, Louisiana. OpenReview.net.

Xabier Soto, Dimitar Shterionov, Alberto Poncelas, and Andy Way. 2020. Selecting Backtranslated Data from Multiple Sources for Improved Neural Machine Translation. In *Proceedings of the 58th Annual Meeting of the Association for Computational Linguistics*, pages 3898–3908, Online. Association for Computational Linguistics.

Nitish Srivastava, Geoffrey Hinton, Alex Krizhevsky, Ilya Sutskever, and Ruslan Salakhutdinov. 2014. Dropout: A Simple Way to Prevent Neural Networks from Overfitting. *Journal of Machine Learning Research*, 15(56):1929–1958.

Ilya Sutskever, Oriol Vinyals, and Quoc V Le. 2014. Sequence to Sequence Learning with Neural Networks. In *Advances in Neural Information Processing Systems 27*, pages 3104–3112, Montreal, Canada. Curran Associates, Inc.

Christian Szegedy, Vincent Vanhoucke, Sergey Ioffe, Jon Shlens, and Zbigniew Wojna. 2016. Rethinking the Inception Architecture for Computer Vision. In *Proceedings of the 2016 IEEE Conference on Computer Vision and Pattern Recognition*, pages 2818–2826, Las Vegas, Nevada. Institute of Electrical and Electronics Engineers.

Toshikazu Tajiri, Mamoru Komachi, and Yuji Matsumoto. 2012. Tense and Aspect Error Correction for ESL Learners Using Global Context. In *Proceedings of the 50th Annual Meeting of the Association for Computational Linguistics*, pages 198–202, Jeju Island, Korea. Association for Computational Linguistics.

Yujin Takahashi, Satoru Katsumata, and Mamoru Komachi. 2020. Grammatical Error Correction Using Pseudo Learner Corpus Considering Learner's Error Tendency. In *Proceedings of the 58th Annual Meeting of the Association for Computational Linguistics: Student Research Workshop*, pages 27–32, Online. Association for Computational Linguistics.

Ashish Vaswani, Noam Shazeer, Niki Parmar, Jakob Uszkoreit, Llion Jones, Aidan N Gomez, Łukasz Kaiser, and Illia Polosukhin. 2017. Attention is All you Need. In *Advances in Neural Information Processing Systems 30*, pages 5998–6008, Long Beach, California. Curran Associates, Inc.

Zhaohong Wan, Xiaojun Wan, and Wenguang Wang. 2020. Improving Grammatical Error Correction with Data Augmentation by Editing Latent Representation. In *Proceedings of the 28th International Conference on Computational Linguistics*, pages 2202–2212, Barcelona, Spain (Online). International Committee on Computational Linguistics.

Chencheng Wang, Liner Yang, Yun Chen, Yongping Du, and Erhong Yang. 2020. Controllable Data Synthesis Method for Grammatical Error Correction. *arXiv preprint arXiv:1909.13302v3 [cs.CL]*.

Lihao Wang and Xiaoqing Zheng. 2020. Improving Grammatical Error Correction Models with Purpose-Built Adversarial Examples. In *Proceedings of the 2020 Conference on Empirical Methods in Natural Language Processing*, pages 2858–2869, Online. Association for Computational Linguistics.

Max White and Alla Rozovskaya. 2020. A Comparative Study of Synthetic Data Generation Methods for Grammatical Error Correction. In *Proceedings of the Fifteenth Workshop on Innovative Use of NLP for Building Educational Applications*, pages 198–208, Seattle, Washington (Online). Association for Computational Linguistics.

Ziang Xie, Guillaume Genthial, Stanley Xie, Andrew Ng, and Dan Jurafsky. 2018. Noising and Denoising Natural Language: Diverse Backtranslation for Grammar Correction. In *Proceedings of the 2018 Conference of the North American Chapter of the Association for Computational Linguistics: Human Language Technologies*, pages 619–628, New Orleans, Louisiana. Association for Computational Linguistics.

Shuyao Xu, Jiehao Zhang, Jin Chen, and Long Qin. 2019. Erroneous data generation for Grammatical Error Correction. In *Proceedings of the Fourteenth Workshop on Innovative Use of NLP for Building Educational Applications*, pages 149–158, Florence, Italy. Association for Computational Linguistics.

Helen Yannakoudakis, Ted Briscoe, and Ben Medlock. 2011. A New Dataset and Method for Automatically Grading ESOL Texts. In *Proceedings of the 49th Annual Meeting of the Association for Computational Linguistics: Human Language Technologies*, pages 180–189, Portland, Oregon. Association for Computational Linguistics.

Helen Yannakoudakis, Øistein E Andersen, Ardeshir Geranpayeh, Ted Briscoe, and Diane Nicholls. 2018. Developing an automated writing placement system for ESL learners. *Applied Measurement in Education*, 31(3):251–267.

Zheng Yuan and Ted Briscoe. 2016. Grammatical error correction using neural machine translation. In *Proceedings of the 2016 Conference of the North American Chapter of the Association for Computational Linguistics: Human Language Technologies*, pages 380–386, San Diego, California. Association for Computational Linguistics.

Yi Zhang, Tao Ge, Furu Wei, Ming Zhou, and Xu Sun. 2019. Sequence-to-sequence Pre-training with Data Augmentation for Sentence Rewriting. *arXiv preprint arXiv:1909.06002v2 [cs.CL]*.

Wei Zhao, Liang Wang, Kewei Shen, Ruoyu Jia, and Jingming Liu. 2019. Improving Grammatical Error Correction via Pre-Training a Copy-Augmented Architecture with Unlabeled Data. In *Proceedings of the 2019 Conference of the North American Chapter of the Association for Computational Linguistics: Human Language Technologies*, pages 156–165, Minneapolis, Minnesota. Association for Computational Linguistics.

Wangchunshu Zhou, Tao Ge, Chang Mu, Ke Xu, Furu Wei, and Ming Zhou. 2020a. Improving Grammatical Error Correction with Machine Translation Pairs. In *Findings of the Association for Computational Linguistics: EMNLP 2020*, pages 318–328, Online. Association for Computational Linguistics.

Wangchunshu Zhou, Tao Ge, and Ke Xu. 2020b. Pseudo-Bidirectional Decoding for Local Sequence Transduction. In *Findings of the Association for Computational Linguistics: EMNLP 2020*, pages 1506–1511, Online. Association for Computational Linguistics.

Parallel sentences mining with transfer learning in an unsupervised setting

Yu Sun
Zhengzhou University of Light Industry

Shaolin Zhu *
Zhengzhou University of Light Industry
zhushaolin003@163.com

Chenggang Mi
Northwestern Polytechnical University
michenggang@nwpu.edu.cn

Yifan Feng
Zhengzhou University of Light Industry

Abstract

The quality and quantity of parallel sentences are known as very important training data for constructing neural machine translation (N-MT) systems. However, these resources are not available for many low-resource language pairs. Many existing methods need strong supervision and hence are not suitable. Although there have been several attempts at developing unsupervised models, they ignore the language-invariant between languages. In this paper, we propose an approach based on transfer learning to mine parallel sentences in an unsupervised setting. With the help of bilingual corpora of rich-resource language pairs, we can mine parallel sentences without bilingual supervision of low-resource language pairs. Experiments show that our approach improves the performance of mined parallel sentences compared with previous methods. In particular, we achieve good results at two real-world low-resource language pairs.

1 Introduction

Parallel sentences are known as very important training data for constructing machine translation (MT) systems (Belinkov and Bisk, 2018). The volumes of quality parallel sentences heavily affect the performance of trained machine translation systems. However, these resources are only available for a handful of language pairs and domains while the others suffer from the scarcity problem (Bouamor and Sajjad, 2018). In this situation, parallel sentences are very crucial for training machine translation systems.

Transfer learning is an effective approach to mine parallel data in low-resource scenarios. (Artetxe and Schwenk, 2019) brought the evidence of cross-lingual transfer to mine parallel data for low-resource language pairs. However, their method is not unsupervised and relies on bilingual supervision (e.g, bilingual lexicon or sentences), which is not available for low-resource language pairs. Although (Kvapilíková et al., 2020) solved the supervised limitation by employing an unsupervised MT, the performance heavily depended on MT's quality.

In this paper, we propose a parallel sentences mining model based on transfer learning in an unsupervised setting[1]. As illustrated in Figure 1, we obtain sentence embeddings by mean-pooling the outputs of multilingual BERT (Lample and Conneau, 2019), which is trained on monolingual corpora. In particular, we use a language discriminator to learn shared and refined language-invariant representations for transfer learning. (Chen et al., 2018; Ziser and Reichart, 2018) pointed out the language-invariant is helpful for transfer learning. Then, we treat detecting parallel sentences as a classification task and generate multi-view semantic representations for the classifier. Generally, data from different views contain complementary information and multi-view learning exploits the consistency from multiple views (Li et al., 2018; Fei and Li, 2020). In our model, we use two views for the classifier: (i) word representations; (ii) sentence representations. In addition to achieving good results on BUCC 2018[2] shared task, we demonstrate the effectiveness of our model using an example of two low-resource language pairs where parallel corpora are almost not available.

In summary, our contributions in this paper are as follows:

(1) We propose an unsupervised method based on transfer learning to mine parallel sentences without any bilingual data for low-resource language

*Corresponding author: Shaolin Zhu, zhushaolin003@163.com

[1] The unsupervised setting means we only have monolingual corpora for a pair of language that bilingual resources are not available, while there are some language pairs have bilingual resources which we use for unsupervised transfer learning in low-resource language pairs.

[2] 11th Workshop on Building and Using Comparable Corpora

Proceedings of NAACL-HLT 2021: Student Research Workshop, pages 136–142
June 6–11, 2021. ©2021 Association for Computational Linguistics

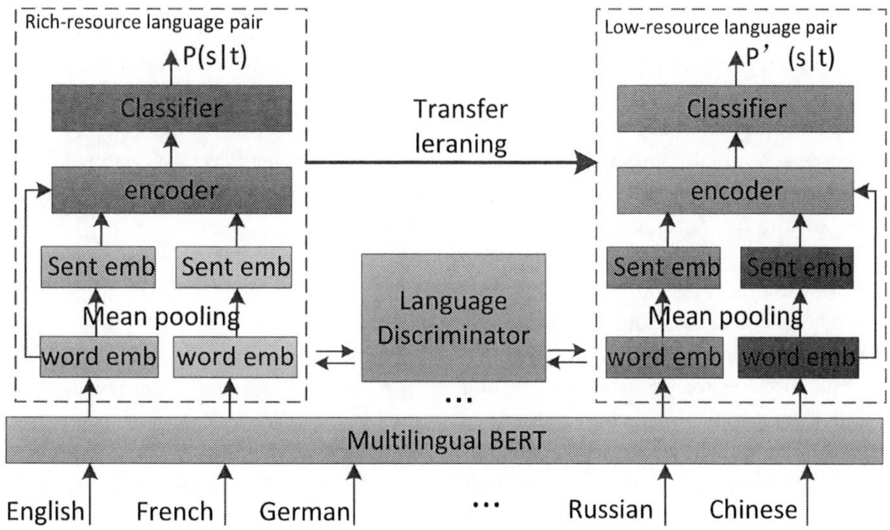

Figure 1: Our proposed method that based on multi-view transfer training for parallel phrase detection on a non-parallel sentence pair.

pairs. By designing a multi-view model, we encode the representations on word-level and sentence-level to obtain high-quality parallel data.

(2) We extensively consider the language-invariant by constructing a language discriminator to well capture the semantic similarity among languages. This makes the robustness of our model for transfer learning.

2 Related Work

Many works mine parallel corpora from monolingual data which contain potential mutual translations. Previous methods depended on engineering features. (Shi et al., 2006; Esplà-Gomis et al., 2016) used metadata information from web crawls to mine parallel data. Recent methods used cross-lingual word embeddings to obtain parallel corpora (Guo et al., 2018; Schwenk, 2018; Bouamor and Sajjad, 2018; Schwenk et al., 2019b,a). (Artetxe and Schwenk, 2019) encoded the universal language embeddings that are agnostic to languages. They used transfer learning to mine parallel sentences of low-resource language pairs. This transfer learning method inspired our work and the main difference is that they required bilingual supervision (e.g, bilingual lexicon, parallel sentences), which is not available for many low-resource language pairs.

Recently, several works developed unsupervised method to mine parallel data (Hangya et al., 2018; Hangya and Fraser, 2019; Kvapilíková et al., 2020; Keung et al., 2020). These approaches mainly rely on unsupervised cross-lingual embeddings (Artetxe et al., 2018; Lample and Conneau, 2019) that be trained on monolingual corpora. However, several researchers question that these methods may not well capture the semantic similarity among languages (Karthikeyan et al., 2019; Pires et al., 2019). Some researchers proposed to use transfer learning to solve cross-lingual applications for low-resource language pairs (Lakew et al., 2018; Kocmi, 2020). (Eriguchi et al., 2018) used a multilingual neural machine translation system to learn the word representations of rich-resource language pairs. Then, they used transfer learning to identify parallel sentences for low-resource language pairs. However, it has an implicit dependency on multilingual NMT that requires pre-training on large parallel sentences. Our transfer learning is inspired by (Fei and Li, 2020). The difference is that they mainly solve cross-lingual unsupervised sentiment classification.

3 Proposed Method

The overview of the model architecture is as shown in Figure 1. Our proposed approach based on transfer learning to mine parallel data is composed of three components: an unsupervised multilingual BERT, a language discriminator, and a multi-view classifier. Motivated by the success of unsupervised cross-lingual word embeddings (Artetxe et al., 2018; Lample and Conneau, 2019) and its application in mining parallel data (Hangya and Fraser, 2019; Keung et al., 2020), we use multilingual BERT to initialize word and sentence embeddings. Although previous methods are effective, they may ignore sentential context on using multilingual word embeddings, which could harm the performance of mining parallel corpora. In our work, we use multi-view representations to mine parallel data. We can get good performance on rich-resource language pairs. However, our aim is to obtain parallel data for low-resource language pairs. For this purpose, we use transfer learning to mine parallel data of the low-resource scenarios using rich-resource language pairs. Note that our method doesn't rely on any bilingual data of low-resource language pairs. Therefore, we can call that our method is unsupervised for low-resource language pairs.

3.1 Language Discriminator

Previous works (Chen et al., 2018; Fei and Li, 2020) indicate that cross-lingual transfer learning work well when their representations are language-invariant. We use the unsupervised multilingual BERT to map the word representations into a shared space. Although we can generate shared word representations for different languages by using the unsupervised multilingual BERT, there is still a semantic gap between languages. Following (Chen et al., 2018; Lample et al., 2018), we employ a language discriminator for getting fine-tuned word representations, which is necessary to preserve language-invariant on language transfer. In detail, the language discriminator is trained to distinguish between the mapped source and target embeddings. Then, we refine-turn the two language embeddings with a cross-lingual Procrustes method according to (Lample et al., 2018). The language discriminator contains a feed-forward neural network with two hidden layers as an encoder and one softmax layer. The objective of the discriminator is to maximize its ability to identify the source and target embeddings. The discriminator loss can be written as follows:

$$\begin{aligned} L(\theta_D|W) = & -\log P_{\theta_D}(source = 1|Wx) \\ & + \log P_{\theta_D}(target = 1|y) \end{aligned} \tag{1}$$

Where Θ_D denotes parameters of the discriminator, (x, y) corresponds to source and target language. $P_{\theta_D}(source = 1|z)$ is a probability that a vector z is the mapping W of a source embedding, $P_{\theta_D}(target = 1|z)$ is similar. In parallel, we use the Procrustes analysis to fine-tune the mapping W as follows (Lample et al., 2018). We can obtain universal language-agnostic embeddings when the discriminator is not able to identify the origin of an embedding.

3.2 Transfer Learning for Mining Parallel Data

In this paper, we propose to use transfer learning to mine parallel data of the low-resource scenarios by rich-resource language pairs. In this paper, we first consider two views of input for classifier in rich-resource language pairs:(i) the word-level representations from languages; (ii) the sentence-level representations from languages. The multi-view classifier has been demonstrated useful as data from different views contains complementary information (Chen and Qian, 2019; Fei and Li, 2020). In this paper, we use a feed-forward neural network based on LSTM with two hidden layers as an encoder to balance two view representations. Then, we train a classifier to match predicted labels with ground truth from the parallel sentences in rich-resource language pairs as follows:

$$P(s|t) = \frac{e^{enc(\theta)}}{1 + e^{enc(\theta)}} \epsilon(0, 1) \tag{2}$$

Where $enc(\theta)$ denotes parameters of the encoder. Then, we use transfer learning to mine parallel data for low-resource language pairs. The detail process is as follows: We firstly train a classifier on rich-resource language pairs (such as English-Chinese or English-French). In parallel, we use the language discriminator to fine-tune the different language representations into a shared space to keep language-invariant between languages. After that, we transfer the pre-trained classifier to detect parallel sentences for low-resource pairs. Finally, we use detected parallel data to train the classifier again in low-resource language pairs for better performance.

4 Experimental Setting

In this section, we mainly present our experimental settings and describe the datasets used.

Dataset: We test our proposed method on four language pairs of BUCC sample data (English-French, English-German, English-Russian, English-Chinese). The shared task of

	En-Fr			En-De			En-Ru			En-Zh		
	P	R	F_1	P	R	F_1	P	R	F_1	P	R	F_1
supervised methods												
Bouamor and Sajjad, 2018	87.5	65.8	75.1	-	-	-	-	-	-	-	-	-
Schwenk, 2018	84.8	68.6	75.8	84.1	70.7	76.9	81.1	67.6	73.8	77.7	66.4	71.6
Artetxe and Schwenk, 2019	91.5	93.3	92.3	95.6	95.1	95.4	90.6	94.0	92.2	91.9	91.3	91.6
unsupervised methods												
Hangya and Fraser, 2019	50.5	38.1	43.4	48.5	39.1	43.3	37.4	18.7	24.9	-	-	-
Keung et al., 2020	-	-	73.0	-	-	74.9	-	-	69.6	-	-	60.1
Hangya et al., 2018	39.0	52.6	44.8	23.7	44.5	30.9	17.3	24.9	20.4	-	-	-
Kvapilíková et al., 2020	-	-	78.7	-	-	80.1	-	-	77.1	-	-	67.0
Proposed method	81.6	79.5	80.6	88.5	85.5	86.9	80.4	78.1	80.6	78.4	76.3	77.3

Table 1: Results of our proposed systems on the BUCC shared task's training set for the 4 language-pairs. We also report the results of baselines as described in their paper. "-" represents the result are not reported in ther paper, respectively.

the workshop on Building and Using Comparable Corpora (BUCC) is a well-established evaluation framework for mining parallel corpora (Zweigenbaum et al., 2018). The shared task provides a gold standard to assess retrieval systems for precision, recall, and F_1-score. We applied our approach to all language pairs of the BUCC18 shared task. Moreover, we carry out an experiment on real-world low-resource scenarios (English-Esperanto, Chinese-Kazakh). For the monolingual data, we extract corpora from Wikipedia using WikiExtractor[3]. As there is no gold standard to evaluate mining parallel sentences, we use mined parallel sentences to train a machine translation system that can reflect the quality of mined parallel sentences.

Baselines: In our experiments, we consider supervised baselines (Bouamor and Sajjad, 2018; Schwenk, 2018; Artetxe and Schwenk, 2019). We also compare several unsupervised baselines which contains (Hangya and Fraser, 2019; Keung et al., 2020; Hangya et al., 2018; Kvapilíková et al., 2020).

5 Results and Discussions

In this section, we present the results of mining parallel sentences and our comparison to previous work. We also present results on real-world low-resource language pairs and demonstrate our obtained parallel corpora can improve the performance of machine translation.

[3]https://github.com/attardi/wikiextractor

5.1 Results on BUCC

As BUCC provides a gold standard to assess mined parallel data, we test our method on the BUCC dataset. Although the language pairs used for evaluation are all high-resources, we only simulate the low-resource scenario to justify our method here and we will present results on real-world low-resource language pairs in the section 5.3. We show precision (P), recall(R) and F_1 scores in Table 1 for the four language pairs. Noted that, we use English-German as the rich-resource language pair to initialize our model. Then, we transfer this model into other low-resource language pairs. We also test different rich-resource language pairs for transfer learning as Table 2.

Noted that, our method doesn't rely on any bilingual data of low-resource language pairs. Therefore, we can call that our method is unsupervised for low-resource language pairs. This is a fair comparison to other unsupervised methods. From Table 1, we achieve an increase of F_1 compared with unsupervised baselines for all language pairs. It also can be seen that the precision and recall of the proposed method is significantly increased for all language pair than unsupervised methods. (Artetxe and Schwenk, 2019) also used transfer learning to mine parallel sentences. However, their method needs strong supervision which is not available in low-resource language pairs. The proposed method overcomes the limitation and obtains relatively good results against (Artetxe and Schwenk, 2019).

	En-Fr			En-De			En-Ru			En-Zh		
	P	R	F_1	P	R	F_1	P	R	F_1	P	R	F_1
-language discriminator												
(En-Fr)	87.5	85.8	86.6	78.1	76.8	77.4	63.6	63.4	62.5	63.1	61.8	62
(En-Ru)	66.3	63.1	64.7	64.2	60.7	62.4	86.8	83.6	85.2	63.7	63.4	63.5
(En-Zh)	61.2	63.3	62.2	60.6	62.1	61.3	60.8	64.2	62.5	83.7	81.6	82.6
(En-De)	75.5	74.5	75.0	88.5	85.5	86.9	74.1	74.2	74.2	71.7	70.7	71.3
+language discriminator												
(En-Fr)	87.5	85.8	86.6	82.3	81.2	81.7	79.6	76.6	78.1	77.2	74.6	75.9
(En-Ru)	80.6	82.3	81.4	81.1	80.7	80.9	86.8	83.6	85.2	76.8	75.3	76.1
(En-Zh)	78.2	76.1	77.1	80.7	78.6	79.6	77.6	78.8	78.2	83.7	81.6	82.6
(En-De)	81.6	79.5	80.6	88.5	85.5	86.9	80.4	78.1	80.6	78.4	76.3	77.3

Table 2: Ablation study on the BUCC shared task. Note that, the first column indicates that we use different rich-resource language pairs for transfer learning.

5.2 Ablation Study

To understand the effect of different components in our model on the overall performance, we conduct an ablation study in Table 2 to test the language discriminator whether affects transfer learning or not. "-language discriminator" is not adding the language discriminator and "+language discriminator" is adding the language discriminator. In Table 2, the first column is that we use different rich-source language pairs to implement transfer learning for mining parallel sentences. We firstly can find that different sources have similar results for transfer learning of our model. Then, we can find that when we don't add the language discriminator, the performances of the model are not good for transfer learning. When we add the language discriminator for transfer learning, we can find that our model gets an obvious and stable improvement in all language pairs. So from Table 2, we can conclude that language-invariant is very important for transfer learning.

5.3 Results on Low-resource Language Pair

In the above section, we simulate the low-resource scenario to justify our method on the BUCC dataset. In this section, we evaluate our mined parallel sentences on real-world low-resource language pairs. We apply our method to the English-Esperanto(En-Es) and Chinese-Kazakh(Zh-Kz) language pairs. As there is no gold standard to evaluate mining parallel sentences, we use mined parallel sentences to train a machine translation system that can reflect the quality of mined parallel sentences.

Methods	**En-Es**	**Zh-Kz**
(Hangya and Fraser, 2019)	18.5	21.6
(Keung et al., 2020)	20.2	22.8
(Hangya et al., 2018)	16.3	19.3
(Kvapilíková et al., 2020)	23.6	22.7
Proposed method	24.3	25.8

Table 3: BLEU scores on different language pairs.

We use openNMT[4] to train the machine translation system. The results are as in Table 3. Based on the scores in Table 3 it can be seen that we achieve a significant performance increase compared to the unsupervised baseline. It is well-known that the quality and quantity heavily affect the performance of machine translation. The results of Table 3 demonstrate that the proposed method is effective, especially for low-resource language pairs.

6 Conclusion

In this paper, we propose an unsupervised method that uses multi-view transfer learning to mine parallel sentences. Our method can effectively use the bilingual data of rich-resource language pairs. We transfer the model of rich-resource language pairs into a low-resource situation without any supervision of low-resource language pairs. In particular, we employ a language discriminator to capture language-invariant for benefiting transfer learning. In the experiments, the results show that our method significantly and consistently outperforms the baselines.

[4]https://opennmt.net/

For the future, we would like to apply our model on other low-resource language pairs to test universal applicability in different language pairs.

Acknowledgements

This work is supported by the National Natural Science Foundation of China (61906158), the Project of Science and Technology Research in Henan Province (212102210075).

References

Mikel Artetxe, Gorka Labaka, and Eneko Agirre. 2018. A robust self-learning method for fully unsupervised cross-lingual mappings of word embeddings. In *Proceedings of the 56th Annual Meeting of the Association for Computational Linguistics (Volume 1: Long Papers)*, pages 789–798.

Mikel Artetxe and Holger Schwenk. 2019. Massively multilingual sentence embeddings for zero-shot cross-lingual transfer and beyond. *Transactions of the Association for Computational Linguistics*, 7:597–610.

Yonatan Belinkov and Yonatan Bisk. 2018. Synthetic and Natural Noise Both Break Neural Machine Translation. In *International Conference on Learning Representations.*

Houda Bouamor and Hassan Sajjad. 2018. H2@ bucc18: Parallel sentence extraction from comparable corpora using multilingual sentence embeddings. In *Proc. Workshop on Building and Using Comparable Corpora.*

Xilun Chen, Yu Sun, Ben Athiwaratkun, Claire Cardie, and Kilian Weinberger. 2018. Adversarial deep averaging networks for cross-lingual sentiment classification. *Transactions of the Association for Computational Linguistics*, 6:557–570.

Zhuang Chen and Tieyun Qian. 2019. Transfer capsule network for aspect level sentiment classification. In *Proceedings of the 57th Annual Meeting of the Association for Computational Linguistics*, pages 547–556.

Akiko Eriguchi, Melvin Johnson, Orhan Firat, Hideto Kazawa, and Wolfgang Macherey. 2018. Zero-shot cross-lingual classification using multilingual neural machine translation. *arXiv preprint arXiv:1809.04686.*

Miquel Esplà-Gomis, Mikel L Forcada, Sergio Ortiz Rojas, and Jorge Ferrández-Tordera. 2016. Bitextor's participation in WMT'16: shared task on document alignment. In *Proceedings of the First Conference on Machine Translation: Volume 2, Shared Task Papers*, pages 685–691.

Hongliang Fei and Ping Li. 2020. Cross-lingual unsupervised sentiment classification with multi-view transfer learning. In *Proceedings of the 58th Annual Meeting of the Association for Computational Linguistics*, pages 5759–5771.

Mandy Guo, Qinlan Shen, Yinfei Yang, Heming Ge, Daniel Cer, Gustavo Hernandez Abrego, Keith Stevens, Noah Constant, Yun-Hsuan Sung, Brian Strope, et al. 2018. Effective Parallel Corpus Mining using Bilingual Sentence Embeddings. In *Proceedings of the Third Conference on Machine Translation: Research Papers*, pages 165–176.

Viktor Hangya, Fabienne Braune, Yuliya Kalasouskaya, and Alexander Fraser. 2018. Unsupervised Parallel Sentence Extraction from Comparable Corpora. In *Proc. IWSLT.*

Viktor Hangya and Alexander Fraser. 2019. Unsupervised parallel sentence extraction with parallel segment detection helps machine translation. In *Proceedings of the 57th Annual Meeting of the Association for Computational Linguistics*, pages 1224–1234.

Kaliyaperumal Karthikeyan, Zihan Wang, Stephen Mayhew, and Dan Roth. 2019. Cross-lingual ability of multilingual bert: An empirical study. In *International Conference on Learning Representations.*

Phillip Keung, Julian Salazar, Yichao Lu, and Noah A Smith. 2020. Unsupervised Bitext Mining and Translation via Self-trained Contextual Embeddings. *arXiv preprint arXiv:2010.07761.*

Tom Kocmi. 2020. Exploring Benefits of Transfer Learning in Neural Machine Translation. *arXiv preprint arXiv:2001.01622.*

Ivana Kvapilíková, Mikel Artetxe, Gorka Labaka, Eneko Agirre, and Ondřej Bojar. 2020. Unsupervised Multilingual Sentence Embeddings for Parallel Corpus Mining. In *Proceedings of the 58th Annual Meeting of the Association for Computational Linguistics: Student Research Workshop*, pages 255–262.

SM Lakew, A Erofeeva, M Negri, M Federico, and M Turchi. 2018. Transfer Learning in Multilingual Neural Machine Translation with Dynamic Vocabulary. In *15th International Workshop on Spoken Language Translation*, pages 54–62.

Guillaume Lample and Alexis Conneau. 2019. Cross-lingual language model pretraining. *arXiv preprint arXiv:1901.07291.*

Guillaume Lample, Alexis Conneau, Marc'Aurelio Ranzato, Ludovic Denoyer, and Hervé Jégou. 2018. Word translation without parallel data. In *International Conference on Learning Representations.*

Yingming Li, Ming Yang, and Zhongfei Zhang. 2018. A survey of multi-view representation learning. *IEEE transactions on knowledge and data engineering*, 31(10):1863–1883.

Telmo Pires, Eva Schlinger, and Dan Garrette. 2019. How Multilingual is Multilingual BERT? In *Proceedings of the 57th Annual Meeting of the Association for Computational Linguistics*, pages 4996–5001.

Holger Schwenk. 2018. Filtering and Mining Parallel Data in a Joint Multilingual Space. In *Proceedings of the 56th Annual Meeting of the Association for Computational Linguistics (Volume 2: Short Papers)*, pages 228–234.

Holger Schwenk, Vishrav Chaudhary, Shuo Sun, Hongyu Gong, and Francisco Guzmán. 2019a. WikiMatrix: Mining 135M Parallel Sentences in 1620 Language Pairs from Wikipedia. *arXiv*, pages arXiv–1907.

Holger Schwenk, Guillaume Wenzek, Sergey Edunov, Edouard Grave, and Armand Joulin. 2019b. C-cmatrix: Mining billions of high-quality parallel sentences on the web. *arXiv preprint arXiv:1911.04944*.

Lei Shi, Cheng Niu, Ming Zhou, and Jianfeng Gao. 2006. A dom tree alignment model for mining parallel data from the web. In *Proceedings of the 21st International Conference on Computational Linguistics and 44th Annual Meeting of the Association for Computational Linguistics*, pages 489–496.

Yftah Ziser and Roi Reichart. 2018. Deep pivot-based modeling for cross-language cross-domain transfer with minimal guidance. In *Proceedings of the 2018 Conference on Empirical Methods in Natural Language Processing*, pages 238–249.

Pierre Zweigenbaum, Serge Sharoff, and Reinhard Rapp. 2018. Overview of the third BUCC shared task: Spotting parallel sentences in comparable corpora. In *Proceedings of 11th Workshop on Building and Using Comparable Corpora*, pages 39–42.

Sentence Concatenation Approach to Data Augmentation for Neural Machine Translation

Seiichiro Kondo, Kengo Hotate[*] **Tosho Hirasawa,**
Masahiro Kaneko[†] and **Mamoru Komachi**
Tokyo Metropolitan University
kondo-seiichiro@ed.tmu.ac.jp, kengo_hotate@r.recruit.co.jp
hirasawa-tosho@ed.tmu.ac.jp, masahiro.kaneko@nlp.c.titech.ac.jp
komachi@tmu.ac.jp

Abstract

Neural machine translation (NMT) has recently gained widespread attention because of its high translation accuracy. However, it shows poor performance in the translation of long sentences, which is a major issue in low-resource languages. It is assumed that this issue is caused by insufficient number of long sentences in the training data. Therefore, this study proposes a simple data augmentation method to handle long sentences. In this method, we use only the given parallel corpora as the training data and generate long sentences by concatenating two sentences. Based on the experimental results, we confirm improvements in long sentence translation by the proposed data augmentation method, despite its simplicity. Moreover, the translation quality is further improved by the proposed method, when combined with back-translation.

1 Introduction

Neural machine translation (NMT) can be used to achieve high translation quality. However, it has certain drawbacks, such as the degradation in the translation quality for long sentences. Koehn and Knowles (2017) reported that the translation quality of NMT is superior to that of statistical machine translation (SMT) for input sentences within a certain length. However, they also stated that when the sentence length exceeds a particular value, the quality of NMT becomes inferior to that of SMT, and the greater the sentence length, the lower the translation quality.

Additionally, they presented the correlation between the size of the training data and the translation quality (Koehn and Knowles, 2017). In other words, the less training data we have, the lower will be the accuracy of the translation. This issue is prevalent in low-resource languages. Therefore, various data augmentation methods for low-resource parallel corpora have been studied. For instance, the generation of pseudo data was proposed by back-translating the monolingual corpora or paraphrasing the parallel corpora as additional training data (Wang et al., 2018; Sennrich et al., 2016; Li et al., 2019).

Hence, this study proposes a data augmentation method that can be effective in long sentence translations. The proposed method is illustrated in Figure 1. Long sentences were obtained by concatenating two sentences at random and adding them to the original data. The translation quality is expected to be improved by this method because the low quality of translation of long sentences was caused by insufficient number of long sentences in the training data, which reduces this concern in the proposed method.

This study presents an improved BLEU score and higher quality in long sentence translations on English–Japanese corpus. Moreover, the BLEU score further increases by incorporating back-translation. In addition, human evaluation shows that fluency is increased more than adequacy.

In summary, the main contributions of this paper are as follows:

- We propose a simple yet effective data augmentation method, involving sentence concatenation, for long sentence translation.
- We show that the translation quality can be further improved by combining back-translation and sentence concatenation.

2 Related Works

NMT exhibits a significant decrease in the translation quality for very long sentences. Koehn and Knowles (2017) analyzed the correlation between the translation quality and the sentence length by comparing NMT with SMT. They showed that the

[*]Current affiliation: Recruit Co., Ltd.
[†]Current affiliation: Tokyo Institute of Technology

Proceedings of NAACL-HLT 2021: Student Research Workshop, pages 143–149
June 6–11, 2021.

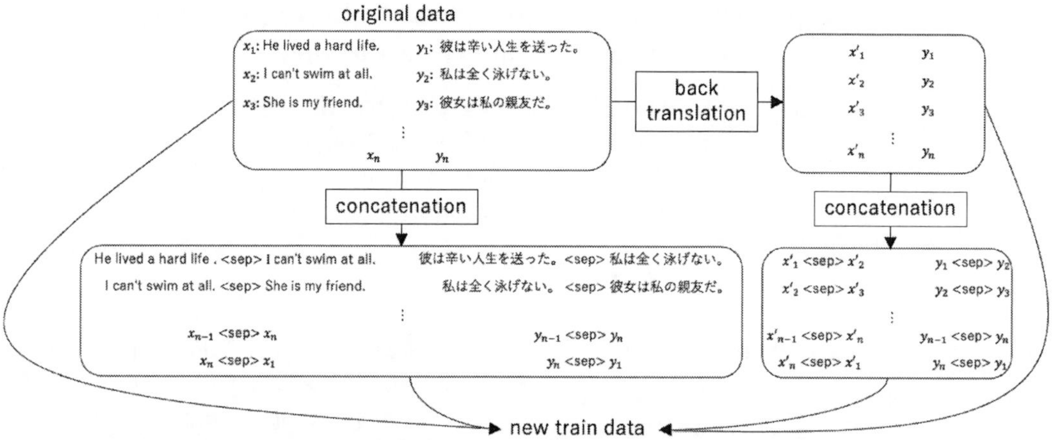

Figure 1: Proposed method: Augmentation of data by combining the back-translation and the concatenation of two sentences. During concatenation, each sentence is randomly sampled, so that they do not have context overlap with each other.

overall quality of NMT is better than that of SMT but that SMT outperforms NMT on sentences of 60 words and longer. They stated that this degradation in quality was caused by the short length of the translations. Additionally, Neishi and Yoshinaga (2019) propose to use the relative position information instead of the absolute position information to mitigate the performance drop of NMT models for long sentences. They conducted an analysis of the translation quality and sentence length on length-controlled English–to–Japanese parallel data and showed that the absolute positional information sharply drops the BLEU score of the transformer model (Vaswani et al., 2017) in translating sentences that are longer than those in the training data.

Several data augmentation methods have been proposed for NMT, such as back-translation, which involves translating the target-side monolingual data to create a pseudo dataset (Sennrich et al., 2016). In their method, the back-translation model is first learned by using parallel corpora from the target-side to the source-side. Once converged, this model generates pseudo data by translating the target-side monolingual corpora to the source-side language. A translation model is then trained using both the pseudo-parallel and original-parallel data. Li et al. (2019) analyzed multiple data augmentation methods. In their experiments, they applied self-training and back-translation. In self-training, they fixed the source-side and used a forward translation model to generate the target-side, and in back-translation, they fixed the target-side and used a backward translation model to generate the source-side. It was observed that these methods can effectively improve the translation accuracy for infrequent tokens. These methods can be used with the sentence concatenation method proposed in this study.

In multi-source neural machine translation, Dabre et al. (2017) proposed concatenating source sentences in different languages corresponding to a target sentence in training. However, they did not aim to improve the translation accuracy of long sentences. Our method concatenates two source sentences in the same language at random.

3 Data Augmentation by Sentence Concatenation

The proposed method augments the parallel data by back-translation and concatenation. A schematic overview of the proposed method is shown in Figure 1.

First, we back-translate the target-side of the parallel corpus (Li et al., 2019; Sennrich et al., 2016) to create pseudo data as additional training data. Note that we do not use external data in back-translation, and the diversity of target sentences does not change.

Then, we randomly select two sentences exclusively in the original or pseudo data and concatenate them to create another training data. Technically, we concatenate two source sentences and insert a special token, "<sep>," between them. Corresponding target sentences are concatenated in the same way. Afterwards, we remove the sentences

length	all	1 – 10	11 – 20	21 – 30	31 – 40	41 – 50	51 – 60	61 – 70	71 –
sentences	1,812	73	529	600	341	164	74	18	13
vanilla (400K)	26.5	22.9	23.0	26.2	27.1	29.6	28.5	28.8	23.6
+ concat (+ 400K)	26.6	21.4	23.3	25.7	27.5	29.5	28.7	28.2	29.0
+ ST (+ 400K)	28.2	23.9	24.8	27.4	28.6	31.4	31.4	29.6	27.6
+ BT (+ 400K)	28.8	24.3	25.5	28.3	29.5	31.6	30.6	28.7	28.7
+ BT + concat (+ 1.2M)	**29.4**	**25.4**	**25.6**	**28.6**	**30.1**	**33.1**	**31.5**	**29.9**	**30.1**

Table 1: BLEU scores for each sentence length breakdown on the test data set: "vanilla + BT + concat" consists of data from vanilla, BT, and concatenation of both.

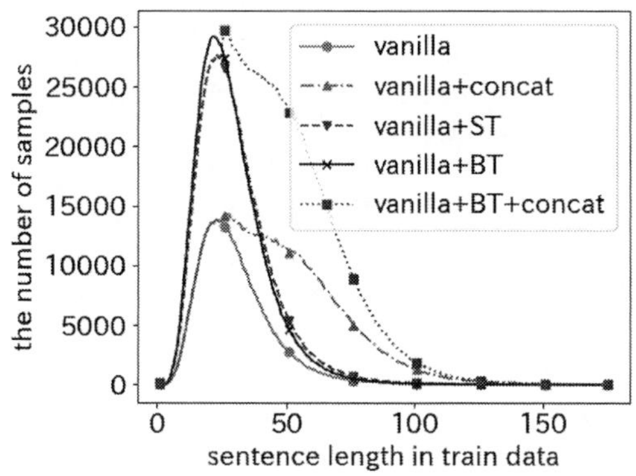

Figure 2: Distribution of each data set.

consisting of less than 25 words from the pseudo data.

Finally, we obtain an augmented training data comprising original, pseudo, and concatenated sentences, which has the quadruple data size of the original training data.

We train our models on both single and concatenated sentences first because models can learn to translate single sentences. We also expect models to acquire a better absolute position encoding to translate long sentences in the better quality without generating a special token (i.e., <sep>) contained in concatenated sentences in the inference process.

During the testing process, a single sentence is fed as the input, even though the training data contains concatenated sentences.[1]

4 Experiments

4.1 Models

To investigate the effectiveness of the proposed method when combined with previous data augmentation methods, five types of training data were prepared from the original training data.

Figure 2 shows the number of training data used in this experient. Note that the total number of sentences in "vanilla + concat," "vanilla + ST" and "vanilla + BT" are nearly equal. In the source language, the average sentence length of "vanilla" is 30.39, and that of "vanilla+concat" is 46.18.

We train the forward translation models using the training data and compare the BLEU scores obtained for the output of the test data.

vanilla. Original data.

vanilla + concat. Original data and augmented data by sentence concatenation. Sentences with length of less than 25 words after concatenation were removed to improve the translation quality of long sentences.

vanilla + ST. Original data and augmented data by self-training.

vanilla + BT. Original data and augmented data by back-translation.

vanilla + BT + concat. The composite data of the original data, the back-translated data, and their sentence concatenation.[2]

4.2 Setup

We used ASPEC[3] from WAT17 (Nakazawa et al., 2017) to perform English-to-Japanese translation. This dataset contains 2M sentences as training data, 1,790 as valid data and 1,812 as test data. We also followed the official segmentation using SentencePiece (Kudo and Richardson, 2018) with a vocabulary size of 16,384. A total of 400K sentences were randomly extracted from the original training

[1]We also conducted an experiment with two sentences as input during the test, but the BLEU score was worse than the proposed method.

[2]The results of the experiment showed that the score of "vanilla + BT" was higher than that of "vanilla + ST." Therefore, in this study, the proposed method was combined only with "vanilla + BT."

[3]http://lotus.kuee.kyoto-u.ac.jp/WAT/WAT2017/snmt/

	adequacy			fluency		
length	win	tie	lose	win	tie	lose
1 – 10	**4**	5	3	**3**	7	2
11 – 20	20	39	**29**	**21**	47	20
21 – 30	**34**	35	31	**33**	42	25
31 – 40	**23**	21	13	**17**	24	16
41 – 50	10	6	**11**	6	10	**11**
51 –	**6**	5	**6**	**7**	6	4
overall	**97**	111	93	**87**	136	78

Table 2: Human evaluation: Pairwise comparison of "vanilla + BT" and "vanilla + BT + concat." "win" denotes the sentence generated by our proposed method, "vanilla + BT + concat," is superior to that of "vanilla + BT," and "lose" denotes the opposite of "win."

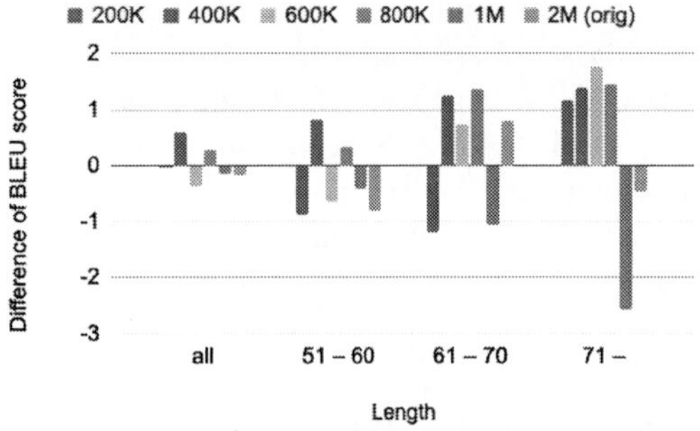

Figure 3: Effectiveness of the proposed method for each data size by sentence length: Vertical axis represents BLEU score of "vanilla + concat + BT" minus BLEU score of "vanilla + BT."

data and selected as the training data to be used in this experiment. Regarding self-training and back-translation models, we used only the training corpus, following Li et al. (2019).

The transformer models from Fairseq were used in the experiment (Ott et al., 2019)[4]. Adam was set as the optimizer with a dropout of 0.3, a maximum of 300,000 steps in the training process, and a total batch size of approximately 65,536 tokens per step. The same architecture was also used to train the self-training and the back-translation models.

The BLEU score (Papineni et al., 2002) was used for automatic evaluation. We computed the average of the BLEU scores of three runs with different seeds. Human evaluation was also conducted. For three native Japanese evaluators, 100 sentences were randomly selected from the test set per evaluator. They performed pairwise evaluation between "vanilla + BT" and "vanilla + BT + concat" from two perspectives: adequacy and fluency.

[4]https://github.com/pytorch/fairseq

length	sentences	vanilla + BT	vanilla + BT + concat
all	999,998	22.1	**22.2**
1 – 10	22,725	18.2	**18.3**
11 – 20	232,829	**17.9**	**17.9**
21 – 30	329,597	20.1	**20.2**
31 – 40	219,845	22.1	**22.3**
41 – 50	109,528	23.2	**23.4**
51 – 60	47,851	24.3	**24.4**
61 – 70	20,526	24.6	**24.8**
71 – 100	15,557	25.1	**25.4**
101 – 200	1,540	20.1	**22.3**

Table 3: BLEU scores for each sentence length breakdown on the pseudo test data set: pseudo test data consists of 1M sentences from the training data that were not used for training.

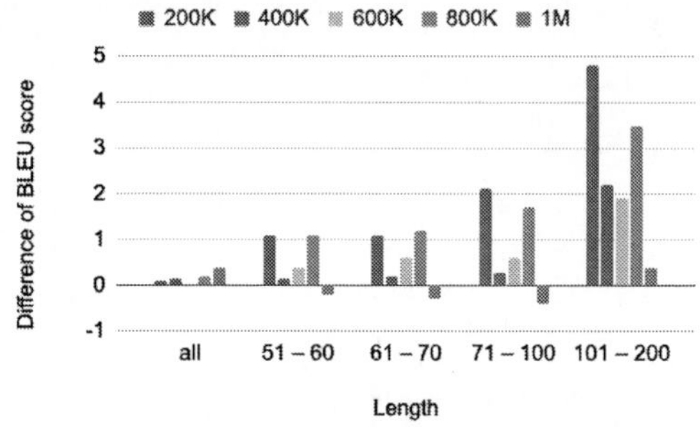

Figure 4: Effectiveness of the proposed method for each data size by sentence length in 1M pseudo test set.

4.3 Results

Automatic evaluation. The result of this experiment is presented in Table 1. It describes the BLEU scores measured for each test data classified by the sentence length.

The BLEU score of "vanilla + concat" is more stable when applied for translation with sentence lengths of longer than 51 words, which are the majority of data augmented by the sentence concatenation, although the score for the sentences classified as 61–70, is slightly lower than that of "vanilla." Conversely, the quality of the translation of short sentences is greatly reduced.

Additionally, the overall score of "vanilla + BT + concat" is higher than that of "vanilla + BT" by 0.6. In particular, the score of the sentence lengths of longer than 41 is significantly improved, which indicates that the proposed method is more effective for long sentence translation. In Addition, the score of "vanilla + BT + concat" is much higher than that of "vanilla + concat." Consequently, it is shown that the back-translation and concatenation

src	Myanma is behind in market economization together with Laos, Canbodia, Vietnam, and the GDP per one person is the lowest in the 4 countries, and it remains $ 180, but Myanma is thought to remarkably develop if political problems are solved, because flatland occupies $7 \times 10\%$ of the land and natural resources are rich, and because personnel expenses are extremely cheap.
tgt	ミャンマーは自国とともに後発ＡＳＥＡＮ４カ国といわれるラオス，カンボディア，ベトナムと比較しても市場経済化が遅れ，一人あたりのＧＤＰは最低で１８０ドルにとどまっているが，平地が７割で天然資源もあり，人件費が極端に安価なので，政治的問題が解決されれば著しく発展すると見られる。
vanilla	ミャマは，陸上と自然資源の７割を占めるため，平地は土地と自然資源の７割を占めるので，人件費が極端に安く，４か国で１人当たりＧＤＰが最低である。
vanilla +concat	ミャンマーはラオス，カンボジア，ベトナムと共に市場経済化に遅れ，４国ではＧＤＰが１人あたり最低であるが，国土の７割を占める平坦な土地と自然資源が豊富で人件費が極端に安く政上の問題が解決されれば，顕著に発展すると考えられる。

Table 4: An example of the effectiveness of the proposed method.

are independent factors that improve the accuracy of the translation.

Human evaluation. Table 2 presents the results of human evaluation. We observed that the output of the proposed method improved or were comparable under almost all conditions except for "11–20" on adequacy and "41–50" on fluency. The proposed method added the sentences whose length is more than 25 words and is effective in improving the translation of such sentences.

4.4 Discussion

Test set. Figure 3 depicts the breakdown in the difference between the BLEU scores of the proposed method for each training data size per sentence length. Notably, for sentences with 51 words or longer, the translation quality improves when the size of data is between 400K and 800K. However, the translation quality degrades when there are more than 1M sentences. The proposed method is not suitable when a large amount of training data is available.

In the human evaluation, we observe that the proposed method is more effective in terms of fluency than adequacy. It is assumed that the translation model can handle absolute positional encoding for long sentences by the proposed method.

Pseudo test set. In this experiment, the number of bilingual sentences in the test set was small, especially in long sentences. For this reason, additional experiments were carried out to confirm the validity of the results. For evaluation, we extracted 1M sentences from the training data that were not used for training and used them as the pseudo test data. Table 3 shows the average of the BLEU scores for the three runs with 400K training data with different seeds. Note that the overall BLEU score is, however, lower than when using the test data, but this is probably because the quality of the training data is lower than that of the test data.

By comparing the results of "vanilla + BT" and that of the proposed method, the proposed method was shown to have a slightly better overall score. Examining the scores by sentence length, there was a significant increase in scores for longer sentences, especially for "101 – 200" sentences. It indicates that the proposed method is effective in improving the translation accuracy of long sentences.

Also, a comparison similar to the one using the test set was conducted using this 1M pseudo test data. The results are shown in Figure 4. In this setting, it is more evident that for sentences with a sentence length of 51 words or more, the translation accuracy improves when the data size is 800K or less and decreases when the data size exceeds 1M.

4.5 Case Study

Tables 4 and 5 show the cases in which the proposed method worked effectively in this experiment, whereas Table 6 shows the cases in which the translation quality deteriorated.

The example in Table 4 shows that the sentence output by "vanilla" is shorter than expected, which indicates that necessary information for translation is missing. Conversely, the output of "vanilla + concat" is a longer sentence, which reduces the missing information.

The example in Table 5 shows an example of improved translation by using the proposed method. Similar to the previous example, "vanilla + BT" completely loses the information in the first half of the sentence, while "vanilla + BT + concat" produces a translation that includes the information of

src	Results of the analysis shows high accuracy properties, such as the reproducibility of relative standard deviation 0.3~0.9% varified by repetitive analyses of ten times, the clibration curves with correlation coefficient of 1 verified by tests of standard materials in using six kinds of acetonitrile dilute solutions, and the formaldehyde detection limit of 0.0018μg/mL.
tgt	結果は，相対標準偏差０．３～０．９％の再現性（１０回の繰返し分析），相関係数１の検量線（６種類のアセトニトリル希釈溶液による標準資料の検定），０．００１８μｇ／ｍＬのホルムアルデヒド検出限界，など高い精度を得た。
vanilla +BT	６種のアセトニトリル希薄溶液を用いた標準物質の試験及びホルムアルデヒド検出限界は０．００１８μｇ／ｍＬであった 。
vanilla +BT +concat	分析の結果は１０回の繰り返し解析で相対標準偏差０．３～０．９％の再現性，６種のアセトニトリル希薄溶液を用いた標準物質の試験により検証された１の相関係数を持つクライテリア曲線，及び０．００１８μｇ／ｍＬのホルムアルデヒド検出限界など高い精度を示した。

Table 5: An example where the proposed method worked well.

src	These seemed to be noticeable complications in case of extracorporeal circulation for umbilical hernia repair.
tgt	さい帯ヘルニア修復術における体外循環の合併症として注目すべきと思われた 。
vanilla	さい帯ヘルニア修復術における体外循環の合併症として注目すべきと思われた 。
vanilla +concat	以上の所見より，さい帯ヘルニアに対する体外循環では，特に合併症として特に合併症として，特に，さい帯ヘルニアでは体外循環がより注意を要すると考えられた。

Table 6: An example where the proposed method may have caused errors.

the entire sentence.

However, as shown in the example in Table 6, there were cases where the output of the model trained including concatenated data showed repetitive outputs that were not seen in the output of the model trained on the original data. This type of output occurs more frequently in the case of short sentences. This suggests that the ability to output long sentences may lead to unnatural repetition of the output because of the attempt to generate long sentences.

5 Conclusion

This study proposes a data augmentation method to improve the translation quality of long sentences. The experimental results confirmed that the data augmentation method is straightforward but useful, especially for the translation of very long sentences. However, the quality of the translation of short sentences is reduced.

In the future, we would like to develop a method that works well when there is a large amount of available parallel data. Moreover, since the adequacy of the translation of short sentences is considerably low in the proposed method, we would like to compensate for this weakness by considering the reconstruction loss (Tu et al., 2017). Also, it would be interesting to explore the use of interpolation of hidden space for data augmentation considering long sentences (Chen et al., 2020).

Acknowledgements

We would like to thank Aomi Koyama, Tomoshige Kiyuna and Hiroto Tamura for their evaluation. We would also like to thank the anonymous reviewers for their valuable feedback.

References

Jiaao Chen, Zichao Yang, and Diyi Yang. 2020. MixText: Linguistically-informed interpolation of hidden space for semi-supervised text classification. In *Proceedings of the 58th Annual Meeting of the Association for Computational Linguistics*, pages 2147–2157, Online. Association for Computational Linguistics.

Raj Dabre, Fabien Cromierès, and Sadao Kurohashi. 2017. Enabling multi-source neural machine translation by concatenating source sentences in multiple languages. In *Proceedings of MT Summit XV*, volume 1, pages 96–107, Nagoya, Japan.

Philipp Koehn and Rebecca Knowles. 2017. Six challenges for neural machine translation. In *Proceedings of the First Workshop on Neural Machine Translation*, pages 28–39, Vancouver. Association for Computational Linguistics.

Taku Kudo and John Richardson. 2018. SentencePiece: A simple and language independent subword tokenizer and detokenizer for neural text processing. In *Proceedings of the 2018 Conference on Empirical*

Methods in Natural Language Processing: System Demonstrations, pages 66–71, Brussels, Belgium. Association for Computational Linguistics.

Guanlin Li, Lemao Liu, Guoping Huang, Conghui Zhu, and Tiejun Zhao. 2019. Understanding data augmentation in neural machine translation: Two perspectives towards generalization. In *Proceedings of the 2019 Conference on Empirical Methods in Natural Language Processing and the 9th International Joint Conference on Natural Language Processing (EMNLP-IJCNLP)*, pages 5689–5695, Hong Kong, China. Association for Computational Linguistics.

Toshiaki Nakazawa, Shohei Higashiyama, Chenchen Ding, Hideya Mino, Isao Goto, Hideto Kazawa, Yusuke Oda, Graham Neubig, and Sadao Kurohashi. 2017. Overview of the 4th workshop on Asian translation. In *Proceedings of the 4th Workshop on Asian Translation (WAT2017)*, pages 1–54, Taipei, Taiwan. Asian Federation of Natural Language Processing.

Masato Neishi and Naoki Yoshinaga. 2019. On the relation between position information and sentence length in neural machine translation. In *Proceedings of the 23rd Conference on Computational Natural Language Learning (CoNLL)*, pages 328–338, Hong Kong, China. Association for Computational Linguistics.

Myle Ott, Sergey Edunov, Alexei Baevski, Angela Fan, Sam Gross, Nathan Ng, David Grangier, and Michael Auli. 2019. fairseq: A fast, extensible toolkit for sequence modeling. In *Proceedings of the 2019 Conference of the North American Chapter of the Association for Computational Linguistics (Demonstrations)*, pages 48–53, Minneapolis, Minnesota. Association for Computational Linguistics.

Kishore Papineni, Salim Roukos, Todd Ward, and Wei-Jing Zhu. 2002. BLEU: a method for automatic evaluation of machine translation. In *Proceedings of the 40th Annual Meeting of the Association for Computational Linguistics*, pages 311–318, Philadelphia, Pennsylvania, USA. Association for Computational Linguistics.

Rico Sennrich, Barry Haddow, and Alexandra Birch. 2016. Improving neural machine translation models with monolingual data. In *Proceedings of the 54th Annual Meeting of the Association for Computational Linguistics (Volume 1: Long Papers)*, pages 86–96, Berlin, Germany. Association for Computational Linguistics.

Zhaopeng Tu, Yang Liu, Lifeng Shang, Xiaohua Liu, and Hang Li. 2017. Neural machine translation with reconstruction. In *Proceedings of the AAAI Conference on Artificial Intelligence*, volume 31, pages 3097–3103.

Ashish Vaswani, Noam Shazeer, Niki Parmar, Jakob Uszkoreit, Llion Jones, Aidan N. Gomez, undefinedukasz Kaiser, and Illia Polosukhin. 2017. Attention is all you need. In *Proceedings of the 31st International Conference on Neural Information Processing Systems*, NIPS'17, page 6000–6010, Red Hook, NY, USA. Curran Associates Inc.

Xinyi Wang, Hieu Pham, Zihang Dai, and Graham Neubig. 2018. SwitchOut: an efficient data augmentation algorithm for neural machine translation. In *Proceedings of the 2018 Conference on Empirical Methods in Natural Language Processing*, pages 856–861, Brussels, Belgium. Association for Computational Linguistics.

Emotion Classification in a Resource Constrained Language Using Transformer-based Approach

Avishek Das, Omar Sharif, Mohammed Moshiul Hoque and **Iqbal H. Sarker**
Department of Computer Science and Engineering
Chittagong University of Engineering & Technology
Chittagong-4349, Bangladesh
u1504018@student.cuet.ac.bd,{omar.sharif,moshiul_240,iqbal}@cuet.ac.bd

Abstract

Although research on emotion classification has significantly progressed in high-resource languages, it is still infancy for resource-constrained languages like Bengali. However, unavailability of necessary language processing tools and deficiency of benchmark corpora makes the emotion classification task in Bengali more challenging and complicated. This work proposes a transformer-based technique to classify the Bengali text into one of the six basic emotions: anger, fear, disgust, sadness, joy, and surprise. A Bengali emotion corpus consists of 6243 texts is developed for the classification task. Experimentation carried out using various machine learning (LR, RF, MNB, SVM), deep neural networks (CNN, BiLSTM, CNN+BiLSTM) and transformer (Bangla-BERT, m-BERT, XLM-R) based approaches. Experimental outcomes indicate that XLM-R outdoes all other techniques by achieving the highest weighted f_1-score of 69.73% on the test data. The dataset is publicly available at `https://github.com/omar-sharif03/NAACL-SRW-2021`.

1 Introduction

Classification of emotion in the text signifies the task of automatically attributing an emotion category to a textual document selected from a set of predetermined categories. With the growing number of users in virtual platforms generating online contents steadily as a fast-paced, interpreting emotion or sentiment in online content is vital for consumers, enterprises, business leaders, and other parties concerned. Ekman (Ekman, 1993) defined six basic emotions: happiness, fear, anger, sadness, surprise, and disgust based on facial features. These primary type of emotions can also be extracted from the text expression (Alswaidan and Menai, 2020).

The availability of vast amounts of online data and the advancement of computational processes have accelerated the development of emotion classification research in high-resource languages such as English, Arabic, Chinese, and French (Plaza del Arco et al., 2020). However, there is no notable progress in low resource languages such as Bengali, Tamil and Turkey. The proliferation of the Internet and digital technology usage produces enormous textual data in the Bengali language. The analysis of these massive amounts of data to extract underlying emotions is a challenging research issue in the realm of Bengali language processing (BLP). The complexity arises due to various limitations, such as the lack of BLP tools, scarcity of benchmark corpus, complicated language structure, and limited resources. By considering the constraints of emotion classification in the Bengali language, this work aims to contribute to the following:

- Develop a Bengali emotion corpus consisting of 6243 text documents with manual annotation to classify each text into one of six emotion classes: anger, disgust, fear, joy, sadness, surprise.
- Investigate the performance of various ML, DNN and transformer-based approaches on the corpus.
- Proposed a benchmark system to classify emotion in Bengali text with the experimental validation on the corpus.

2 Related Work

Substantial research activities have been carried out on emotion analysis in high-resource languages like English, Arabic, and Chinese (Alswaidan and Menai, 2020). A multi-label

Proceedings of NAACL-HLT 2021: Student Research Workshop, pages 150–158
June 6–11, 2021. ©2021 Association for Computational Linguistics

with multi-target emotion detection of Arabic tweets accomplished using decision trees, random forest, and KNN, where random forest provided the highest f_1-score of 82.6% (Alzu'bi et al., 2019). Lai et al. (2020) proposed a graph convolution network architecture for emotion classification from Chinese microblogs and their proposed system achieved an F-measure of 82.32%. Recently, few works employed transformer-based model (i.e., BERT) analyse emotion in texts. (Huang et al., 2019; Al-Omari et al., 2020) used a pretrained BERT for embedding purpose on top of LSTM/BiLSTM to get an improved f_1-score of 76.66% and 74.78% respectively.

Although emotion analysis on limited resource languages like Bengali is in the preliminary stage, few studies have already been conducted on emotion analysis using ML and DNN methods. Irtiza Tripto and Eunus Ali (2018) proposed an LSTM based approach to classify multi-label emotions from Bengali, and English sentences. This system considered only YouTube comments and achieved 59.23% accuracy. Another work on emotion classification in Bengali text carried out by Azmin and Dhar (2019) concerning three emotional labels (i.e., happy, sadness and anger). They used Multinomial Naïve Bayes, which outperformed other algorithms with an accuracy of 78.6%. Pal and Karn (2020) developed a logistic regression-based technique to classify four emotions (joy, anger, sorrow, suspense) in Bengali text and achieved 73% accuracy. Das and Bandyopadhyay (2009) conducted a study to identify emotions in Bengali blog texts. Their scheme attained 56.45% accuracy using the conditional random field. Recent work used SVM to classify six raw emotions on 1200 Bengali texts which obtained 73% accuracy (Ruposh and Hoque, 2019).

3 BEmoC: Bengali Emotion Corpus

Due to the standard corpus unavailability, we developed a corpus (hereafter called 'BEmoC') to classify emotion in Bengali text. The development procedure is adopted from the guidelines stated in (Dash and Ramamoorthy, 2019).

3.1 Data Collection and Preprocessing

Five human crawlers were assigned to accumulate data from various online/offline sources. They manually collected 6700 text documents over three months (September 10, 2020 to December 11, 2020). The crawler accumulated data selectively, i.e., when a crawler finds a text that supports the definition of any of the six emotion classes according to Ekman (1993), the content is collected, otherwise ignored. Raw accumulated data needs following pre-processing before the annotation:

- Removal of non-Bengali words, punctuation, emoticons and duplicate data.
- Discarding data less than three words to get an unerring emotional context.

After pre-processing the corpus holds 6523 text data. The processed texts are eligible for manual annotation. The details of the preprocessing modules found in the link[1].

3.2 Data Annotation and Quality

Five postgraduate students working on BLP were assigned for initial annotation. To choose the initial label majority voting technique is applied (Magatti et al., 2009). Initial labels were scrutinized by an expert who has several years of research expertise in BLP. The expert corrected the labelling if any initial annotation is done inappropriately. The expert discarded 163 texts with neutral emotion and 117 texts with mixed emotions for the intelligibility of this research. To minimize bias during annotation, the expert finalized the labels through discussions and deliberations with the annotators (Sharif and Hoque, 2021). We evaluated the inter-annotator agreement to ensure the quality of the annotation using the coding reliability (Krippendorff, 2011) and Cohen's kappa (Cohen, 1960) scores. An inter-coder reliability of 93.1% with Cohen's Kappa score of 0.91 reflects the quality of the corpus.

3.3 Data Statistics

The BEmoC contains a total of 6243 text documents after the preprocessing and annotation process. Amount of data inclusion in BEmoC

[1]https://github.com/omar-sharif03/NAACL-SRW-2021/tree/main/Code%20Snippets

varies with the sources. For example, among online sources, Facebook contributed the highest amount (2796 texts) whereas YouTube (610 texts), blogs (483 texts), and news portals (270 texts) contributed a small amount. Offline sources contributed a total of 2084 texts, including storybooks (680 texts), novels (668 texts), and conversations (736 texts). Data partitioned into train set (4994 texts), validation set (624 texts) and test set (625 texts) to evaluate the models. Table 1 represents the amount of data in each class according to the train-validation-test set.

Class	Train	Validation	Test
Anger	621	67	71
Disgust	1233	155	165
Fear	700	89	83
Joy	908	120	114
Sadness	942	129	119
Surprise	590	64	73

Table 1: Number of instances in the train, validation, and test sets

Since the classifier models learn from the training set instances to obtain more insights, we further analyzed this set. Table 2 shows several statistics of the training set.

Class	Total words	Unique words	Avg. words per text
Anger	14914	5852	24.02
Disgust	27192	7212	22.35
Fear	14766	5072	21.09
Joy	20885	7346	23.40
Sadness	22727	7398	24.13
Surprise	13833	5675	23.45
Total	114317	38555	-

Table 2: Statistics of the train set of BEmoC

The *sadness* class contains the most unique words(7398), whereas the *fear* class contains the least(5072). In average all the classes have more than 20 words in each text document. However, a text document in *sadness* class contained the maximum number of words (107) whereas *fear* class consisting of a minimum number of words (4). Figure 1 represents the number of texts vs the length of texts distribution for each class of the corpus. Investigating this figure revealed that most of the data varied a length between 15 to 35 words. Interestingly, most of the texts of *Disgust* class have a length less than 30. The *Joy* & *Sadness* classes seem to have almost similar number of texts in all length distributions.

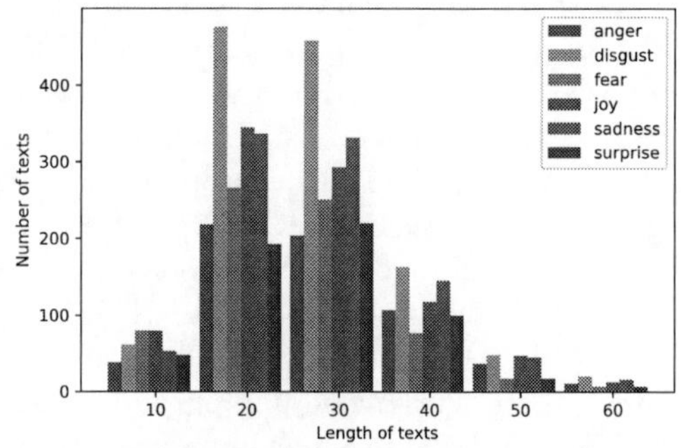

Figure 1: Corpus distribution concerning number of texts vs length

For quantitative analysis, the *Jaccard* similarity among the classes has been computed. We used 200 most frequent words from each emotion class, and the similarity values are reported in table 3. The *Anger-Disgust* and *Joy-Surprise* pairs hold the highest similarity of 0.58 and 0.51, respectively. These scores indicate that more than 50% frequent words are common in these pair of classes. On the other hand, the *Joy-Fear* pair has the least similarity index, which clarifies that this pair's frequent words are more distinct than other classes. These similarity issues can substantially affect the emotion classification task. Some sample instances of BEmoC are shown in Table 9 (Appendix B).

	C1	C2	C3	C4	C5	C6
C1	1.00	0.58	0.40	0.43	0.45	0.47
C2	-	1.00	0.41	0.45	0.47	0.44
C3	-	-	1.00	0.37	0.45	0.46
C4	-	-	-	1.00	0.47	0.51
C5	-	-	-	-	1.00	0.48

Table 3: *Jaccard* similarity between the emotion class pairs. Anger (c1), disgust (c2), fear (c3), joy (c4), sadness (c5), surprise (c6).

4 Methodology

Figure 2 shows an abstract view of the used strategies. Various feature extraction techniques such as TF-IDF, Word2Vec, and FastText are used to train ML and DNN models. Moreover, we also investigate the Bengali text's emotion classification performance using transformer-based models.All the models are trained and tuned on the identical dataset.

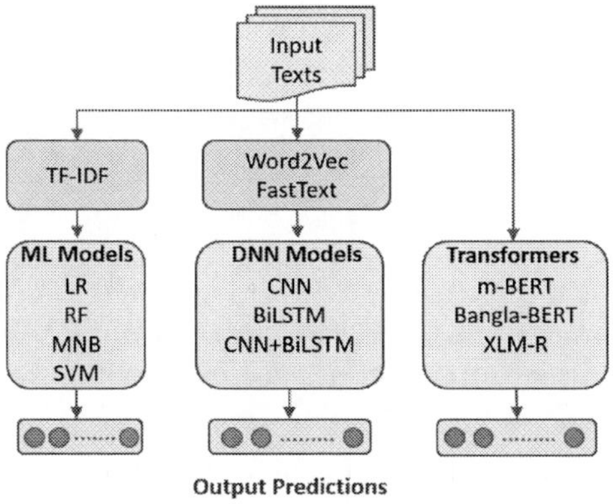

Figure 2: Abstract process of emotion classification

4.1 Feature Extraction

ML and DNN algorithms are unable to learn from raw texts. Therefore, feature extraction is required to train the classifier models.

TF-IDF: Term frequency-inverse document frequency (TF-IDF) is a statistical measure that determines the importance of a word to a document in a collection of documents. Uni-gram and bi-gram features are extracted from the most frequent 20000 words of the corpus.

Word2Vec: It utilizes neural networks to find semantic similarity of the context of the words in a corpus (Mikolov et al., 2013). We trained Word2Vec on Skip-Gram with the window size of 7, minimum word count to 4, and the embedding dimension of 100.

FastText: This technique uses subword information to find the semantic relationships (Bojanowski et al., 2017). We trained FastText on Skip-Gram with character n-grams of length 5, windows size of 5, and embedding dimension of 100.

For both Word2Vec and FastText, there are pre-trained vectors available for the Bengali language trained on generalized Bengali wiki dump data (Sarker, 2021). We observed that the deep learning models perform well on vectors trained with our developed BEmoC rather than the pre-trained vectors.

4.2 ML Approaches

We started an investigation on emotion detection system with ML models. Logistic Regression (LR), Support Vector Machine (SVM), Random Forest (RF) and Multinomial Naive Bayes (MNB) techniques are employed using TF-IDF text vectorizer. For LR *lbfgs'* solver and *'l1'* penalty is chosen and C value is set to 1. The same C value with *'linear'* kernal is used for SVM. Meanwhile, for RF *'n_estimators'* is set to 100 and *'alpha=1.0'* is chosen for MNB. A summary of the parameters chosen for ML models are provided in Table 6 (Appendix A).

4.3 DNN Approaches

Variation of deep neural networks (DNN) such as CNN, BiLSTM and a combination of CNN and BiLSTM (CNN+BiLSTM) will investigate the performance of emotion classification task in Bengali. To train all the DNN models, 'adam' optimizer with a learning rate of 0.001 and a batch size of 16 is used for 35 epochs. The 'sparse_categorical_crossentropy' is selected as the loss function.

CNN: Convolutional Neural Network (CNN) (LeCun et al., 2015) is tuned over the emotion corpus. The trained weights from the Word2Vec/FastText embeddings are fed to the embedding layer to generate a sequence matrix. The sequence matrix is then passed to the convolution layer having 64 filters of size 7. The convolution layer's output is max-pooled over time and then transferred to a fully connected layer with 64 neurons. 'ReLU' activation is used in the corresponding layers. Finally, an output layer with softmax activation is used to compute the probability distribution of the classes.

BiLSTM: Bidirectional Long-Short Term Memory (BiLSTM) (Hochreiter and Schmidhuber, 1997) is a variation of recurrent neural network (RNN). The developed BiLSTM network consists of an Embedding layer similar to CNN, a BiLSTM layer with 32 hidden units, and a fully connected layer having 16 neurons with 'ReLU' activation. An output layer with 'softmax' activation is used.

CNN+BiLSTM: An embedding layer followed by a 1D convolutional layer with 64 filters of size three and a 1D max-pool layer is employed on top of two BiLSTM layers with 64 and 32 units. Outputs of BiLSTM layer fed to an output layer with 'softmax' activation.

Table 7 (Appendix A) illustrates the details

of the hyperparameters used in the DNN models.

4.4 Transformer Models

We used three transformer models: m-BERT, Bangla-BERT, and XLM-R on BEmoC. In recent years transformer is being used extensively for classification tasks to achieve state-of-the-art results (Chen et al., 2021). The models are culled from the Huggingface[2] transformers library and fine-tuned on the emotion corpus by using Ktrain(Maiya, 2020) package.

m-BERT: m-BERT (Devlin et al., 2019) is a transformer model pre-trained over 104 languages with more than 110M parameters. We employed 'bert-base-multilingual-cased' model and fine-tuned it on BEmoC with a batch size of 12.

Bangla BERT: Bangla BERT (Sarker, 2020) is a pre-trained BERT mask language modelling, trained on a sizeable Bengali corpus. We used the 'sagorsarker/Bangla-bert-base' model and fine-tuned to update the pre-trained model fitted for BEmoC. A batch size of 16 is used to provide better results.

XLM-R: XLM-R (Liu et al., 2019) is a sizeable multilingual language model trained on 100 different languages. We implemented the 'xlm-Roberta-base' model on BEmoC with a batch size of 12.

All the transformer models have been trained with 20 epochs with a learning rate of $2e^{-5}$. By using the checkpoint best intermediate model is stored to predict on the test data. Table 8 (Appendix A) shows a list of parameters used for transformer models.

[2]https://huggingface.co/transformers/

5 Results and Analysis

This section presents a comprehensive performance analysis of various ML, DNN, and transformer-based models to classify Bengali texts emotion. The superiority of the models is determined based on the weighted f_1-score. However, the precision (Pr), recall (Re) and accuracy (Acc) metrics also considered. Table 4 reports the evaluation results of all models.

Among ML approaches, LR achieved the highest (60.75%) f_1-score than RF (52.78%), MNB (48.67%) and SVM (59.54%). LR also performed well in Pr, Re and Acc than other ML models. In DNN, BiLSTM with FastText outperformed other approaches concerning all the evaluation parameters. It achieved f_1-score of 56.94%. However, BiLSTM (FastText) achieved about 4% lower f_1-score than the best ML method (i.e., LR).

After employing transformer-based models, it observed a significant increase in all scores. Among transformer-based models, Bangla-BERT achieved the lowest of 61.91% f_1-score. However, this model outperformed the best ML and DNN approaches (56.94% for BiLSTM (FastText) and 60.75% for LR). Meanwhile, m-BERT shows almost 3% improved f_1-score (64.39%) than Bangla-BERT (61.91%). XLM-R model shows an immense improvement of about 6% compared to Bangla-BERT and 5% compared to m-BERT, respectively. It achieved a f_1-score of 69.73% that is the highest among all models.

Method	Classifier	Pr(%)	Re(%)	F1(%)	Acc(%)
ML models	LR	61.07	60.64	60.75	60.64
	RF	55.91	54.72	52.78	54.72
	MNB	60.23	54.08	48.67	54.08
	SVM	61.12	60.10	59.54	60.00
DNN models	CNN (Word2Vec)	53.20	52.12	51.84	52.12
	CNN (FastText)	54.54	53.45	52.52	53.48
	BiLSTM (Word2Vec)	56.81	55.78	53.45	57.12
	BiLSTM (FastText)	57.30	58.08	56.94	58.08
	CNN + BiLSTM (Word2Vec)	56.48	56.64	56.39	56.64
	CNN + BiLSTM (FastText)	55.74	55.68	55.41	55.68
Transformers	Bangla-BERT	62.08	62.24	61.91	62.24
	m-BERT	64.62	64.64	64.39	64.63
	XLM-R	**70.11**	**69.61**	**69.73**	**69.61**

Table 4: Comparison of various approaches on test set. Here Acc, Pr, Re, F1 denotes accuracy, weighted precision, recall, and f_1-score

5.1 Error Analysis

It is evident from Table 4 that XLM-R is the best performing model to classify emotion from Bengali texts. A detailed error analysis is performed using the confusion matrix. Figure 3 illustrates a class-wise proportion of the number of predicted labels. It is observed from the matrix that few data classified wrongly. For example, 8 instances among 71 of the *anger* class predicted as *disgust*. In *fear* class, 6 data out of 83 mistakenly classified as *sadness*. In the *sadness* class, misclassification ratio is the higest (15.13%). That means, 18 data out of 119 in *sadness* class misclassified as *disgust*. Moreover, among 73 data in *surprise* class 9 are predicted as *sadness*. The error analysis reveals that *fear* class achieved the highest rate of correct classification (77.15%) while *surprise* gained the lowest (61.64%).

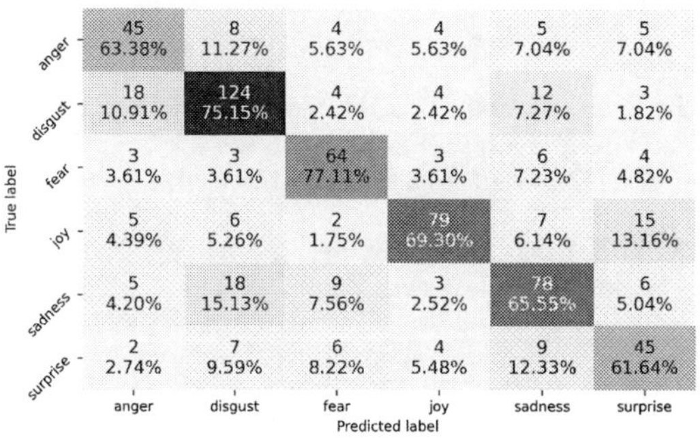

Figure 3: Confusion matrix of XLM-R model

The possible reason for incorrect predictions might be the class imbalance nature of the corpus. However, the high value of *Jaccard similarity* (Table 3) also reveals some interesting points. Few words are used multi-purposely in multiple classes. For instance, hate words can be used to express both *anger* and *disgust* feelings. Moreover, emotion classification is highly subjective, depends on the individual's perception, and people may contemplate a sentence in many ways (LeDoux and Hofmann, 2018). Thus, by developing a balanced dataset with diverse data, incorrect predictions might be reduced to some extent.

5.2 Comparison with Recent Works

The analysis of results revealed that XLM-R is the best model to classify emotion in Bengali texts. Thus, we compare the performance of XLM-R with the existing techniques to assess the effectiveness. We implemented previous methods (Irtiza Tripto and Eunus Ali, 2018; Azmin and Dhar, 2019; Pal and Karn, 2020; Ruposh and Hoque, 2019) on BEmoC and reported outcomes in f_1-score. Table 5 shows a summary of the comparison. The results show that XLM-R outperformed the past techniques with achieving the highest f_1-score (69.73%).

Methods	F1(%)
Word2Vec + LSTM (Irtiza Tripto and Eunus Ali, 2018)	53.54
TF-IDF + MNB (Azmin and Dhar, 2019)	48.67
TF-IDF + LR (Pal and Karn, 2020)	60.75
BOW + SVM (Ruposh and Hoque, 2019)	59.17
XLM-R (**Proposed**)	**69.73**

Table 5: Performance comparison. Here F1 denotes weighted f_1-score.

6 Conclusion

This paper investigated various ML, DNN and transformer-based techniques to classify the emotion in Bengali texts. Due to the scarcity of benchmark corpus, we developed a corpus (i.e., BEmoC) containing 6243 Bengali texts labelled with six basic classes. Co-hen's Kappa score of 0.91 reflects the quality of the corpus. Performance analysis on BEmoC illustrated that XLM-R, a transformer model provided a superior result among all the methods. Specifically, XLM-R achieved the highest f_1-score of 69.61% which indicates the improvement of 8.97% (than ML) and 11.53% (than DNN). Although XLM-R exhibited the most elevated scores, other technique (such as the ensemble of the transformer models) can also investigate enhancing performance. Additional categories (such as love, hate, and stress) can also include generalization. Moreover, transformer-based models can also investigate extending the corpus, including text with sarcasm or irony, text with comparison and mixed-emotion.

Acknowledgements

We sincerely acknowledge the anonymous reviewers and pre-submission mentor for their insightful suggestions, which help improve the work. This work was supported by the Directorate of Research & Extension, CUET.

References

H. Al-Omari, M. A. Abdullah, and S. Shaikh. 2020. Emodet2: Emotion detection in english textual dialogue using bert and bilstm models. In *2020 11th International Conference on Information and Communication Systems (ICICS)*, pages 226–232.

Nourah Alswaidan and Mohamed El Bachir Menai. 2020. A survey of state-of-the-art approaches for emotion recognition in text. *Knowledge and Information Systems*, pages 1–51.

S. Alzu'bi, O. Badarneh, B. Hawashin, M. Al-Ayyoub, N. Alhindawi, and Y. Jararweh. 2019. Multi-label emotion classification for arabic tweets. In *2019 Sixth International Conference on Social Networks Analysis, Management and Security (SNAMS)*, pages 499–504.

S. Azmin and K. Dhar. 2019. Emotion detection from bangla text corpus using naïve bayes classifier. In *2019 4th International Conference on Electrical Information and Communication Technology (EICT)*, pages 1–5.

Piotr Bojanowski, Edouard Grave, Armand Joulin, and Tomas Mikolov. 2017. Enriching Word Vectors with Subword Information. *Transactions of the Association for Computational Linguistics*, 5:135–146.

Ben Chen, Bin Chen, Dehong Gao, Qijin Chen, Chengfu Huo, Xiaonan Meng, Weijun Ren, and Yang Zhou. 2021. Transformer-based language model fine-tuning methods for covid-19 fake news detection. *arXiv preprint arXiv:2101.05509*.

Jacob Cohen. 1960. A coefficient of agreement for nominal scales. *Educational and Psychological Measurement*, 20(1):37–46.

Dipankar Das and Sivaji Bandyopadhyay. 2009. Word to sentence level emotion tagging for bengali blogs. In *Proceedings of the ACL-IJCNLP 2009 Conference Short Papers*, pages 149–152.

Niladri Sekhar Dash and L Ramamoorthy. 2019. *Utility and application of language corpora*. Springer.

Jacob Devlin, Ming-Wei Chang, Kenton Lee, and Kristina Toutanova. 2019. Bert: Pre-training of deep bidirectional transformers for language understanding.

Paul Ekman. 1993. Facial expression and emotion. *American psychologist*, 48(4):384.

Sepp Hochreiter and Jürgen Schmidhuber. 1997. Long Short-Term Memory. *Neural Computation*, 9(8):1735–1780.

Chenyang Huang, Amine Trabelsi, and Osmar R. Zaïane. 2019. ANA at semeval-2019 task 3: Contextual emotion detection in conversations through hierarchical lstms and BERT. *CoRR*, abs/1904.00132.

N. Irtiza Tripto and M. Eunus Ali. 2018. Detecting multilabel sentiment and emotions from bangla youtube comments. In *2018 International Conference on Bangla Speech and Language Processing (ICBSLP)*, pages 1–6.

Klaus Krippendorff. 2011. Agreement and information in the reliability of coding. *Communication Methods and Measures*, 5(2):93–112.

Yuni Lai, Linfeng Zhang, Donghong Han, Rui Zhou, and Guoren Wang. 2020. Fine-grained emotion classification of chinese microblogs based on graph convolution networks. *World Wide Web*, 23(5):2771–2787.

Yann LeCun, Yoshua Bengio, and Geoffrey Hinton. 2015. Deep learning. *nature*, 521(7553):436–444.

Joseph E LeDoux and Stefan G Hofmann. 2018. The subjective experience of emotion: a fearful view. *Current Opinion in Behavioral Sciences*, 19:67–72. Emotion-cognition interactions.

Yinhan Liu, Myle Ott, Naman Goyal, Jingfei Du, Mandar Joshi, Danqi Chen, Omer Levy, Mike Lewis, Luke Zettlemoyer, and Veselin Stoyanov. 2019. Roberta: A robustly optimized BERT pre-training approach. *CoRR*, abs/1907.11692.

D. Magatti, S. Calegari, D. Ciucci, and F. Stella. 2009. Automatic labeling of topics. In *2009 Ninth International Conference on Intelligent Systems Design and Applications*, pages 1227–1232.

Arun S Maiya. 2020. ktrain: A low-code library for augmented machine learning. *arXiv preprint arXiv:2004.10703*.

Tomas Mikolov, Kai Chen, Greg Corrado, and Jeffrey Dean. 2013. Efficient estimation of word representations in vector space. *arXiv preprint arXiv:1301.3781*.

Aditya Pal and Bhaskar Karn. 2020. Anubhuti–an annotated dataset for emotional analysis of bengali short stories. *arXiv preprint arXiv:2010.03065*.

Flor Miriam Plaza del Arco, Carlo Strapparava, L. Alfonso Urena Lopez, and Maite Martin. 2020. EmoEvent: A multilingual emotion corpus based on different events. In *Proceedings of the 12th Language Resources and Evaluation Conference*, pages 1492–1498, Marseille, France. European Language Resources Association.

H. A. Ruposh and M. M. Hoque. 2019. A computational approach of recognizing emotion from bengali texts. In *2019 5th International Conference on Advances in Electrical Engineering (ICAEE)*, pages 570–574.

Sagor Sarker. 2020. Banglabert: Bengali mask language model for bengali language understading.

Sagor Sarker. 2021. Bnlp: Natural language processing toolkit for bengali language. *arXiv preprint arXiv:2102.00405*.

Omar Sharif and Mohammed Moshiul Hoque. 2021. Identification and classification of textual aggression in social media: Resource creation and evaluation. In *Combating Online Hostile Posts in Regional Languages during Emergency Situation*, pages 9–20, Cham. Springer International Publishing.

Appendices

A Model Hyperparameters

Classifier	Parameters
LR	optimizer = 'lbfgs', max_iter = 400, penalty = 'l1', C=1
SVM	kernel='linear', random_state = 0, γ='scale', tol='0.001'
RF	criterion='gini', n_estimators = 100
MNB	α = 1.0, fit_prior = true, class_prior = none,

Table 6: Optimized parameters for ML models

Hyperparameter	Value
Fit method	'auto_fit'
Learning rate	2e-5
Epochs	20
Batch size	12,16
Max sequence length	70

Table 8: Optimized hyperparameters for transformers models

Hyperparameters	Hyperparameter Space	CNN	BiLSTM	CNN + BiLSTM
Filter Size	3,5,7,9	7	-	3
Pooling type	'max', 'average'	'max'	-	'max'
Embedding Dimension	30, 35, 50, 70, 90, 100, 150, 200, 250, 300	100	100	100
Number of Units	16, 32, 64, 128, 256	64	32	64,64,32
Neurons in Dense Layer	16, 32, 64, 128, 256	64	16	-
Batch Size	16, 32, 64, 128, 256	16	16	16
Activation Function	'relu', 'tanh', 'softplus', 'sigmoid'	'relu'	'relu'	'relu'
Optimizer	'RMSprop', 'Adam', 'SGD', 'Adamax'	'Adam'	'Adam'	'Adam'
Learning Rate	0.5, 0.1, 0.05, 0.01, 0.005, 0.001, 0.0005, 0.0001	0.001	0.001	0.001

Table 7: Hyperparameters for DNN methods

B Data Examples

Data	Class
যা শুনলাম সত্যিই অসাধারণ ছিল। কিছু মানুষের জীবনে জমা স্বপ্ন গুলো সত্যি হয়। তোমায় না দেখলে তা বুঝতে পারতাম না। (What I heard was really awesome. Some people's dreams come true. I couldn't understand it without seeing you.)	Joy
রিয়াকে আমি কয়েক বছর আগে দেখেছিলাম।অনেক হাসিখুশি, মিষ্টি একটা মেয়ে ছিল।কিন্তু আজকে সেই উচ্ছলতা কোথায় যেন বিলীন হয়েছে। (I saw Riya a few years ago. She was a very happy, sweet girl. But today, that fun seems to have disappeared.)	Sadness
ফালতু নিউজ, পত্রিকা বিক্রি বন্ধ হয়ে যাচ্ছে তাই এরকম মিথ্যা তথ্য দিচ্ছে আর মানুষকে মৃত্যুর মুখে ঠেলে দিতে চাচ্ছে এই পুজিবাদী শালারা। (False news, magazines are being stopped selling so they are giving such false information and these capitalist bastards are trying to push people to the brink of death.)	Anger
লাশের মিছিল হবে এবার। চোখের সামনে লাশ পড়ে থাকবে, দাফন করতে আসবেনা কেউ। সেই দিন আসতেসে, বেশি দেরী নাই ভাই। There will be a procession of corpses this time. The dead bodies will be lying in front of the eyes, no one will come to bury it. That day is coming soon brother.)	Fear
বলতে লজ্জা হয় কিন্তু সত্য হচ্ছে জাতি হিসাবেই আমরা ধর্ষণকামী এবং বর্বর প্রকৃতির। নাহলে কিভাবে সম্ভব, অন্যের মোবাইল নম্বর সোশ্যাল মিডিয়াতে পোস্ট করা! (It is a shame to say but the truth is that as a nation we are rapist and barbaric in nature.) Otherwise, how is it possible to post someone else's mobile number on social media !)	Disgust
আমি সিগারেটের ধোঁয়া ছাড়তে গিয়ে বিষম খেয়ে গেলাম!ছোট্ট একটা মেসেজ।"আমি আসছি!" নিজের চোখকে বিশ্বাস করতে পারছিলামনা যে সে আসলেই আসছে। (I was smoking and got shocked! A short message. "I'm coming!" I couldn't believe my eyes that he was really coming.)	Surprise
পাত্রী দেখতে এসে পাত্রীর মুখে এমন অদ্ভুত প্রশ্ন শুনে আমার সামনে বসে থাকা ভদ্রলোক যে বেশ অবাক হয়েছেন তা আমি বুঝতে পারছি(I understand that the gentleman sitting in front of me was quite surprised to hear such a strange question on the face of the bride when she came to see him)	Surprise
মহিলার চেহারায় কোন অভিব্যক্তি নেই তিনি হাউমাউ কান্নায় ভেঙ্গে পড়লেন।(There was no expression on the woman's face and she broke down in tears.)	sadness
সেই তিনি মাস্ক না পরার জন্য তিনজন বয়স্ক লোককে কানে ধরাচ্ছে খুবই দুঃখজনক।(It is very sad that he is holding the ears of three old men for not wearing a mask.)	sadness
অনেকেই তাদের ব্যস্ততার মাঝে সময় করে উইশ করছেন, অনেকে উইশ করেন নাই, কিন্তু মন থেকে দোয়া করছেন। সকলের নিকট আমি কৃতজ্ঞ।(Many are wishing in their busy time, many are not wishing but praying from the heart. I am grateful to everyone.)	joy
শত চেষ্টা থাকার সত্ত্বেও এই আতংকিত পরিস্থিতির মধ্যে বাসা থেকে যেতে না দেওয়ায় উপস্থিত হতে পারলাম নাহ।(Despite hundreds of attempts, I could not attend because I was not allowed to leave the house in this panic situation.)	fear
বাংলাদেশের মানুষদের মধ্যে একটা আইডেন্টিটি ক্রাইসিসে ভুগার মেন্টালিটি আছে, যে যে পেশায় না ঠিক অন্য পেশার মানুষকে গালি দিতে এক সেকেন্ডও সময় নেয়না।(There is an identity crisis mentality among the people of Bangladesh that they don't take even a second to abuse people of other professions.)	disgust
পাপন মাদারচোদ একে একে সব ক্রিকেটারের ক্যারিয়ারে এভাবে ধ্বংস করে ছাড়বে যেমন সাকিবকে করছে।(Papon Motherchod will destroy the careers of all cricketers one by one as done to Shakib.)	anger

Table 9: Sample instances in BEmoC.

Hie-BART: Document Summarization with Hierarchical BART

Kazuki Akiyama
Ehime University
k_akiyama@ai.cs.ehime-u.ac.jp

Akihiro Tamura
Doshisha University
aktamura@mail.doshisha.ac.jp

Takashi Ninomiya
Ehime University
ninomiya@cs.ehime-u.ac.jp

Abstract

This paper proposes a new abstractive summarization model for documents, hierarchical BART (Hie-BART), which captures the hierarchical structures of documents (i.e., their sentence-word structures) in the BART model. Although the existing BART model has achieved state-of-the-art performance on document summarization tasks, it does not account for interactions between sentence-level and word-level information. In machine translation tasks, the performance of neural machine translation models can be improved with the incorporation of multi-granularity self-attention (MG-SA), which captures relationships between words and phrases. Inspired by previous work, the proposed Hie-BART model incorporates MG-SA into the encoder of the BART model for capturing sentence-word structures. Evaluations performed on the CNN/Daily Mail dataset show that the proposed Hie-BART model outperforms strong baselines and improves the performance of a non-hierarchical BART model (+0.23 ROUGE-L).

1 Introduction

In recent years, improvements to abstractive document summarization models have been developed through the incorporation of pre-training. The BERTSUM model (Liu and Lapata, 2019) has been proposed as a pre-training model for document summarization tasks. For sequence-to-sequence tasks, the T5 model (Raffel et al., 2020) and the BART model (Lewis et al., 2020) have been proposed as part of generalized pre-training models. Among the existing pre-training models, the BART model achieves state-of-the-art performance on document summarization tasks. However, the BART model does not capture the hierarchical structures of documents when generating a summary.

Neural machine translation has been improved by the capture of multiple granularities of information in input texts such as "phrases and words" and "words and characters". In particular, Transformer-based machine translation model has been improved by incorporating multi-granularity self-attention (MG-SA) (Hao et al., 2019), which considers the relationships between words and phrases by decomposing an input text into its elements using multiple granularity (i.e., words and phrases) and assigning each granular element (i.e., a word or a phrase) to a head in multi-head Self-Attention Networks (SANs). This method enables interactions not only between words but also between phrases and words, through self-attentions.

Inspired by previous work, this paper proposes a new abstractive document summarization model, hierarchical BART (Hie-BART), which captures a document's hierarchical structures (i.e., sentence-word structures) through the SANs of the BART model. Here, a document is divided into elements with word-level and sentence-level granularity, where each element is assigned to a head of the SANs layers of the BART encoder. Then, information with multi-granularity is captured by combining the output of the SANs layers, where the ratio of combining word-level and sentence-level information is controlled by a hyperparameter.

We evaluated the proposed model in an abstractive summarization task with the CNN/Daily Mail dataset. Our evaluation shows that our Hie-BART model improves the F-score of ROUGE-L by 0.23 points relative to the non-hierarchical BART model, and the proposed model is better than the strong baselines, BERTSUM and T5 models.

2 Background

2.1 BART

The BART model (Lewis et al., 2020) is a generalized pre-training model based on the Transformer

Proceedings of NAACL-HLT 2021: Student Research Workshop, pages 159–165
June 6–11, 2021. ©2021 Association for Computational Linguistics

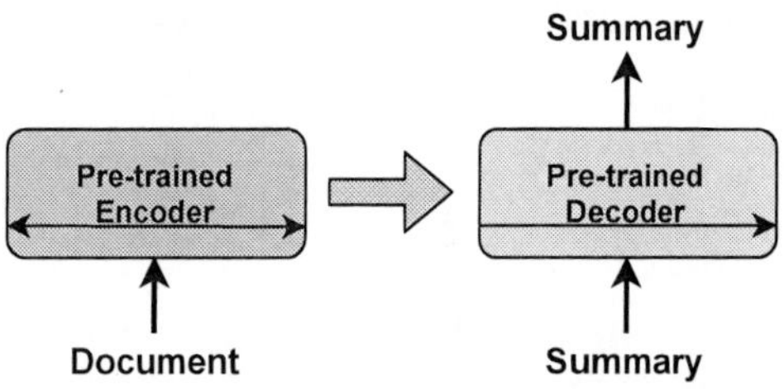

Figure 1: The overview architecture of BART. The encoder is a bidirectional model and the decoder is an autoregressive model.

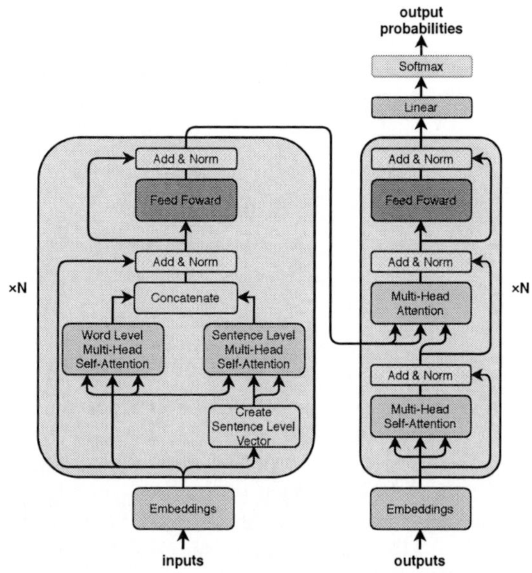

Figure 2: Overview architecture of Hie-BART. This is based on the Transformer model. The SANs in the encoder are divided into word and sentence levels and computed.

model (Vaswani et al., 2017). Five pre-training techniques are introduced: token masking, sentence permutation, document rotation, token deletion, and text infilling.

Each of these is a denoising autoencoder technique that adds noise to the original text and restores the original text. **Token masking**, as used in BERT (Devlin et al., 2019), randomly masks tokens. **Sentence permutation** randomly shuffles the sentences in a document. **Document rotation** randomly selects a token from a sentence and then rotates the sentence so that it begins with that token. **Token deletion** randomly deletes a token from the original sentence. **Text infilling** replaces word sequences with a single mask token or inserts a mask token into a randomly selected position. A combination of sentence permutation and text infilling achieves the best accuracy of all techniques.

An overview of the BART model is given in Figure 1. The encoder is a bidirectional model and the decoder is an autoregressive model. This pre-trained BART model is fine-tuned to various tasks, such as the summarization task, for which, a document is provided to the encoder, and the decoder generates a document summary.

2.2 Multi-Granularity Self-Attention (MG-SA)

MG-SA (Hao et al., 2019) is used to capture multi-granularity information from an input text by dividing the input into elements with several types of granularity and preparing heads of multi-head SANs for each type of granularity. Provided with the word-level matrix H, which is an input to the SANs, this method first generates a phrase-level matrix H_g representing phrase-level information, as follows:

$$H_g = F_h(H),$$

where $F_h(\bullet)$ is a function that generates a phrase-level matrix for the h-th head. Specifically, a phrase-level matrix is generated by running a max pooling operation on word-level vectors in a word-level matrix. After a phrase-level matrix is generated, SANs perform the following computations:

$$Q^h, K^h, V^h = HW_Q^h, H_gW_K^h, H_gW_V^h, \quad (1)$$

$$O^h = \mathbf{ATT}(Q^h, K^h)V^h, \quad (2)$$

where $Q^h \in \mathbb{R}^{n \times d_h}$, $K^h \in \mathbb{R}^{p \times d_h}$, $V^h \in \mathbb{R}^{p \times d_h}$ are respectively the query, key, and value representations, $W_Q^h, W_K^h, W_V^h \in \mathbb{R}^{d \times d_h}$ are parameter matrices, and d, d_h, n, and p are the dimensions of the hidden layer, one head, a word vector, and a phrase vector, respectively. In addition, **ATT(X,Y)** is a function that calculates the attention weights of X and Y. From these computations, the output O^h of each head in the SANs is generated. Then, the output of MG-SA is generated by concatenating the outputs from all heads: $\mathbf{MG\text{-}SA(H)} = [\mathbf{O^1}, ..., \mathbf{O^N}]$. The outputs of each head O^h contain information between words or between words and phrases. Thus, in addition to relationships between words, the relationships between words and phrases can be captured with MG-SA.

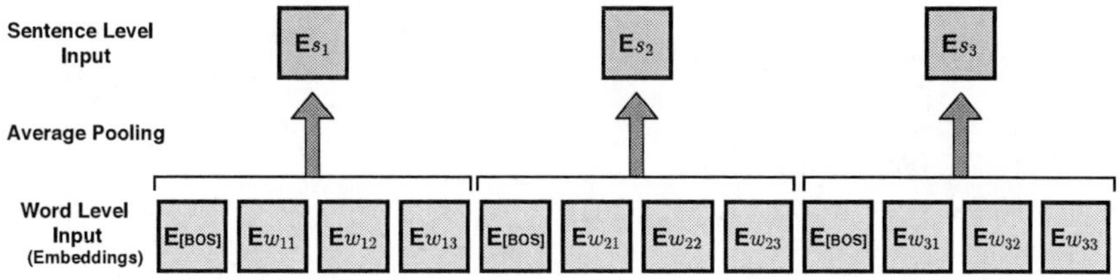

Figure 3: Behavior of the create sentence level vector layer. $E_{w_{ij}}$ and $E_{[BOS]}$ are embedded vectors for the word w_{ij} (j-th word in i-th sentence) and $[BOS]$ token, respectively. E_{s_i} is the sentence-level embedded vector for the i-th sentence s_i.

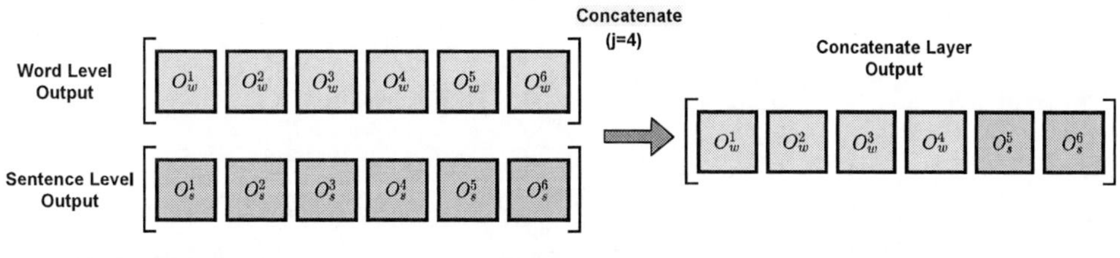

Figure 4: An example of the behavior of the concatenate layer where the number of heads of the multi-head is 6 and the join point $j = 4$. The blue $[O_w^1, ..., O_w^6]$ designates the outputs of the word-level SANs and the red $[O_s^1, ..., O_s^6]$ shows the outputs of the sentence-level SANs.

3 Hie-BART

3.1 Architecture

The Hie-BART (Hierarchical-BART) model has a sentence-to-word (sentence-level) SANs in addition to the word-to-word (word-level) SANs of the original BART model. An overview of Hie-BART is shown in Figure 2. Hie-BART has sentence-level SANs, a create sentence level vector layer and a concatenate layer, in addition to BART. In the create sentence level vector layer, a sentence-level matrix is created from a word-level matrix. The concatenate layer concatenates the outputs of word-level and sentence-level SANs. The outputs of the concatenate layer are forwarded to the subsequent feed-forward layer. To provide boundary information between the sentences, each sentence is prefixed with a $[BOS]$ token.

3.2 Create Sentence Level Vector Layer

The behavior of the create sentence level vector layer is shown in Figure 3. $E_{w_{ij}}$ and $E_{[BOS]}$ are embedded vectors for word w_{ij} (j-th word in the i-th sentence) and $[BOS]$ token, respectively. E_{s_i} is the sentence-level embedded vector for the i-th sentence s_i.

The create sentence level vector layer uses average pooling to generate a sentence-level vector from word-level vectors. Given the word sequence $W = (w_1, ..., w_N)$, it is divided into sentences $S = (s_1, ..., s_M)$, where N is the total number of words, M is the total number of sentences, and each s_i is the i-th sentence consisting of a word subsequence $w_{i1}, \ldots w_{iN_i}$, where N_i is the total number of words in the sentence. For each element of S, we apply average pooling as follows: $g_m = \mathbf{AVG}(s_m)$, where the $\mathbf{AVG}(\bullet)$ is average pooling. From this formula, $G = (g_1, ..., g_M)$ is generated. Each element of W, S, and G is an embedded vector. G is forwarded to the sentence-level SANs as its input.

3.3 Concatenate Layer

The outputs of each of the word-level and sentence-level SANs are combined in the concatenate layer. The outputs of the word-level and sentence-level SANs layer are as follows:

$$\mathbf{SANs(W)} = [O_w^1, \ldots, O_w^H] = O_w^{ALL}, \quad (3)$$

$$\mathbf{SANs(G)} = [O_s^1, \ldots, O_s^H] = O_s^{ALL}, \quad (4)$$

where H is the number of heads, $[O_w^1, \ldots, O_w^H] = O_w^{ALL}$ is the output of the word-level SANs, consisting of the word-level head's outputs, and $[O_s^1, ..., O_s^H] = O_s^{ALL}$ is the output of the sentence-level SANs, consisting of the sentence-level head's outputs. The outputs of these word/sentence-level SANs are combined as follows:

$$\mathbf{CONCAT}(\mathbf{O_w^{ALL}}, \mathbf{O_s^{ALL}}, \mathbf{j}) = [\mathbf{O_w^1}, ..., \mathbf{O_w^j}, \mathbf{O_s^{j+1}}, ..., \mathbf{O_s^H}], \quad (5)$$

Model	ROUGE-1	ROUGE-2	ROUGE-L
LEAD-3 (Nallapati et al., 2017)	40.42	17.62	36.67
PTGEN (See et al., 2017)	36.44	15.66	33.42
PTGEN+COV (See et al., 2017)	39.53	17.28	36.38
BERTSUMEXTABS (Liu and Lapata, 2019)	42.13	19.60	39.18
T5 (Raffel et al., 2020)	43.52	21.55	40.69
BART (Lewis et al., 2020)	44.16	21.28	40.90
BART (ours)	44.06	21.22	40.82
Hie-BART (ours)	**44.35***,**	**21.37**	**41.05****

Table 1: Results on the CNN/Daily Mail test set.

Word : Sentence	ROUGE 1	ROUGE 2	ROUGE L
16 : 0	44.72	21.73	41.43
15 : 1	44.95	**21.92**	41.68
14 : 2	**45.01**	**21.92**	**41.75**
13 : 3	44.91	21.87	41.64
12 : 4	44.74	21.66	41.49
11 : 5	44.88	21.81	41.62
10 : 6	44.78	21.75	41.51
9 : 7	44.70	21.71	41.46
8 : 8	44.79	21.77	41.58

Table 2: Results on the CNN/Daily Mail validation set. The leftmost column shows the ratio of the number of multi-heads to combine. The highest score was achieved for the ratio "Word:Sentence = 14:2".

where **CONCAT(X, Y, j)** is a function that concatenates X and Y at the join point j of the multi-heads. In the combined multi-head, the heads from 1 to j are word-level outputs, and the heads from $j+1$ to H are sentence-level outputs.

Figure 4 shows an example of the behavior of the concatenate layer in Hie-BART, where the number of heads of the multi-head is 6 and the join point $j = 4$. The output of the word-level SANs $[O_w^1, ..., O_w^6]$ and the output of the sentence-level SANs $[O_s^1, ..., O_s^6]$ are joined at the join point $j = 4$, resulting in the output $[O_w^1, O_w^2, O_w^3, O_w^4, O_s^5, O_s^6]$.

The output of the concatenate layer is forwarded to the feed-forward layer in the encoder.

4 Experiments

4.1 Dataset

We used the CNN/Daily Mail dataset[1] (Hermann et al., 2015), a summary corpus of English news articles, consisting of 287,226 training pairs, 13,368 validation pairs, and 11,490 test pairs. On average, the source documents and summary sentences have 781 and 56 tokens, respectively. For data preprocessing, we followed the instruction provided in the CNN/Daily Mail dataset[1] and fairseq[2].

4.2 Parameters

We used the pre-trained BART model "bart.large", provided in fairseq[2] for Hie-BART. The hyperparameters for BART and Hie-BART were determined for the validation set; the gradient accumulation parameter (update-freq) was 10, the total number of training steps was 20,000, and the number of multi-heads was set to 16. The ratio of the number of combined heads of output in word-level and sentence-level SANs was set to "Word:Sentence = 14:2" for Hie-BART. We followed fairseq's settings[2] for the other hyperparameters. In our environments, the model had 406,291,456 parameters for Hie-BART and 406,290,432 parameters for BART.

4.3 Results

The results of the evaluation of the Hie-BART model for the CNN/Daily Mail test data are shown in Table 1. The F-score for ROUGE-1, ROUGE-2, and ROUGE-L (Lin, 2004) were used as evaluation metrics. To calculate the ROUGE score, we

[1] CNN/Daily Mail dataset: https://github.com/abisee/cnn-dailymail

[2] Usage of BART by faireseq: https://github.com/pytorch/fairseq/tree/master/examples/bart

[Source Document]
(CNN)About a dozen Native American actors have walked off the set of an Adam Sandler movie comedy, saying the satirical Western's script is insulting to Native Americans and women, according to a report. ... According to ICTMN, a Native American adviser hired to help ensure the movie's cultural authenticity also walked off the set in protest. Hill, the Choctaw actor, seemed to hold out hope that differences between the producers and Native American cast members could be resolved . ... .
[Baseline Model's Summary]
The walkout occurred on the set of "The Ridiculous Six" near Las Vegas, New Mexico, according to a report . The script called for native women's names such as "Beaver's Breath" and "No Bra" and an actress portraying an Apache woman to squat and urinate while smoking a peace pipe, ICTMN reports .
[Proposed Model's Summary]
About a dozen Native American actors walked off the set of an Adam Sandler movie comedy, a report says . They say the script is insulting to Native Americans and women, according to the Indian Country Today Media Network . "The Ridiculous Six" also stars Will Forte, Taylor Lautner, Steve Buscemi and John Turturro .
[Gold Summary]
About a dozen Native American actors walk off set of Adam Sandler comedy, says report . Actors say satirical Western's script is insulting to Native Americans and women .

Table 3: An example of improved summaries. Note that the source document is partially omitted.

[Source Document]
(CNN)It's the kind of thing you see in movies, like Robert Redford's role in "All Is Lost" or Ang Lee's "Life of Pi." But, in real life, it's hard to swallow the idea of a single person being stranded at sea for days, weeks, if not months and somehow living to talk about it. Miracles do happen, though, and not just in Hollywood. We're not talking about people who float aimlessly or run aground after running out of gas or being let down by faltering winds only to be picked up a few hours later by the U.S. Coast Guard. ... After being spotted by crew aboard a Japanese Maritime Self-Defense Force destroyer and picked up in a smaller rescue boat, he took a drink offered to him and burst into tears, Kyodo reported. Shinkawa told his rescuers, "I thought today was the last day of my life."
[Base Model's Summary]
It's hard to swallow the idea of a single person being stranded at sea for days, weeks, if not months and somehow living to talk about it . Miracles do happen, though, and not just in Hollywood . Jose Salvador Alvarenga says his journey began in Paredon Viejo, a port on Mexico's Pacific coast in late 2012 .
[Proposed Model's Summary]
It's hard to swallow the idea of a single person being stranded at sea for days, weeks, if not months and somehow living to talk about it . Miracles do happen, though, and not just in Hollywood . Jose Salvador Alvarenga says his journey began in Paredon Viejo, a port on Mexico's Pacific coast, in late 2012 . Louis Jordan says he used laundry to trap and scoop up fish, rigged a makeshift mast and sail .
[Gold Summary]
A South Carolina man says he spent 66 days alone at sea before being rescued . Other sole survivor stories include a Japanese man washed away by a tsunami . An El Salvador man says he drifted from Mexico to Marshall Islands over a year .

Table 4: An example of summaries that are not improved.

used files2rouge[3]. Hie-BART was compared with LEAD-3 (Nallapati et al., 2017), PTGEN, PTGEN+COV (See et al., 2017), BERTSUMEXTABS (Liu and Lapata, 2019), T5 (Raffel et al., 2020), BART with our environment, and BART with Lewis et al. (2020). The **LEAD-3** method uses the first three sentences of the source document as a summary. **PTGEN** is a sequence-to-sequence model that incorporates a pointer generator network. **PTGEN+COV** introduces the coverage mechanism into PTGEN. **BERTSUMEXTABS** is a pre-training model that adapts BERT for summarization tasks. **T5** is a generalized pre-training model for sequence-to-sequence tasks based on the Transformer model. The statistical significance test was performed by the Wilcoxon-Mann-Whitney test. In Table 1, * and ** indicate that the comparisons with BART (ours) are statistically significant at 5% significance level and 10% significance level, respectively.

Hie-BART improved the F-score of ROUGE-1/2/L by 0.223 points on average relative to BART with our environment, and by 0.143 points on average from BART reported in (Lewis et al., 2020). Table 1 also shows that our Hie-BART model significantly improved ROUGE-1 and ROUGE-L scores of the baseline BART model.

4.4 Analysis

Table 2 shows a comparison of ROUGE scores for the ratio of the number of multi-heads at the word and sentence levels with the validation set of the CNN/Daily Mail dataset. The leftmost column shows the ratio of the number of multi-heads to combine. As can be seen in Table 2, the maximum ROUGE-1/2/L score was achieved for "Word:Sentence = 14:2". In ROUGE-1/2/L, smaller ratios of multi-heads at the sentence level that are compared to the word level, the higher the score tends to be. However, when the number of multi-heads at the sentence level is 0 (the original BART), the accuracy is lower than that of Hie-BART.

Table 3 shows an improved example of summaries: summaries generated by the baseline model (BART) and the proposed model (Hie-BART), and the gold summary. As can be seen in Table 3, the summary of the proposed model is fluent and close to the contents of the gold summary, which indicates that the summary of the proposed model includes the important parts of the source document.

Table 4 shows an example of summaries that are not improved. In this example, the baseline model's summary and the proposed model's summary include almost the same contents, but they are far from and longer than the gold summary.

5 Conclusion

In this study, we proposed Hie-BART to can take into account the relationship between words and sentences in BART by dividing the self-attention layer of encoder into word and sentence levels. In the experiments, we confirmed that Hie-BART improved the F-score of ROUGE-L by 0.23 points relative to the non-hierarchical BART model, and the proposed model was better than the strong baselines, BERTSUM and T5 models for the CNN/Daily Mail dataset.

As future work, we intend to investigate methods to incorporate information between sentences in addition to word-to-word and word-to-sentence information.

References

Jacob Devlin, Ming-Wei Chang, Kenton Lee, and Kristina Toutanova. 2019. BERT: Pre-training of deep bidirectional transformers for language understanding. In *Proceedings of the 2019 Conference of the North American Chapter of the Association for Computational Linguistics: Human Language Technologies, Volume 1 (Long and Short Papers)*, pages 4171–4186, Minneapolis, Minnesota. Association for Computational Linguistics.

Jie Hao, Xing Wang, Shuming Shi, Jinfeng Zhang, and Zhaopeng Tu. 2019. Multi-granularity self-attention for neural machine translation. In *Proceedings of the 2019 Conference on Empirical Methods in Natural Language Processing and the 9th International Joint Conference on Natural Language Processing (EMNLP-IJCNLP)*, pages 887–897, Hong Kong, China. Association for Computational Linguistics.

Karl Moritz Hermann, Tomas Kocisky, Edward Grefenstette, Lasse Espeholt, Will Kay, Mustafa Suleyman, and Phil Blunsom. 2015. Teaching machines to read and comprehend. In *Advances in neural information processing systems*, pages 1693–1701.

Mike Lewis, Yinhan Liu, Naman Goyal, Marjan Ghazvininejad, Abdelrahman Mohamed, Omer Levy, Veselin Stoyanov, and Luke Zettlemoyer. 2020. BART: Denoising sequence-to-sequence pre-training for natural language generation, translation,

[3]files2rouge usage : https://github.com/pltrdy/files2rouge

and comprehension. In *Proceedings of the 58th Annual Meeting of the Association for Computational Linguistics*, pages 7871–7880. Association for Computational Linguistics.

Chin-Yew Lin. 2004. ROUGE: A package for automatic evaluation of summaries. In *Text Summarization Branches Out*, pages 74–81, Barcelona, Spain. Association for Computational Linguistics.

Yang Liu and Mirella Lapata. 2019. Text summarization with pretrained encoders. In *Proceedings of the 2019 Conference on Empirical Methods in Natural Language Processing and the 9th International Joint Conference on Natural Language Processing (EMNLP-IJCNLP)*, pages 3730–3740, Hong Kong, China. Association for Computational Linguistics.

Ramesh Nallapati, Feifei Zhai, and Bowen Zhou. 2017. SummaRuNNer: A recurrent neural network based sequence model for extractive. In *Proceedings of In Association for the Advancement of Artificial Intelligence*.

Colin Raffel, Noam Shazeer, Adam Roberts, Katherine Lee, Sharan Narang, Michael Matena, Yanqi Zhou, Wei Li, and Peter J. Liu. 2020. Exploring the limits of transfer learning with a unified text-to-text transformer. *Journal of Machine Learning Research*, 21(140):1–67.

Abigail See, Peter J. Liu, and Christopher D. Manning. 2017. Get to the point: Summarization with pointer-generator networks. In *Proceedings of the 55th Annual Meeting of the Association for Computational Linguistics (Volume 1: Long Papers)*, pages 1073–1083, Vancouver, Canada. Association for Computational Linguistics.

Ashish Vaswani, Noam Shazeer, Niki Parmar, Jakob Uszkoreit, Llion Jones, Aidan N Gomez, Ł ukasz Kaiser, and Illia Polosukhin. 2017. Attention is all you need. In *Advances in Neural Information Processing Systems*, volume 30, pages 5998–6008. Curran Associates, Inc.

Association for Computational Linguistics
209 N. Eighth Street
Stroudsburg, Pennsylvania 18360

ISBN 978-1-7138-3012-2

CURRAN ASSOCIATES INC.
proceedings
.com